STUDIES IN FRENCH LITERATURE

presented to

H. W. LAWTON

by colleagues
pupils and friends

STUDIES IN FRENCH LITERATURE

presented to

H. W. LAWTON

by colleagues
pupils and friends

Edited by J. C. Ireson, I. D. McFarlane
and Garnet Rees

Manchester University Press

Barnes & Noble Inc, New York

© Manchester University Press, 1968

Published by the University of Manchester at
THE UNIVERSITY PRESS
316–324 Oxford Road
Manchester 13

First published 1968

U.S.A.
BARNES & NOBLE, INC.
105 Fifth Avenue, New York, N.Y. 10003

GB SBN 7190 0310 5

Printed in Great Britain by Butler & Tanner Ltd, Frome and London

CONTENTS

ACKNOWLEDGEMENTS

The Editors wish to express their thanks to the University of Sheffield for generous financial assistance towards the publication of this book, and also to Dr W. H. Lyons, Dr Majorie Shaw and Miss S. J. Shipside, who gave valuable assistance at various stages in the preparation of the volume.

R. W. Ladborough

INTRODUCTION

This book is to be primarily and inevitably a tribute to Professor H. W. Lawton's work as scholar and as administrator in two universities. Its contents and the bibliography of Lawton's own writings will stress the fact, known to all students of French, that his interests have lain since his student days chiefly in the sixteenth century. His doctorate thesis, *Térence en France au XVIe siècle*, published forty years ago, still the standard work on the subject, is referred to by French as well as by English scholars, and has inspired several works on similar lines. It is obviously written by someone well versed in classical Latin as well as in sixteenth-century France, and who is also a student of the theories and techniques of drama—which of course Lawton has never ceased to be. And he seems to write and to speak in French as clearly and as forcibly as in English. It is perhaps worth remarking that this most English of Englishmen received his higher education in the Universities of Wales (Bangor) and of Paris. Rarely has parochialism been less absent in a professor than in this cosmopolitan humanist.

It is, therefore, with Harold Lawton as a person rather than as a specialist that this short introduction will deal. For it was his wisdom as well as his teaching ability which soon made its mark at his first post in what was then the University College of Southampton. His kindliness and flair in dealing with students were of the sort which used to be expected from tutors in the older universities. His influence extended to young men and women outside his own department, and after 1937, when he succeeded to the chair, to his junior colleagues as well. When a new hall of residence was built for the College, it surprised no one that Lawton should be appointed its first Warden. And the legend of his reign there persists today. His interest in each of its inmates, his tolerance and tact, his capacity for administration, and above all his sense of humour set a standard which could not be bettered.

He resigned from his wardenship on the occasion of his marriage, but his own extremely happy home was soon to be another focus in the life of the College. Indeed, before the war, when Southampton as a place of higher education was still struggling to maintain its existence, the shortage of staff, students and money was largely compensated for by the sense of intimacy and common effort with which those who knew the place in those days will always associate the name of Lawton.

It may be a surprise to those acquainted with him only through his writings that Lawton's teaching activities extended far beyond the bounds of the sixteenth century. Indeed, there seemed no field in which he was not at home; and as a lecturer he was first-rate. He taught (as a professor should) beginners as well as fourth-year students. He was witty in prose and translation classes, learned but clear in the history of the language, stimulating in teaching literature of the seventeenth, eighteenth and nineteenth centuries. He was also a first-rate administrator of his department.

His skill in administration was not confined to his own special duties. He took a great interest in the Library of which he was a wise curator. He was a prominent and popular member of Senate, as well as of seemingly innumerable committees both in College and outside it. He was an assiduous president of the local branch of the Alliance française, for which he often lectured, and he was in demand as a speaker on topics other than French in Southampton and its neighbourhood. It is a marvel that he found time; yet nothing seemed to harass him or to tax his patience too much. He seemed to enjoy everything he did; rarely was he heard to complain. Before the war he enrolled as a special constable, and although his nocturnal tasks in the less seemly parts of the city would have intimidated many of his colleagues, the few who were privileged to hear some of his more hair-raising experiences were given the treat of listening to a first-class raconteur and humorist.

It is to be hoped that one day there will be added to his bibliography a list of his occasional verse, both in French and English. He is one of the lucky ones who has the knack of spotting the *double-entendre* or the loose word or phrase, and of immortalizing it in rhyme, often in parody. This would be accomplished with a poker-face during a solemn meeting, and passed round to the élite, who would often be reduced to hysterics, especially if the poem was accompanied, as it often was, by an apt drawing or caricature. For Lawton is also an accomplished draughtsman in pen and ink, and occasionally in oils. Of course he used this talent, as well as the art of improvising on the piano, for entertaining his children as well as adults.

The coming of the war forced his attention to wider horizons. Undaunted by a yet more depleted staff, Lawton somehow managed to keep his department going by his inspiration and vigour, and at the same time threw himself into the job of post-war planning. The College set up a development committee of which he was one of the leading lights. When, after the war, the College became the University of Southampton, it could with truth be said that it owed much to his wise vision and to his enthusiasm tempered with moderation.

The same qualities were displayed during his distinguished tenure of the Chair at Sheffield University, of which he became a pro-vice-chancellor. The French department flourished, and during his many activities inside and outside the university, he never allowed his high standards as scholar to flag. He somehow, *par miracle*, kept abreast of the latest research in his field, as well as indulging in it himself. And once more his wise advice was unstintingly given on matters academic or otherwise. It is hardly necessary to add how much his services were appreciated on the board of what eventually became the Society for French Studies, and on the editorial committee of its journal. The many reviews he wrote for *French Studies* and other learned periodicals were always perceptive, charitable and to the point.

Last, and perhaps for Lawton most important, there is one other aspect of his life and work which might go undetected by a casual student of his scholarly writings—his interest in theology. As a devout Anglican, he has not only interested himself in religious matters, but is able to speak about them with authority informed by wide reading. He would be too modest to admit that it is his attempt to practise what he preaches that has affected the whole ethos of his professional life. But many of his colleagues and pupils would insist that this was so. Again, a future comprehensive bibliography would give an impressive list of sermons and addresses, some of them (such as the French ones delivered in the French Church at Southampton) unprinted, but as good to read as they were to hear.

This volume, then, is designed to do honour to one who has not only been an adornment to French studies in this country, but who as a man has been an inspiration to many in many walks of life. Perhaps this time it would not be a cliché to quote the words of one to whom Harold Lawton devoted his great work: 'Humani nil a me alienum puto.'

BIBLIOGRAPHY OF THE WORKS OF H. W. LAWTON

BOOKS

Térence en France au XVIe siècle: éditions et traductions. Paris, Jouve, 1926, 570 pp. (Thèse présentée à la Faculté des Lettres en vue de l'obtention du Doctorat de l'Université de Paris.)

Handbook of French Renaissance Dramatic Theory. Manchester University Press (French Classics, Extra Series), 1949, xxvii + 147 pp.

Joachim du Bellay, *Poems,* Selected and Edited by H. W. Lawton. Oxford, Basil Blackwell (Blackwell's French Texts), 1961, xxvii + 178 pp. (Revised and corrected reprint, 1967.)

INAUGURAL LECTURE

'The Classical Tradition and Classicism in France'. Inaugural Lecture 31 Jan. 1951. University of Sheffield, 1951, 19 pp.

ARTICLES

'The Teaching of Early British History'. *Teachers' World,* 4 Mar. 1925, p. 1132.

'Notes sur un traducteur: Jean Baudoin'. *Revue de Littérature Comparée,* Oct. 1926, pp. 673–81.

'Charles Estienne et le théâtre'. *Revue du Seizième Siècle,* XIV, 1927, pp. 336–47.

'Note sur le décor scénique au XVIe siècle'. *Revue du Seizième Siècle,* XV, 1928, pp. 161–4.

'The Religion of the Gallo–Romans' in *Speculum Religionis: being Essays and Studies in Religion and Literature from Plato to Von Hügel, Presented by Members of the Staff of University College, Southampton, to their President, Claude G. Montefiore.* Oxford, Clarendon Press; London, Milford, 1929, pp. 71–98.

'Bishop Godwin's *Man in the Moone'. Review of English Studies,* VII, Jan. 1931, pp. 23–55.

'French Work in Progress'. *Modern Humanities Research Assn.,* July 1939, pp. 4–5.

'Comparative Humanism'. *Comparative Literature Studies,* I, Cardiff, 1941, pp. 18–20.

'The Confidant in and before French Classical Tragedy'. *Modern Language Review,* XXXVIII, 1 Jan. 1943, pp. 18–31.

'L. Febvre, *Autour de l'*Heptaméron. *Revue de Psychologie des Peuples,* Le Havre, Nov. 1946, pp. 275–8.

'Les variations du goût littéraire et la psychologie collective'. *Revue de Psychologie des Peuples*, Juillet 1947, pp. 285–301.

Articles in *The Guardian*, 16 Sept. to 25 Nov. 1949: series on 'Religious Literature in France'.

Articles in *Chambers's Encyclopædia*, 1950 on: Fable; Charles Perrault; Tallemant des Réaux; Catherine de Vivonne, Marquise de Rambouillet; Pierre de Ronsard.

'The Bases of Franco-British Friendship'. *Britain–France*, VII, no. 33, 1951, pp. 3–5.

'*L'Heautontimorumenos* de Térence, J.-C. Scaliger et les unités dramatiques'. *Mélanges . . . offerts à Henri Chamard*, Paris, Nizet, 1951, pp. 205–9.

'Note on *l'œuvre Salomon*'. *M.L.R.*, Jan. 1955, pp. 50–2.

'Vernacular Literature in Western Europe, 1493–1520'. *New Cambridge Modern History*, I, *The Renaissance, 1493–1520*, Cambridge U.P., 1957, pp. 169–93.

Sixteenth-Century French Tragedy and Catharsis'. *Essays presented to C. M. Girdlestone*, University of Durham, 1960, pp. 171–80.

'La survivance des personnages térentiens'. *Bulletin de l'Association Guillaume Budé*, mars 1964, pp. 85–94.

'The Sixteenth Century'. *Year's Work in Modern Language Studies:*
Vol. V. O.U.P., 1935, pp. 50–6.
  VI. C.U.P., 1936, pp. 48–57.
  VII. C.U.P., 1937, pp. 42–51.
  VIII. C.U.P., 1938, pp. 54–60.

REVIEWS

P. Jourda, *Marguerite d'Angoulême, Duchesse d'Alençon, Reine de Navarre (1492–1549): étude biographique et littéraire*. 2 vols. Paris, Champion, 1930. *Times Literary Supplement*, 17 Sept. 1931, p. 697.

W. B. Cornelia, *The Classical Sources of the Nature References in Ronsard's Poetry*. New York, Publ. of Inst. of Fr. Studies, 1943. *M.L.R.*, XXX, 1935, p. 132.

C. R. Baskerville, *Pierre Gringore's Pageants for the Entry of Mary Tudor into Paris*. Chicago U.P., 1934. *M.L.R.*, XXXI, 1936, p. 264.

W. Mönch, *Frankreichs Literatur im XVI. Jahrhundert*. Berlin, de Gruyter, 1938. *M.L.R.*, XXXIV, 1939, pp. 273–4.

L. Wencelius, *L'esthétique de Calvin* and *Calvin et Rembrandt*. Paris, Belles-Lettres, 1937. *M.L.R.*, XXXIV, pp. 275–6.

E. V. Telle, *L'œuvre de Marguerite d'Angoulême, Reine de Navarre, et la*

Querelle des Femmes. Toulouse, Lion et fils, 1937. *M.L.R.,* XXXV, 1940, pp. 103–4.

M. Bishop, *Ronsard, Prince of Poets.* Oxford U.P., 1940. *M.L.R.,* XXXVI, 1941, p. 269.

L. C. Keating, *Studies on the Literary Salon in France, 1550–1615.* Harvard U.P., 1941. *M.L.R.,* XXXVII, 1942, pp. 517–8.

La Boétie, *Anti-Dictator: The* Discours sur la servitude volontaire *of Etienne de la Boétie, Rendered into English by Harry Kurz.* Columbia U.P., 1942. *M.L.R.,* XXXVIII, 1943, p. 74.

R. J. Clements, *Critical Theory and Practice of the Pléiade.* Harvard U.P., 1942. *M.L.R.,* XXXVIII, pp. 157–8.

G. D. Hocking, *A study of the* Tragœdiæ Sacræ *of Father Caussin (1583–1651).* Baltimore, Johns Hopkins Press, 1943. *M.L.R.,* XXXIX, 1944, pp. 315–16.

D. Delacourcelle, *Le sentiment de l'art dans la* Bergerie *de Remy Belleau.* Oxford, Blackwell, 1945. *M.L.R.,* XLI, 1946, p. 438.

L. Febvre, *Autour de* l'Heptaméron. Paris, Gallimard, 1944. *M.L.R.,* XLII, 1947, p. 142.

A. J. George, *Pierre-Simon Ballanche, Precursor of Romanticism.* New York, Syracuse U.P., 1945. *M.L.R.,* XLII. p. 143.

B. W. Bates, *Literary Portraiture in the Historical Narrative of the French Renaissance.* New York, Stechert, 1945. *M.L.R.,* XLII, pp. 143–4.

N. F. Osborne, *The Doctor in the French Literature of the Sixteenth Century.* New York, King's Crown Press, 1946. *M.L.R.,* XLII, p. 278.

Pierre de Ronsard, *Poèmes.* Choisis et commentés par André Barbier. Oxford, Blackwell, 1946. *F.S.,* I, 1947, pp. 58–9.

Jean Lemaire de Belges, *La Concorde des deux langages.* Edition critique publiée par Jean Frappier. Paris, Droz, 1947. *F.S.,* II, 1948, pp. 263–5.

Jean Lemaire de Belges, *Les Epistres de l'amant vert.* Edition critique publiée par Jean Frappier. Lille, Giard and Geneva, Droz, 1948. *F.S.,* III, 1949, pp. 75–6.

The French Bandello. Edited with an introduction by F. S. Hook. Missouri U.P., 1948. *F.S.,* III, pp. 162–3.

Sponde, *Poésies.* Edited by A. Boase and F. Ruchon. Geneva, Cailler, 1949. *F.S.,* IV, 1950, pp. 354–5.

The Universe of Pontus de Tyard. A critical edition of *L'Univers* with introduction and notes by J. C. Lapp. Cornell U.P., 1950. *M.L.R.,* XLVI, 1951, pp. 105–6.

B. Weinberg, *Critical Prefaces of the French Renaissance.* Evanston, Illinois, Northwestern U.P., 1950. *F.S.,* V, 1951, pp. 69–70.

J. Marouzeau, *Aspects du français*. Paris, Masson, 1950. *Archivum Linguisticum*, Dec. 1951, pp. 219–21.

Dépouillements de *Bibliothèque d'Humanisme et Renaissance*, Vols. XII–XXIV. *F.S.*, VI, 1952–XVII, 1963.

F. Desonay, *Ronsard, poète de l'amour*. Vol. I. Brussels, Gembloux, 1952. *F.S.*, VIII, 1954, pp. 63–4.

R. Hallowell, *Ronsard and the Conventional Roman Elegy*. Univ. of Illinois Press, 1945. *F.S.*, VIII, pp. 353–5.

Hans Urs von Balthasar, *Thérèse of Lisieux*. Transl. D. Nicholl. London, Sheed and Ward, 1953. *Theology*, Nov. 1954, pp. 436–7.

P. P. Morphos, *The Dialogues of Guy de Brués*. Baltimore, Johns Hopkins Press, 1953. *M.L.R.*, L, 1955, pp. 79–80.

Jean Rotrou, *Le véritable Saint Genest*. Edited with an essay on Rotrou's life and works by R. W. Ladborough. Cambridge U.P., 1954. *M.L.R.*, L, p. 367.

R. Heppenstall, *Léon Bloy*; E. Starkie, *André Gide*; M. Jarrett-Kerr, *Mauriac*. Cambridge, Bowes and Bowes, 1953 and 1954. *Theology*, Jan. 1955, pp. 85–6.

Remy Belleau, *La Bergerie*. Ed. D. Delacourcelle. Lille, Giard; Geneva, Droz, 1954. *F.S.*, IX, 1955, pp. 65–6.

C. A. Mayer, *Bibliographie des Œuvres de Clément Marot. I., Manuscrits. II. Editions.* Geneva, Droz, 1954. *F.S.*, IX, pp. 160–2. *B.H.R.*, XVII, 1955, pp. 337–9.

Jean de Sponde, *Méditations avec un Essai de Poèmes Chrétiens*. Intr. A. Boase. Paris, Corti, 1954. *F.S.*, IX, pp. 259–61.

F. Desonay, *Ronsard, poète de l'amour*. Vol. II. Brussels, Gembloux, 1954. *F.S.*, IX, pp. 257–9.

Ronsard, *Poésies choisies*, ed. P. de Nolhac. Paris, Garnier, 1954. *F.S.*, X, 1956, pp. 164–5.

Literature and Science. Proceedings of the Sixth Triennial Congress, Oxford, 1954. (International Federation for Modern Languages and Literatures). Oxford, Blackwell, 1955. *F.S.*, X, pp. 347–9.

A Critical Bibliography of French Literature. Vol. II. *The Sixteenth Century.* Ed. A. H. Schutz. Syracuse U.P. 1956. *M.L.R.*, LII, 1957, p. 113.

D. Thickett, *Bibliographie des Œuvres d'Estienne Pasquier*. Geneva, Droz, 1956. *M.L.R.*, LII, pp. 139–40.

Estienne Pasquier, *Choix de Lettres*. Ed. D. Thickett. Geneva, Droz, 1956. *M.L.R.*, LII, pp. 437–8.

H. Weber, *La création poétique au XVIᵉ siècle en France de Maurice Scève à Agrippa d'Aubigné.* 2 vols. Paris, Nizet, 1956. *F.S.*, XI, 1957, pp. 344–6.

Vauquelin de la Fresnaie, *Les Foresteries*. Ed. M. Bensimon. Lille, Giard; Geneva, Droz, 1956. *F.S.*, XI, pp. 346–7.

La Renaissance dans les Provinces du Nord. Entretiens d'Arras, 17–20 juin, 1954. Etudes réunies et présentées par F. Lesure. Paris, C.N.R.S., 1956. *F.S.*, XII, 1958, pp. 62–3.

O. Reverdin, *Quatorze Calvinistes chez les Topinambous. Histoire d'une mission genevoise au Brésil (1556–1558)*. Geneva, Droz; Paris, Minard, 1957. *F.S.*, XII, pp. 66–8.

I. Buffum, *Studies in the Baroque from Montaigne to Rotrou*. Yale U.P., 1958, *M.L.R.*, LIII, pp. 258–9.

J. von Stackelberg, *Humanistische Prosatexte aus Mittelalter und Renaissance*. Tübingen, Max Niemayer Verlag, 1957. *M.L.R.*, LIII, p. 461.

Philippe Desportes, *Cartels et Masquerades, Epitaphes*. Ed. V. E. Graham. Geneva, Droz; Paris, Minard, 1958. *F.S.*, XII, 1958, p. 367.

Bonaventure des Périers, *Cymbalum Mundi*. Ed. P. Nurse. Manchester U.P., 1958. *F.S.*, XIII, 1959, pp. 59–60.

Pierre Sala, *Tristan*. Ed. L. Muir. Geneva, Droz; Paris, Minard, 1958. *F.S.*, XIII, pp. 265–7.

Clément Marot, *Les Epîtres*. Ed. C. A. Mayer. London, Athlone Press, 1958. *F.S.*, XIII, pp. 351–2.

R. Mortier, *Un pamphlet jésuite 'Rabelaisant'. Le 'Hochepot ou Salmigondi des Folz' (1596). Etude historique et linguistique suivie d'une édition du texte*. Brussels, Palais des Académies, 1959. *M.L.R.*, LIV, 1959, p. 604.

Philippe Desportes, *Les Amours de Diane*. Ed. V. E. Graham. 2 vols. Geneva, Droz; Paris, Minard, 1959. *F.S.*, XIV, 1960, pp. 246–7.

F. Desonay, *Ronsard, poète de l'amour*. Vol. III. Brussels, Gembloux, 1959. *F.S.*, XIV, pp. 358–9.

Philippe Desportes, *Les Amours d'Hippolyte*. Ed. V. E. Graham. Geneva, Droz; Paris, Minard, 1960. *F.S.*, XV, 1961, pp. 262–3.

G. Gadoffre, *Ronsard par lui-même*. Paris, Seuil, 1960. *F.S.*, XV, pp. 364–6.

G. Dickinson, *Du Bellay in Rome*. Leiden, Brill, 1960. *F.S.*, XVI, 1962, pp. 57–8.

A. W. Satterthwaite, *Spenser, Ronsard and Du Bellay. A. Renaissance Comparison*. Princeton U.P., 1960; London, Oxford U.P., 1961. *F.S.*, XVI, pp. 174–6.

Philippe Desportes, *Elégies*. Ed. V. E. Graham, Geneva, Droz; Paris, Minard, 1961. *F.S.*, XVI, pp. 370–1.

Clément Marot, *Œuvres Satiriques*. Ed. C. A. Mayer. London, Athlone Press, 1962. *F.S.*, XVII, 1963, pp. 54–5.

B

I. Silver, *Ronsard and the Hellenic Renaissance in France*. Vol. I. *Ronsard and the Greek Epic*. St Louis, Washington U.P., 1961. *F.S.*, XVII, pp. 161–2.

Philippe Desportes, *Cléonice. Dernières Amours*. Ed. V. E. Graham. Geneva, Droz; Paris, Minard, 1962. *F.S.*, XVII, pp. 253–4.

G. Saba, *La Poesia di Joachim de Bellay*. Messina–Firenze, Casa Editrice G. d'Anna, 1962. *F.S.*, XVII, pp. 359–60.

Mythistoire Barragouyne de Fanfreluche et Gaudichon. Reproduction photographique de l'édition de Rouen [1578] avec des notes par M. Françon. Cambridge, Massachusetts, Schœnhof 1962. *F.S.*, XVII, pp. 361–3.

P. Mansell Jones, *The Assault on French Literature and other essays*. Manchester U.P., 1963. *The Economist*, 4 Jan. 1964.

Pierre de Ronsard, *Les Amours*. Ed. H. and C. Weber. Paris, Garnier, 1963. *F.S.*, XVIII, 1964, pp. 150–1.

Pierre de Ronsard, *Œuvres Complètes*. Vol. VIII. *Les Hymnes de 1555. Le Second Livre des Hymnes de 1556*. Ed. P. Laumonier and R. Lebègue. Paris, Didier, 1963. *F.S.*, XVIII, pp. 249–50.

Philippe Desportes, *Diverses Amours et Autres Œuvres Meslées*. Ed. V. E. Graham. Geneva, Droz; Paris, Minard, 1963. *F.S.*, XVIII, p. 256.

Clément Marot, *Œuvres Lyriques*. Ed. C. A. Mayer. London, Athlone Press, 1964 *F.S.*, XIX, 1965, pp. 53–4.

Jacques Lefèvre d'Etaples et ses disciples, *Epistres et Evangiles pour les cinquante et deux sepmaines de l'an*. Fac-similé de la première édition Simon du Bois, avec introduction etc. par M.A. Screech. Geneva, Droz, 1964. *F.S.*, XIX, pp. 177–8.

G. Castor, *Pléiade Poetics: a study in sixteenth-century thought and terminology*. Cambridge U.P., 1964. *F.S.*, XIX, pp. 179–80.

Conteurs français du XVIᵉ siècle. Ed. P. Jourda. Paris, Gallimard (Pléiade), 1965. *F.S.*, XX, 1966, p. 177.

Sixteenth-Century French Poetry. Ed. V. E. Graham. Toronto U.P., 1964. *F.S.*, XX, p. 178.

Currents of Thought in French Literature. Essays in Memory of G. T. Clapton. Oxford, Blackwell, 1965. *Yorkshire Post*, 19 May, 1966.

The 'Délie' of Maurice Scève. Ed. I. D. McFarlane. Cambridge U.P., 1966. *F.S.*, XX, pp. 394–5.

F. P. Bowman, *Montaigne: Essays*. London, Arnold, 1965. *F.S.*, XX, p. 397.

Dépouillements de *Bibliothèque d'Humanisme et Renaissance*, Vols. XII–XXIV *F.S.* 1952–63.

Joachim du Bellay, *Les Regrets et autres Œuvres Poétiques suivis des Anti-*

quitez de Rome. Plus un Songe ou Vision sur le mesme subject. Texte établi par J. Jolliffe. Intr. et comm. par M. A. Screech. Geneva, Droz, 1966. *F.S.*

J. A. de Baïf, *Les Amours de Francine.* Vol. I. *Sonnets.* Ed. E. Caldarini. Geneva, Droz, 1966. *F.S.*

Clément Marot, *Œuvres Diverses.* Ed. C. A. Mayer. London, Athlone Press, 1966. *F.S.*

D. Stone, Jr., *Ronsard's Sonnet Cycles.* Yale U.P., 1966. *F.S.*

H. T. Barnwell

SEVENTEENTH-CENTURY TRAGEDY:
A Question of Disposition

The tragic writers of seventeenth-century France were the first to consider their plays from the point of view of subject and sources. It is perhaps not altogether surprising, therefore, that modern scholars should have assumed that the meaning of the word *subject* was clear and required no definition, and that the sources were—chiefly, at any rate—of the kind admitted by the dramatists. There has obviously been a close connexion between the alleged subject and the acknowledged source, and this is not to be wondered at. Racine, for example, begins his prefaces to *Andromaque* with some lines from the third book of the *Æneid*, and follows them with the statement: 'Voilà, en peu de vers, tout le sujet de cette tragédie (...)' Subject is virtually identified with source.

My purpose in the following pages is to try to determine, however tentatively, whether this identification is valid; but this can only be done in the light of a definition of the subject of a play based on what we grasp of the dramatists' conception of their craft as revealed in their critical writings and in the plays themselves. We may then be in a position to suggest some of the uses to which the alleged sources were put. In all this much is bound to remain conjectural, but my aim will have been fully satisfied if these few reflections lead to a reconsideration, no matter how slight, of the essential nature of seventeenth-century tragedy. They will no doubt suggest more questions than answers. For I would make no claim to erudition, and shall confine myself to material which is already familiar, and, in particular, to the works of Corneille and Racine.

It is quite clear to me, as I have indicated elsewhere,[1] that Corneille's defence of his art as a tragedian is based on his conception of the subject—what he calls *le beau sujet*. Whatever sacrifices or concessions he felt bound to make to the views of his critics, he consistently refused to give any ground in the matter of the subject. Thus the modifications made in *Le Cid* appear insignificant when one considers the points on which the dramatist did not yield. The passionate behaviour of Chimène remained unchanged, for any change would have entailed abandoning the subject of the play as Corneille understood it; likewise, the possibility—to put it no higher than that—of the eventual marriage of hero and heroine is safeguarded by the retention of the original *dénouement*: if the ending had been altered to bring it into line with the conventional moral preconceptions of Chapelain and Scudéry, the subject of the play would have collapsed at the centre, since then its entire scale of moral values would have been inverted. In the same way, in spite of D'Aubignac's strictures, Corneille never accepted that the last part of Act IV and the whole of Act V of *Horace* were anything more than technically defective; but in making this admission he was at the same time maintaining the essence of his subject which was, I believe, authentically tragic—but only so long as the last part of the play remained intact.[2] Again, the only serious charge brought against *Théodore* concerned the essence of the subject,[3] and again Corneille neither abandoned nor modified it. Much later, his defence of *Sophonisbe* was a defence of the subject of the play which, so D'Aubignac averred, was unacceptable on the grounds of conventional morality: Mairet had handled the subject more satisfactorily because he had made concessions to that morality— and had thereby changed the supposed historical subject almost beyond recognition.

Not that fidelity to historical sources was in itself considered an indispensable or even valid criterion. Like Racine after him, Corneille was often quite prepared to show the points at which he departed from them, but the admission of such departures constituted on the one hand a demonstration of technical orthodoxy, and on the other a defence of the subject. In his Prefaces, Racine adopted the same kind of tactics as Corneille: thus, with regard to Pyrrhus, he played his critics off against each other. For some Pyrrhus was too remote from his Greek counterpart because of his resemblance to the seventeenth-century courtly lover; for others he was too near to the character in antiquity on account of his ferocity and violence.[4] Whatever suggestions may be advanced

that Racine was concerned primarily here with arguments relating to doctrinal questions of *bienséance* and *vraisemblance*, his
remarks constituted in effect a defence of the subject of *Andromaque* as conceived by him and in so far as it concerned Pyrrhus.

If then the subject of a play was so obviously central to both the
leading tragic dramatists, our first task must be to attempt to
establish in what it consisted. It is clear that when writing of the
constitution of the subject, these two authors adopted an am-
bivalent and sometimes quite cavalier attitude to their alleged
sources. It would be as well, therefore, if to begin with we were to
ignore those sources and to concentrate on the subjects of some of
the plays in themselves. And if we are in the ordinary way asked
what is the subject of a play, we usually begin by defining the
initial situation and the relationships between the characters. We
then pass on to describe the consequences and working-out of
those relationships as seen in plot and *dénouement*.

In the first place, we are probably inclined to consider the
subject as the story of certain individuals: in seventeenth-century
tragedy, the story for example of Nicomède, Prusias and Arsinoé,
or of Titus and Bérénice, or of Phèdre, Hippolyte and Thésée.
But once we have said this we are immediately faced with two
facts of literary history: one is that the story is often differently
told by each of two or more playwrights, and the other that a
story attached to one set of historical or mythological personages
may, at the hands of a particular dramatist, more closely resemble
the story of a different set of personages which may already have
been the subject of a tragedy written by another dramatist. In the
light of these facts, what *is* the subject? Is it the story, in whatever
version, of a particular group of individuals? Or does it consist in a
certain situation in which characters—however named, and
irrespective of historical and mythological connexions—stand in
certain relationships to each other?

Aristotle considered that the poet was chiefly a poet in the
sense of being a maker of plots, and that even if he took a well-
known theme or story (and he was not absolutely bound to do so)
as his subject, he need be faithful only to the broad outline of the
story, the rest—its particular development—being matter for
invention. The broad outline would consist in certain elements of
the initial situation, but chiefly in the nature of the catastrophe:
Corneille therefore had every right to distinguish between the
invented *acheminements* and the traditional *effet*.[5] The *Examen* of

Rodogune is particularly instructive in this connexion. Corneille begins by saying: 'Le *sujet* de cette tragédie est *tiré* d'Appian Alexandrin ...', and then goes on to quote some sentences from that historian. He claims as additional sources Justin, the book of *Maccabees* and Josephus. But, he says, 'c'est à lui [Appian] que je me suis attaché pour la narration que j'ai mise au premier acte [i.e. a definition of the initial *situation*], et pour l'effet du cinquième [i.e. the *catastrophe*] (...) Le reste sont des épisodes d'*invention*, qui ne sont pas incompatibles avec l'histoire (...)' In the next paragraph, Corneille explains his particular preference for this play by referring again to the 'incidents surprenants qui sont purement de mon invention et n'avaient jamais été vus au théâtre'. This tragedy is characterized first and foremost by 'la beauté du sujet, la nouveauté des fictions'. In the same way, Racine claimed the right to invent anything except 'le principal fondement d'une fable'.[6] Indeed, it was through this process of invention that a dramatist made a subject his own and attained that *nouveauté* for which the seventeenth-century public clamoured, and which was presumably a mark of originality.

We are confronted here with something of a paradox, which is surely enhanced by the contrast between Corneille's pride in venturing along new paths of inventiveness and Racine's claim, at certain stages in his career, merely to imitate the masters of antiquity. And the paradox is that in tragedy the traditional stories, as Aristotle called them, were to all intents and purposes unavoidable, but that they had to be made to appear new. Clarification on this point comes from a somewhat unexpected source—the writings of the painter Poussin:

> La nouveauté dans la peinture ne consiste pas surtout dans un sujet non encore vu, mais dans *la bonne et nouvelle disposition* et expression, et ainsi de commun et vieux, le sujet devient singulier et neuf.[7]

At this point, it is as well that we should observe that we have now found writers using two of the terms of formal Rhetoric: *inventio* and *dispositio*. Dr Peter France has admirably elucidated many features of Racine's characteristic style by considering them in the light of Rhetoric. He writes:

> *Inventio* was obviously useful in finding the characters something to say ... *Dispositio* enables him to put together the tirades ...; on a larger scale the spirit of *dispositio* might influence him in the orderly overall construction of the play (...)

He also says:

> (. . .) The preface to *Bérénice* for instance contains many references to rhetoric.[8]

It is, however, clear that those references may well be to the terms of Rhetoric, but that Racine does not use those terms as the rhetoricians did. When he says that 'il y en a qui pensent que cette simplicité est une marque de peu d'*invention*', he is referring specifically to the number of episodes in a play; and after the famous 'toute l'invention consiste à faire quelque chose de rien' he enumerates those things in which invention consists: *action, passions, sentiments* and, only in last place, *l'élégance des expressions.* Indeed, the advantage of the truncated sentence from Suetonius which opens the Preface was that it left Racine free virtually to invent his play almost in its entirety and not only in its words. As for *dispositio*, Dr France's second remark, detaching the word from Rhetoric proper, is certainly as apt and as important as his first, and it clearly links up with what Poussin had to say about *la bonne et nouvelle disposition* of the subject.

Two quotations, from works written more than a century apart, will help to clarify the point still further. The first is in Jean de La Taille's *Art de la tragédie* (1572):

> Or c'est le principal point d'une Tragedie de la sçavoir bien disposer, bien bastir, et la deduire de sorte qu'elle change, transforme, manie, et tourne l'esprit des escoutants de çà, de là... Quant à l'art qu'il fault pour la disposer et mettre par escript, c'est de la diviser en cinq actes (...)

The second quotation comes from Saint-Évremond's *Défense de Corneille* (1677) and is strikingly similar:

> J'ai soutenu que pour faire une belle comédie il fallait choisir un beau sujet, le bien disposer, le bien suivre, et le mener naturellement à sa fin (...)

To these we may add some other remarks of Poussin, taken from a letter containing his definition of painting:

> [La matière] doit être prise noble [cf. Corneille's *beau sujet*]... Il la faut prendre capable de recevoir la plus excellente forme. Il faut commencer par la disposition, puis par l'ornement (...) [etc.][9]

It is obvious that however little faith we may place in Louis Racine's gloss, 'comptant le reste pour rien', on the words he put into his father's mouth, 'ma tragédie est faite', those words have an air of probability if taken in conjunction with the kind of *disposition* of which the prose draft of Act I of the projected *Iphigénie en Tauride* gives us some slight evidence. Again Poussin is enlightening. In a letter written to his patron Chantelou in March, 1658, we read these words:

> J'ai arrêté la disposition de la *Conversion de Saint Paul* et la dépeindrai en temps d'élection.[10]

It would seem now, therefore, that invention, in terms of tragedy, consisted in making plot and action, and in developing a situation whose newness arose out of an original disposition of a dramatic situation. The first aspect of the subject lies in that disposition—making the subject new (or even 'inventing' it)—means effecting the disposition of its elements into a certain order or pattern. If, as we have so far done, we detach the subject from its supposed sources, we have to carry this process to its logical consequence: we must try to discern those elements in abstract terms by removing from them those things by which they are particularized—names, places, a specific historical or mythological context—those things by virtue of which they belong to a particular 'story'.

The situation made up of such elements has two facets, which I will call the circumstantial and the emotional. While these cannot, in the organic work of art, be separated, we can, for purposes of analysis, look at them separately.

Let us take two specific examples, each consisting of one play by Corneille, one by Racine and one by Rotrou. First, then, what is the circumstantial situation of *Nicomède* reduced to general and abstract terms? It is that of a weak old king who has two sons: the elder, by his first wife, is heir to the throne; the younger, by his second wife, has been brought up in a country which now threatens his own. The king can choose resistance, as advocated by the patriotic elder son, or what we should call appeasement, as suggested by the younger son, abetted by his mother. Now Corneille tells us[11] that he found his story in Roman history, he quotes chapter and verse, and he admits to having made certain far-reaching modifications to the alleged sources. He has eliminated the assassination of the king by the elder son and the king's intention to have the son killed; he has made the sons suitors of the queen of a country allied to their own; and he has invented the role of the ambassador of the strong foreign power. Now in doing this, Corneille has in fact created an entirely new disposition of the situation as it is to be found in Justin. He may not have invented this disposition in a strict sense, for one which is strikingly similar is to be found in Rotrou's *Cosroès*, as Professor Knight has observed.[12]

But whereas Rotrou develops the initial situation in such a way as to exploit its pathetic potential and writes a fundamentally sentimental tragedy, Corneille exploits its heroic potential and, as he himself says in the *Examen*, minimizes the sentimental element. The different purpose to which Corneille puts the circumstantial situation does not preclude the possibility that he took his cue from Rotrou's play. What is more to the point, however, is the contrast between the ways in which the situation is developed by the two playwrights. We can take this a stage further by moving on from *Nicomède* to *Mithridate*.[13] Here again several of the elements in the *Cosroès-Nicomède* situation are to be found, but Racine, in his turn, exploits it along his own lines, accentuating the love element and complicating it by making the king, as well as his sons, the suitor of the foreign princess (who is, furthermore, virtually his captive). So Racine's play becomes one largely of tempestuous love and jealousy; and he, like Corneille, has achieved his purpose by radically altering the disposition of the circumstantial situation he claims to have found in history.

Now in analysing these plays in this way, we discover that it is possible that, in spite of the variety of particularities drawn from quite different historical narratives, Corneille borrowed suggestions, at least, of the disposition of his play from Rotrou, and that Racine likewise borrowed from Corneille. There would be nothing surprising in this in view of the habits of seventeenth-century dramatists and the rivalries between them. I am not concerned, however, to argue for and against the sources of the plays.

A second point emerges, which is of greater importance. The disposition of the situation, as defined so far, has merely established certain relationships between characters which depend on their circumstances—family connexions, international alliances or hostilities, etc. But, once more, if we read Corneille's *Examen* of *Nicomède*, we find some valuable clues to his reasons for adopting or creating this situation. The projected marriage of Nicomède to Laodice will give 'plus d'ombrage aux Romains'; Nicomède is made the disciple of Hannibal 'pour lui prêter plus de valeur et plus de fierté contre les Romains'; Flaminius's mission is occasioned by the jealousy of the Romans; the situation is so contrived as to demonstrate Arsinoé's ambition and the budding 'gloire' and 'grandeur' of her stepson. Furthermore, the whole play illustrates, through the development of the situation, 'la grandeur de courage' and 'une prudence généreuse', and is calculated to excite the 'admiration' of the spectator.

These clues are crucial, because what they reveal to us is that the emotional aspect of the situation is described in terms of conflicting passions, as the seventeenth century understood the word. The characters are not the historical personages of Justin's narrative, but the embodiment of one or more of the passions. At the same time, the spectacle of the play will arouse certain passions in the audience. But to this point I shall return.

Now let us look briefly at our second group of plays. One could multiply comparisons of abstract situation, of course. For example, in the case of *Phèdre*, this has been done by scholars like Professors Pommier and Knight, showing Racine's possible debts not only to Euripides and Seneca and to modern writers (from Garnier to Bidar) who had used the same theme, but to Grenaille and Tristan, who had used the analogous theme of Crispus. But here, I am primarily concerned with *Andromaque*. In his two Prefaces, Racine, like Corneille in the *Examen* of *Nicomède*, first points to his alleged source, in Virgil, and then explains that he has departed from it in certain particulars. These changes are well known, but perhaps the most significant are that the heroine, although the captive of a foreign king, is not his chattel and concubine, as in antiquity, but a virtuous widow, devoted and faithful to the memory of her dead husband; and that the allied princess is betrothed but not married to the king. For these and other changes, Racine may have been indebted, as Voltaire suggested,[14] to Corneille's *Pertharite*, or, as Rudler wished to prove,[15] to Rotrou's *Hercule mourant*. But here, as with our first group of plays, we have to remember that the similarities lie chiefly in the external and circumstantial situation abstracted from its particular context, and that each of the three playwrights develops it in his own way. Lancaster maintained that Racine 'created little in his situations that was new': this remark is true only if we limit the nature of the situation to its external aspects.[16]

Racine's Prefaces to *Andromaque* are less rich in suggestions of his reasons for modifying his supposed source material than is Corneille's *Examen* of *Nicomède*. Yet one can see even there how Pyrrhus's love is thought of as his dominant passion, as is Andromaque's fidelity as hers. Indeed, Racine, like Corneille, obviously conceives of the circumstantial situation in terms of the emotional relationships between the characters. It would not be an exaggeration to say that he makes his whole play out of his two most important changes to the external situation (those I have already mentioned), for the whole action depends on Andromaque's resistance to the advances of Pyrrhus and on Hermione's passionate desire to possess him. It could well be that, in attributing the changes in the Greek myth and Virgilian narrative to the needs of *bienséance* and *vraisemblance*, Racine was not only defending himself against possible criticism from the *doctes*, but was also using precisely this kind of argument in order to distract attention from the real point, which was that he did *not* find his subject in the *Æneid* or in Euripides. It is significant that in listing the elements he claims to have used in Virgil's story, he does not mention situation.[17] What we have once more, then, is a circumstantial situation adopted or created in order to bring passions embodied in certain characters into conflicting relationships with each other; and that situation is developed through the logic and interaction of those relationships. This is quite clear when we compare Racine's play with those of Rotrou and Corneille, where the development is different because the passions and relationships are different. Again too, the tragedy is spoken of by its author in his second Preface in terms of the emotional response of the spectator.

There has, of course, always been much discussion of the passions in French tragedy, but that discussion has often been bedevilled by failure to distinguish between the passions experienced by the characters on the stage and those aroused in the audience. This was so in the controversy over the morality of drama as early as the seventeenth century itself. The distinction, however, has to be made, as Corneille made it at the beginning of the second *Discours*,[18] for the two sets of passions not only have different subjects and objects, but are of two different kinds. We must also be quite clear that, as Dr Anthony Levi's book[19] shows, the theory of the passions was a universal preoccupation central to the thought of the men of seventeenth-century France, and that it was in terms of the passions that all human behaviour was explained. There is no reason to suppose that the dramatists were any exception to the general rule which is illustrated by the abundance of moral treatises on this subject from Du Vair to Senault. Another important point is that during that period, the word *passion* was attached to a remarkably wide range of feelings or reactions: there is evidence enough of this in Descartes's *Les Passions de l'âme*, but his list is by no means exhaustive.

A reading of this treatise, published in mid-century, can have an important bearing on our enquiry in several respects. Remembering, as Corneille and Racine did, that according to Aristotle action is the essential feature of tragedy, we find that from the outset (Articles 1 and 2) Descartes virtually identifies action with passion:

> (...) Je considère que tout ce qui se fait ou qui arrive de nouveau est généralement appelé par les philosophes une passion au regard du sujet auquel il arrive, et une action au regard de celui qui fait qu'il arrive; en sorte que bien que l'agent et le patient soient souvent fort différents, l'action et la passion ne laissent pas d'être toujours une même chose qui a ces deux noms (...)
> (...) Nous devons penser que ce qui est en [l'âme] une passion est communément en [le corps] une action...

To read, say, the *Examen* of *Nicomède* or the Preface to *Phèdre* is to realize that their authors had a clear understanding of this relationship between action and passion. To read their plays is of course to be made aware that action springs from passion (provided that this word is interpreted as broadly as it was three hundred years ago). It is obvious, too, that if dramatic action consists in conflict, its sources must be in conflicting passions; and it is equally obvious, therefore, that the playwright has so to contrive his situation as to dispose the passions in conflicting relationships with each other.

A second important point is that the passions can be extremely complex and that they are closely linked to each other. Any given passion may engender a variety of frequently conflicting passions:[20] thus desire to attain some object may lead either to hope of possessing it or to fear of not doing so; hope, in its turn, may lead to courage, or if it alternates with fear, to irresolution; while fear may bring in its train despair and cowardice. Furthermore, each passion has its opposite. It is clear from Descartes's analysis that there may be conflict not only between opposing passions embodied in different dramatic characters, but also between conflicting passions within the same character. This goes a long way towards explaining the kind of disposition we find in Cornelian or Racinian situations and their development.

Descartes, of course, does not consider the passions to be bad in themselves, but only in excess or misuse. The greatest danger (see Articles 138, 160, 211) is that, lacking self-control through the will or *générosité*, we may be led into hasty action and that our passions may give us a false estimate of the good or evil inherent in the object of our passions. Again this provides us with some explanation of behaviour and conflict in the plays of both our tragic poets. What is more, Descartes points out the dangers (Article 145) of allowing our actions to be directed, thanks to uncontrolled passion, to false or unattainable ends: is this not the tragedy of Cléopâtre in *Rodogune*, or of Phèdre? And the essence of tragedy— of psychological tragedy as written in the seventeenth century—is to be found in Articles 41 and 45, for instance, where Descartes insists that we are not capable, by the mere exercise of the will, of arousing or suppressing the passions.

What we usually somewhat loosely call psychological tragedy is rightly considered to be the modern (particularly Elizabethan and seventeenth-century) contribution to the tragic genre. As far as Corneille and Racine and their French contemporaries are concerned, the adjective is perhaps not particularly well chosen. It tends to make us think that these writers were concerned with character-study 'in the round' and perhaps even static. But the word they are always using—and of course it features in their translations of Aristotle, too—is *les mœurs*, and that means not so much 'character' as 'behaviour' or 'habits of behaviour'. Men like Pascal, Méré and La Rochefoucauld are called *moralistes*, not *psychologues*. The point is important, because they are interested chiefly in behaviour, which implies action, and action, according to contemporary theory, springs from passion, as we have seen. So it is that La Rochefoucauld's moral system and observations are based on the notion of *amour-propre*, for example, considered as a passion. That the thinkers of the seventeenth century were aware of the novelty of their interest in the passions is evident from Descartes's opening remarks in *Les Passions de l'âme*:

> Il n'y a rien en quoi paraisse mieux combien les sciences que nous avons des anciens sont défectueuses qu'en ce qu'ils ont écrit des passions... C'est pourquoi je serai obligé d'écrire ici en même façon que si je traitais d'une matière que jamais personne avant moi n'eût touchée (...)

If, then, the representation and disposition of the passions in the characters on the stage may rightly be thought of as a distinctly modern characteristic in seventeenth-century tragedy, and if it is also the passions which are seen to be the very seeds of tragedy itself, the same cannot of course be said of those passions which the spectacle of the victims of passion is supposed to excite in the spectator. Pity and fear, at any rate, come from antiquity, even if Corneille and Racine add to them the 'Cartesian' passions of *admiration* (or wonder) and *tristesse*.[21] And just as the passions experienced by the characters are the source of action in the plot, so those experienced by the spectators are the source of the 'poetic' action in their minds. Neither kind of action, however, would be possible without conflict, and conflict has to be arranged by the poet in the making of a dramatic situation. It is this situation and its development which properly constitute the *subject*.

If this is so, what are we to make of the dramatists' claims about their sources? They almost invariably point to some classical source—history, poetry or drama—and say something like 'Voilà le sujet de ma tragédie'. It is perfectly clear, as we have seen, that the 'source' does not provide the real subject.

Part of the explanation for this lies in the polemical nature of the prefaces, etc. Yet, behind the apparent striving after some semblance of doctrinal or scholarly orthodoxy, writers like Corneille and Racine display ambiguous attitudes to their 'sources', and those attitudes reveal their true preoccupations as dramatists. On the one hand, they may protest fidelity to history or legend if that provides them with justification for portraying situations, episodes or human characteristics which would otherwise be thought of as so extraordinary as to be incredible; on the other hand, they may admit departures from the traditional story when the dramatic needs of the situation, episode or character demand it. Arguments about historical truth, *vraisemblance* and *bienséance* may, as often as not, be blind alleys, while the playwright manipulates his treatment of the alleged sources in the light of his dramatic preconceptions. And those preconceptions will appear first and most obviously in the creation of the initial situation.

Then, one may ask, why worry about the sources at all? The answer to this question is twofold. First, the doctrinal answer. It is part of orthodox theory, from Aristotle onwards, that tragedy concerns itself with traditional stories. Those stories can be modified, as Aristotle himself points out—hence the several versions or interpretations of many of the traditional stories. Both

Corneille and Racine were quick to follow this lead both in their dramatic practice and in its defence. Linked to this theory was the idea of tragedy being concerned with a few families and therefore being associated with a few well-known names.

But if the 'sources' were virtually a doctrinal necessity, they could also be turned to practical use. The mention of Rome, for instance, was sufficient in seventeenth-century France to suggest an aura of grandeur and heroism, and this could certainly be made more precise and more telling by the addition of the name of some well-known person or event. There was no question of seventeenth-century readers obtaining or even seeking an authentic picture of Roman history: it provided them very largely with an idealized state characterized by certain moral values. If, then, Corneille chose to set his dramatic situation in some period of Roman history and to give his characters Roman names, he was doing so because he could be assured that his audience would immediately recognize and respond to the moral climate and the kind of passions displayed. In the same way, evocation of the mythological world of the Greeks provided an aura of fatality: when Racine set his situations in that world, he counted on provoking an immediate, if vague and rather ill-informed, response, and could then display the fatality of the passions through the symbols of the ancient myths.

It is probably a delusion to think that Corneille was any more 'authentic', historically, than Racine. He does not hesitate to invent a character where that is necessary to his situation, nor to prolong a life, nor to arrange an impossible meeting between two characters, nor to suppress facts which loomed large in his sources. Both Corneille and Racine become involved in tortuous arguments in which what they are really trying to do is to fit purely imaginary situations, involving imaginary characters and their passions and relationships, to a 'traditional story'. That story—or at least certain elements in it—is useful and even essential, for it enables the playwright not only to make use of an atmosphere or setting, but, even more important, to give his characters names, an identity, an air of reality, a time and place for their activities. It is through the story, then, that abstract concepts of situation, passion and relationships are particularized.

Since no writer in the age of Louis XIII or Louis XIV would ever admit to making use of the work of a contemporary, and since the polemics were directed largely against pedants with little dramatic sense and no creative genius, it is of course quite impossible to know in any particular instance whether Corneille or Racine found the first suggestion for a tragic situation in the supposed source, in the work of a contemporary or in his own imagination. It does seem likely, however, that the situation is what came first, and that, since nothing in that situation was ever sacrificed for the sake of historical accuracy or even doctrinal orthodoxy—the arguments are often means of twisting the doctrine to fit the situation and subject—, the situation contained the essence of the drama. On the other hand, the 'sources' were undoubtedly a powerful agent in the creation of the 'world' of the tragedy— a world dominated by a certain set of values and passions, but a world also constructed in order precisely to demonstrate those values and passions in action and requiring its 'climate' to make them flourish. That is not to say that those values and passions belong exclusively to the world of the 'source': on the contrary, they are universal, but the world of the play enables the poet to intensify them to the tragic pitch. We notice the same kind of thing in a novel like *La Princesse de Clèves*. It is immaterial whether the setting is that of the reign of Henri II or of Louis XIV: what it provides is a society which could not possibly exist but which is so closed in on itself that no one's actions or feelings escape public notice. This setting must be provided for the intense development of the passions which make up Mme de La Fayette's situation: love, jealousy, fear, shame.

The setting of the 'source' and the attendant names and major events of a tragedy may well, therefore, be dictated by the exigencies of the subject, which could possibly be conceived quite apart from them. We might, accordingly, derive some profit from refraining from thinking of the plays of Corneille and Racine in terms either of character-study or of their supposed sources. Instead, taking a lead from Poussin, we might consider the disposition first—the disposition of passions embodied in the characters—, and see the dramatic situation thus conceived developing in the action to which (if I may be excused the pun) the passions dispose the characters, as Descartes puts it:

> …L'usage de toutes les passions consiste en cela seul qu'elles disposent l'âme à vouloir les choses que la nature dicte nous être utiles, et à persister en cette volonté…[22]

That remark could well be the epigraph for a study of the tragedies of the two French masters of the genre, which, in their hands, displays the dire effects of man's persistence in pride or sensual passion.

NOTES

[1] See 'Some reflections on Corneille's theory of *vraisemblance* as formulated in the *Discours*'. *Forum for Modern Language Studies*, Vol. I (1965), pp. 295–310.

[2] Cf. my lecture, *The Tragic in French Tragedy*, Belfast, The Queen's University (1966), pp. 13–14.

[3] D'Aubignac, *La Pratique du Théâtre*. Ed. Martino, Paris, Champion (1927), pp. 66, 133–4.

[4] First Preface to *Andromaque*.

[5] Corneille, *Second Discours*, in *Writings on the Theatre*, Oxford, Blackwell (1965), pp. 46.

[6] Second Preface to *Andromaque*.

[7] *Lettres et propos sur l'art*. Ed. Sir Anthony Blunt, Paris, Hermann (1964), pp. 172–3.

[8] *Racine's Rhetoric*, Oxford, Clarendon Press (1965), pp. 31, 13.

[9] J. de La Taille, *De l'Art de la tragédie*. Ed. F. West, Manchester University Press (1939), pp. 26–7; Saint-Evremond, *Œuvres*, 1740, Paris ed., Vol. IV, pp. 52–3; Poussin, Letter to Chambray, 1 March 1665, in *Lettres*, Ed. P. du Colombier, Paris, Cité des Livres (1929), p. 310. It is not without interest that, in his preface to *Samson Agonistes*, Milton wrote of the 'economy and disposition of the fable'.

[10] *Lettres*, p. 298. Racine's correspondence is also revealing. In a letter to Le Vasseur (28 March 1662), he writes of his poem, *Les Bains de Vénus:* 'Ce n'est pas une pièce, ce semble, tout à fait nouvelle pour vous; mais vous la trouverez pourtant toute nouvelle. Je l'avais mise en l'état qu'elle est huit jours devant ma maladie, et je l'avais même montrée à deux personnes seulement... Et ils étaient tous deux amoureux du dessein et de la conduite de cette fable.' In June 1661, Racine had written to the same correspondent about his work on his *Amours d'Ovide*: '...J'ai fait, refait et mis enfin en sa dernière perfection tout mon dessein... Avec cela, j'ai commencé même quelques vers...'

[11] *Examen* of *Nicomède*.

[12] '*Cosroès* and *Nicomède*.' *The French Mind: Studies in honour of Gustave Rudler*, Oxford, Clarendon Press (1952), pp. 53–69.

[13] G. G. Rudler's introduction to *Mithridate*, Oxford, Blackwell (1960), pp. xxiii–xxv.

[14] *Commentaire sur Pertharite*. It is significant that Voltaire uses the word 'ordonnance' here, analogously to 'disposition'.

[15] 'Une source d'*Andromaque: Hercule Mourant* de Rotrou'. *Modern Language Review*, Vol. XII (1917), pp. 286–301, 438–49.

[16] *A History of French Dramatic Literature in the Seventeenth Century*, Baltimore, Johns Hopkins (1940), Part IV, Vol. I, p. 55. Lancaster, like Mornet, points to other possible sources for the situation of *Andromaque*.

[17] It is also of some importance that, in the second Preface, Racine states

expressly, writing of Euripides's *Andromache:*' ... Quoique ma tragédie porte le même nom que la sienne, le sujet en est pourtant très différent.'
[18] *Writings on the Theatre*, pp. 28–9.
[19] *French Moralists. The Theory of the Passions, 1585 to 1649*, Oxford, Clarendon Press (1964).
[20] *Les Passions de l'âme*, Articles 53 ff.
[21] For example, Articles 53 and 61.
[22] Article 52. In fact, Descartes takes this matter of disposition a stage further when in the *Traité de l'Homme*, ed. Adam and Tannery, Paris, Cerf (1909), Vol. XI, pp. 166–7, he connects the passions with the humours: '...Ces (...) humeurs, ou du moins les passions auxquelles elles disposent, dépendent (...) beaucoup des impressions qui se font dans la substance du cerveau.'

A short study complementary to this article appears in the *Australian Journal for French Studies*, IV, 2 (May–August 1967) under the title 'Some notes on Poussin, Corneille and Racine'.

E. Beaumont

LA FEMME PAUVRE AND FEMININE MYTHOLOGY

In her rogues' gallery of myth-makers Simone de Beauvoir gives
Bloy no place, an omission which will perhaps surprise few readers.
Yet, lightly as we may take some of the ideas of Léon Bloy, his
view of woman, in its fusion of pungent earthiness and religious
symbolism, offers a refreshingly original perception of the meaning
of womanhood in the only world that existed for Bloy, the valley
of tears separating the lost Eden from the apocalyptic manifestation of God's glory on earth. Of the many who have written on
Bloy, only two critics have devoted much attention to his view of
woman: Stanislas Fumet, writing in 1935,[1] and a Luxembourg
critic, Hubert Juin, writing in 1957.[2] In his important, though
too enthusiastically censorious work, infused as it is with the
spirit of a narrow Tridentine dogmatism, Raymond Barbeau
gives only passing mention to the subject, promising a future
book, *Léon Bloy l'Initié*, which will explain the arcanum of the
earthly paradise symbolized by the sex of woman.[3] He thus
makes the mistake of inverting the symbols, for in fact Bloy
maintained that it was the earthly paradise that symbolized
woman's sex.[4] This explanation of a misunderstood notion remains, however, among the pleasures in store. What is noteworthy in the case of all these writers and others, illuminating as
are the comments of Fumet and Juin, is that none seems to have
realized the full scope of *La Femme pauvre* (1897), the grandiosity
of the vision that Bloy was seeking to convey. This is no cause for
wonder, as Bloy did not in fact entirely succeed in presenting the
fulness of his vision. It is only in the light of Bloy's ideas, to be
gleaned elsewhere in his work, that we can fully comprehend the
striking conception of woman's destiny that he tried to embody in
his second and last novel.

While Bloy was still contemplating the composition of *La Désespérée*, to be a companion novel to *Le Désespéré*, he wrote on 24 February 1887, to the editor of the Editions Quantin, outlining the shape of his projected work.

> Le central concept de ce roman [he wrote], est le sexe *physiologique* de la femme, autour duquel s'enroule où se débobine implacablement sa psychologie tout entière. Pour parler net, entre nous, la femme dépend de sa vulve comme l'homme de son cerveau. L'idée n'est pas neuve. Elle pourrait avoir soixante millions de siècles, si l'histoire humaine avait elle-même cet âge ridicule. Mais il est possible de la renouveler et d'en donner même une impression terrifiante, en la poussant à ses plus extrêmes conséquences et c'est précisément ce que je me propose avec l'espoir de démontrer la vérité absolue.[5]

It was, of course, ever Bloy's way to push ideas to their extreme consequences; it was by this means that he achieved his startling originality. The idea that the psychology of woman derives from her physiological nature is a commonplace, now incorporated in every form of psychological thinking on the subject. Schwartz, for instance, refers to 'the matrix from which the feminine character springs'[6] and affirms that 'for the woman, her sexuality is part of herself, of her being (...)'[7] Similarly, Buytendijk tells us at the end of his essay on existentialist psychology that 'le corps féminin est le centre du monde féminin (...)'[8] This fundamental notion Bloy always held. Thus, when the project of *La Désespérée* had become the project of *La Prostituée*, the passage quoted above was copied textually, save for the omission of the words *entre nous* and the substitution of *sexe* for *vulve*, in the long letter written to Johanne Molbech at 4 a.m. on 27 November 1889,[9] a letter which is a most valuable source for Bloy's view of woman.

Bloy's differentiation between brain and vulva as the respective centres of man and woman is no doubt a simplification devised for its striking effect; we should not, I think, understand it too literally. He cannot have meant, one hopes, that woman is unable to think, but he probably meant that her thinking is informed, or directed, by her sexual nature, by her sexual reactions. Schwartz refers to 'a conflict inherent in woman's existence. She has a brain and a womb', he tells us; 'like an ellipse she has, as it were, two centres compared with the one centre of the man's existence, which may be likened to a circle. For the woman her sexual function is essential, whereas it is only accidental to the man'.[10] Bloy would certainly not have subscribed to the notion of conflict, as he clearly regarded the womb, or rather the vulva, as dominant in the woman. Later in the work from which I have just quoted, Schwartz affirms that 'it is difficult for a woman to erect such a partition between brain and womb (...)'[11] Again, Bloy would probably have contended that there is no such partition, that in fact the thought-processes of women are determined to a large extent by their sexual reactions. However, these quotations from contemporary psychologists have been introduced merely for the purpose of indicating the psychological respectability of Bloy's basic notion about the nature of woman. He is at one with twentieth-century psychologists in regarding the sexual nature of woman as colouring her whole being.

For Bloy no natural phenomenon has a purely natural cause. The sexuality of woman, the fact, as he wrote so many times, that woman worships the exterior sign of her sex, which he believed that she unconsciously considers to be the threshold of paradise, is fully justified, perfectly explained, through the Incarnation.[12] Woman is right to regard her primary sexual characteristics as being of such inestimable value, 'cause of our joy' and 'gate of heaven'—attributes of Mary from the Litany of Loreto that Bloy applies in this context without thought of irreverence—because this part of her body was the tabernacle of the living God, the womb in which Christ was conceived and brought to birth. No one, wrote Bloy, can assign limits to the solidarity of this stupendous mystery;[13] that is to say, no one can set any limit to the implications this event involves. Bloy himself, as we shall see, drew far-reaching conclusions from it.

Often enough in the thought of Christian poets the role of Mary has been linked with that of every woman, of whom she is the archetype, woman in her perfection. As Mary was instrumental in giving birth to Christ, in presenting him to the world, in thus bearing man's salvation in general, so may a particular woman bring Christ, as it were, to a particular man. Through a certain woman met at a certain juncture, a man may see God, may begin the ascent towards God, whatever the obstacles to be overcome. Frequently this notion of a woman being the bearer of salvation is associated, consciously or not, with the Platonic idea of the image through which reality is perceived. It is of course Dante who has provided the world with the literary prototype of this woman, the Beatrice, though there have been in successive centuries many heroines cast in her mould, the best-known being probably those of Fogazzaro and Claudel. For Bloy, however, there is no question of a Beatrice; moreover, he knew neither Plato nor Plotinus. As he confided to Johanne Molbech, 'la philosophie m'ennuie, la théologie m'assomme, les paroles sans amour me sont inintelligibles, les raisonnements des sages m'apparaissent comme un cloaque de ténèbres et l'orgueil de l'esprit me fait vomir'.[14] Bloy's thinking on this subject follows a firmly physiological course: through Mary's conception of Christ, the matrix of woman, every woman, has been sanctified. It will have been noticed that Bloy tends to identify womb and vulva, or at least closely associates them, an association for which there is obvious anatomical justification. It is through the conception of Christ that woman is entitled to regard herself as a dispenser of joy by means of the entry to paradise which her body promises. The Virgin Birth is not commonly interpreted in this fashion and we shall have occasion to examine the implications that Bloy derives from Mary's conceiving through the Holy Ghost.

Bloy's isolation of the womb as being especially sanctified by the Incarnation may seem arbitrary. One might perhaps maintain that every part of the body of man has been made sacred by Christ's assumption of a human body, of a male body in particular. Though this is true, it is also evident that a woman, Mary, formed Christ's body within her, from her own body gave birth to the God-man. This fact does seem to give to woman's body an intimacy with the divine that no man's body has and it would seem to confer on it an exclusive privilege. This elevated view of woman's body, of her sexual and generative organs in particular, has, however, to be brought into relationship with the actual behaviour of existing, imperfect women. Though women may, as Bloy affirms, all consider their bodies as the portal of paradise, possibly few, if any, tremble at the thought that they may conceive an *alter Christus*, or that this is the high purpose for which their matrix is designed. Such a notion is none the less implicit in Christian belief, if it is logically regarded. Basing himself on this lofty view, Bloy fulminates against women who sell themselves, for they are guilty of an incalculable sacrilege. For Bloy, whose view is always fresh and free from conformism, women who sell themselves are those who make a marriage of self-interest, a *mariage raisonnable*.

Cette jeune fille d'esprit léger et de cœur frivole [he wrote to Johanne Molbech], qui, pour échapper à sa famille, pour être appelée Madame, pour avoir des toilettes et des parures ou, pour d'autres raisons plus méprisables encore, livre au premier drôle venu qui s'appellera son mari le tabernacle *possible* d'un Dieu,—cette jeune fille fait sangloter la Troisième Personne divine, elle fixe pour mille ans peut-être, sur sa Croix de feu, Notre patient Seigneur Jésus qui allait en descendre, elle décourage les esprits d'en haut, et fait gronder effroyablement les esprits d'en bas, elle pousse le verrou sur tous les captifs, aggrave la désolation des créatures et désespère les agonisants.[15]

For prostitutes, on the other hand, Bloy had, in common with the earlier romantics, an inalienable sympathy, because prostitutes are often poor and are always numbered among the despised and rejected. Bloy did not consider the prostitute as a woman who sells her body—he ignored this inconvenient aspect of her trade— but as a woman who provides pleasure. Having made of the sex of woman the basis of her being—as contemporary psychologists also tend to do—and having conferred on her sexual characteristics a capital importance, indeed a supernatural significance, he is obliged to make of the woman who lives, as it were, on her sex a being at least virtually privileged. Minimizing the venal side, he emphasizes the gift of self. Bloy in fact recognises only two modes of existence for woman: the prostitute who gives herself to any-body and everybody and the saint who gives herself totally to God, what he calls Mary Magdalene before and Mary Magdalene afterwards. Between the two there is only the respectable woman, 'c'est-à-dire la femelle du *Bourgeois*, du réprouvé que nul holo-causte ne peut racheter. Une sainte peut tomber dans la boue et une prostituée monter dans la lumière, mais l'affreuse pécore sans entrailles et sans cerveau qu'on appelle une honnête femme et qui refusa naguère l'hospitalité de Bethléem à l'Enfant Dieu, est dans une impuissance éternelle de s'évader de son néant par la chute ou par l'ascension'.[16] This is not of course a theological statement that the Redemption was intended for only a section of mankind, but merely a strongly pointed paradox.

This gift of self, as Bloy sees it, this universally bestowed 'love', coupled with the evident abjection of her condition, brings the prostitute in close relationship with the Holy Ghost as Bloy con-ceives the Third Divine Person. The prostitute is woman reduced to the lowest state to which she may descend *qua* woman. In view of the supernatural importance that Bloy attributes to woman's sexual function, the prostitute's life is a sort of continuous sacrilege, a parody of the perfect gift of herself made by Mary, a parody of true love, but it is a parody and not a negation, not a refusal. We know that Bloy liked to picture the Holy Ghost in the form of some despised and mocked individual, living in poverty and ignominy, as he did himself. He thus considered Naundorff, whose claim to be Louis XVII he took seriously, as a last prefiguration of the Holy Ghost.

> Et maintenant [he wrote in his book on this personage], quand viendra L'AUTRE? 'Il m'est impossible, écrivais-je en 1894, de penser à cet homme de rêve et de prodige [Naundorff], sans être atteint dans l'intime de mon âme. La figure de Louis XVIII, errant et renié par toute la terre, n'est-elle pas la plus étonnante *prophétie*? Je songe qu'il y a certainement QUELQU'UN de très-pauvre, de très-inconnu et de très-grand, qui souffre de la même manière, *en ce moment*, et qu'il faut avoir peur de méconnaître, quand on LE rencontrera'. Ceux qui pensent avec moi que ce Consolateur des désespérés ne peut apparaître que lorsque le monde sera en agonie, doivent, aujourd'hui, l'attendre d'heure en heure.[17]

For Bloy the Third Divine Person is best figured by an outcast, a wandering beggar, as well as by the Cross of Christ, the Cross of ignominy and suffering to which Christ was so closely attached.[18] With less picturesque use of symbolism, we may see the Holy Ghost as the perfect gift of love, that which the Father and Son have for one another and which is offered freely to the whole of mankind through the Cross, within the Church, and in every act of human love, but which is nevertheless often spurned and sometimes derided. Even within this more conventional interpretation of the function of the Holy Spirit, it is easy to see the analogy which Bloy points between the Third Divine Person and the idealized prostitute. Bloy is in any case not alone in establishing the parallel. Baudelaire had done so before him.[19] The projected novel, *La Prostituée*, was to reveal this relationship in fictional terms. 'As-tu compris, chère amie', he wrote to Johanne Molbech, 'que je veux montrer, pour l'étonnement des âmes médiocres, la miraculeuse connexité qui existe entre le Saint Esprit et la plus lamentable, la plus méprisée, la plus souillée des créatures humaines, la Prostituée?'[20] Among the manifold aims of Léon Bloy is always to be found the desire to scandalize, so that it is not always easy to distinguish, in the expression of his thought, between what is intended to shock and what corresponds to his inner conviction. Usually, however, the two things coincide admirably.

A further complication arises in the labyrinth of Bloy's system of multiple analogies with the nature of the relationship between

Mary and the Holy Ghost. It is a commonplace of mystical
theology to refer to Mary as the Spouse of the Holy Ghost, 'sa
chère et indissoluble Epouse', wrote Grignion de Montfort in his
Traité de la vraie dévotion à la Sainte Vierge,[21] a work which deeply
influenced Léon Bloy. If we bear in mind that in the sphere of
conjugal relations, viewed in the light of Christian symbolism, the
man and woman constitute 'one flesh', we may perhaps understand something of what Bloy, with his basic earthiness, his
emphasis on the body, means when he states that 'entre elle
[Woman] et le Saint Esprit il y a une telle affinité qu'on peut
humainement les confondre et qu'il est difficile de ne pas imaginer, avec certains Mystiques, le Troisième Règne, c'est-à-dire le
triomphe du Paraclet, procuré par Celle dont il est dit qu'elle
rira au Dernier Jour'.[22] Woman is for Bloy essentially Mary. In
the thought of Grignion de Montfort, the Second Coming which
for Bloy takes a Joachimite form, the Third Reign, that of the
Holy Ghost, is to be coincident with the manifestation of the
glory of Mary.[23] Bloy expresses the same notion in this way in his
unfinished *Symbolisme de l'apparition*:

> C'est Elle-même [Mary] qui sera ce Paradis de volupté arrosé par les
> quatre fleuves des mains et des pieds du Rédempteur crucifié et dont
> l'Eden perdu n'était qu'une image; Jardin fermé et Fontaine scellée
> (Cant., IV, 12) jusqu'à ce que Celui dont elle est en même temps la
> Mère, la Sœur et l'Epouse vienne dans son règne et fasse sanctifier son
> Nom sur la terre aussi bien qu'au Ciel.[24]

Those words need to be borne in mind when we come to consider
the relationship that Bloy saw between woman and the earthly
paradise which is for him an image of woman and which is to be
identified with Mary herself.[25]

The close relationship of the Holy Ghost with the feminine is
frequently encountered in the more mystical speculations of
Christian theology, particularly in the Eastern Churches.
Evdokimov, a Russian Orthodox thinker of our own times, tells
us that there is a deep connexion between the Holy Ghost, Sophia,
the Virgin and the feminine. He points out that: 'En langue
sémitique, l'Esprit a deux genres, il peut être féminin; les textes
syriaques sur le Consolateur disent la Consolatrice. *L'Evangile des
Hébreux* met dans la bouche du Christ l'expression 'ma mère
l'Esprit-Saint'. Selon l'expression du Père Boulgakoff il est *la
maternité hypostatique*, il révèle le Fils au Père et le Père au Fils'.[26]
At the same time Evdokimov takes care to indicate that these

expressions are not intended to introduce any feminine element in God but refer to the feminine aspect of certain manifestations of God in the world. Other Russian theologians seem less prudent, as Bulgakov has in fact been accused of postulating the feminine principle within the Godhead.[27] However, my purpose in mentioning these Russian writers is merely to show that the thinking of Bloy is related to a current of thought still being developed within the Russian Orthodox Church.

Surprisingly enough, Bloy does not seem to have made use of *Proverbs*, the eighth chapter of which so much struck Claudel that it coloured all his thinking on woman and which is also the basis of the theological notion of Sophia or Divine Wisdom as being essentially feminine.[28] Claudel came eventually to identify Divine Wisdom and Mary, greeting the latter in *Le Chant de marche de Noël* with words taken from *Proverbs*. So does C. G. Jung, in his *Antwort auf Hiob*, regard her as the incarnation of Sophia. 'The divine immaculateness of her status', he there writes, 'makes it immediately clear that she not only bears the image of God in undiminished purity, but, as the bride of God, is also the incarnation of her prototype, namely Sophia'.[29] Though these words of Jung correspond more to the thinking of Claudel than to that of Bloy, there is much elsewhere in the *Answer to Job* that is strikingly in harmony with the ideas of Bloy.[30]

The imagery of the eighth chapter of *Proverbs*, of inspiration not only to Claudel but to many other poets, including Milton[31] and Patmore,[32] may help to throw light on Bloy's analogical reasoning with regard to woman and the earthly paradise:

The Lord possessed me in the beginning of his way,
Before his works of old.
I was set up from everlasting from the beginning,
Or ever earth was,
When there were no depths, I was brought forth;
When there were no fountains abounding with water
. . . .
When he established the heavens I was there:
. . . .
When he marked the foundations of the earth:
Then I was by him, as a master workman:
And I was daily his delight,
Rejoicing always before him;
Rejoicing in his habitable earth;
And my delight was with the sons of men.[33]

It is easy to see how this personification of Divine Wisdom in a feminine figure may give rise to the notion of womanhood pre-existent in the divine order before the world was created and, being the delight of God, constituting paradise. It is no less easy to see how she becomes identified with Mary, so that the latter readily acquires the characteristics there attributed to creative Wisdom. Other Sophianic texts from *Ecclesiastes* and the *Song of Solomon*, quoted by Jung,[34] reinforce the notion of divine delight in feminine activity, reminding us that in Jewish thought the creation of the world was itself the consequence of an act of divine fecundation.[35] These biblical passages evoke the heavenly paradise of which the earthly paradise is but an image, one, more-over, which contemporary theological thinking, spurred by the discoveries of paleontology and anthropology, has had to con-fine to the domain of meta-history.[36] Bloy's analogies, how-ever, remain independent of the discoveries of science, as they do of the categories of theologians. For him Mary *is* the earthly paradise. The earthly paradise is the symbol of woman. 'La première femme venue', he wrote in his book on Joan of Arc, 'est déjà tout un mystère, puisqu'on ne trouve pas mieux que le Paradis terrestre pour la symboliser. Elle centralise tellement toutes les convoitises et concupiscences humaines! Mais la Vierge est l'objet de la concupiscence divine et l'Esprit-Saint qui est l'Amour même n'y résiste pas'.[37] In the eyes of Bloy, God's love of Mary is not an etherealized concept, but a real love with all the delight that that entails; she is his paradise, as woman is man's paradise, as indeed Johanne Molbech was, so he said, Léon Bloy's paradise.[38] The liturgical terms applied to Mary have a meaning, as Evdokimov affirms: 'Ce n'est point seulement du lyrisme, lorsque la liturgie appelle la Vierge "Paradis" ', 'Porte du Royaume', 'Ciel', 'le réalisme liturgique donne comme axe à l'histoire la réalité très concrète exprimée dans ces noms'.[39] Grignion de Montfort, whose imagery may well have influenced Bloy's thought, goes even farther. He expressly affirms that Mary is the earthly paradise of the new Adam, Christ.[40]

Conceived without sin, Mary herself belongs to the state be-fore the Fall, to the earthly paradise, as Jung so clearly per-ceives.[41] Alone of human beings, she lived in that state of inno-cence. In that sense she *is* the earthly paradise persisting in the fallen world. But, Bloy also affirms, the earthly paradise is a symbol of woman. Woman is therefore more basic than the earthly paradise, she is the reality of which the earthly paradise is but an image. We have already seen that for Bloy woman's body is the portal of paradise, not only in her own possibly unconscious view of it, but in reality, through Mary's conception of Christ. Woman's body gives the promise of joy, in every sense, from physical delight to the redemption of mankind. In the timelessness of God, this must always be so. It is perhaps now easier to see how the earthly paradise, the ideal state that man should have enjoyed on earth and to which access still seems possible, in some sense, under certain conditions, symbolizes woman. Psychology, with its emphasis on child images of the mother and on sexuality as a prime factor in human life, would not perhaps give the lie to Bloy's vision.

Further light may possibly be brought to this complex subject by reference to Coventry Patmore. When he affirms that 'heaven becomes very intelligible and attractive when it is discovered to be —Woman',[42] he is following a line of thought different from Bloy's, yet fully in harmony with it. For Patmore there is a universal bi-polarity; the masculine and the feminine run through the whole cosmos. All love for the higher is feminine, all love for the lower masculine, a notion which could hardly fail to anger Simone de Beauvoir. All love for God is feminine and, in so far as heaven expresses love for God, it is woman. The Word made flesh is the Word made Woman, since all 'descent' is a transition from the masculine mode to the feminine; the whole of mankind is feminine in relation to God and Christ also is feminine in relation to the Father. 'Woman', wrote Patmore, 'is the sum and complex of all nature, and is the *visible* glory of God'.[43] The glory of God, Bloy never tires of saying, is Mary.[44] Thus, for the inveterate lover of woman, as both Patmore and Bloy were, all things lead to woman.

In Bloy's system of exegesis all oppositions are resolved. As much as Jung, he sees in mankind, and possibly in the Godhead as well, a *conjunctio oppositorum*. The opposites meet, become even identified, in some sense, in Bloy's thought. As we have seen, Mary is the joy of man, *causa nostræ laetitiæ*, she is the mother of Christ, she who gave birth to the Saviour of mankind; but she is also the *mater dolorosa*, she who, at the foot of the Cross, suffered more than any other human being has ever done, because of her perfect nature, and who, if we take account, as Bloy so wholeheartedly did, of the message of La Salette,[45] is still suffering

because of the sins of mankind. The earthly paradise, affirms
Bloy, is not only joy, it is also suffering:

> Marie est le Paradis terrestre, je ne le dirai jamais assez. Mais qu'est-il
> donc, ce paradis terrestre et où est-il? Aux temps de foi, il y eut des
> chrétiens pour le chercher. Raymond Lulle paraît y avoir pensé et on
> raconte que Christophe Colomb ne désespérait pas de le rencontrer
> aux Antilles ou un peu plus loin. Mélanie seule a trouvé le paradis
> terrestre,[46] bien connu pourtant avant elle, mais sans dénomination
> précise—comme on découvre un trésor qui est sous les pieds de tout le
> monde—et elle l'a reconnu tel par l'effet d'un miracle d'illumination
> intérieure. *Le Paradis terrestre, c'est la Souffrance*, et il n'y a pas d'autre.
> En réalité, l'homme est toujours dans le Jardin de Volupté et son
> expulsion n'est qu'apparente. Seulement, depuis la Désobéissance, il
> s'est vu nu, il a vu nus la terre et tout ce qui est sur la terre, il a connu
> que la souffrance n'est autre chose que la volupté toute nue. Des saints
> innombrables ont pu avoir ce pressentiment, mais rien de plus qu'un
> pressentiment, parce que l'Ere de l'Absolu n'avait pas commencé.[47]

The condition wrought in man by the Disobedience, by the
Fall, has of course been most diversely interpreted. Among recent
glosses, a strikingly optimistic view, cosmogonically, is provided
by Charles Williams, for whom the Fall was but a change in the
mode of knowledge, since, according to him, there can only be
good to know: therefore the Adam and Eve knew good as
antagonism. Their descendants may prolong the Fall by their
own will or they may reduce the antagonism by their conformity
with the divine will,[48] the realization of their essential selves.
Bloy's conception of the Fall is not, perhaps, very much different:
suffering is the new mode of knowledge that man has inflicted on
himself by his disobedience. Suffering, experienced to the full and
accepted, is the only means now accessible to man—and especially
to woman, since she is herself symbolized by the garden of Eden—
to live as wholly as possible in the earthly paradise, which is the
anticipation of paradise proper.[49]

In the passage which I have quoted from the introduction to
the *Vie de Mélanie*, Bloy equates suffering with 'volupté toute nue',
an expression which may perhaps be understood in variously
different ways. The nakedness may refer to the withdrawal of
God's intimacy. Without God's felt presence, having forfeited his
confidence, man saw himself in his nakedness, saw everything
naked, stripped as it were of its proper fulfilment. In these circumstances, man could only experience pleasure as suffering. If,
however, we interpret Bloy's terms at the level of human experience alone, existentially, then this equation of pleasure with

pain reveals itself completely in harmony with psychological thinking. Indeed, what Bloy does is to offer a supernatural key to human causality. That there is an intimate connexion between pleasure and pain we all know: pleasure at its most intense becomes or is replaced by pain, whilst pain, physical or moral, constitutes for some people, of pathological condition, the only form of pleasure they are able to enjoy. Moreover, it would seem that it is in woman that these two opposites tend to be most clearly associated. In the concept of masochism which Hélène Deutsch sees as the basis of feminine nature, the two modes of pleasure and suffering are clearly related. 'The attraction of suffering', she writes, 'is incomparably stronger for women than for men'.[50] Most psychologists would probably subscribe to this view. 'We must reflect on the indissoluble bond which links love, sacrifice and suffering', writes Buytendijk, 'only then shall we reach the heart of feminine existence'.[51]

Those psychologists, such as Buytendijk, who recognize a spiritual dimension, also associate woman closely with it. 'Cette métamorphose, cette renaissance, cette sanctification, cette spiritualisation, cette élévation—ou quelque nom qu'on y donne', writes Buytendijk, 'est possible pour tout être humain; elle n'est pas spécifiquement féminin mais forme pourtant le mystère de l'intériorité féminine'.[52] Evdokimov goes even farther, making of woman the stronger sex in all that has to do with religion:

> On comprend ce rôle [the infinitely significant role of woman in future history and in religious revival, according to Berdyaev], si on comprend la valeur métaphysique de la nature féminine; *dans la sphère religieuse c'est la femme qui est le sexe fort*. L'erreur classique de tous les commentateurs du récit de la chute est d'expliquer la démarche de Satan auprès d'Eve comme étant faite auprès du 'sexe faible', de la partie la plus vulnérable de l'être humain. En réalité c'est juste le contraire. Eva a été tentée en tant que principe religieux de la nature humaine, c'est dans ce principe avant tout qu'il fallait blesser l'homme et le corrompre.[53]

This relationship of woman to the religious principle of human nature is expressed by Bloy with customary trenchancy in the phrase that Gertrud von le Fort takes as epigraph for *Die ewige Frau*:[54] 'Plus une femme est sainte, plus elle est femme'.[55] The order is, as always, significant. The closer woman comes to God, the more her feminine nature is realized, a statement fraught with vast implications. In the last chapter of *La Femme pauvre*, Clotilde thus fulfils her destiny. She is, really and truly, in so far as this is possible on earth, in paradise, therefore wholly Woman. 'Je suis heureuse,' she tells a priest. 'On n'entre pas dans le Paradis demain, ni après-demain, ni dans dix ans, on y entre *aujourd'hui*, quand on est pauvre et crucifié'.[56]

The movement that we follow in *La Femme pauvre* is from the superficial form of the earthly paradise, mere pleasure, which is only a parody of paradise, the appearance of it, to the deepest and most authentic experience of the earthly paradise, in the condition created by the Fall, suffering at its most extreme: woman deprived of home, husband, child and of all but fortuitous means of subsistence. One may see how this is prostitution spiritually understood: Clotilde has given everything, she has nothing left to give but her life itself, offered at every moment to God himself, who may thus entirely possess her: 'Elle a même compris, et cela n'est pas très loin du sublime, que la Femme n'*existe* vraiment qu'à la condition d'être sans pain, sans gîte, sans amis, sans époux et sans enfants, et que c'est comme cela seulement qu'elle peut forcer à descendre son Sauveur'.[57] As Mary was the tabernacle of the living God, the flesh from which he took his own flesh, so potentially is every other woman, but for woman born with original sin the tabernacle is perfectly created in her only when she is deprived of all else; Mary, too, knew the keenness of grief, the maximum of sorrow.

The theme of the earthly paradise runs through the whole of *La Femme pauvre*, as it does throughout Bloy's work.[58] In her banal *liaison*, ending in the usual abandonment, Clotilde experiences but a parody of the earthly paradise. Closer association with the lost Eden comes with the knowledge of the cult of Eve, mother of all the living (Gen. iii, 20), an Eastern devotion taught her by a missionary.[59] In her dreams Clotilde now enters the inaccessible Garden:

Je me rappelle qu'en mon sommeil Vous [Eve] me preniez par la main et qu'on allait ensemble dans un pays adorable où les lions et les rossignols périssaient de mélancolie. Vous me disiez que c'était le Jardin perdu, et Vos grandes larmes, qui ressemblaient à de la lumière, étaient si pesantes qu'elles m'écrasaient en tombant sur moi. Cela me consolait, pourtant, et je m'éveillais en me sentant *vivre*.[60] M'abandonnerez-Vous aujourd'hui, parce que d'autres ont eu pitié de Votre enfant?[61]

Clotilde is a child of Eve, as all women must be. Throughout the first part of the novel she and the others live in exile from Eden,

D

entering it only in dreams or seeking it through art. The very
animals bespeak this sense of exile, seeming to retain a secret they
are unable to tell.[62]

All sorrow is that of exclusion from the earthly paradise: 'On a
beau chercher, on ne trouvera pas une souffrance hors du cercle
de feu de la tournoyante Epée qui garde le Jardin perdu. Toute
affliction du corps ou de l'âme est un mal d'exil, et la pitié
déchirante, la compassion dévastatrice inclinée sur les tout petits
cercueils est, sans doute, ce qui rappelle avec le plus d'énergie le
Bannissement célèbre dont l'humanité sans innocence n'a jamais
pu se consoler'.[63] A child is for his parents an image of the earthly
paradise, but for Clotilde this image is removed. Marriage with
Leopold, happy beyond expression, had brought with it participation in the earthly paradise, but never completely enduring: 'Une
Joie mélancolique, surnaturellement douce et calme, arrivait,
chaque matin, pour eux seuls, d'une contrée fort inconnue.
Laissant à leur porte toutes les poussières des chemins, toutes les
rosées des bois et des plaines, tous les arômes des monts lointains,
elle les éveillait gravement pour le travail et le poids du jour'.[64]
There can be no doubt of the identity of the 'contrée fort inconnue'.[65] But the husband, too, is lost, after the child. When all is
lost, then all is possessed. The earthly paradise may be experienced
anew, in a suffering fully understood and accepted.

At first sight, it may seem that Bloy takes as harsh a view of
sanctity as Bernanos, with his devil-tormented Donissan, his
clumsy cancer-plagued country priest, his raped and murdered
Chantal. Indeed, both writers regard the deepest joy as the fruit of
suffering and associate holiness with continuous self-offering. Yet
there is in the closing chapter of La Femme pauvre a serenity, a
luminosity which, even in Dialogues des Carmélites, Bernanos never
achieves. On the human level, as well as the eschatological, Bloy
is profoundly optimistic. Not only does his heroine survive in
paradisiacal beatitude, but she has previously known, as well as,
of course, squalor, seduction, exploitation and persecution, the
altruistic kindness of the sculptor and the full joy of reciprocated
love in marriage. This basically optimistic view of the human
condition that characterizes Bloy stands out all the stronger if we
compare the turn that Clotilde's life takes after her initial mis-
adventure, with the fate of Bernanos's two Mouchettes; their
background is essentially the same as that of Clotilde, their
disillusioning experience not dissimilar. Both kill themselves;

beforehand, the first Mouchette, Germaine Malorthy, eaten up with self-hatred, murders her first lover and subsequently lives in a world of falsehood, even of mental derangement for a time, desecrating with perverse pleasure her disappointed and misused self, indeed giving herself up to Satan. Undoubtedly, our sense of tragic fatalism is better satisfied by Bernanos who is in any case much the superior artist, one of the greatest of the twentieth century. Both the darkness and the light convince us in Bernanos, fitful as the light may seem in the vast expanse of darkness. In *La Femme pauvre* Bloy expresses only one side of his nature, the luminous: Clotilde, Gacougnol, Marchenoir and Léopold are all idealized, even sentimentalized. The darkness is exterior, embodied in wicked secondary figures, Chapuis, Mme Maréchal, Mme Poulot, Mme le Grand. The value of the novel lies in the ultimate vision; there and there only does Bloy reach aesthetic authenticity, revealing, by an imaginative transference entirely different in intention from Flaubert's, what it *means* to be a woman, what womanhood is in its essence.

Certainly, the vision that *La Femme pauvre* provides is of woman as victim. Clotilde is first a victim of her environment, of her mother and of her mother's lover, a victim, too, of the 'bellâtre quelconque'[66] who seduces her. Finally, she is the victim of God's love, as in a sense Christ is. She is shown in the last chapter as 'poor and crucified'. In his first play, *Tête d'Or*, Claudel too portrays woman in similar fashion: the Princess sees her father killed and herself disinherited and outcast, ultimately nailed to a tree, a crucifixion which could hardly symbolize more clearly the Passion on Mount Calvary. She brings Grace, of which she is also an image, as she is an image of Sophia, but she is none the less a victim, suffering crucifixion. The idea of woman's close association with Christ, primarily deriving from the dogma of the Virgin Birth, takes many strange forms. Charles Williams, for instance, saw woman as living the bleeding on the Cross in her monthly cycles, involuntary and inescapable stigmata. Women are sharers, he maintains, in the victimization of the blood: 'They are mothers and, in that especial sense, victims: witnesses, in the body, to the suffering of the body, and the method of Redemption'.[67] In *Taliessen in the Rose-Garden*, one of Williams's Arthurian poems, the king's poet expressly links this shedding of blood on the part of women with the Dolorous Blow and with the healing Christ.[68] It is perhaps noteworthy that both Bloy and

Williams intimately link the sexual and genetic characteristics of woman with her closeness to Christ' primarily as an instrument of joy in Bloy and as a participation in Christ's Passion in Williams. But, even in the latter's thought, as possibly best illustrated in this respect in his last novel, *All Hallow's Eve*, the body, 'Creation's and Creator's crowning good', as Patmore wrote,[69] is an occasion of joy; after the death of his wife, Richard visualizes 'the high thing which was now in his mind, the body that had walked and lain by his, (...) itself celestial and divine'.[70] She herself, in the state following death that Williams imagines, still feels joy in her sexual nature,[71] though ultimately both she and her living husband must will their separation.[72]

When he came to write his novel, Bloy muted the themes of prostitution and the sexual dependency of woman, which almost any novel of Zola's illustrates more effectively than *La Femme pauvre*. The nearest Clotilde comes to actual prostitution is the visit to Gacougnol's in the guise of artist's model, a profession which she regards as a form of prostitution, for the model sells the artist the nudity of her body and sacrifices to him her modesty, which is intimately associated in Bloy's unifying symbolism with the image of the Holy Ghost which for him woman presents.[73] As it happens, Clotilde is spared the humiliation she fears, being allowed to pose draped. Indeed, the 'central concept of this novel', so clearly expressed in the various letters written by Bloy between 1887 and 1889, has obviously been modified: the notion of woman which it was to have imaginatively embodied is instead summarized in Chapter XX of Part One, which is transcribed with few alterations from the letter of 14 March 1887, to Georges Khnopff, and that of 27 November 1889, to Johanne Molbech. The existence of this chapter is itself an admission of failure. Bloy was not able to achieve his vision in all its complex grandiosity. Emphasis is given in the novel itself to the attainment of the earthly paradise through maximized suffering. This culminating vision overshadows all else; unless one reads the work with an eye well versed in Bloy's symbolism, the full meaning of the transformation that takes place in the heroine, the gradual realization in her of the earthly paradise which is itself but a symbol of womanhood, that human nature which is nearest to divine nature, may well not be grasped. Salvation will come only from saintliness, writes Evdokimov:

or celle-ci est plus intérieure à la femme dans les conditions de la vie actuelle. La Vierge *conserve les paroles du Fils dans son cœur* (Luc, 2, 51), toute femme a une intimité innée, presqu'une complicité avec la tradition, la continuité de la vie. En Dieu, l'existence coïncide avec l'essence, la femme est plus apte à rapprocher dans la sainteté l'essence et l'existence par la force de l'humilité, car 'L'Humilité est l'art de se trouver exactement à sa place'. A l'opposé de tout égalitarisme et revendication, c'est le rayonnement le plus naturel de son état charismatique. C'est le ministère du Paraclet, la grâce de consolation et de joie, et qui postule l'être féminin en tant que mère pour qui tout être est son enfant. La Beauté sauvera le monde; non point n'importe quelle beauté, mais celle de l'Esprit-Saint, celle de la *Femme habillée de soleil*.[74]

It is this same vision which, over sixty years earlier, *La Femme pauvre* embodies. Essence and existence are indeed brought into the closest relationship in the forty-eight year old Clotilde, this 'column of prayer',[75] for whom there is only one sorrow, not to be a saint. It is a remarkable vision, unique in literature, and the thought-processes which gave rise to it and which I have tried to elucidate in this essay, odd as they may seem to the rationalist, are hardly less remarkable. Bloy really relates religious data with the very act of living, with the basic elements of human life itself; moreover, he relates them as closely as possible. This is no small and no ordinary achievement.

NOTES

[1] Stanislas Fumet, *Mission de Léon Bloy*, Paris, Desclée de Brouwer (1935).
[2] Hubert Juin, *Léon Bloy*, Paris, Editions du Vieux Colombier (1957).
[3] Raymond Barbeau, *Un prophète luciférien, Léon Bloy*, Paris, Aubier (1957), p. 133.
[4] Léon Bloy, *La Femme pauvre*, Paris, Livres de Poche (1964), p. 162; Léon Bloy, *Jeanne d'Arc et l'Allemagne*, Paris, Crès (1915), p. 31; Léon Bloy, *Lettres à sa Fiancée*, Paris, Stock (1947), p. 52 (letter of 3 November 1889).
[5] Quoted by Joseph Bollery, *Léon Bloy, essai de biographie, Vol. II, 1882–1892*, Paris, Albin (1949), p. 235, and to be found also in Léon Bloy, *Lettres à sa Fiancée*, p. 78 (letter of 27 November 1889).
[6] Oswald Schwartz, *The Psychology of Sex*, London, Penguin Books (1949), p. 122.
[7] *Ibid.*, p. 136.
[8] F. J. J. Buytendijk, *La Femme, ses modes d'être, de paraître, d'exister: essai de psychologie existentielle*, Paris, Desclée de Brouwer (1954), p. 377. (This is a French translation from the Dutch by Alphonse de Waelhens and René Mich.)
[9] *Lettres à sa Fiancée*, p. 78.
[10] *Op. cit.*, p. 121.
[11] *Ibid.*, p. 132.

[12] See the letter to the editor of Editions Quantin, quoted by Joseph Bollery, *op. cit.*, p. 235, a copy of which was sent to Georges Khnopff on 14 March, 1887 (Léon Bloy, *Lettres à Georges Khnopff*, Liège, Editions du Balancier (1929), pp. 22–3, also quoted by Joseph Bollery, *op. cit.*, p. 236), and the letter to Johanne Molbech of 27 November 1889 (*Lettres à sa Fiancée*, p. 79).

[13] *Lettres à sa Fiancée*, p. 81 (letter of 27 November 1889); *La Femme pauvre*, p. 163.

[14] *Lettres à sa Fiancée*, p. 47 (letter of 31 October 1889).

[15] *Ibid.*, p. 75 (letter of 27 November 1889).

[16] *Lettres à Georges Khnopff*, p. 25; letter to Denise T . . . ., of 21 March 1887 (Léon Bloy, *Lettres aux Montchal*, Paris, Bernouard, undated, pp. 301–2); letter to Johanne Molbech of 27 November 1889 (*Lettres à sa Fiancée*, p. 80); *La Femme pauvre*, p. 162.

[17] Léon Bloy, *Le Fils de Louis XVI*, Paris, Mercure de France (1926), p. 221.

[18] *Lettres à sa Fiancée*, pp. 42–3 (letter of 24 October 1889).

[19] Baudelaire, *Mon cœur mis à nu* (fragment non numéroté, *Œuvres complètes*, Paris, Bibliothèque de la Pléiade (1961), pp. 1286–7): 'L'être le plus prostitué, c'est l'être par excellence, c'est Dieu, puisqu'il est l'ami suprême pour chaque individu puisqu'il est le réservoir commun, inépuisable de l'amour.' Cf. *Fusée*, I, 'L'amour, c'est le goût de la prostitution. Il n'est même pas de plaisir noble qui ne puisse être ramené à la Prostitution.'

[20] *Lettres à sa Fiancée*, p. 81 (letter of 27 November 1889).

[21] Louis-Marie Grignion de Montfort, *Traité de la vraie dévotion à la Sainte Vierge*, 6me édition canadienne (1916), p. 11. Grignion de Montfort was a seventeenth-century religious who founded the Company of Mary (Montfort Fathers). He was canonized by Pope Pius XII in 1947.

[22] *Jeanne d'Arc et l'Allemagne*, pp. 31–2.

[23] *Op. cit.*, pp. 30 seq.

[24] Léon Bloy, *Le Symbolisme de l'Apparition*, Paris, Lemercier (1925), p. 260.

[25] This identification is made especially in *Vie de Mélanie, Bergère de la Salette, écrite par elle-même en 1900, son enfance (1831–46)*, introduction de Léon Bloy, Paris, Mercure de France (1954), p. 25.

[26] Paul Evdokimov, *La Femme et le Salut du Monde*, Tournai, Casterman (1958), p. 215.

[27] N. O. Lossky, *History of Russian Philosophy*, London, Allen and Unwin, 1952, p. 231.

[28] With regard to Claudel, see Paul Claudel, *J'aime la Bible*, Paris, Fayard (1955), p. 8, and Paul Claudel, *Mémoires improvisés*, Gallimard (1954), p. 51. With regard to the sense in which Sophia is feminine in Orthodox theology, see in particular Serge Bulgakof, *Du Verbe incarné 'Agnus Dei'*, Paris, Aubier (1943), pp. 7–63 and pp. 121–37, and Lossky, *op. cit.*, pp. 103–4, pp. 206–10, pp. 227–31.

[29] C. G. Jung, *Collected Works, vol. 11, Psychology and Religion: West and East*, London, Routledge and Kegan Paul (1958), p. 398. (This work is translated from the German by R. F. C. Hull.)

[30] Jung sees in man—and in God—a *conjunctio oppositorum*. Christ (and Mary) were exempted from the 'dark' side of man's (and God's) nature. After the Assumption (the definition of which by Pope Pius XII was the occasion of Jung's *Antwort auf Hiob*), the way is open for God's continuing Incarnation, but now in *total* man, comprehending the 'dark' as well as the 'light' side. It is not clear to me whether Jung understood this Incarnation as taking place in man collectively (as Teilhard de Chardin seems to do) or in one person in particular (as Bloy seems to do). In any case, Jung sees Satan as the elder brother of Christ, the 'dark' son of God, and he regards the story of Cain and Abel as a prefiguration of the relationship of Satan and Christ. With the new era, upon which we are supposedly entering, woman is closely associated, being indeed the religious figure *par excellence*. All this echoes, with much less caution, much less veiling of meaning, the thinking of Bloy, particularly as interpreted by Raymond Barbeau.

[31] Milton, *Paradise Lost, Book VII*, ll. 1–12.

[32] Coventry Patmore, *The Angel in the House*, Part I, Book I, Canto VIII, Prelude IV.

[33] *Proverbs*, VIII, 22–31 (RV).

[34] *Op. cit.*, pp. 386–90.

[35] S. Karppe, *Etude sur les origines de la nature du Zohar*, Paris, Alcan (1901), p. 64.

[36] See I.-H. Dalmais, o.p., *La Justice originelle*, in *Initiation théologique, tome II, Dieu et sa Création*, Paris, Editions du Cerf (1957), p. 402.

[37] *Jeanne d'Arc et l'Allemagne*, p. 31.

[38] *Lettres à sa Fiancée*, pp. 51–2 (letter of 3 December 1889): 'C'est toi-même, ma chère épouse bien-aimée, qui seras alors (after marriage), qui es déjà mon paradis de délices et remarque bien, mon amour, que ce mot n'est pas une simple caresse de langage, une de ces tendres exagérations par lesquelles les cœurs épris essayent de mettre un peu d'infini dans leurs sentiments. Il est rare, tu le verras, que je parle, sans savoir profondément ce que je dis. Le deuxième chapitre de la Génèse où se trouve décrit le paradis terrestre est, à mes yeux, une figure symbolique de la *Femme*. C'est une des découvertes dont je suis le plus fier, car je t'assure que cette exégèse est d'une beauté incomparable (...)'

[39] *Op. cit.*, p. 32.

[40] *Op. cit.*, p. 3.

[41] *Op. cit.*, p. 398.

[42] Coventry Patmore, *The Rod, the Root and the Flower*, Aurea Dicta, LXXII.

[43] *Ibid.*, Homo X.

[44] E.g. *Le Symbolisme de l'Apparition*, p. 169.

[45] On 19 September 1846, two shepherd children, Mélanie Calvat and Maximin Giraud, claimed to have received a message from Mary who had appeared to them at La Salette, in the mountains not far from Grenoble. This was a message of penitence and referred to the suffering of Mary on account of the sins of mankind. For various reasons, to do both with the nature of the two children, especially Maximin Giraud, and the contents of the message, ecclesiastical encouragement of devotion to

the shrine was long hesitant and never wholehearted. Bloy, introduced to the shrine by Abbé Tardif de Moidrey in 1879, was immediately attracted by the message, which corresponded well with his own expectations. For an intelligent examination of the subject, see J. Jaouen, *La Grâce de la Salette*, Paris, Editions du Cerf (1946).

⁴⁶ For Bloy, Mélanie Calvat is 'l'annonciatrice et la prophétesse du *Christianisme absolu*' (*Vie de Mélanie*, p. 25). It is inconceivable how any one could take her so-called autobiography seriously. It is clearly a tissue of imaginative inventions in which she attributes to herself supernatural contact with the Child Jesus in earthly form from earliest childhood. R. P. Jaouen regards her as an hysteric. She took the Carmelite habit at Darlington on 25 February 1855, but was relieved of her vows on her return to France on 28 September 1860. In November 1860, she entered another religious community in Marseille, but left in 1867 without having taken any vows. She then lived with a companion until 1889, when the latter died, and thereafter lived alone, frequently changing her abode. She died at Altamura, in Italy, in 1904. Bloy was not alone in rating her so highly. At her funeral oration in Messina, Canon Annibal-Marie de France paid eloquent farewell to this 'angelic creature' (see Léon Bloy, *Celle qui pleure*, Paris, Mercure de France (1949), p. 235).

⁴⁷ *Vie de Mélanie*, p. 25.

⁴⁸ Charles Williams, *He came down from Heaven*, London, Heinemann (1938), p. 19, p. 42.

⁴⁹ In one of his 'further paradoxes', Henri de Lubac writes that pain and joy are correlatives and more than correlatives. 'La douleur est l'envers de cette unique étoffe dont l'endroit est—ou sera—la joie... Sous les espèces de la douleur, la substance de la joie est là, déjà' (Henri de Lubac, s.j., *Nouveaux Paradoxes*, Paris, Editions du Cerf, 1955, p. 71). The thought, expressed in more scholastic terms, is identical with Bloy's.

⁵⁰ Hélène Deutsch, *The Psychology of Women: a Psychanalytical Interpretation*, London, Research Books, 1946, Vol. I, *Girlhood*, p. 216.

⁵¹ *Op. cit.*, p. 375.

⁵² *Ibid.*, p. 279.

⁵³ *Op. cit.*, pp. 153-4.

⁵⁴ Gertrud von le Fort, *Die ewige Frau—Die Frau in der Zeit—die zeitlose Frau*, Munich, Kösel-Pustet (1934). In his introduction to the French translation of this book, RP H.-Ch. Desroches, o.p., claims with evident approval, that Gertrud von le Fort's whole book is 'un commentaire éblouissant' of this phrase of Bloy's, Gertrud von le Fort, *La Femme éternelle*, Paris, Editions du Cerf (1952), p. xxviii. (The book is translated from the German by André Boccon-Gibod.)

⁵⁵ *La Femme pauvre*, p. 83.

⁵⁶ *Ibid.*, p. 445.

⁵⁷ *Ibid.*, p. 446.

⁵⁸ See Marie-Joseph Lory, *La Pensée religieuse de Léon Bloy*, Paris, Desclée de Brouwer (1951), pp. 115-20.

⁵⁹ *La Femme pauvre*, p. 45.

⁶⁰ *Vivre* appears in italics because *Eve* means *life* (Gen. iii, 20). According to Evdokimov, the name was conferred on Eve on account of the Christ-

bearing destiny of the second Eve, as Mary is so often called. See
Evdokimov, *op. cit.*, p. 152.

[61] *La Femme pauvre*, p. 186.

[62] *Ibid.*, p. 132.

[63] *Ibid.*, p. 332.

[64] *Ibid.*, p. 310.

[65] According to Orthodox tradition, the sacrament of marriage is
fraught with paradisal grace, enabling the married partners to participate in the edenic conjugal state. See Paul Evdokimov, *Sacrement de
l'Amour: le mystère conjugal à la lumière de la tradition orthodoxe*, Paris, Editions
de l'Epi (1962), pp. 174, 177, 197, 206, 210.

[66] *La Femme pauvre*, p. 48.

[67] Charles Williams, *The Forgiveness of Sins*, London, Bles (1942), p. 41.

[68] Charles Williams, *The Region of the Summer Stars*, London, O.U.P.
(1944), pp. 26-7.

[69] Coventry Patmore, *The Unknown Eros*, Book II, VII.

[70] Charles Williams, *All Hallows' Eve*, London, Faber (1945), pp. 189-90.

[71] *Ibid.*, p. 152.

[72] *Ibid.*, p. 226.

[73] The passage of the letter of 2 December 1889 to Johanne Molbech
concerning this subject is omitted from the published edition of *Lettres à sa
Fiancée*, but the omitted passage is quoted by Raymond Barbeau, *op. cit.*,
pp. 140-1.

[74] *La Femme et le Salut du Monde*, p. 221. The 'woman arrayed with the sun,
and the moon under her feet, and upon her head a crown of twelve
stars', comes of course from the *Apocalypse* or *Revelation*, XII, I. She is
commonly identified with Mary in mystical speculations. Indeed, this
verse of the *Apocalypse* is incorporated in the Introit for the Mass on 15
August, the feast of the Assumption. The 'woman arrayed with the sun'
occurs not only in the work of Bloy (*Le Symbolisme de l'Apparition*, p. 65),
Claudel (e.g. *La Rose et le Rosaire*, Egloff (1946), p. 64) and many others,
such as Abbé Pernety and Abbé Constant, but also in Jung's *Answer to
Job*, (*op. cit.*, pp. 438-9).

[75] Cf. Paul Evdokimov, *Sacrement de l'Amour: le mystère conjugal à la
lumière de la tradition orthodoxe*, p. 46: 'La femme est l'orante, l'image de
l'âme en adoration, l'être humain devenu prière' and p. 85: 'Dans les
catacombes, l'image la plus fréquente est une figure de femme en prière,
'l'orante', elle représente la seule attitude vraie de l'âme humaine. Il ne
suffit pas *d'avoir* la prière, il faut devenir, *être*, prière, prière incarnée. Il
ne suffit pas d'avoir des moments de louange, il faut que toute la vie, tout
acte, tout geste, jusqu'au sourire du visage humain, devienne chant
d'adoration, offrande, amour'. This is in fact what Clotilde achieves.

Madeleine Blaess

LE GRAND MYSTÈRE DE JÉSUS

When, in 1885, the Vicomte Hersart de la Villemarqué completed
his self-imposed task of publicizing Breton works by publishing
the only known Breton Passion play, he made little stir. Paul
Meyer, in the *Revue Critique d'Histoire et de Littérature*, I (1866), pp.
219–29, was more concerned with refuting the claims that de la
Villemarqué made as to the antiquity of the play than with
passing more than a hasty (though essentially correct) judgement on the work itself:

> Le mystère breton est l'abrégé du mystère français [the Jean Michel
> *Passion*]. Plusieurs scènes sont supprimées, presque toutes resserrées: de
> nombreux détails ont été élagués, quelques-uns ont été ajoutés, et ceux-là
> ont une couleur assez moderne qui contredit l'opinion de M. de la
> Villemarqué sur la date de l'ouvrage. On remarque aussi dans le
> drame breton un tour emphatique que ne présente pas le texte fran-
> çais . . . (p. 225).

By an examination of the death of Judas, he then went on to show
that the Breton author undoubtedly had the Jean Michel *Passion* of
1486 before him, but all this was merely incidental to demolishing
Hersart de la Villemarqué's preface.

Almost 20 years later, Emile Roy, in his *Le Mystère de la Passion
en France du XIVe au XVIe siècles*, (1905), refers to the Breton
Passion several times (pp. vi, 59*, 270, 293) before discussing it
briefly.[1] It has 'de curieuses particularités' (p. 306), notably the
type of 'peines d'Enfer' that Lazarus describes (and which is the
only 'particularité' to attract Emile Roy[2]). Apart from this, the
Breton play seems to fall into oblivion.

And is this oblivion justified? Perhaps the time has now come
for a re-appraisal of this much-neglected play.

Le Grand Mystère de Jésus (to give it the French title bestowed on

it by de la Villemarqué) is a reasonably accurate transcription of a
Passion play in Breton printed in Paris in 1530. It is part of the
contents of a 24mo volume, gilt-edged, and bound in red
morocco, with its pages unnumbered, and two of them missing.[3]
The book was printed by Yves Quilleveré in Paris, near the
Petit-Pont, at the sign of the Black Cross, Rue de la Bucherie, and
is one of the five books still extant from the press of this Breton
'libraire-juré' who had established himself in the French capital.[4]
It contains the *Passion*, the *Resurrection*, the *Death of Our Lady*, the
Fifteen Joys of Our Lady, and the *Life of Man*. The *Passion*, which is
the only part to be considered here, is in Breton and written in 12-
line strophes (which de la Villemarqué prints as 'sixains',
following the practice of a later edition of this play to be discussed
below). One of the earliest owners of the book (if not the earliest)
appears to have been a certain Simon Biell (or Byiel) who, in a
hand of the first part of the 16th century, wrote his name on
several of the pages, being more explicit on the second leaf of the
text of the play itself where he wrote: 'A simon bieel suis† tout ma
vie.'[5] The next known possessor of this volume was the Capuchin
Grégoire de Rôtrenen, priest of the diocese of Quimper, who
wrote on the fly-leaf that he had had 'bien de la peine à l'avoir,
parce qu'on ne voulait pas s'en défaire à aucun prix'. This in 1730,
exactly 200 years after it was first printed. Eventually the book
found its way to the Bibliothèque Impériale, and so under the
eyes of Hersart de la Villemarqué.

But there existed another edition of this book, which de la
Villemarqué discovered misplaced among the theological works
in Latin prose of the Bibliothèque Impériale. This was the edition
by Georges Allienne, of Morlaix (Brittany), printed there in 1622,
and including all that the Quilleveré edition had contained, but
'An oll corriget hac amantet gant Tanguy Gueguen, boelec hag
organist, natiff a Leon' (the whole corrected and emended by
Tanguy Guéguen, priest and organist, native of Léon).

In fact, this 32mo volume, bound in calf, shows no radical
differences, only a slightly more modern Breton spelling which de
la Villemarqué often gives in the footnotes to his edition of the
1530 text. But the verses are six lines in length, a division the
nineteenth-century editor adopts, instead of the 12-line division
favoured by the first text, while a later hand has added page
numbers. This text was practically complete, with only a few
unimportant lacunae and some imperfect verses, as in the 1530

edition; but, with its help, de la Villemarqué was able to include the text of the two missing pages of the Quilleveré book. He also supplied a reasonably close French translation, and it is de la Villemarqué's translation that we shall use throughout this article. He moreover divided the play into scenes, a task made easy by the structure, supplied a long dissertation on the theatre, and sought to prove by means of reasoning clear only to himself (and which justifiably roused the wrath of Paul Meyer) that the play was written in 1365[6] at the very latest. All this need not detain us.

However, in view of the fact that the *Grand Mystère de Jésus*, even in its nineteenth-century 2nd (1866) edition is particularly difficult to come by, perhaps it would be as well to offer a synopsis of the play.

The *Grand Mystère de Jésus*, despite its title, is a short play, involving only a limited number of speaking parts—53 (not 43, as alleged by de la Villemarqué).[7] Only six of the disciples have separate speaking parts, though the others were certainly on the stage, and would join in the *Amen* when required, or help to produce the Breton equivalent of 'Rhubarb' in the crowd scenes. Cooks, officers, soldiers, Jews (male and female) were also 'dumb' parts, and their numbers would depend on the resources available to the stage-manager—if the play was ever produced.

Though there is no scene division in the text, one is provided by *An test*, 'the Witness', who, before each 'action' recites a commentary in 5-syllable verse (the rest of the play being mainly in octo-syllables). Throughout, he acts as a narrator, much as in a modern radio play, though at times the commentary overruns the forthcoming action, reading more like a meditation on the Passion with thoughts flying to the painful End, and then, in the next scene, returning to a previous point in the narrative, before again mentioning the death of the Cross. For instance, the Witness introduces Scene XII:

> Au Calvaire, on le dépouilla sans égards devant tout le monde, et, après l'avoir couché sur la croix de bois, on le détira violemment;
> Si violemment qu'on pouvait compter tous ses os sacrés; et, par un raffinement de cruauté et de haine, on l'attacha au bois à l'aide de deux, puis de trois clous.
> Quand il y eut été attaché, au prix de grandes douleurs, on le remit debout lui et sa croix de bois, au milieu de la place, pour mourir tout nu.
> Sa chair une fois cuite au feu des tourments, on lui donna le coup de

la mort, comme à un malfaiteur ou à un traître; et personne ne le secourut (pp. 133–4).

Yet the Introduction to the following scene (XIII) starts:

> Etant en croix, le larron le pria, et il lui pardonna. Suspendu par les bras, accablé d'angoisse et de douleur, il eut soif;
> Mais il ne but point.
> Puis, quand l'heure vint, il pria son Père pour chacun de ceux qui, par haine, le crucifièrent. (. . .) (pp. 139–40).

Then he gives the rest of the scene, which is the committing of Our Lady to St John.

Since each 'scene' starts with a short narrative by the Witness, this will not be mentioned in the synopsis, and the page references will be to the 2nd (1866) edition, which is the more accessible of the two.

Synopsis:

1 Simon invites Jesus and the apostles to a meal; asked by Jesus to do so, Lazarus describes the pains of Hell;[8] Mary Magdalen pours ointment over Jesus; the Devil taunts Judas, who is horrified at the loss of 300 deniers' worth of perfume (pp. 3–16).

2 Annas and Caiphas take counsel; Judas resolves to betray Jesus for cash; Caiphas gives him 30 deniers in a purse (pp. 16–19).

3 Mary tries to dissuade her Son from going back to Jerusalem and facing the Passion; Jesus asks Peter and John to prepare the Upper Room; they find the water-carrier who leads them to the host; the room is prepared; the washing of the feet; the consecration of the bread and wine and the Last Supper; Judas leaves to betray Jesus; Peter is told he will deny Christ; prophecy of the death and resurrection (pp. 19–63).

4 Jesus pleads with Reason in the Garden of Olives, and is comforted by an angel; Judas' kiss; the guards fall twice; Christ arrested; Peter cuts off Malchus' ear, which is healed by Christ (pp. 64–75).

5 Christ before Annas; Peter denies Christ twice and is driven out of Annas' courtyard (pp. 75–8).

6 Jesus before Caiphas; Peter denies Christ for the third time and leaves in tears (pp. 78–83).

7 Judas' remorse; he returns the money; dialogue of Judas and Despair; Judas' testament; Despair strangles Judas; Jesus is sent to Pilate who forthwith sends Him to Herod (pp. 83–102).

8 Jesus before Herod (pp. 102–4).

9 Jesus returns to Pilate; is scourged, crowned with thorns, spat on and derided; the Jews ask a reluctant Pilate to crucify Christ (pp. 105–14).

10 The devil plagues Progilla, Pilate's wife, who sends a letter to her husband; Pilate offers to release Christ or Barabbas; Barabbas is released; Pilate washes his hands; Christ is condemned to death (pp. 114–22).

11 Mary's anguish; St John sees Jesus setting out for Calvary; he goes to seek Mary; Veronica and her veil; the Women of Jerusalem; Mary meets John; her lamentations; Simon carries the Cross and collapses under its weight (pp. 122–33).

12 Christ nailed to the Cross; the Cross is raised into position; *Scripsi, scripsi*; 'Father, forgive them' (pp. 133–9).

13 Jesus gives Mary into St John's care; the Bad Thief and the Good Thief; 'I thirst' (pp. 139–43).

14 Dice are cast for Jesus' garments; Jesus dies; the centurion marvels at the earthquake and the darkness; Longinus pierces Jesus' side, recovers his sight and is converted; lamentation of Mary at the foot of the Cross (pp. 143–51).

15 Joseph of Arimathea begs the body of Jesus from Pilate; he, Nicodemus and Gamaliel go off to collect it (pp. 151–5).

16 The deposition; Mary's lament; the burial; Magdalen and Martha persuade Mary to go with them to Bethany; the angel Gabriel consoles Mary; Caiphas arraigns Joseph of Arimathea and imprisons him; Annas and Caiphas ask Pilate for troops to guard the tomb; Pilate orders the Jews to provide their own guard; they hire mercenaries and seal the tomb (pp. 156–69).

AMAN EZ FIN AN PASSION

What at first sight is so striking about this play, apart from the narrative introduction to each scene, is the way the action has been condensed to its bare essentials, and yet how such dialogues as occur take up a vast proportion of the play—just under one-third, to be exact. Indeed, the dialogue between Christ and His Mother alone takes up almost one-sixth of the whole play. These dialogues are mostly theological arguments expressed in a sequence of lyrical stanzas. With only a few exceptions, they are taken almost word for word from the *Passions* of Arnoul Gréban and of Jean Michel,[9] where, though extensive, they occupy a very small proportion of the play indeed.

The remainder of the Breton play (which includes the Witness narrative) provides action that is swift to the point of bareness. Here, for instance, is the whole of the scene which deals with the Council of the Jews and the Bargain with Judas:

ANNE

Tenons prudemment un conseil secret, et cherchons le moyen et la manière de prendre promptement Jésus. Ne perdons point de temps; car si nous tardons, croyez-le, nous nous trouverons pris nous-mêmes.

CAYPHE

Il est clair que vous dites vrai; en effet, nous sommes abandonnés du peuple; il a même à sa suite sans cesse des hommes considérables. Croyez-moi, s'il vit, dans peu de temps il gagnera tous les gens du pays, et nous ne trouverons plus personne qui nous estime.

JUDAS (seul).

Mon maître est maintenant en Béthanie; il n'en bougera pas d'aujourd'hui; mon parti est donc pris, je cours à la ville, dans mon ardeur; je vais trouver les Princes, qui sont, je crois, réunis en conseil privé.

Certes, je vais leur vendre mon maître, s'ils veulent m'en donner un bon prix, et, avant tout, me payer comptant; puis je le leur livrerai sans délai, en peu de temps, avec plaisir, quand je devrais mourir à la peine.

(Aux princes des prêtres).

Je sais ce que vous faites ici: que me donnerez-vous, et, sous peine d'être mis à mort, je vous le livrerai la corde au cou, secrètement,— mais ne soufflez mot,— à l'heure et dans le temps qu'il vous plaira?

CAYPHE

Qui es-tu, et d'où viens-tu? D'après tes paroles, tu as entendu notre secret, je le présume.

JUDAS

Croyez-moi, ne parlez plus; je ferai très-bien votre affaire, car je suis un habitué de la maison.

CAYPHE

Trente deniers de belle monnaie, sans qu'il en manque un seul, sur ma parole, te seront donnés: tiens, les voici dans une bourse; compte-les; ne t'attarde pas ici; fais ton coup; n'ouvre plus la bouche.

JUDAS

Soyez discrets.

ANNE

N'en doutez pas.

(pp. 17–19)

It will be noticed that the council itself, which occupied several hundred lines in both the Gréban and the Michel *Passions* is here condensed into two short conversations between Annas and Caiphas; Judas bursts into the secret council (were there no guards?); Caiphas expresses only mild surprise, and does not seek unduly to find out who Judas is before handing over without prompting the required 30 deniers. Judas and the Council then part as equals. The whole episode was obviously well known to the audience, and the author relies more than once on the undoubted knowledge of the Passion story by his audience in order to get through the action as rapidly as possible. The author also cuts severely the account of the Passion as it appears in the Gréban/ Michel plays. After the meal at Simon's house, these plays continue with Palm Sunday and several other events. But not our author. The meal is immediately followed by a long dialogue between Christ and His Mother, which comes to an end when Jesus asks John and Peter to go to prepare the Pasch (in the Gréban/Michel *Passions* the disciples are the first to bring up the matter). In this, the Breton author follows the Gospels of Matthew and Mark, except for the addition of the dialogue between Jesus and Mary. Another cut occurs in the Garden of Olives, where the scene is entirely taken up by Christ's prayers and Reason's arguments. There is no mention of the disciples being unable to keep awake, and only at the end of the scene does Christ go to wake them, merely saying:

> Levez-vous! hâtons-nous, mes frères; allons, de l'air le plus tranquille, nous présenter à notre ennemi. Dans un instant, le traître détestable, avec sa troupe que rien n'arrête, va venir s'emparer de moi.
>
> (p. 69)

(In this, the author tends to follow the Gospel of St Luke.) And so with the rest of the Passion. As a result, it is rather surprising to find that every now and again the author adds something to the action, instead of cutting it to the bone. For instance, at Herod's court, he adds an angry Fool, distressed at seeing his dress put on Jesus. Another example comes on the *Via Dolorosa*, when Simon the Cyrenian has to carry the Cross. Both Gréban and Michel make quite a play of Jesus' escort persuading Simon to carry the Cross, ending the lengthy argument with this lively exchange:

GADIFER
Maistre vilain, songemalice,
et remply de rebellion,
vous le ferés, vueillés ou non;
chargez a coup, chargez ce fais.
SYMON
Je me oppose.
ROULLART
   Vilain punais,
Jouez-vous de la reculoyre?

E

SYMON
Si on me fais tort sans mesfais,
Je m'oppose.
CLAQUEDENT
                     Vilain punais,
vous aurés tant de coups infais
qu'on vous cassera la machouere.
SYMON
Je m'oppose.
MALCHUS
                     Vilain punais,
Jouez vous de la reculoire?
BRUYANT
Tu quiers pour neant escapatoire;
il te convient passer par la.

                                        (Michel, vv. 26986–26999)

Then the mood changes as Simon looks at Christ whilst they
remove the Cross from His shoulders:

SYMON
Or, avant donc, puis que ainsi va,
je feray vostre volunté;
mais il me poise, en verité,
de la honte que vous me faictes.
O Jesus, de tous les prophetes
le plus saint et le plus bening,
vous venés a piteuse fin,
veue vostre vie vertueuse,
quant vostre croix dure et honteuse
pour vostre mort fault que je porte.
Ce c'est a tort, je m'en rapporte
a ceulx qui vous y ont jugé.
GRIFFON
Messeigneurs, il est bien chargé;
cheminons, depeschons la voye.[10]

                                        (vv. 27000–27013)

And that is the last one hears of Simon.

In the *Grand Mystère*, the long persuasion that precedes and
culminates in the above is reduced to:

GADIFFER
Çà! brave homme, qui passez, approchez.
SYMON LE CYRÉNÉEN
Pour quoi faire?
DRAGON
Pour prendre cette croix, vassal; pour aider celui-ci qui n'en peut plus.
SIMON
Moi? excusez-moi; je n'en ferai rien.

BRUYANT
Vous n'en ferez rien? Vous le ferez, ou je vous casse le nez.

SIMON
Portez-la vous-même si vous voulez; pour moi, je n'y toucherai point;
voilà la vérité.

BRUYANT
Vilain, tu la porteras sur ton dos! la vérité, la voilà. (*Il le frappe*) En
veux-tu encore?

SIMON
Au meurtre! [The Breton has simply: Alas]. C'est une monstrueuse
infamie!

DANTART
Voyons! voyons! marchez! faites votre besogne.

SIMON
Ah! il faut donc que je la porte moi-même.—Hélas!

GADIFFER
Oui, et à l'instant!

SIMON
Donnez-moi alors le timon de la croix; si lourde et si grande qu'elle soit,
je la porterai sans me plaindre. Hâtez-vous donc de m'en charger, que
je la porte vers ce haut lieu, hors de la ville.   (pp. 131-2)

When Simon has been loaded with the Cross, there is no respect-
ful address to Jesus as when the Gréban/Michel Simon was
waiting for the load to be transferred, but:

SIMON
Ouf! Ouf! quelque fort que je sois, j'ai ici une lourde charge; j'étais
trop osé de la prendre; je ne pourrai jamais porter ce fardeau jusqu'au
but. Laissez-moi ici, car je suis déjà rendu.

DRAGON
Allons, vilain; en avant! en avant!

SIMON
Oh! je vais; mais si vous me frappez je ne pourrai plus avancer. Vous
avez tort de me presser; accordez-moi un moment de repos, ou je reste
ici sous mon faix. (*Il tombe*) Je m'évanouis, je n'en puis plus.

BRUYANT
Debout! ou je vous coupe la face!   (pp. 132-3).

In view of the extreme compression of the story, such additions
come as a surprise, and when they do, there is a liveliness about
the speech that contrasts with the rather stiffer dialogues that
precede them.

There does indeed exist a certain variety of style in the play,
despite the rigid *aabccbbbdeed* rhyme-scheme used throughout.[11]
On the whole, it can be seen that the style tends to follow what is
happening on the stage, as is natural, and so falls into four main
categories: the style of the Witness; the style used in the lyrical

dialogues taken from the Michel *Passion*; the style of the action
proper; and the style of what does *not* occur in the Michel.

The Witness, as has already been stated, speaks in 5-syllable
verse, and owing to the shortness of the line and the exigencies of
the rhyme-scheme, uses much padding and make-rhyme, as:

> *Eno, gant dazlou*
> *Ez golchas, hep gou,*
> *Treit hon Autrou fur ...*
> (Là, de ses larmes, sans mentir, elle baigna les pieds de notre Seigneur
> ...)   (p. 4)

It is rather more difficult to decide whether the numerous
adjectives in the Witness' introductions are due to padding or to
an attempt at provoking a certain attitude of mind in the hearer,
as for instance in the introduction to Scene II:

> Qui fut traître envers le sang royal, et conseiller perfide, et fourbe au
> premier chef, et faux marchand à froid? Ce fut Judas lui-même.
> Sans honte, par avarice, après avoir été le majordome d'une
> grande maison, pour la modique somme de trente deniers, il vendit
> son maître, le Roi des astres.
> Quand fut réuni le conseil des Princes et des Scribes et des docteurs
> de la Loi pour la mort de notre Sauveur, Judas, un mercredi, Judas,
> l'avare, le meurtrier fieffé,
> Alla, sans pudeur aucune, comme un chien effronté,—plusieurs y
> prirent garde,—pour vendre son Père, et recevoir l'argent de ceux qui
> conclurent le marché.   (pp. 16–17)

The emotional content is highly charged by the choice of adjective, and by the use of contrast.

After this type of introduction, the scenes themselves, which are
mainly in octosyllables, have a more sober complexion. Though
the longer line gives greater freedom, some padding still exists,
mostly in the longer speeches, as witness Annas' exposé in Scene
II (already quoted):

> Tenons prudemment un conseil secret, et cherchons le moyen et la
> manière de prendre promptement Jésus...   (p. 17)

But when the dialogue consists of only very short speeches, or of
rapid conversation, the action naturally moves much more
swiftly, as can be seen from any of the scenes already quoted. This
seems to be in part due to an attempt at translating Michel's
lively style.

Where there are long lyrical passages which are a translation of
the Gréban/Michel plays, there is a little unavoidable padding
due to the rhyme-scheme, but remarkably few emotional

adjectives. As in the French models, the lyrical verses depend for their impact on their theological content, as witness one of Christ's replies to His Mother:

> Je ne puis, soyez-en certaine, vous accorder cela non plus, ma chère mère: il faut en vérité que chacune des lettres de l'Ecriture soit justifiée, et que toutes les prophéties s'accomplissent qui ont été faites sur moi, croyez-le.
> Vous me verrez étendu en croix, flagellé, battu... (p. 32)

In view of the material, there is much soberness in the words of Christ, which contrasts naturally with the rather more impassioned lyrical complaints of the Virgin, a contrast which also existed in the French.

As has been noted above in the Herod's Fool scene, or in that of Simon the Cyrenian, where there are additions to the action of the French models, there is a tendency to greater vivacity and freedom of expression.

But when we turn to the lyrical passages which do not conform to the Gréban/Michel model, there is a change, not in the rhyme-scheme, but in the length of the line, octosyllables being replaced by decasyllables. One passage in question—the Torments of Hell —has an apocalyptic style in keeping with its subject, as shown for instance, in the Torments for the Sin of Lechery:

> Une montagne élevée, difficile, exécrable, se dresse, creusée de haut en bas de puits profonds remplis de chiens, de dragons, d'horreurs de tout genre; de ces puits-là s'élancent des flammes cruelles destinées aux impudiques, aux libertins, aux luxurieux, et des exhalaisons fétides où ils roulent confusément. (p. 13)

This series of descriptions is so unlike the rest of the play that one is tempted to believe that the author was following the model[12] not only in substance.

On the whole it is fair to suggest that where the author had a model he followed it also in style, as closely as his versification would allow; and the diversity of his sources makes for variety of style within the play itself.

Having briefly treated the peculiarities of the Breton author, it may be desirable to consider the question of his possible sources, and more particularly the question of whether the author depended on the *Passion* of Arnoul Gréban, or the *Passion* of Jean Michel; leaving aside all discussion of the sources of what is not to be found in these two authors, and which it is hoped to deal with elsewhere.

Paul Meyer's reaction, as was noted above, was to observe that the Breton *Passion* derived from the Jean Michel *Passion*; and he used as argument the despair and death of Judas, which, as he points out (*op. cit.*, pp. 225–8) are closer to the Michel *Passion* than to the Gréban one, both in detail and in development. But this is one example only, and though conclusive in this instance, may not be representative as a whole. There has been so much condensation of the action in the Breton play, that it might prove useful to know whether it was the shorter Gréban play that was used, or whether, in spite of the condensation, any of the Jean Michel additions or reworkings were followed.

For instance, when Jesus comes to the house of the Last Supper, Gréban has St Peter, and Michel has Zachée, the host, notifying the arrival of Christ; in the *Grand Mystère* there is no announcement. But then Christ says in the Gréban:

> Paix soit en cest hostel notable
> et a tout habitans en luy!   (vv. 17850–1)

whilst Michel simply has Jesus state:

> La paix soit en ceste maison!   (v. 18277)

The *Grand Mystère de Jésus* follows the Gréban greeting:

> La paix de Dieu soit avec vous, tous tant que vous êtes dans cette maison.   (p. 50)

The three plays then follow the same pattern in the Host's reply, but from that point on, the *Grand Mystère* is closer to the Michel than to the Gréban (allowing for cuts). Similarly, Peter's reference to the preparing of the meal followed immediately by Judas' mention of the lateness of the hour and the need for haste (though the reasons stated for this haste are not the same) echo, in the Breton play, the Michel play exactly. The Gréban play gives a different type of conversation, and between different people. When Christ pronounces the blessing, Gréban's reads:

> JHESUS
> *Benedicite*
>   TOUS *respondent*
>   *Dominus*
> JHESUS
> *Posita et apponenda*
> *benedicat Dei dextra. Amen*

but both the Michel and Breton formula, after the *Benedicite*. Resp. *Dominus* is:

que sumpturi sumus
Benedicat trinus et unus.

However, this evidence cannot perhaps be pressed very far, since a different type of grace may have been used in 1458 (the date of the Gréban manuscript) from that usual in 1486 or 1530, the dates of the two other texts.

After this blessing, the Breton Passion proceeds directly to the Washing of the Feet, and this episode follows only in general outline the Gréban/Michel texts, which agree quite closely with each other. However, when it comes to the blessing of the Bread and Wine, and the Communion of the disciples, the Breton Passion no longer stands by itself. In Gréban, the disciples are given the Bread and Wine, then they all start putting their hand into the dish with Christ who remarks:

> L'ung de mes douze principaulx
> qui de la main ose touchier
> avec moy ou plat a mengier,
> me traïra sans nulle doubte. (vv. 18124–7)

This is followed by the shocked enquiries of most of the disciples, ending with Judas remarking:

> Puisqu'on fait enqueste si forte
> *numquid tunc ego sum rabi?*
> Suis je pas lëal en la sorte?
> Serez vous de par moy trahy?
>> JHESUS
> Tu l'as dit. (vv. 18156–60)

In both the Michel and the Breton Passions, when Christ has given the bread and wine, it is Judas who is the first to speak, followed by Peter. Moreover, both in the Michel and the Breton plays Judas expresses the same thoughts, which in the Breton play run:

> Ni moi non plus je ne faillirai pas; je suis toujours prêt et courageux; je ne manquerai pas de faire tout ce que vous voudrez,
> Maître, car vous m'avez donné votre corps, votre chair, votre sang précieux par lequel notre âme est bénie sans nul doute. (pp. 56–7)

But in the Michel, all the disciples in turn have their say, before Christ starts his soliloquy:

> Je suis en mon ame troublé
> et prens en moy turbacïon,
> tant pour la recordacion
> des doleurs qu'i fault que j'endure
> que pour la tres dampnable injure
> que l'un d'entre vous me fera (vv. 18934–9)

and talks of the betrayal, with the apostles protesting until it comes to Judas' turn who, in two lines only, asks

Numquid ego sum, raby?
N'esse pas moy, maistre   (vv. 18974–5)

whilst Jesus': 'Tu le dis' is slipped in almost unnoticed amongst the anxious questions of SS. Bartholomew, James the Less, and Philip.

Here, the Breton author follows the extended Michel pattern very closely, though exercising his normal method of compression. Peter speaks immediately after Judas has said: 'Maître, car vous m'avez donné …' which we have quoted above, and Peter speaks for all of the disciples, since Christ follows him immediately with: 'Je suis tout troublé dans mon âme …' (p. 57) as in the Michel; but the dialogue which follows this soliloquy lacks the vivacity (for once) of the French *Passions* as can be seen from the somewhat stilted question that Judas poses:

Maître, est-ce moi celui qui doit être dur envers Vous? (p. 59)

It is unnecessary to follow the whole Passion through line by line. One more example must suffice, that of Peter's denials. In Gréban, according to the Gospel of St Mark, Christ says to Peter:

Et vrayement, Pierre, je te dis
que ains que le coq chante deux fois,
ceste nuyt, tu m'en nyras trois;   (vv. 18288–90)

and this is precisely what happens at Annas' court; Peter denies Jesus three times before the cock crows twice, Christ looks at Peter, who flees in tears and lamentations. In Michel, however, Christ tells Peter that before the cock crows thrice, Peter will have denied Him thrice. (The Gospels of Matthew, Luke and John simply state that Peter will deny Christ three times before the cock crows). And indeed Peter denies Christ twice in Annas' court, with the cock crowing twice; then he leaves Annas' court, and when Christ is taken to Caiphas, slips in again near the fire, where he is again recognized, and denies Christ vehemently. The cock crows for the third time, and immediately Peter remembers, repents, and flees lamenting, without a look from Christ. The Breton Passion follows this version almost exactly: two denials at Annas' courtyard fire, the third at Caiphas'; but in the Breton play Christ turns to him with:

Pierre, mon ami, toi qui m'aimais, tu le sais; pourquoi, sans rougir,
me renies-tu?   (p. 82)

before Peter is struck by remorse.

From the few examples quoted, it is manifest that the Breton author had before him some version of the Jean Michel *Passion*. The correspondences are too striking for there to be any doubt of this. But he also certainly had with him the Arnoul Gréban, or some very closely allied play, for his cuts correspond in the main, though not always, to the additions Michel has made to the older play; and every now and again the Gréban beginning or end of a scene is used, as in the reply to the host at the house of the Last Supper, and in the end of the episode of Peter's denial. Elsewhere, we hope to pursue the theme of the Gréban influences more thoroughly, and to trace the various other sources. So far, only one has been identified. Emile Roy has been able to show[12] that the description of the Torments of Hell by Lazarus comes from the 'Légende de Lazare' (B.N. fr. 923, fol. 116 r., ff). This description is new in that it gives seven torments appropriate to the seven Deadly Sins, instead of the more conventional description of the four parts of Hell, or even a list of torments without special attribution. The 'Légende de Lazare' passed through several versions before being printed from 1492 onwards, in the *Calendrier des Bergers* which became so popular in the sixteenth century. It is possible that Gréban and Michel had not read this legend, though they could have done so. The Breton author seized upon a description that seemed more vivid to him, and this is but one instance of his wide knowledge of the religious literature of the time. This knowledge he used extensively, not always, admittedly, in soliloquies as long as the Lazarus description, but here and there throughout the play, as with the Dialogue of Christ and Reason, or Simon's comments on carrying the Cross, to quote but two examples. And these examples also show that this knowledge ranged from the theological to the trivial.

This religious literature the Breton author draws upon seems to be used because he is not overly concerned with a simple depicting of the Passion of Christ. He has omitted enough Passion scenes (notably in the Garden of Olives, to quote only one) to make that manifest. The author's intentions seem to have been more to provide themes for meditation on the Passion itself, and these themes for meditation occur not only in the brief introductions of the Witness, but more plentifully, more lyrically, and at greater length in, for instance, the dialogues between Christ and Mary, Christ and Reason, Judas and Despair, or the various soliloquies of the Virgin. Theology is taught, and the emotions appealed to, not by the happenings of Holy Week, but against its familiar back-cloth. Some of this is indeed present in both the Gréban and the Michel plays, but there they are very definitely subordinate to the whole action of the drama, so that the theology is incidental, and the appeal to the emotions comes, not through long sequences of lyrical verse, but through the portrayal in action of Christ's sufferings.

It is naturally impossible for us, with so little Breton background material available, to know why the author of the *Grand Mystère de Jésus* chose this particular way of conveying the message of the Passion, or indeed why it is that only this particular *Passion* has survived, in two editions almost one hundred years apart. But it certainly presented a considerable attraction to the deeply religious Breton mind, mainly, it may be, because it commented on, and suggested different meditative approaches to, the well-known incidents of the Passion of Christ.

NOTES

[1] *Op. cit.*, pp. 306–7.
[2] This will be discussed later.
[3] *Le Grand Mystère de Jésus*, Paris (1886), p. iv, note 1.
[4] In Renouard (P), *Répertoire des Imprimeurs Parisiens*, Paris (1965) under Quilleveré (Yves), né au pays de Léon, libraire-juré, 1498(?)–1540.
[5] I am indebted to the Paleographical Department of the Bibliothèque Nationale in Paris for this information. To me, the name sometimes seemed like 'Borel', but in view of the fragile state of this unique volume it was not possible to have it photocopied.
[6] *Op. cit.*, p. cxvij.
[7] *Ibid.*, p. cxxiii.
[8] Not those described by Gréban and Michel.
[9] *Le Mystère de la Passion d'Arnoul Gréban*, Ed. O. Jodogne, Brussels, (1965), t. I.; Michel (Jean), *Le Mystère de la Passion*. Ed. O. Jodogne, Gembloux, (1959). I would like to thank Professor Jodogne for his help and kindness in discussing the Breton play with me.
[10] The Gréban text is practically identical.
[11] The 1530 edition uses the 12-line scheme, but the 1622 edition and de la Villemarqué employ the 'sixain'. This is no real change, except that the shorter stanza is easier on the eye.
[12] E. Roy, *op. cit.*, pp. 306–7.

A. M. Boase

THE EARLY HISTORY OF THE *ESSAI* TITLE IN FRANCE AND BRITAIN

Montaigne is usually credited with the invention of the *essai* or 'essay'; both of the word as a title and of the concept—namely that of a critical but personal, tentative and non-exhaustive discussion in prose of any topic whatsoever. The word, native in this sense to France and England since the end of the sixteenth century, has proved so essential that every main European language has sooner or later adopted its equivalent for it. Its use, however, for more than a century after Montaigne's time, both in France and in Britain presents a much wider variety than is commonly realized, and a development in which there are some indications that England led the way.

In the first place, not only is the earliest title in which the word figures that of a volume of verse—*Le coup d'essai* of François Sagon,[1] the poem in which he attacked Marot, only to be told by Fripelipes *alias* Marot that he had stolen the only good thing in his pamphlet—but sixteenth- and earlier seventeenth-century usage seems to show a connection with poetry at least as much as with prose.

Thus (so far as I know) the earliest title of this kind in French after the first edition of Montaigne is the *Essays poétiques de Hierosme d'Avost de Laval sur les Sonets du divin Petrarque avec quelques pièces de son invention*, in 1584.

Next, in 1588 Jean de Sponde gives to the poems which follow his *Méditations sur les Pseaumes* a similar title (though in the singular form): *Un Essay de Quelques Poèmes Chrestiens*—they include the *Stances et Sonnets de la Mort*. In the following year Antoine Favre's attempt to emulate Robert Garnier in his *Les Gordians et les Maximins* carries as the sub-title of its frontispiece:

Premiers et Derniers Essais de Poesie d'Antoine Favre. In 1593 we may note the *Essays poétiques de Guillaume de Peyrat.* Nor indeed does this modest way of presenting one's verse die out very rapidly. It is even chosen by the self-advertising Nervèze (1605); it is favoured by more than one satirist—by Jean Le Blanc (1628), by Anthoine Garaby de La Luzerne (1642), as also by the obscure Sieur de la Vergne (1643). Of these, only La Luzerne seems to have been an admirer or disciple of Montaigne.[2]

Before leaving the application of this title to a collection of verse (*essais poétiques, essai de poèmes, essais de poésie*) it is interesting to note that already in 1584 King James the First and Sixth had published his juvenile verse in Edinburgh under the title of *Essayes of a Prentice in the Divine Art of Poesy.* The book, by its translations of Du Bartas and the acquaintance shown with Ronsard and Du Bellay, suggests that the title may be directly borrowed from France. Furthermore, in the case of Samuel Daniel who collected some of his verse under the title of *Poetical Essays* (1599), there is no doubt of the connexion with Montaigne. Daniel (who was John Florio's brother-in-law) was an enthusiastic admirer of the *Essais,* as is shown by many passages, not least the well-known lines in a poem addressed to the Countess of Cumberland which echo the end of the *Apologie*:

> Knowing the heart of man is set to be
> The centre of the world, about the which
> These revolutions of disturbances
> Still roll: (...)
> And that unless above himself he can
> Erect himself how poor a thing is man.

It will, however, have been noticed that Montaigne's book remains the only prose work and the only one to be called *essais* absolutely, without any further description. The absolute use of the term, no doubt, baffled some of his earliest readers, in spite of such declarations as: 'ce sont ici purement l'essai de mes facultés naturelles et nullement des acquises'. This is shown, as I pointed out many years ago,[3] by the speculations of La Croix du Maine who, not content with a reference to the 'coup d'essai ou apprentissage' also suggests 'essais ou expériences, c'est-à-dire Discours pour façonner sur autrui', thus doing his best to fit Montaigne's book into the then familiar category of *leçons,* where the author fashioned his views on what he read, and implied that others might well do the same (thus importing a didactic intention which Montaigne was careful to disclaim). It is also shown, however, by the various renderings of Montaigne's title which gave rise to contemporary discussion in at least one instance. Thus Antoine de Laval—who can claim personal acquaintance with Montaigne[4]—comments in his copy of Montaigne on the sentence of the *Essais* which I have quoted above in the following terms:

> De ce mot je tire un argument que Lipsius et ses semblables étrangers qui n'entendent pas nostre langue, ont mal rendu le titre de ce livre *Essais* par *Gustus* en latin qu'ils ont pris et mal [pris] de *pregustare* qui est l'essay que fait le gentilhomme servant devant le roi. Cela s'appelle bien essay. Mais les Essays de ce livre signifient autre chose que goûter. Il a entendu *Conatus*, comme dit le Poëte *quicquid conabor dicere versus est*. Tout ce que j'essayois à dire estoi vers, c'est à dire essayer, tenter pour voir s'il ne réussiroit a écrire, à faire des livres, comme pour les apprentis. Ils essayent de faire un ouvrage. C'est un mot ici qui marque la modestie de l'autheur qui se mocque des grands faiseurs de livres.[5]

This attitude is borne out by the choice of *Conatus* by Scévole de Sainte-Marthe in his *Elogiarum Liber II*—who incidentally also finds Montaigne's title unduly modest[6]—and also by the historian J.-A. de Thou in his *Historiae sui temporis* (1604-48). On the other hand Bishop Huet (1630-1721) was later to use *Specimina* as a title, and F. G. Freytag *Adparatus litterarius* (1752) the word *Tentamina*.

It was, however, Bacon who was the first to follow Montaigne in any real sense. The *Essayes or Counsels Civill and Moral* grew from a mere ten in first edition of 1597 to fifty-eight by 1625, the year before his death. For the English public they thus anticipated by six years Florio's translation of Montaigne under the title of *Essayes on Morall, Politike and Militarie Discourses* (1603). As has been sometimes observed, Bacon's essays, like Montaigne's, show a development which emphasizes similarities. What is less often realized is that in Florio's and Bacon's wake there is hardly a year from the opening of the century which does not bring a new volume or a reprinted volume of *Essayes*. Thus in 1601 Robert Johnson publishes his *Essayes or Rather Imperfect Offers*, reprinted in 1607 and again in 1638. In 1608 Daniel Turvill (Tuvill) issues *Essayes Political and Moral* and in 1609 *Essayes Moral and Theological*, the whole to be republished in 1629 as *Vade Mecum: a Manuall of Essayes*. John Stephens in 1615—with a different formula which shows a connection with Earle and Overbury—

publishes his *Satirical Essayes, characters and other; or accurate and quick descriptions, fitted to the life of their subjects*; to be followed up by his *New Essayes and Characters* in 1631. In the following year, 1616, it is the turn of Sir William Cornwallis's *Essais of Certain Paradoxes* and in 1620 Richard Brathwaite's *Essayes upon the Five Senses*.

No doubt, most of these books and their authors are quite insignificant, but the list is far from exhaustive, the crop of *Essayes* in the Baconian rather than Montaigne tradition goes on. The title is used to cover an ever wider range of works, which after 1650 tended to be religious or ethical in character.

It remains to be added that before Bacon's death he had twice been translated into French; in 1619 by Sir Francis George, *Chevalier Anglais* under the title *Essais moraux* and by J. Baudouin (*Essais politiques et moraux*). Sir Tobias Matthews had indeed already published an Italian version in 1618, *Saggi morali*.[7]

It would seem, then, that the English or specifically the Baconian influence was the prime factor in first stages of the evolution of the sense of this title towards its modern acceptation.

This is fully confirmed if we look at the early seventeenth century in France. It is surprising that such enthusiastic *Montaignisants* as Marie de Gournay and Jean-Pierre Camus, Bishop of Belley,[8] should have avoided the title, for the latter's *Diversités* (1609–18), or the former's *Ombre de Marie de Gournay* (1626) seem to cry out for it. As a matter of fact, Camus does tell us he had thought of adopting it, and in one instance actually does so. This is the *Essai Sceptique* to be found in the fourth volume and dedicated to Monsieur Tambonneau, Seigneur de Courcelles.[9] By way of excuse for certain *boutades*, the Bishop tells us that it was written when he was only nineteen—he was incidentally a *docteur en droit* at eighteen—and before his vocation to become a priest had declared itself (1605):

> J'estois lors tout frais esmoulu de la boutique de l'Empirique Sextus, de sorte que la teste pleine de ses maximes, je me proposai ce problème bizarre de l'opinion, de la vérité, de l'indifference, ainsi l'avois-je premièrement baptisé, comme vous savez.

Camus's thesis 'que tout ce que nous jugeons est faux, et puis vrai, pour establir en fin l'indifference des Sceptiques' is naturally full of echoes of the *Apologie pour Remond Sebond*. Indeed it is here that Camus referring to the final development of the *Apologie* with a marginal *Montaigne ès Essaiz* declares:

Un des plus beaux esprits de nostre temps, et peut-estre le plus beau selon mon jugement, du moins celuy qui me semble joindre le plus pres l'antiquité s'essaie en quelqu'unes de ses conceptions, toutefois après Plutarque, de révoquer en doute le nombre des sens.

Despite this admiration for Montaigne and for Montaigne's scepticism it is not clear that the term *essai sceptique* as used by Camus has anything more than its original etymological sense. Apart indeed from the translations of Bacon, the only prose volume published in France under this title[10] during the first quarter of the seventeenth century is the curious *Essay des Merveilles de Nature et des Plus Nobles Artifices* of René François, *prédicateur du Roy* (1622). The author's intention may be said to be that of providing preachers, barristers and writers with the technical vocabulary of such subjects as hunting (in all its branches, including hawking) seafaring, gardening, precious stones, architecture and painting by means of minute, picturesque and fairly technical descriptions—in fact a contribution to practical Rhetoric which is not without a certain mannered charm and is still of great interest to the lexicographer. In other words, it has absolutely nothing in common with Montaigne or Bacon, and we are back, as with the poets, at square one, the etymological sense of trial. This is shown, moreover, by the way in which the whole volume is referred to as an *Essay* but also each little group of chapters is also so described on its own prefatory page.

It is indeed true that in 1626 appeared in London a few pages written by a Protestant Soldier of Fortune (he had spent eight years in Russian and Polish service) under the title of *Essais: et Observations sur les Essais du seigneur de Montagne par le sieur Jonatan de Sainct-Sernin*. This opuscule,[11] written by the amateur author while confined to his house in London by the plague, is of quite minor interest. There is no evidence that it ever reached the French public nor that Sainct-Sernin was aware of the English essayists, though one of them, Stephens, had also been published by the same firm, Edmond Alde.

In short, with the exceptions of René François, Sainct-Sernin and the two translations of Bacon, we have no French use of *essai* as a title for prose between Montaigne and Descartes' *Discours de la Méthode* the title page of which informs us that the treatises on Geometry, Meteors and Dioptrics 'sont les essais de cette Methode', and which Descartes himself in his correspondence habitually refers to as his *Essais*.

It is to be noted that Descartes employs the form *Essais de* and it is only gradually that either in France or in England the modern usage of *Essai sur*, or *Essay on*, *Essay concerning* is reached and confirms a weakening of the original sense of trial or prentice venture.

Thus in the 1650's we have Seth Ward's *Philosophical Essay towards an eviction of the being or attributes of God*. Neither William Master's Λόγοι εὔχειροι, *essayes and observations theological and moral* (1653), nor Wm. Spriggs's *Philosophical Essayes* (1657), nor Launay's *Essais Physiques* allow of any conclusion on this point, but Abraham Cowley writing of his *Pindaric Odes* (1656) speaks of this '*Essay*' as 'but to show how it will look in English'. When Nicole publishes his *Essais de Morale* in 1671 he is at pains to explain that his title implies that Christian Ethics are too vast a subject for him to do more than *attempt* to deal with parts of it, but not in the least that he is uncertain of his own views. Thus to Nicole's mind *essai* is still connected with Montaigne and with some notion of avoiding total responsibility for the opinions he expresses. More than ten years later Robert Boyle can still phrase one of his titles as *An Essay of the Great Effects of even languid and unheeded Motion*, and Dryden whose *Essay of Dramatick Poesie* dates from 1668, in 1700 still says of his *Fables*: 'The first of Homer's *Iliad* which I intended as an Essay to the whole work', while Defoe in a variety of pamphlets prefers the formula *An Essay at* (1706 and 1711). On the other hand, John Locke appears to write indifferently *Essay on*, *Essay concerning* or *Essay of*. (See the title of his letter to the Bishop of Worcester and the Abstract of his most famous work.) In 1688 Le Clerc in his *Bibliothèque Universelle* refers to the as yet unpublished *Essai concernant l'Entendement Humain*, while Pierre Coste in his translation of 1700 writes *Essai sur l'Entendement Humain*. In 1694 Dangeau publishes an *Essai de grammaire*. It would seem, then, that it is shortly after 1700 that the trend sets definitely in favour of the modern usage with Shaftesbury's *Sensus Communis, an Essay on the Freedom of Wit and Humour* (1707), and the French translation of A. Collins' *Essai sur l'usage de la raison*.

One may say that this is all confirmed by Addison and Steele whose *Tatler* and *Spectator* essays (between 1709 and 1712) provide a model for the English essay as a commentary on men, manners and morals which brings it closer than ever before to Montaigne. On the other hand, their great contemporary, Pope, is a reminder that the title can still be applied to verse, as it was by him throughout his career. It remains to add, so far as France is concerned, that Fénelon's posthumous *Essai sur le Gouvernement Civil* (1722) and Voltaire's *Essai sur la poésie épique* confirm the 'sur' usage in France. It is perhaps symbolic of the road travelled that this very work of Voltaire's first appeared, as is well known, in an English version.

NOTES

[1] See 1912 Reprint. (Société rouennaise de Bibliophiles. Querelle de Marot et Sagon.)

[2] See Boase, *Fortunes of Montaigne*, pp. 157–62.

[3] *Fortunes of Montaigne*, pp. 2–4.

[4] *Desseins de Professions Nobles* (1605), p. 189a.

[5] See *Essais* (Courbet et Roger), Vol. 5, p. 252.

[6] Amabilis Miscellaneorum libri ab eo Gallice conscripti, quos titulo sane superbiori dignos modestissime *Conatus* appellavit (*loc. cit.*).

[7] Whereas the Italian adoption of *Saggio* for *Essai* is thus vouched for at an early date, a modern Spanish encyclopedia (Espasa—Calpera) reveals the fact that a modern Spanish authority (P. Juan Mir, *Hispanismo y Barbarismo*) still regards *ensayo* as an exotic loan word.

[8] Both merited (in my eyes) no less than two chapters each of my *Fortunes of Montaigne*, 1935.

[9] Michel Tambonneau, Président à la Chambre des Comptes from 1605, and died in 1634. It appears that he and Camus were together *dans une docte compagnie à la campagne*, and the latter was induced to promise *an essai de son art universel* and to read it out to the party on the following days. It was taken down by Tambonneau and sent back to Camus with the earnest request to publish it.

[10] The *Essais Politiques et Militaires* (*Enrichis de diverses maximes et remarques tirées des anciens auteurs*), published by le sieur de Mouchembert (Paris 1627) is merely a literal translation of Sir Robert Dallington's *Aphorismes* (1613). It may be noted, however, that in his dedication to the Marquis d'Effiat the author writes in praise of the Maréchal's services (marriage of Charles I and Henrietta Maria): '*De sorte que je pens à bon droit vous présenter ces Essais politiques et militaires ausquels vous donnez tous les jours le lustre et la perfection dans le maniment des affaires d'Estat...*' Mouchembert translated Barclay's *Argenis* into French.

[11] See *Fortunes of Montaigne*, p. 203, note 1.

S. J. Collier

LE THÉÂTRE DE MARCEL AYMÉ

> Le faux et le merveilleux sont plus
> *humains* que l'homme vrai.
> Paul Valéry[1]

Marcel Aymé se tourna vers le théâtre en 1932. Il avait derrière lui trente ans de vie rustique et citadine, des études de mathématiques supérieures, plusieurs faux-départs dans des métiers divers et deux romans, *Brûlebois* (1926) et *La Table aux Crevés* (1929). Sa première pièce, *Lucienne et le Boucher*, resta seize ans dans les cartons avant d'être présentée par Douking sur la scène du Vieux-Colombier. Après *Clérambard* en 1950, *Vogue la Galère* (1951) et *La Tête des Autres* (1952), Aymé quitta un certain ton de véhémence et de satire mordante pour composer des pièces dont le style et la présentation sont plus proches de ceux de ses contes et romans. *Les Quatre Vérités* (1954), *Les Oiseaux de Lune* (1956) et *La Mouche Bleue* (1957) sont des fables scéniques où la satire toujours latente cède le pas à l'invention cocasse et au burlesque. *Louisiane* (1961) est une pièce anti-raciste dont l'action se passe aux Etats-Unis, tandis que *Les Maxibules* de cette même année (le maxibule est à l'industrie ce que le snark de Carroll est à la zoologie) sont une farce incohérente à la manière d'Achard. Aymé a, en outre, adapté pour la scène française *Les Sorcières de Salem* et *Vu du Pont* de Miller et *Le Placard* d'Arthur Kopit. Une nouvelle farce a été annoncée pour 1966, *La Convention Belzébir*, dont le texte n'est pas encore publié.

Dans un des rares commentaires qu'Aymé a faits sur ses intentions d'auteur dramatique[2] on relève les phrases suivantes:

> Quand je vais écouter une pièce j'ai presque toujours l'impression que l'auteur s'interpose entre les personnages et moi. Je ne serais donc pas

surpris si j'avais voulu écrire une pièce ayant l'ambition d'établir entre
les personnages et le spectateur un contact, direct, immédiat... Ma
matière, ce n'est ni le merveilleux, ni la réalité; mais ce qui change de
la vie...

Cette matière, il l'exploite dans toutes ses comédies, comme
dans ses contes, romans et nouvelles. Ce qui frappe d'abord, c'est
l'audace de la situation initiale liée habituellement à un personnage banal et prosaïque, situation qui nous est présentée non
comme une possibilité qui exige toute notre crédulité de spectateurs mais comme un fait extraordinaire mais indéniable. Dans *Les
Oiseaux de Lune*, par exemple, c'est Valentin le gendre du Directeur, personnage modeste, qui explique les origines de son don
miraculeux de métamorphoser ses collègues en oiseaux:

VALENTIN
Tout a commencé par la lecture des œuvres de Jules Verne et de la
comtesse de Ségur. Je crois vous l'avoir déjà dit, j'ai eu une enfance un
peu triste, sans affection, sans jeux, sans lectures non plus. Il y a trois
mois, en lisant Jules Verne et la comtesse, j'ai enfin découvert le
monde avec les yeux et la sensibilité de l'enfance. Ces lectures ne
m'ont rien appris de positif, mais par les chemins de l'enfance re-
trouvée elles m'ont amené à découvrir certaines dispositions contem-
platives que, sans le savoir, je portais en moi. C'est ainsi que je suis
parvenu très vite à connaître une région de l'être où l'esprit, délivré des
simplifications de la pensée, se trouve en communion avec l'univers et,
dans une faible mesure, dispose de la matière même de la vie.

Quatre ans avant le *Rhinocéros*, Aymé fustige d'une part
l'enseignement qui charge le destinataire d'un fardeau asphyxiant
et cette libération de la condition humaine qui liquide la person-
nalité. Son professeur, comme celui d'Ionesco, est ici bourreau et
victime mais la critique des formes d'instruction imposées à
l'enfant par les parents avec la complicité arrogante des pro-
fesseurs qui reste implicite chez Ionesco, se mue chez Aymé en
une simple revanche de l'humanité sur les humanités. Le pouvoir
miraculeux de Valentin est celui dont rêve tout cancre de
quatrième et ses effets ressembleraient plutôt à l'apothéose
d'Amédée. Ce n'est que par la technique que *Les Oiseaux de Lune*
rejoignent *Rhinocéros* et encore faut-il préciser que les intentions
d'Aymé n'y sont nullement politiques, ni métaphysiques. Cette
pièce courte, pathétique, constitue comme une mise en pratique
de la 'recette' d'Ionesco:

Tragique et farce, prosaïsme et poétique, réalisme et fantastique,
quotidien et insolite, voilà peut-être les principes contradictoires (il n'y

a de théâtre que s'il y a des antagonismes) qui constituent les bases d'une construction théâtrale possible.[3]

Or, il est évident que, dans son œuvre romanesque, Marcel Aymé se plaît à dépister son lecteur en lui présentant avec un phlegme imperturbable des faits extra-rationnels ou atroces:

> Il y avait à Montmartre, au troisième étage du 75 *bis* de la rue d'Orchampt, un excellent homme nommé Dutilleul qui possédait le don singulier de passer à travers les murs sans en être incommodé. Il portait un binocle, une petite barbiche noire et il était employé de troisième classe au ministre de l'Enregistrement. En hiver, il se rendait à son bureau par l'autobus, et, à la belle saison, il faisait le trajet à pied, sous son chapeau melon.[4]

Cette irruption brusque, et toujours de sang-froid, de l'insolite dans le quotidien—un employé parisien qui passe par les murs, une belle femme douée du don de l'ubiquité, une jument qui naît verte, un percepteur réclamant des épouses et non des impôts, des bêtes qui dialoguent, des cabaretiers qui composent des vers raciniens—n'est, entre les mains d'Aymé, qu'un instrument pour démasquer la quotidienneté, pour mettre en évidence l'affreuse machinerie qui règle notre existence. 'Je tiens compte seulement de deux bêtises', dit Giraudoux dans *La Guerre de Troie n'aura pas lieu*, 'celle des hommes et celle des éléments.' Pour Marcel Aymé aussi l'existence est une affaire d'hommes et son fantastique, une fois accompli sa courte trajectoire, nous enfonce encore plus profondément dans le réel. A l'instar de nos auteurs de comédies noires, Aymé ne quitte la réalité que pour mieux la déchiffrer. La gamme de son théâtre, comme celle de ses contes, va de la pure fantaisie et de la traînée éphémère du rêve vécu jusqu'à la cuisante vérité du fait, observé, noté, rapporté. Nous partons sur les activités titillantes de Dutilleul (l'un des pôles d'attraction de l'œuvre d'Aymé comme de celle d'Ionesco est la sexualité) pour échouer pendant l'Occupation devant cette épicerie de la rue Coulaincourt, parmi cette poignée d'humains affamés, désespérés, condamnés. Parmi les plaintes et doléances de ce bétail angoissé se trouve, isolée du texte, cette phrase terrible:

—Moi, dit un Juif, je suis juif.[5]

C'est aussi par pure pitié—ou par discrétion?—qu'il ajoute, entre autres, cette note à une page du *Chemin des Ecoliers*:

> Un jour de décembre 1943, la belle jeune femme rencontra, dans un magasin des Champs-Elysées, un important fonctionnaire de la Gestapo française, qui lui offrit de coucher avec elle. Ayant essuyé un

refus, il la fit arrêter et transporter dans un local où il la viola et la dépouilla de ses bijoux. Au bout d'une quinzaine, il la repassa à ses subordonnés et au bout d'un mois, la fit mettre à mort. Le cadavre fut jeté à la Seine après avoir été coupé en plusieurs morceaux pour la commodité du transport.

Telle est la vérité nue de l'existence sous des circonstances données et nous savons que ce sont précisément ces circonstances-là, celles de la défaite et de l'humiliation, qui ont fourni à Aymé la matière première de ses œuvres les plus saisissantes. Seuls ce refus de se scandaliser devant telle ou telle atrocité, devant tel ou tel exemple de la sottise meurtrière, son horreur de la sensiblerie, son scepticisme fait de doses égales de réalisme et de compassion peuvent expliquer la violente attaque qu'il lança en 1949 contre 'l'hypocrisie, le pompiérisme, la confusion et ambiguïté criminelles du romantisme'.[6] Nous ne nous attarderons pas sur les arguments de Monsieur Lepage qui vise avant tout le langage déliquescent qui, à son avis, aurait mis la littérature sur la voie de la dégradation et du confusionnisme.[7] Ce que Marcel Aymé semble reprocher aux extrémistes des mouvements romantique et surréaliste c'est un langage creux, fait d'ornements, d'arabesques et de coups d'archet, qui tombe dans l'insignifiance grâce à une séparation de fond et de forme. Par contre, et s'avouant moins 'artiste', Aymé se contente d'exprimer l'absurdité du système social avec simplicité et exactitude dans un style qui s'adapte *parfaitement* à la situation ou au personnage et qui est la traduction fidèle de son univers. Malheureusement, l'esprit libre qui a fait d'Aymé 'l'Anatole France de notre époque'[8] et qui lui a valu le titre de 'pessimiste qui se penche sur une humanité inguérissable', cet esprit libre amène trop souvent la parole trop franche qui le trahit à la scène; il n'y arrive pas toujours à maîtriser le tranchant de la satire.

Si l'on peut regarder *Lucienne et le Boucher* comme une simple pièce policière (où la naïve victime d'une femme diabolique n'est disculpée que par l'intelligence d'un commissaire qui, pour une fois, n'est pas un de ces déformés professionnels qui peuplent les farces de Feydeau et de Courteline), la satire de certaines formes de cruauté et d'exploitation n'en est pas moins explicite. Le pathétique—dans le bon sens du terme—est ici celui du *Proverbe* ou de la *Légende Poldève* et explique en partie le fait que certains critiques ont rapproché Marcel Aymé d'une part de La Fontaine et de Perrault, de l'autre de Céline et de Giono. Il s'y manifeste le même humour cruel, le même désir d'enduire le lecteur de miel avant de le dépecer, la même violence, la même impassivité devant l'affreux; les personnages sont, en général, des gens simples, impuissants, incapables pour peu qu'ils la voient foncer sur eux de contourner ou d'éviter la catastrophe. *Lucienne* n'est peut-être qu'un conte, mais *Vogue la Galère*, présentée trois ans plus tard, démontre encore plus clairement ses procédés dramatiques.

Les préoccupations morales n'y sont que trop évidentes. La galère est notre société en microcosme, où l'ordre, toujours précaire, repose sur l'esclavage (justifié) des uns et l'autorité (appuyée par la loi) des autres. L'engrenage, comme celui de la magistrature qu'Aymé attaquera plus tard, est la condition préalable de toute communauté post-primitive et ante-marxiste. Marcel Aymé établit sa satire sur le triple édifice: liberté, égalité, fraternité, et son titre est suffisamment révélateur. Cette discipline, pour nécessaire qu'elle soit, est une affaire entre hommes ne fût-ce que par l'isolement du vaisseau—donc, rien du procédé claudélien dans *Partage de Midi*. Entre les habitants de la chiourme compagnons de bagne, il s'est forgé un genre d'amitié, une fraternité de forçats, dont Lazare, fils de bonne famille protestante, et Simon, corsaire pour ainsi dire de carrière, homme d'action, se décident à profiter. La présence à bord des deux femmes, Clotilde et sa servante Marion, rescapées d'un naufrage en mer, leur en fournit l'occasion. Cette situation initiale, Aymé la présente avec clarté et précision mais surtout en évoquant dans un langage mi-poétique, mi-réaliste la misère des galériens, l'arrogance des officiers, l'obséquieuse hypocrisie de l'argousin et du comite qui font parmi les bagnards le trafic du vin et du tabac. Lazare est le rêveur, l'idéaliste pour qui la révolte à venir ne représente pas une simple issue hors de la servitude immédiate:

NICAISE
Oh! tu sais... la liberté... ça ne me démange pas...
LAZARE
Qu'est-ce que tu me chantes là?
NICAISE
La vérité. Vois-tu, Lazare, ici, je suis ton vieil ami. C'est le miracle des galères, que toi et moi, nous puissions être des amis. Suppose qu'on nous rende la liberté demain.
LAZARE
Eh bien?

NICAISE

Fh bien? Mais tu redeviens M. Lazare de Barrals, gentilhomme huguenot. La vie t'apparaît comme du haut d'un cheval, et moi je suis si petit que ton regard me passe par-dessus la tête.

LAZARE

Comment peux-tu parler ainsi? Ce qui m'occupe, ce n'est pas tant ma liberté que la tienne et celle de tous nos compagnons, tu le sais bien. Et penses-tu que je n'aie rien appris de la misère en deux années de bagne? Quand je les aurai délivrés de leurs chaînes, je ne me croirai pas quitte envers mes compagnons. Ma tâche ne fera que commencer. Il me restera à leur rendre le goût d'une existence honnête, à leur donner la passion de la justice, de l'honneur, de la vérité. Et il faudra bien que tu restes mon ami, pour m'aider...

NICAISE

Mon pauvre petit!... mais tu n'y penses pas! Faire la morale à toute cette crapule! Une racaille que la justice aurait donnée au bourreau si ce n'était que la marine manque de bras! La passion de la vérité! Il n'y a que les gens bien de chez eux, pour avoir de ces idées-là...[9]

Simon a beau lui dire—et ici on rappelle le dialogue Jupiter-Oreste dans l'Acte III des *Mouches* et l'inquisition nocturne dans la cellule de Séville[10]—que l'homme libéré de ses chaînes ne demande qu'à être dirigé et que, quels que puissent être les sentiments qui l'inspirent, une révolte s'accomplit dans la haine et la vengeance:

SIMON

Tu te trompes. Aujourd'hui, les forçats se réchauffent à ton amitié, mais c'est qu'ils sont enchaînés. Quand ils seront libres, tes beaux sentiments les gêneront comme une dette à payer. Crois-moi, tu es d'un métal trop fin pour mener de pareils hommes. Le moment venu, laisse-moi prendre les choses en main... Quand il s'agit de mener des hommes, un chef vraiment résolu ne s'amuse pas à poursuivre un but; il le rencontre.[11]

A la faveur d'une petite comédie jouée à bord en présence des officiers—emploi très efficace de la présentation «en abime»—la révolte est déclenchée. A la discipline succèdent le désordre, le viol, le pillage, la gabegie, tandis que la galère va à la dérive. Fatigués enfin de la débauche, désœuvrés, les forçats regagnent leurs bancs; c'est maintenant Simon qui assume le commandement avec une brutalité encore plus féroce que celle des anciens officiers. Il comble de son mépris ces criminels qu'il n'a jamais aimés:

SIMON

Non, je ne suis pas des vôtres. Je ne suis pas de l'espèce des tire-laine et des sorgueurs qui préparent leurs voleries en tremblant. J'ai navigué vingt ans sous le pavillon noir des gentilshommes de fortune... Je pillais, je brûlais des villes. Capitaine, j'ai eu des révoltes à mon bord... Mais quels hommes c'étaient! J'avais de vrais matelots, de vrais équipages, fins gabiers et durs au combat. Et aujourd'hui, c'est à vous que je commande, chiens que vous êtes!

Les protestations que fait Lazare au nom de l'humanité et de l'amour restent inutiles et la pièce se termine sur le décret de Simon:

> Tout à l'heure sur l'espale il sera procédé à la mise à mort des officiers, du comite et de leur complice Lazare de Barrals. Les deux filles seront consignées dans une chambre où elles se tiendront à la disposition des rameurs qui n'auront encouru aucun reproche dans l'accomplissement de leur tâche.

> FORÇATS
> Vive Simon! Vive la justice! Mort aux traîtres! Vive Simon!
> NICAISE
> Faites passer parmi les vogavants qu'il va falloir défourneller tout d'un temps!

> (*L'argousin se penche sur les deux premiers vogavants. Nicaise siffle. La chiourme se lève. Deuxième coup: les forçats ôtent leurs bonnets. Troisième coup: leurs casaques. Quatrième coup: leurs chemises. Cinquième coup: se rassoient. Sixième coup: prennent les rames.*)

Nous avons insisté sur l'action et le dialogue de cette pièce parce qu'elle semble cristalliser les préoccupations et l'attitude de son auteur. On pourrait conclure, d'après cette démonstration quasi-brechtienne, que les galériens, l'humanité s'entend, sont veules, lâches, incapables de se libérer, prisonniers consentants, proches parents des «salauds» sartriens, et que l'ordre social est synonyme d'un règne de terreur et de chantage savamment administré. Ce serait oublier que la vision de Lazare est dictée par un sentiment tout aussi suspect aux yeux de l'équipage que le chantage pratiqué par les patrons; l'amitié est moins sûre que la crainte. Les arguments et les promesses du théoriste sonnent faux et c'est finalement l'humaniste-tyran aux mains capables qui l'emporte. Simon triomphe parce qu'il comprend et dirige les condamnés sans toutefois les aimer; Lazare échoue parce que, en réalité, il n'aime que des idées, des mots. En dépit de sa compassion, Aymé ne saurait tricher. Sartre, dans *La Putain Respectueuse* ne pouvait pas fausser les réactions de Lizzie au point de lui faire braver le Sénateur pour dénoncer son fils et sauver le nègre. Elle est ce qu'elle est—c'est-à-dire *respectueuse* (de la supériorité blanche) et se sachant en outre par sa profession un être en

marge de la société. De même, Aymé se refuse à juger les galériens,
se contentant tout simplement de les peindre tels qu'ils sont. La
liberté telle que l'on veut la leur imposer est un non-sens. Ils sont
doublement victimes: de la société qui les condamne et de
l'égoïsme de leurs prétendus messies.

Si le public parisien s'est efforcé de voir dans *Tête des Autres*
une veine comique, c'est sans doute parce que l'exposé du vice
sur lequel repose, selon Aymé, notre justice, s'est toujours prêté
naturellement à la farce et au vaudeville. Magistrats et commis-
saires, une fois transportés sur une scène de théâtre, ont été de
tous temps des personnages burlesques. Au fait, et en dépit du
mélange de genres discordants—farce, drame, satire, vaudeville
noir, comédie de mœurs, pièce policière,—l'image que l'on en
retient est justement celle d'un condamné à mort, pris comme un
animal dans la machinerie judiciaire, incapable de prouver son
innocence qu'au prix d'un scandale, et traqué par des tueurs à
gages. Ce serait peut-être exagéré que d'essayer de rapprocher
cette pièce, de par sa structure, à la machine infernale de la
tragédie grecque. Et pourtant, le procédé de l'entrave qui laisse
au protagoniste l'apparente échappatoire qui lui permet de
s'enliser plus profondément, rappelle tantôt Kafka, tantôt *Le
Professeur Taranne* d'Adamov, tandis que la fidélité scrupuleuse
avec laquelle Aymé restitue le langage administratif, les lieux
communs gigantesques, les monstrueuses idioties et l'ignoble
pantomime des tribunaux fait penser à *La Leçon*, à *Rhinocéros* et
aux *Chaises* d'Ionesco où celui-ci débusque les inanités du jargon
professoral, les solécismes du logicien et les interminables banalités
du vieux couple.

Si nous revenons sur cette parenté entre Aymé et Ionesco, c'est
qu'en 1959 Anouilh avait déjà perçu certains rapports entre
Beckett, Ionesco et Aymé:

> Moi, je serais plutôt pour Molière, que je trouve sous ses joyeusetés
> infiniment plus noir et mystérieux, comme d'ailleurs tout notre XVIIe
> siècle. Ce sont les psychanalysés de maintenant qui sont clairs comme
> de l'eau de roche à force de s'expliquer. Nos classiques gardaient les
> clefs de leurs abîmes... *En attendant Godot* est un des chefs-d'œuvre du
> jeune théâtre, une des rares pièces qui m'aient plongé dans mon âge
> mûr (avec *Clérambard*) dans ce désespoir du créateur maladroit... Je
> tiens *En attendant Godot* pour une des trois ou quatre pièces-clefs du
> théâtre contemporain, depuis que le vieux sorcier sicilien nous a fait
> éclater au nez *Six Personnages en quête d'auteur*. Quel que soit le talent de
> Beckett et de l'insondable Marcel Aymé, je croyais pouvoir souffler un

peu. L'expérience m'a appris que les chefs-d'œuvre étaient rares. Et voilà que Ionesco sort ses *Chaises*, je ne sais d'où…[12]

Les qualificatifs dont se sert Anouilh en essayant de définir *Clérambard* ('noir à la Molière,' 'affreux', 'cocasse, poignant et toujours authentique') pourraient s'appliquer aussi bien aux *Pièces Grinçantes*—à *Ardèle*, à *La Répétition* ou à *La Valse des Toréadors*. Il est naturel qu'Anouilh admire chez Marcel Aymé précisément les éléments dont se composent ses propres pièces. Quoi qu'il en soit, *Clérambard* reste la meilleure création théâtrale de Marcel Aymé non seulement par sa parfaite maîtrise de la matière dramatique qui semble lui avoir échappé depuis, mais aussi parce que, avec une objectivité remarquable, se dissimulant totalement derrière son écriture, son auteur réussit à établir ce contact, cette étroite communion entre scène et salle qui est un phénomène regrettablement rare dans le théâtre des années 1930 à 1950. On comprend facilement qu'Anouilh rapproche *Clérambard* des *Chaises* et *d'En attendant Godot* sur le plan thématique aussi bien que sur le plan théâtral: thèmes entremêlés du salut et du délaissement, de l'absence, de la cruauté (au sens artaudesque), de l'hypocrisie, de la haine et de l'exploitation et, finalement, d'un résidu, presque impalpable et, partant, si précieux, d'*amour*. Ce positif, qui constitue la négation de la charge de nihilisme qu'on a souvent portée contre lui, Marcel Aymé n'a jamais su l'exclure de ses pièces. Il ne cherche ni à condamner l'humanité, ni à lui faire la leçon; il se déclare simplement solidaire avec elle. Dans *Clérambard* il n'y a ni subtilité dans la recherche psychologique, ni expressionnisme intellectualiste, ni cette bouffonnerie gratuite, et parfois de mauvais goût qui est le propre du «boulevardier» et qui affaiblit par exemple *Les Maxibules* et *Les Quatre Vérités*.

Le comte de Clérambard, personnage d'abord grotesque, ubuesque, criblé de dettes, est réduit, ainsi que sa famille (sa belle-mère, Louise sa femme, et son fils Octave) à tricoter à la machine quinze heures par jour pour sauver le château ancestral. Vêtu d'une robe pourpre et coiffé d'un melon, féroce, autoritaire, il brutalise la famille et étrangle, égorge, ou écrase les animaux, oiseaux et insectes du voisinage, jusqu'au chien du curé venu négocier le mariage d'Octave avec la fille laide et sentimentale d'une famille rôturière très riche. Blessées d'abord dans leur orgueil d'aristocrates, la mère et la grand'mère finissent, après quelques façons, par consentir à un marché qui assurera leur fortune. Quant à Octave, veule, grimaçant, négatif sauf dans ses obsessions sexuelles, il est prêt à tout pour échapper à la tyrannie paternelle. Mais il entre silencieusement—seul Clérambard le voit et l'entend—un moine, qui remet au comte un exemplaire des *Fioretti*. Le curé retrouve son chien et Clérambard, foudroyé par la grâce, s'enferme vingt-quatre heures durant dans sa chambre avec le livre de Saint François; il est transformé en pratiquant farouche et passionné de l'amour franciscain. A la fille publique, dite La Langouste, dont il admire l'humilité et la bonté de cœur, il accorde son fils en mariage.

Malgré les protestations de sa femme, il poursuit son dessin, met la demeure familiale en vente, se confesse publiquement et, se sentant comme son fils prêt à sombrer dans le péché d'érotisme, est rappelé à l'ordre par une deuxième vision:

> C'est alors qu'un chant d'oiseau s'est élevé dans la chambre, un chant triste et mélodieux comme le doivent être les sanglots des anges du ciel! Et ma chair brûlante s'est apaisée tout d'un coup! Le repentir est entré en moi comme une eau froide et amère! (*Criant*). Sauvé! J'étais sauvé! (*Il reste un moment haletant, près de la porte*). C'était lui! C'était le petit pauvre! (*Il s'élance dans le couloir*). Il avait eu pitié de moi encore un coup! Il avait eu pitié de mon âme en détresse! Il m'avait averti!

Au dernier acte, Clérambard, ayant vendu son domaine, s'apprête à monter avec sa famille, La Langouste et un dragon de passage dans une roulotte d'où il proclamera dans les villages d'un bout à l'autre de la terre son miracle et son message de joie et d'amour universels. Malheureusement, il retrouve le cadavre décomposé du chien du curé, preuve que son miracle n'aurait été qu'une suite d'illusions et d'impostures. Clérambard chancelle un instant mais déclare:

> Que voulez-vous que cela me fasse? J'ai la foi. Je ne veux rien savoir d'autre. Peu importe d'où elle me vient. Je crois en Dieu, je crois en Notre-Seigneur, je crois à Saint François d'Assise. Je sais qu'à l'heure de la défaillance ils ne m'abandonneront pas. Je sais qu'ils ne dédaignent pas de se pencher sur ce misérable cœur où j'essaie de retenir l'espérance, la foi et la charité. En trouvant ce chien au grenier, j'ai eu un moment d'égarement, j'ai douté. En vous écoutant parler, je me regardais glisser au plus noir de l'abîme, et tout à coup je me suis senti arrêté dans ma chute, je me suis senti soulevé, hissé vers la vérité et vers la lumière. A présent, je remercie Dieu qu'il n'y ait pas eu de miracle. Heureux ceux qui n'auront pas vu et qui auront cru! Le miracle, c'est qu'il n'y en ait pas eu et que ma foi s'en trouve affermie, exaltée...

Là-dessus, nouvelle apparition de Saint François devant laquelle tous cette fois s'agenouillent, sauf le curé qui ne voit rien. Même le médecin-psychiâtre, appelé pour raisonner Clérambard, est touché par la grâce et accepte de monter dans la roulotte.

Comédie noire, guignolesque, comédie de la sainteté, joyeusement applaudie par les anticléricaux qui n'en retiennent que les passages où les croyances sont apparemment tournées en dérision, où un huluberlu qui veut marier son fils à une prostituée invoquent les leçons de Saint François, et où le curé reste seul aveugle en face d'un miracle. Le croyant s'en scandalise car les problèmes graves, de la foi, de la charité, de la rédemption y semblent traités avec désinvolture et irrévérence; le bourgeois bien-pensant s'y voit exposé dans ses attitudes prud-hommesques, son arrivisme et sa moralité factice. Oserait-on rappeler qu'aucune pièce où le grotesque, les personnages extravagants et les effets grossis cachaient un fond sérieux n'a échappé à de telles accusations? Depuis Térence et Plaute, en passant par certaines scènes blessantes de Molière, de Feydeau, jusqu'à *Ubu* et aux coups de scalpel d'Anouilh, d'Ionesco, d'Arrabal et de Beckett ainsi que de toute une génération de jeunes auteurs anglais et américains, le métier de tout auteur comique digne de ce nom est de nous faire rire, impartialement, impitoyablement, de nous-mêmes, de découvrir le ridicule dans toutes les attitudes humaines, fussent-elles les plus sacrées, les plus respectables, de nous empêcher de nous prendre trop au sérieux.

Si Clérambard est un grotesque, un imposteur, alors le curé a raison de se montrer réticent devant le miracle de sa conversion, et c'est le curé qui représente le bon sens. Si le curé est dans son tort, c'est que Clérambard est vraiment un saint. Il est plus probable que Marcel Aymé estime à la fois l'extravagante charité du converti et la prudence de l'ecclésiastique. Après sa révélation, Clérambard n'est pas moins despotique, naïf et intransigeant dans sa nouvelle vocation—mais il y a sur lui, malgré son extravagance, le signe d'une vraie générosité, la lumière d'un véritable amour. Ce qui rend pitoyablement comique le départ du comte vers les moulins du doute et de l'incroyance, c'est justement le spectacle de cette foi enfantine, moyenâgeuse dans le monde moderne.

Il conviendrait peut-être, en guise de conclusion, de faire allusion à *Louisiane*, pièce où Marcel Aymé, avec un sérieux qui lui est peu coutumier, s'attaque au problème le plus délicat et le plus complexe de notre époque—celui du racisme. Or, pour des raisons qui restent difficiles à préciser, mais qui tiennent sans doute au caractère émotionnel inhérent du théâtre lui-même et au fait que le racisme représente un domaine d'interrogations passionnantes, de questions sociales, métaphysiques, physiologiques même, c'est un phénomène qui semble résister totalement à toute transposition artistique satisfaisante. Les passions que soulève, par exemple, un traitement anecdotique du racisme nous éloignent le plus souvent d'une considération rationnelle de ses données et, par conséquent, de sa solution. Pour le dramaturge contemporain, c'est évidemment un problème de *fond* artistique et non de forme. Dans *La Putain Respectueuse*, Sartre, voulant situer le problème dans le domaine réaliste-socialiste, c'est-à-dire marxiste, adopte la forme théâtrale du drame et ses personnages souffrent d'un manque de conviction qui frise le caricatural. Avec *Les Nègres*, Genet se sert du jeu de miroirs déjà employé pour *Les Bonnes*, une série de déguisements et de dédoublements, destinée à centrer la culpabilité, mais qui finit par laisser à leur place bourreaux et victimes, blancs et noirs dans une contradiction non-résolue, non-assimilable. Dans *Louisiane*, Aymé rejette à la fois la conception de la lutte des classes et celle, métaphorique, de Genet, pour tenter *d'expliquer* et de comprendre l'esprit raciste, d'isoler et d'étudier le virus de la maladie. Malheureusement— le mot de 'non-intégration' étant pour le Français un mot d'étymologie étrangère—Marcel Aymé se concentre trop sur l'aspect sexuel du problème. La dégradation d'une femme blanche qui se croit métisse se solde par l'assassinat de son amant. L'action de la pièce est factice, mais les personnages, comme toujours chez Aymé, sont vivants et denses. L'agencement des effets manque de subtilité et le langage, se voulant naturel, tombe trop souvent dans la banalité.

Il est évident que Marcel Aymé, comme Giraudoux, se trouve mal à l'aise dans le tragique et que ses pièces ne sont efficaces sur le plan artistique et social que quand il les situe dans le fantastique et dans l'ambigu. Ce fantastique n'est jamais gratuit; il est sa façon d'être réel dans l'irréel, la brèche pratiquée dans la muraille du quotidien qui ouvre au spectateur cette perspective sur l'absurde qui lui permet de supporter le poids de l'existence. Dans *Notes et Contre-Notes*, Ionesco prend la défense des auteurs dits irrationnels:

> La fantaisie est révélatrice; tout ce qui est imaginaire est vrai; rien n'est vrai s'il n'est imaginaire. Pour ce qui est de l'humour, il n'est pas

seulement la seule vision critique valable, il n'est pas seulement l'esprit critique même, mais—contrairement à l'évasion—l'humour est l'unique possibilité que nous ayons de nous détacher—mais seulement après l'avoir surmontée, assimilée, connue—de notre condition humaine comico-tragique, du malaise de l'existence. Prendre conscience de ce qui est atroce et en rire, c'est devenir maître de ce qui est atroce... La nature authentique des choses, la vérité ne peut nous être révélée que par la fantaisie plus réaliste que tous les réalismes.[13]

C'est précisément ce que fait depuis trente ans, et peut-être sans le savoir, Marcel Aymé.

NOTES

[1] *Tel Quel*, Paris, Gallimard (1941), t. I, p. 26.
[2] *Vogue la Galère*, Paris, Grasset (1944), Préface.
[3] *Notes et Contre-notes*, Paris, Gallimard (1962), p. 15.
[4] *Le Passe-Muraille*, Paris, Gallimard (1943), p. 5.
[5] *Op. cit.*, p. 241.
[6] *Le Confort Intellectuel*, Paris, Flammarion (1949).
[7] *Op. cit.*, pp. 94–100.
[8] Le mot est de François Mauriac.
[9] *Vogue la Galère*, Acte I, sc. 3.
[10] Dostoïevski, F., *Les Frères Karamazov*, Livre V.
[11] *Vogue la Galère*, Acte I, sc. 4.
[12] Dans *Cahier des Saisons*, 15 (hiver 1959), p. 219.
[13] *Notes et contre-notes*, Paris, Gallimard (1962), pp. 122–3.

J. Cruickshank

KNOWLEDGE AND BELIEF IN PASCAL'S APOLOGY

Traditionally, we trace our Western European intellectual legacy to three distinct sources: the Hebraic, the Greek and the Roman. In practice, our mental habits have chiefly been formed by the post-Renaissance tradition. This tradition, because it was largely built on Aristotelian thought and confined the Hebraic element to the sphere of religious speculation, created a distinction between knowledge and belief, between what is demonstrably rational and what is purely speculative. Eventually, it implanted the widespread and popular view that only the Cartesian-Newtonian world is real and that knowledge must be something explicit, objective, impersonal and permanent. Although this has proved to be the dominant Western intellectual tradition, it has lately been subject to severe attack from the 'new physics', from biology and psychology and from various phenomenologically-inclined thinkers.[1] In fact a very different kind of epistemology, closer in emphasis to Hebraic thought, has always existed and has not been confined to neo-Platonic apologetics. This is the theory of knowledge associated with the Old and New Testament writers (reality as moral rather than scientific) and of which there are distinct traces in Plato. It can also be found in later thinkers as different as Kierkegaard and Dilthey. More recently still existentialism and phenomenology, with their view that knowledge involves some sort of acquaintance (the known is not wholly separable from the knower), have revived serious interest in a whole tradition of thought at variance with that which hitherto distinguished confidently between knowledge and belief, reason and feeling.

This shift in thought is one which has contributed to a new interest, not wholly confined to theological considerations, in the Pascal of the *Pensées*. Of course Pascal has always been thought of as representing some of the more important features of the anti-cartesian outlook. And in recent years he has frequently been presented—with varying degrees of historical sense—as one of the founding fathers of existentialism. The time has now come, I think, to look more closely at the further significance of those Pascalian attitudes which have prompted both these interpretations of his thought. My own starting-point for the comments which follow was a passage from the *Pensées* which has not received much comment. Pascal writes:

> La foi est différente de la preuve. L'une est humaine et l'autre est un don de Dieu. *Justus ex fide vivit.* C'est de cette foi que Dieu lui-même met dans le cœur, dont la preuve est souvent l'instrument, *fides ex auditu*, mais cette foi est dans le cœur et fait dire non *scio* mais *Credo*.[2]

On the face of it, this looks like the familiar, traditional distinction between knowledge and opinion with Pascal, in the interests of Christian apologetics, throwing rationality overboard and preferring *credo* to *scio*. It is the distinction made by Marjorie Grene, though she almost reverses the terms used, when she says that Othello was of the opinion (*believed*) that Desdemona loved Cassio, while Iago—and Desdemona herself—*knew* that she did not.[3] But Pascal claims in this fragment that proof can be instrumental to faith, even though the kind of proof he has in mind is not clear at this stage. He appears to be prepared to establish some kind of relationship between rationality and faith. The question therefore arises whether what he conceives of as 'knowledge' of God is *belief*, in the sense of Othello's belief above, or *knowledge*, in the sense in which Iago and Desdemona both knew the nature of her relationship with Cassio. What emerges from a fuller scrutiny of the *Pensées* is that such a question is ultimately misconceived. Pascal's distinctive claim, backed up by a complicated and fascinating epistemology, is that knowledge and belief are in one sense distinguishable yet so intimately related that belief *is* knowledge in the theological sphere.

Perhaps the most striking way in which Pascal departs from the dominant Western tradition lies in the fact that he rejects the whole concept of rational proofs of God's existence. Furthermore, he does so by a particular method which never retreats into mere fideism. His rejection of rational proofs is not a rejection of all reasonableness in theology. In fact, Pascal insists, 'si on choque les principes de la raison notre religion sera absurde et ridicule'.[4] His dismissal of a purely rational starting-point for his apologetics is composed of several different elements all of which are important.

In the first place, Pascal is too intelligent not to be aware of the inadequacies of rational discourse as such. Indeed, reason is the instrument which enables us to discover and categorize its own inadequacies. Pascal's many references to the unreliability of reason in ordinary life are well known and based on a realistic psychology (since there is strictly no 'reason' but 'a person who reasons'). He lists the senses, the emotions and sheer mental inadequacy among the 'puissances trompeuses'[5] which contribute to the perpetual 'guerre intestine de l'homme'.[6] Marjorie Grene, though she does not mention Pascal, is arguing from a modern viewpoint the position he adopted when she writes:

> (. . .) the knowing mind is always and inalienably the *whole* person, not a separate part of him. The achievement of insight does not cut us off from our whole psycho-physical nature nor rescue it from decay. Separate mind, as Aristotle briefly but definitely declares it to exist, is unthinkable in terms of the metaphysical situation also. For if our knowledge of concrete individual aspects of reality is tied to our bodily orientation, to the orientation of our whole, ineradicably psycho-physical situation, so are our ultimate metaphysical beliefs.[7]

In fact, not the least modern and impressive aspect of Pascal's epistemology is the way in which he bases it on an awareness of the many-faceted wholeness of individual personality. Like so much of his thought, his epistemology is no abstract intellectual construct but is grounded in the sharp observation of his own and other people's multiplicity.

It is ultimately through this same confrontation of epistemology and psychology that Pascal arrives at his fundamental distinction between the *esprit de géométrie* and the *esprit de finesse*. His use of the term *esprit* should remind us that he is not distinguishing two kinds of reason (since reason is at best a useful term to refer to something which is not itself abstract and independent) but two casts of mind. The *esprit de géométrie*, which we may perhaps call *numerative thinking*, is associated with the kind of mind which finds itself at home in the exercise of scientific method. The *esprit de finesse*—something more like *evaluative judgement*—is the kind of mind which operates most readily in the sphere of history, art, ethics, theology, etc. One is reminded of Kant's distinction between the knowing mind as *passivity* (e.g. knowledge of the theorems of geometry) and as *activity* (e.g. knowledge of God as creator and redeemer through worship and prayer). It is true that Pascal himself possessed both kinds of mental equipment to a remarkable degree, and critics have rightly emphasized the way in which his scientific and mathematical work is reflected in his writings on moral and religious questions.[8] But in an age that has become so conscious of the 'two culture' dichotomy we can readily assent to the reality of the distinction which he draws. No doubt, too—particularly in view of the clear exposition contained in the 'Préface: Sur le Traité du Vide'—we can agree that it would be as useless to apply the *esprit de géométrie*, without qualification, to religious questions as it would be foolish to adopt the *esprit de finesse*, also without qualification, in the realm of science.

The third strand in Pascal's rejection of a purely rational starting-point in theology has to do with his strongly anti-cartesian position. It is noticeable that, whatever his borrowings,[9] his explicit references to Descartes in the *Pensées* are all antagonistic. There are many reasons for this attitude. Pascal regards Descartes' scientific work as much too abstract and lacking a proper experimental method—it is rational, but without sufficient empirical checks, and therefore virtually useless. Again, he questions the assumptions about human personality lying behind the *cogito*. Not least of all, he can accept neither Descartes' confidence in the capacity of men for rational argumentation nor his claim that rational discourse leads to certainty. More immediately relevant in the present context is Pascal's objection to cartesian metaphysics and the ontological argument as set out in the *Discours de la Méthode*. He states the grounds of this objection when he writes:

> Les preuves de Dieu métaphysiques sont si éloignées du raisonnement des hommes et si impliquées, qu'elles frappent peu et quand cela servirait à quelques-uns, cela ne servirait que pendant l'instant qu'ils voient cette démonstration, mais une heure après ils craignent de s'être trompés.[10]

He adds a further point in another fragment:

> (...) sur ce fondement, ils [les hommes] prennent lieu de blasphémer la religion chrétienne, parce-qu'ils la connaissent mal. Ils s'imaginent qu'elle consiste simplement en l'adoration d'un Dieu considéré comme

grand et puissant et éternel; ce qui est proprement le déisme, presque aussi éloigné de la religion chrétienne que l'athéisme, qui y est tout à fait contraire (...) Et c'est pourquoi je n'entreprendrai pas ici de prouver par des raisons naturelles, ou l'existence de Dieu, ou la Trinité, ou l'immortalité de l'âme, ni aucune des choses de cette nature (...). Quand un homme serait persuadé que les proportions des nombres sont des vérités immatérielles, éternelles et dépendantes d'une première vérité en qui elles subsistent, et qu'on appelle Dieu, je ne le trouverais pas beaucoup avancé pour son salut.[11]

In a word, Pascal rejects rational, *a priori* proofs as a means of persuading men of God's existence because such proofs contain no moral—ultimately no intellectual—force and because they present us only with an abstract idea—something along the lines of the Prime Mover or First Cause of deism.[12] Ontological arguments may lead to a (continually vulnerable) belief in the intellectual idea of a creator; they fail to give knowledge of God. No doubt this position is one which appears to be coloured by theological presuppositions on Pascal's part, but he also argues, using straight cartesian terms, that rational thought and deity are of such radically different natures that the former cannot encompass the latter.[13]

It is on rather similar grounds that Pascal rejects the *a posteriori* arguments of natural theology, particularly the so-called 'argument from design'. Not only does this type of argument also lead to an abstractly conceived creator; it has no objective force since the predisposition to see or fail to see pattern and purpose of this kind in nature depends precisely on one's antecedent theological attitude:

J'admire avec quelle hardiesse ces personnes entreprennent de parler de Dieu. En adressant leurs discours aux impies leur premier chapitre est de prouver la divinité par les ouvrages de la nature. Je ne m'étonnerais pas de leur entreprise s'ils adressaient leurs discours aux fidèles, car il est certain que ceux qui ont la foi vive dedans le cœur voient incontinent que tout ce qui est n'est autre chose que l'ouvrage du Dieu qu'ils adorent, mais pour ceux en qui cette lumière est éteinte et dans lesquels on a dessein de la faire revivre, ces personnes destituées de foi et de grâce (...) ne trouvent qu'obscurité et ténèbres.[14]

Furthermore, the argument from design has no scriptural authority: 'C'est une chose admirable que jamais auteur canonique ne s'est servi de la nature pour prouver Dieu'.[15] The argument from design, in so far as it is valid, could be used in support of many vague forms of transcendental thinking but fails utterly to prove the existence of the Christian God. Thus Pascal concludes—he is speaking of the God of Christianity, not of deism—'Incompréhensible que Dieu soit (...)'[16] He adds immediately, however, '(...)et incompréhensible qu'il ne soit pas'.

This last point leads us on to the remaining major stand in Pascal's refusal to make his approach to Christian apologetics on a strictly rational basis. He works quite deliberately from the assumption—which in his own case is also a conviction—of God's existence. We shall see later that he justifies the making of this assumption itself on rational grounds. More immediately, however, it is now possible to expand slightly the point made at the beginning of this essay that Pascal belongs to the largely lost Hebraic tradition which identifies knowledge with belief rather than to the later classical and Renaissance attitudes which drove a wedge between belief and knowledge, or at least located them in quite different areas of speculation. It has often been pointed out[17] that the prevailing habit of Western philosophy in this respect—which has been to attempt to establish the existence of God by means of rational argument—did not exist in the Hebraic tradition and continued to be unknown later, in Greece, until the period of the Sophists. Plato used rational arguments precisely because he wished to combat the Sophists on their own ground and the familiar phrase, 'proof of the existence of God', is first found in Plato's *Laws*, Bk. X. As John Baillie puts it:

> From Plato this tradition passed into the Academy; through his pupil, Aristotle, it passed into the Lyceum; and finally it passed from both schools alike into the philosophy and theology of the Christian world.[18]

In sharp contrast to the Platonic and Aristotelian traditions, the writers of both the Old and New Testaments, by not regarding God's existence as problematical (they were concerned to answer the question 'which god should I worship?' rather than the question 'do the gods exist?'), had little need to distinguish between knowledge and belief in the way most people would today. This is why it is possible to write:

> In the story of modern thought he [Pascal] is one of the lonely figures who have stood for the Hebraic understanding of human nature and human destiny over against the dominant Hellenic influence (...). At the opening of the modern age in European philosophy, Pascal stands over against Descartes and flings at him a challenge whose might is only now being fully realized.[19]

This statement, firm and assertive though its tone may be, does not explain a great deal and calls for further elucidation and comment. But it is also true that what has been said here so far has been largely negative and concerned to show what Pascal's method is not, rather than what it is. We must now move on to a discussion of the more positive features of his approach to Christian apologetics, noting as we go how this affects his conceptions of knowledge and belief.

What we shall find, I think, is that whereas Descartes moved in his consideration of God's existence (formally at least) from argument to belief, and claimed that his argument led to certain knowledge, Pascal moves in something like the reverse direction—from belief to argument. In fact, his apologetic method is one calculated to bring an antecedent belief to consciousness of itself, reminding us of the *fides quaerens intellectum* of St Anselm's *Proslogion*. It is the first chapter of this work which also sets out, in a celebrated passage, something akin to a description of Pascal's approach: 'For I do not seek to understand in order that I may believe, but I believe in order that I may understand'. Nevertheless, this *credo ut intelligam* is only a part, though an important part, of Pascal's method—the part emphasized when one sees his thought almost solely in terms of Christian apologetics. We must go further and realize that behind this there is an epistemological stance which is concerned to relate what we call knowledge to our own human experience of it. One of Pascal's main objections to Descartes is that so-called 'objective' knowledge is a false ideal (we might formulate this objection nowadays by saying that 'scientific detachment' is no longer a tenable position, even in the exact sciences). Pascal sees that the act of knowing is a human act. In all acts of understanding and knowing there must therefore be some personal participation, and once this is so some prior element of assumption or belief is involved. It should be added that this view of knowledge—and this kind of knowledge—far from being 'merely subjective', takes proper account of human reality and is 'existential' in the proper sense of the term. Indeed, it is in this conception of knowledge, rather than in an allegedly *angst*-ridden response to the 'silence éternel de ces espaces infinis', that Pascal's significant link with the existential tradition is to be found.

It is entirely consistent with these ideas, therefore, that Pascal should begin his exposition of Christian truth with knowledge of man rather than knowledge of God. Fortunat Strowski goes so far as to say: 'Pascal est né "homocentrique" '.[20] What is so persuasive about this aspect of the *Pensées* is the fact that the Christian religion is first presented as an explanation of, and only subsequently as a remedy for, man's contradictory and mysterious nature. Religion is primarily related by Pascal to human concreteness, not to metaphysical abstraction, and as a result human psychology is seen as being naturally and inextricably linked with a transcendental discussion: 'l'homme (...) n'est produit que pour l'infinité'.[21] It follows naturally that this particular kind of 'vision homocentrique' should be, at the same time, a 'vision christocentrique'. The paradoxical nature of man—a creature torn between opposing impulses, between the finite and the infinite—is mirrored in the person of Christ who marks the intersection of finite and infinite, of temporality and eternity, of man and God. It is in a knowledge of Jesus Christ, not in the ontological proof, that Pascal sees the only—but also the natural —means by which man can have knowledge of God. In fact belief (in the divinity of Christ) is a prerequisite of knowledge (of 'reality' in anything beyond a strictly materialist sense of the term).

At this point it is scarcely necessary to rehearse once again the details of Pascal's apology. Commentators have expounded many times his emphasis on the doctrine of the Fall, his claims on behalf of the authority of Scripture, his insistence on the authentication of Christian teaching by the New Testament fulfilment of Old Testament prophecy, by the unique story of the Jewish people, by the history of the Church or by the phenomenon of miracles. To present-day readers, including many present-day Christians, not all these arguments will seem equally convincing and authoritative. In the context of the present discussion, however, they are marginal questions. What is of more immediate relevance is the general attitude to knowledge and belief underlying this kind of evidence. Here, I think, Pascal has often been grossly misunderstood. Perhaps the most frequently quoted fragment from the *Pensées* is his contention that 'le cœur a ses raisons que la raison ne connaît point'.[22] This statement has frequently been interpreted as meaning that Pascal sanctions—indeed that he advocates—a predominantly emotional approach to belief and that he sees Christianity as something to be adhered to blindly—by a faith which grows out of the failure to achieve rational conviction and which is, in fact, its exact opposite. This is a wholly mistaken view of the *Pensées* and one which results from insufficient attention being paid to the particular sense in which Pascal uses the term *cœur* in different contexts along with the related, and the sometimes interchangeable, terms *sentiment* and *instinct*.

Any attempt to understand Pascal's conception of *le cœur* brings us back again to his close connexion with the Hebraic tradition. No doubt it is most obviously in the Old Testament that the term 'heart' is used to indicate the whole personality of a man and, more particularly, that focal point of personality which holds together thought, feeling and will in such a combination that they can provide knowledge which is direct, concrete and, to that extent, intuitive. This, I take it, is the sense in which the translators of Psalm 119 (a psalm much admired by Pascal) use the term in such phrases as: 'Blessed are they that keep his testimonies and seek him with the whole heart', or 'With my whole heart have I sought thee (...)', or 'Princes have persecuted me without cause: but my heart standeth in awe of thy word'. It follows, in more secular contexts, that the 'heart' can be a shortened term for what we would now call existential, as distinct from *a priori*, apprehension of reality. It is in something like this sense— and it certainly cannot be in the sense of irrational emotionalism —that Pascal uses the term when he writes:

> Le cœur a son ordre, l'esprit a le sien qui est par principe et démonstration. Le cœur en a un autre. On ne prouve pas qu'on doit être aimé en exposant d'ordre les causes de l'amour; cela serait ridicule.[23]

Sir Arthur Eddington was making a point closely related to this when he wrote:

> In the case of our human friends we take their existence for granted-not caring whether it is proven or not. Our relationship is such that we could read philosophical arguments designed to prove the non, existence of each other, and perhaps even be convinced by them—and then laugh together over so odd a conclusion. I think it is something of the same kind of security we should seek in our relationship with God. The most flawless proof of the existence of God is no substitute for it; and if we have that relationship the most convincing disproof is turned harmlessly aside.[24]

It is on a different level again that Pascal also writes:

> Le cœur sent qu'il y a trois dimensions dans l'espace et que les nombres sont infinis et la raison démontre ensuite qu'il n'y a point deux nombres carrés dont l'un soit double de l'autre. Les principes se sentent, les

propositions se concluent et le tout avec certitude quoique par différentes voies (...)[25]

It is clear, then, that Pascal uses the term *cœur*—along with *sentiment* and *instinct*—in at least three different senses. Firstly, there is the obvious meaning of the emotional element in our nature: '(...)ce ne sont ni les austérités du corps ni les agitations de l'esprit, mais les bons mouvements du cœur qui méritent, et qui soutiennent les peines du corps et de l'esprit'.[26] Secondly, as we have already seen, emphasis on the rôle of *le cœur* is Pascal's way of insisting that personal participation—will, belief, personality—enters into the search for knowledge and the act of knowing. Thirdly, *le cœur* is that innate acquaintance with certain general principles referred to by Pascal when he writes: 'Nous avons une idée de la vérité, invincible à tout le pyrrhonisme'.[27] And he insists that our failure to 'prove' the contents of this innate knowledge by rational argument 'ne doit donc servir qu'à humilier la raison—qui voudrait juger de tout—mais non pas à combattre notre certitude. Comme s'il n'y avait que la raison capable de nous instruire (...)'[28] In all these cases, of course, Pascal draws religious conclusions. Nevertheless it is important to realize too that in all of them the term *cœur* is first applicable in a purely secular, epistemological analysis.

In using in this way such terms as *cœur* and *sentiment* Pascal was drawing on the available vocabulary of the period. We know, too, of course, that Bérulle offered a theory of knowledge in which a form of intuitive apprehension played an important rôle. Nevertheless, Pascal gave increased meaning and a more active status to these already familiar ideas. One critic sums the position up neatly when he says of Pascal: 'Avant lui, le cœur recevait l'idée; avec lui, il "sent" le vrai'.[29]

As a result of this emphasis on intuitive response, Pascal's conception of the act of knowing depends on a sequence which reverses the terms to which a rationalism derived from Descartes has accustomed us. Instead of proceeding through argument and demonstration to belief, Pascal moves out from belief to retrospectively confirming evidence and rational discourse. However, if this pattern of thinking is to hold good and have 'existential' justification, Pascal is faced with the task of convincing us that it reflects our own experience. He must justify the prior existence of belief on the grounds that, when we begin to think about God's existence, we do so from a natural and innate conviction—conscious or unconscious—of that existence. Several things can be said on this point. In the first place, it is quite clear that many people—explicitly, at least—do *not* have this conviction. On the other hand, it is a striking fact that some of the most vehement atheists use a 'vocabulary of belief'. This vocabulary appears to come not simply from a *verbal tradition* that dies hard, but from a *psychological disposition* which is significantly persistent. For example, despite the rigour of his philosophical training and the watchfulness with which he expresses himself, Sartre describes men as being 'abandoned' and 'condemned to be free'. Inevitably we want to ask: by *whom* are we condemned or abandoned? It seems as though Christian presuppositions, brought out by human response to our moral and metaphysical situation, rise to the surface. In a slightly different way, many observers who are not themselves Christians have pointed to the phenomenon of emotional substitution: the fact that an intellectual rejection of belief in God so often gives rise to an irresistable emotional need for some high-minded replacement. Camus for example, himself an unbeliever, comes near to accepting the traditional *imago dei* argument when he writes that 'rien ne peut décourager l'appétit de la divinité au cœur de l'homme'.

It is this ineradicable 'appétit de la divinité'—groundless in a certain sense for Camus, but a confirmation of God's reality for Pascal—which justifies the latter in adopting the sequence: belief, understanding, knowledge, vision of God. No doubt this is the sense of the celebrated phrase: 'Tu ne me chercherais pas si tu ne me possédais'.[30] The *imago dei* argument is similarly present when Pascal describes men as 'capables de Dieu (...) par leur première nature'.[31] He interprets the 'grandeur de l'homme' as a remnant of the human nature created in God's image before the Fall and still, however muted or unconscious of itself, present in all men and capable of recognizing the divinity from which it initially came.

This kind of theology, which places belief before knowledge, will be unacceptable to many. Some will claim that it shows clearly enough why theology cannot be 'intellectually respectable' —even, perhaps, 'intellectually honest'—in the sense in which we may think ourselves justified in applying such terms to philosophical speculation. In fact, however, this apparently reverse order of rational discourse has increasingly been urged in the sphere of philosophy itself as representing an important feature of all serious acts of thinking. If we look at the matter more closely we realize, indeed, that what might be called Pascal's doctrine of tacit or pre-articulate knowledge—on which genuine knowledge builds—has existed since early times in both Hebrew and Greek thought. There is the weight of meaning carried by the word 'know' in Job's claim: 'I know that my Redeemer liveth'. There is also Plato's explanation, by means of his theory of recollection in the *Meno*, of the way in which it is possible to know already what one seeks knowledge of. Coming to our own times, this is a feature of knowing which Merleau-Ponty underlined in his *Phénoménologie de la perception*, even though he rejected the conclusions which Pascal drew from it. Merleau-Ponty writes: 'L'expérience même des choses transcendantes n'est possible que si j'en porte et j'en trouve en moi-même le project'.[32] This involves the sequence belief-knowledge, and Merleau-Ponty's later comment, 'toute pensée de quelque chose est en même temps conscience de soi',[33] indicates the more general basis of the argument. Pascal and Merleau-Ponty would agree, I think, that thought in a sense creates what it subsequently finds. Where they would disagree is on the question as to whether what religious thought (like other forms of thought) creates has a genuine status outside the subjectivity of the thinker.

Pascal does not claim, however, that an innate sense of the divine—our 'première nature'—leads us to direct knowledge of God. Indeed, he asserts that such direct knowledge is impossible since the finite cannot comprehend the infinite.[34] Hence the significance and function of his christocentrism. Pascal repeatedly insists that we can only know God through the intermediacy of Jesus Christ—and we can do so because Christ was both God and man. Pascal writes:

> Il est non seulement impossible mais inutile de connaître Dieu sans Jésus-Christ.[35]

It is significant here that Pascal should emphasize the uselessness of an approach to God other than through Christ. Only through Christ can contact be made with the 'Dieu d'Abraham, Dieu d'Isaac, Dieu de Jacob, non des philosophes et des savants'. Indeed, Pascal holds that the ontological 'proof' (which takes no account of the person of Christ) can tell us nothing about God[36] or about ourselves—it brings us neither knowledge nor belief. On the other hand, we can learn the truth concerning our own nature and the nature of God through the mediating rôle of Jesus Christ:

> Non seulement nous ne connaissons Dieu que par Jésus-Christ, mais nous ne nous connaissons nous-mêmes que par Jésus-Christ. Nous ne connaissons la vie, la mort que par Jésus-Christ. Hors de Jésus-Christ, nous ne savons ce que c'est ni que notre vie, ni que notre mort, ni que Dieu, ni que nous-mêmes.[37]

In the end, then, it is belief in Christ on the authority of Scripture—which Pascal regards as an unimpeachable intellectual position—that allows us genuine knowledge of God. Jesus Christ is the unique means to knowledge of a God who, in all other ways, remains a *deus absconditus*. Ultimately, indeed, knowledge and belief are inseparable. In the most obvious way, knowledge of Christ Himself is essential to belief since we could not believe in His life and person if we had never heard of Him. At a more important level, to know of Christ's existence and to believe in this authority (on the evidence of prophecies fulfilled, miracles performed, etc.) enables us to know that we *know* and not simply to *believe* that we know. It does so because this is a knowledge involving our whole personality and this, the only genuine kind of knowledge, brings to light both antecedent belief and the tacit or unformulated knowledge from which that belief in its turn grew. Knowledge and belief coalesce in Pascal's apology through the process of reciprocal illumination in which both are continually involved.

NOTES

[1] Two of the most readable recent attacks on traditional epistemology are contained in Michael Polanyi, *Personal Knowledge: towards a post-critical philosophy*, London, Routledge (1958) and Marjorie Grene, *The Knower and the Known*, London, Faber (1966).

[2] *Pensées*, L.7, B.248. In all references to the *Pensées* I have given the numbering of the fragments in both the Lafuma (L) and Brunschvicg (B) arrangements.

[3] Grene, *op. cit.*, p. 36.

[4] *Pensées*, L.173, B.273.

[5] *Pensées*, L.45, B.83.

[6] *Pensées*, L.621, B.412. See also L.410, B.413.

[7] Grene, *op. cit.*, p. 57.

[8] This point is particularly well made in J. H. Broome, *Pascal*, London, Arnold (1965), pp. 54–9 and *passim*.

[9] The most strongly argued—I think excessively argued—case for Pascal's

debt to Descartes is to be found in E. Baudin, *La Philosophie de Pascal* (4 vols.). Vol. I, *Pascal et Descartes*, Neuchâtel, La Baconnière (1946), especially pp. 43–75. There is a very balanced account of the intellectual positions of Pascal and Descartes, in their relationship to one another, in Broome, *op. cit.*, pp. 75–81.

[10] *Pensées*, L.190, B.543.

[11] *Pensées*, L.449, B.556.

[12] Cf. *Pensées*, L.1001, B.77: 'Je ne puis pardonner à Descartes: il voudrait bien, dans toute la philosophie, se pouvoir passer de Dieu; mais il n'a pu s'empêcher de lui donner une chiquenaude pour mettre le monde en mouvement; après cela, il n'a plus que faire de Dieu.'

[13] See *Pensées*, L.418, B.233: 'Nous connaissons donc l'existence et la nature du fini, parce-que nous sommes finis et étendus comme lui (...) Mais nous ne connaissons ni l'existence ni la nature de Dieu, parce qu'il n'a ni étendue ni bornes.'

[14] *Pensées*, L.781, B.242.

[15] *Pensées*, L.463, B.243. There would appear, at first sight, to be obvious exceptions to Pascal's statement, but not if one accepts the following interpretation: 'When psalmist or prophet calls Israel to lift their eyes to the hills, or to behold how the heavens declare the glory of God (...) it is not proofs to doubting minds which he offers: it is spiritual nourishment to hungry souls. These are not arguments—they are sacraments' (Sir George Adam Smith, *The Book of Isaiah* (2 vols.), London, Hodder and Stoughton (1910), Vol. II, p. 90).

[16] *Pensées*, L.809, B.230

[17] E.g., John Baillie, *Our Knowledge of God*, London, O.U.P. (1939) (paperback edition (1963), pp. 107 ff.).

[18] Baillie, *op. cit.*, p. 108.

[19] D. G. M. Patrick, *Pascal and Kierkegaard: a Study in the Strategy of Evangelism* (2 vols.), London, Lutterworth Press (1947), Vol. I, pp. 216–17.

[20] Fortunat Strowski, *Les Pensées de Pascal*, Paris, Eds. de la Pensée Moderne (1965), p. 116. Strowski continues: 'Pascal n'a pas étudié la science pour la vérité pure, mais pour la vérité et pour l'usage humain; il n'a pas réfléchi "dans" la vérité abstraite, mais "dans" la vérité morale. Il a rarement raisonné en dialecticien, il range les idées et les mots selon leur signification "humaine", en auteur dramatique ou en romancier; on dirait que les conceptions ne se présentent à lui que revêtues d'une possibilité humaine.'

[21] 'Préface: Sur le Traité du Vide.'

[22] *Pensées*, L.423, B.277.

[23] *Pensées*, L.298, B.283.

[24] Quoted in Baillie, *op. cit.*, p. 227.

[25] *Pensées*, L.110, B.282.

[26] Letter of December 1656 to Mlle de Roannez.

[27] *Pensées*, L.406, B.395.

[28] *Pensées*, L.110, B.282.

[29] J.-E. d'Angers. *Pascal et ses précurseurs*, Paris, Nouvelles Editions Latines, (1954), p. 116.

[30] *Pensées*, L. 929, B.555. Cf. L.919, B.553: 'Console-toi, tu ne me

chercherais pas, si tu ne m'avais trouvé.' The secular equivalent to this idea is set out very clearly in Michael Polanyi, *The Study of Man*, London, Routledge (1959), p. 35: 'Discovery, invention—these words have connotations which recall what I have said before about understanding as a search for a hidden reality. One can discover only something that was already there, ready to be discovered. The invention of machines and the like does produce something that was not there before; but actually, it is only the knowledge of the invention that is new, its possibility was there before. This is no mere play with words, nor is it meant to derogate from the status of discovery and invention as creative acts of the mind. I am merely referring to the important fact that you cannot discover or invent anything unless you are convinced that it is there, ready to be found. The recognition of this hidden presence is in fact half the battle: it means that you have hit on a real problem and are asking the right questions.'

[31] *Pensées*, L.444, B.557.

[32] Maurice Merleau-Ponty, *Phénoménologie de la perception*, Paris, Gallimard (1945), p. 423.

[33] Merleau-Ponty, *op. cit.*, p. 426.

[34] See *Pensées*, L.418, B.233.

[35] *Pensées*, L.191, B.549.

[36] Cf. *Pensées*, L.418, B. 233: 'Ainsi on peut bien connaître qu'il y a un Dieu sans savoir ce qu'il est (...) on peut bien connaître l'existence d'une chose, sans connaître sa nature.'

[37] *Pensées*, L.417, B.548.

R. Fargher

MOLIÈRE AND HIS REASONERS

> Morbleu! je ne veux point parler,
> Tant ce raisonnement est plein d'impertinence.
>
> (vv. 180–1)

All sound and normal men must sympathize with Alceste's retort. The abnormal is here expressed by Philinte, when he asserts that not even the most heinous offence can ruffle his serene, stoical impassivity:

ALCESTE
Mais ce flegme, Monsieur, qui raisonne si bien,
Ce flegme pourra-t-il ne s'échauffer de rien?
Et s'il faut, par hasard, qu'un ami vous trahisse,
Que pour avoir vos biens, on dresse un artifice,
Ou qu'on tâche à semer de méchants bruits de vous,
Verrez-vous tout cela sans vous mettre en courroux?
PHILINTE
Oui...   (vv. 167–73)

This is not the way Molière reacted under attack, nor does it mirror the attitude of the average theatre audience. And for all his doctrine of sweet reasonableness, Philinte is immoderate and excessive in his preaching of it. Inexorable in his desire to reform Alceste, and blind to his own importunity, he, too, is on occasion ludicrous. When he provokes Alceste into bidding him be silent:

Ah, morbleu! mêlez-vous, Monsieur, de vos affaires.   (v. 1234)

Monsieur, encore un coup, laissez-moi, s'il vous plaît,
Et ne prenez souci que de votre intérêt   (vv. 1243–44)

he puts himself in the same situation as M. Robert in *Le Médecin malgré lui*, whose criticism of wife-beating is received with 'Mêlez-vous de vos affaires (...) vous êtes un fou de venir vous

H

fourrer où vous n'avez que faire', or Jacqueline, whose good advice on marriage is silenced with 'Mêle-toi de donner à téter à ton enfant, sans tant faire la raisonneuse'.[1] If Alceste is incorrigible, so is Philinte. In the face of all evidence that it is futile (Alceste is more realistic when he says 'La raison, pour mon bien, veut que je me retire') Philinte persists in his *Freundverbesserungswahn*. Even after the play is over, he will still continue. It would appear, then, that the most celebrated reasoner in Molière not only acts as a foil to the unreasonable hero, but himself, a prey on occasion to minor folly, is a comic figure in his own right. A survey of the comedies will demonstrate that, to a greater or lesser extent, all Molière's reasoners conform to a basic pattern, which is farcical.

Already in *La Jalousie du Barbouillé* the prototype exists. With a flux of nonsense, the Doctor preaches restraint, sobriety, moderation, peace. He knows that a gentleman must not be a bore. He is aware that bores are ineffectual: 'les grands parleurs, au lieu de se faire écouter, se rendent le plus souvent si importuns qu'on ne les entend pas'. Yet he talks non-stop. For his pains, he is dragged off the stage at the end of a rope, still reasoning. The moral he teaches is sound. But one would have to be as crazy as the Doctor himself to imagine that whoever knocked this farce together did so with moral teaching as his aim.

If the essence of a Molière reasoner is to give restraining counsel to immoderate men, and to become ridiculous in the giving of it, Mascarille, in *L'Étourdi*, must qualify. Something of a *libertin*:

> D'un censeur de plaisirs ai-je fort l'encolure,
> Et Mascarille est-il ennemi de nature?   (vv. 55–6)

and capable of dispassionate thought:

> Mais aussi, raisonnons un peu sans violence   (v. 907)

he unceasingly urges on his master Lélie prudence, caution, deliberation. Lélie is

> un esprit chaussé tout à rebours,
> Une raison malade et toujours en débauche   (v. 886–7)

who cannot be cured. Yet Mascarille exuberantly invents ever new and ineffectual imbroglios to rescue him from his follies:

> Je veux, quoi qu'il en soit, le servir malgré lui,
> Et dessus son lutin obtenir la victoire.   (vv. 1862-3)

Like Philinte, his only part in the *dénouement* is to hope for future
happiness, but lacking Philinte's gravity, he goes out with a quip:

> Allons donc, et que les Cieux prospères
> Nous donnent des enfants dont nous soyons les pères.   (vv. 2067–8)

From the early plays onwards, the words *raisonner, raisonneur,
raisonnement*,[2] occur in a comic or ironical sense. So, in *Le Dépit
amoureux*, Éraste replies 'C'est fort bien raisonné' to Gros-René's
pseudo-rational nonsense proving that 'Les femmes enfin ne
valent pas le diable'. The speeches of Gorgibus in *Les Précieuses
ridicules* show that Molière is not averse to mingling sound
sense with the exaggerated or silly utterances of a stock figure of
fun. There are, indeed, often similarities in style as well as content
between the alexandrines Molière gives to an *honnête homme* and
those spoken by a fool or rogue. The passage on cuckoldry:

>   ... l'invention
> De s'affliger l'esprit de cette vision,
> Et d'attacher l'honneur de l'homme le plus sage
> Aux choses que peut faire une femme volage!

belongs not to Chrysalde the *raisonneur* in *L'École des femmes*, but to
Sganarelle in Scene xvii of *Le Cocu imaginaire*.

    The earliest apparently wise and enlightened reasoner in
Molière is Ariste, of *L'École des maris*, who, like Philinte, teaches
moderation, and conformity to the social norm:

> Toujours au grand nombre on doit s'accommoder,
> Et jamais il ne faut se faire regarder.
> L'un et l'autre excès choque, et tout homme bien sage
> Doit faire des habits ainsi que du langage.
> .   .   .   .
> ... je tiens qu'il est mal, sur quoi que l'on se fonde,
> De fuir obstinément ce que suit tout le monde,
> Et qu'il vaut mieux souffrir d'être au nombre des fous,
> Que du sage parti se voir seul contre tous.   (vv. 41–54)

His high-minded, tolerant benevolence is proved right in the
play, for it brings him a loving wife, whereas his brother Sganarelle, who would keep rebellious women locked up with the
cabbages and poultry, is proved wrong. Nevertheless, the
audience must agree with Sganarelle when (in a scene partly
based on Terence's *Adelphi*) he calls Ariste an old fool. Ariste's
milk-and-water kindliness *is* excessive:

> Hé! qu'il est doucereux! C'est tout sucre et tout miel.   (v. 209)

The habits which this 'goguenard presque sexagénaire' proposes to encourage in his young bride *are* alarmingly emancipated. He perpetually thrusts advice on his brother, instructs him on how to be objective when in a rage:

> Mon frère, doucement il faut boire la chose:
> D'une telle action vos procédés sont cause;　　　　　(vv. 1091–2)

and, like Philinte, will continue to preach after the curtain has fallen:

> Allons tous chez moi. Venez, Seigneur Valère,
> Nous tâcherons demain d'apaiser sa colère.　　　　　(vv. 1111–12)

The device of sage counsel inopportunely given appears yet again in *Les Fâcheux*:

> LA MONTAGNE
> Ah! il faut modérer un peu ses passions;
> Et Sénèque...
> ERASTE
> 　　　Sénèque est un sot dans ta bouche,
> Puisqu'il ne me dit rien de tout ce qui me touche.　　　(vv. 362–4)

Chrysalde in *L'École des femmes* talks mostly sense, but insists on talking it, even when he has promised to be silent:

> ARNOLPHE
> Prêchez, patrocinez jusqu'à la Pentecôte;
> Vous serez ébahi, quand vous en serez au bout,
> Que vous ne m'aurez rien persuadé du tout.　　　　　(vv. 120–3)
> CHRYSALDE
> Je ne vous dis plus mot...

Arnolphe remarks on his obsessions and obstinacy:

> Il est un peu blessé sur certaines matières.
> Chose étrange de voir comme avec passion
> Un chacun est chaussé de son opinion.　　　　　(vv. 196–8)

Chrysalde's discourse in Act IV, Scene viii, has all the air of reasoned moderation:

> Car, pour se bien conduire en ces difficultés,
> Il y faut, comme en tout, fuir les extrémités.　　　　(vv. 1250–1)

But it goes to such excess in proving how every *cocuage* has a silver lining:

> Et, comme je vous dis, toute l'habileté
> Ne va qu'à le savoir tourner du bon côté　　　　　(vv. 1274–5)

that Chrysalde becomes the fool, and Arnolphe the voice of wit and sanity:

Après ce beau discours, toute la confrérie
Doit un remercîment à votre Seigneurie;
Et quiconque voudra vous entendre parler
Montrera de la joie à s'y voir enrôler.   (vv. 1276-9)

Unresponsive to irony, Chrysalde reiterates his point with even
greater relish:

Encore un coup, compère, apprenez qu'en effet
Le cocuage n'est que ce que l'on le fait,
Qu'on peut le souhaiter pour de certaines causes,
Et qu'il a ses plaisirs comme les autres choses.   (vv. 1302-5)

However appropriate this argument may perhaps have been to
the Court of Louis the Great in 1662 (and after all, Amphitryon is
told that:

Un partage avec Jupiter
N'a rien qui déshonore
. . . .
Le seigneur Jupiter sait dorer la pilule)   (*Amphitryon*, vv. 1898-1913)

Chrysalde the reasoner is clearly, in this scene, not preaching
what is normally understood by the golden mean. But, as
L'Impromptu de Versailles explains, all Molière's characters are 'des
personnages en l'air, et des fantômes proprement, qu'il habille à
sa fantaisie pour réjouir les spectateurs'.[3]

Cléante, in *Le Tartuffe*, is no Mascarille or Sganarelle. His
apothegms are closer to Pope than to Polonius. Yet even he talks
to deaf ears, and, besotted with his own sagacity, lacks practical
good sense. He is unimpressive in the first scene, where the
pantomime harridan Madame Pernelle cuts him short after six
syllables, then tells him not to titter. Orgon brushes him aside to
talk to Dorine in Act I:

Dorine ...Mon beau-frère, attendez, je vous prie: (v. 226)

and is still not listening to him in Act IV:

CLÉANTE
Si par quelque conseil vous souffrez qu'on réponde...
ORGON
Mon frère, vos conseils sont les meilleurs du monde,
Ils sont bien raisonnés, et j'en fais un grand cas;
Mais vous trouverez bon que je n'en use pas.   (vv. 1309-12)

He is not a very useful ally in the struggle against Tartuffe. In
Act I, v, it is only after eighty-five lines of discourse that he finds
the courage to make the point which Damis two scenes earlier had
instructed him to make:

ORGON
Monsieur mon cher beau-frère, avez-vous tout dit?
CLÉANTE
Oui.
ORGON
Je suis votre valet. (*Il veut s'en aller*)
CLÉANTE
De grâce, un mot, mon frère.
Laissons là ce discours. Vous savez que Valère
Pour être votre gendre a parole de vous?   (vv. 408–11)

Dorine (to whom he had confided his terror of Madame Pernelle) suspects that he will not help unless she prods him:

Nous allons réveiller les efforts de son frère (i.e. Cléante).   (v. 813)

In the last act, Cléante does realize the serious nature of Tartuffe's threats, and it is he who makes the sensible suggestion that Orgon thank the King. For the rest, his remarks in Act V are pointless, inept, platitudinous.[4] Unrealistic to the last, he goes on hoping that reformation shown impossible in the play will take place in the future. He still preaches moderation to Orgon, and thinks that even Tartuffe may be turned into a good man:

Souhaitez bien plutôt que son cœur en ce jour
Au sein de la vertu fasse un heureux retour,
Qu'il corrige sa vie en détestant son vice
Et puisse du grand Prince adoucir la justice.   (vv. 1951–4)

Perhaps, after all, he is closer to Polonius.

Compared with Sganarelle in *Dom Juan*, Cléante is gravity incarnate. Yet Sganarelle's nonsense is interspersed with sense. His basic beliefs—that a Creator exists, that wickedness is abhorrent, that God is not mocked—are as much a foil to his master's criminal atheism as Philinte's pliancy is to Alceste's arrogance. When in Act IV, Scene i, he states an obvious truth: 'Il n'est rien de plus véritable que ce signe de tête', Dom Juan can counter his argument only by threatening to whip him to death. He is credulous, cowardly, illogical, a caricature of sound reason, but a reasoner he thinks himself to be; and any audience not itself composed of Dom Juans knows that, for all his lunatic *non sequiturs*, Sganarelle is right in condemning his master's behaviour:

Ma foi! j'ai à dire…, je ne sais que dire; car vous tournez les choses d'une manière, qu'il semble que vous avez raison; et cependant il est vrai que vous ne l'avez pas.   (I, ii)

We laugh, with Dom Juan, at him, when, after an unintentional ribald gloss on the theme 'It is he that hath made us, and not we ourselves',[5] his giddy proof of what an excellent creature is man flings him headlong to the ground:

> Bon, voilà ton raisonnement qui a le nez cassé.   (III, i)

His reply to Dom Juan's hypocrisy speech (to which Dom Juan retorts 'O beau raisonnement') is lyrically imbecile. But it begins and ends with true warnings. The proportion of sense and nonsense in Sganarelle differs from that in Ariste and Chrysalde, but his comic function is not entirely different from theirs.

Unreasonable reasonableness abounds in *Le Bourgeois Gentilhomme*. The tutor in philosophy teaches much the same doctrine as Philinte:

> Hé quoi? Messieurs, faut-il s'emporter de la sorte? et n'avez-vous point lu le docte traité que Sénèque a composé de la colère? Y a-t-il rien de plus bas et de plus honteux que cette passion, qui fait d'un homme une bête féroce? et la raison ne doit-elle pas être maîtresse de tous nos mouvements? (...) Un homme sage est au-dessus de toutes les injures qu'on lui peut dire; et la grande réponse qu'on doit faire aux outrages, c'est la modération et la patience.

But more irascible even than Alceste, this 'philosophe de chien' attacks his rivals with fist and pen. M. Jourdain achieves only ludicrousness by his ambition to 'savoir raisonner des choses parmi les honnêtes gens'. Mme Jourdain, excessive in her narrow-mindedness, represents normality when she tells her husband 'Tout ce monde-là est un monde qui a raison, et qui est plus sage que vous'. In the last scene, husband and wife accuse each other of unreason:

> M. JOURDAIN
> Vous venez toujours mêler vos extravagances à toutes choses, et il n'y a pas moyen de vous apprendre à être raisonnable.
> MME JOURDAIN
> C'est vous qu'il n'y a pas moyen de rendre sage, et vous allez de folie en folie.

She is wrong when, unable to penetrate the Grand Turk's disguise, she opposes the marriage. M. Jourdain, right in wanting it, but for the wrong reason, is convinced that his own sanity has gained the victory ('Voilà tout le monde raisonnable'). The play ends in a fantasy where truth and error cease to exist, and the deluded Jourdain enjoys an illusory happiness denied to the clear-sighted fool George Dandin, who, in his frustration, can only cry 'J'enrage de bon cœur d'avoir tort, lorsque j'ai raison'.

Chrysale, in *Les Femmes savantes,* says that

Raisonner est l'emploi de toute ma maison,
Et le raisonnement en bannit la raison.   (vv. 597–98)

A kind of male Mme Jourdain without her vigour, he is less foolish
than his wife, sister, or elder daughter. But in the last act, when
Martine the kitchen-maid speaks on his behalf, Philaminte, for
the moment, is closer to normality than he:

MARTINE
Ce n'est point à la femme à prescrire, et je sommes
Pour céder le dessus en toute chose aux hommes.

. . . .

Les livres cadrent mal avec le mariage;
Et je veux, si jamais on engage ma foi,
Un mari qui n'ait d'autre livre que moi,
Qui ne sache A ne B, n'en déplaise à Madame,
Et ne soit en un mot docteur que pour sa femme.
PHILAMINTE
Est-ce fait? et sans trouble ai-je assez écouté
Votre digne interprète?
CHRYSALE
Elle a dit vérité.   (vv. 1641–2; 1662–72)

Ariste, the *sage de la pièce,* is himself deluded each time he believes
that he has argued Chrysale out of his cowardice, and though,
unlike other reasoners, he does engineer a happy ending to the
play, he does so in a way more befitting a Scapin than a philoso-
pher:

Je ne vous ai porté que de fausses nouvelles;
Et c'est un stratagème, un surprenant secours,
Que j'ai voulu tenter pour servir vos amours.   (vv. 1760–3)

Of all Molière's self-styled reasoners, the Doctors of Medicine are
most bereft of any glimmer of reason. In their mouths, to reason
means to talk maniac gibberish as a preliminary to killing the
patient; it is the language of Bedlam, sinisterly comic by the contrast
between its apparent rigour of logic and the inappropriateness
of its content. Monsieur de Pourceaugnac flees in horror from his
medical tormentors who required of him

Un peu de patience, nous allons raisonner sur votre affaire devant vous
et nous le ferons en français, pour être plus intelligibles.   (I, viii)

Thomas Diafoirus will soon receive his degree as Doctor because

il est ferme dans la dispute, fort comme un Turc sur ses principes, ne
démord jamais de son opinion, et poursuit un raisonnement jusque
dans les derniers recoins de la logique. Mais sur toute chose ce qui me

> plaît en lui, et en quoi il suit mon exemple, c'est qu'il s'attache
> aveuglément aux opinions de nos anciens, et que jamais il n'a voulu
> comprendre ni écouter les raisons et les expériences des prétendues
> découvertes de notre siècle, touchant la circulation du sang, et autres
> opinions de même farine.   (*Mal. Im.*, II, v)

Béralde, the enlightened man in *Le Malade Imaginaire*, defines the
art of medicine as 'un pompeux galimatias(...) un spécieux babil,
qui vous donne des mots pour des raisons, et des promesses pour
des effets'. But, in spite of his enthusiasm for objective reasoning:

> Voulez-vous, mon frère, que je vous demande, avant toute chose, de ne
> vous point échauffer l'esprit dans notre conversation(...)et de raisonner
> ensemble sur les affaires dont nous avons à parler, avec un esprit
> détaché de toute passion   (III, iii)

Béralde is almost as irrationally exaggerated in his scorn for
medicine as Argan in his passion for it. It is ironical that one of the
arguments he uses to try and cure Argan of his folly should be:

> à regarder les choses en philosophe, je ne vois point de plus plaisante
> momerie, je ne vois rien de plus ridicule qu'un homme qui veut se
> mêler d'en guérir un autre.   (*ibid.*)

Incompetent in his task of converting Argan (the stratagem that
saves Angélique's happiness is invented by Toinette), Béralde
himself merges into the comic mummery of that fantastically life-
like Degree Ceremony.

If then, by *raisonneur* is meant a man free from folly and excess,
whose doctrine is self-evidently true and acceptable, we must
conclude that there is only one in Molière's comedies. Nobleman
and valet, enlightened bourgeois and buffoon, each, to a greater
or lesser extent, bears the comic stamp his creator intended. The
only all-wise judge of men, the only infallible Voice of Reason, is
the King and Deus ex machina in *Le Tartuffe*:

> D'un fin discernement sa grande âme pourvue
> Sur les choses toujours jette une droite vue;
> Chez elle jamais rien ne surprend trop d'accès,
> Et sa ferme raison ne tombe en nul excès.   (vv. 1909–12)

For the rest, Molière's comedies portray a world in which error
and excess are incurable by rational argument, and in which the
would-be curer must forever spout unavailingly. Whatever
lesson Molière may conceivably have desired to preach, he knows
that it will be in vain,

> et nous ne prenons guère le chemin de nous rendre sages pour tout ce
> qu'il fait et tout ce qu'il dit.   (*Impromptu*, iv)

The notion that Molière's reasoners present a corpus of doctrine directly expressing Molière's own views has, of course, been disposed of once and for all by Dr W. G. Moore. Not that what the reasoners say is all necessarily false. But the problem of whether Molière has a message is infinitely more complex than the manuals of the 1930's imagined. To those who would deny that the problem exists at all (since Molière wrote comedies, not treatises), two points may be made:

(i) The fact that Molière intended his plays to be acted, not read, does not of itself make it pointless to study them as literary documents, for, as the Preface to *Les Précieuses ridicules* gaily admits, printed they are, 'à la bonne heure, puisque Dieu l'a voulu'.

(ii) Now that the great Jouvet himself is recorded[6] as having pronounced *Dom Juan* to be a problem play, there is less force in the argument that, since actors understand Molière better than university teachers can hope to, and since actors deny any extra-theatrical significance to his comedies, they therefore have no such significance.

The difficulty is not to find social, ethical and religious statements in his plays, but to establish which of them, if any, he stood by. Only a pedant directly descended from one of Molière's own would argue that the presence of a corrupt and sadistic police-force in *Intermède I* of *Le Malade imaginaire*

> Au défaut de six pistoles,
> Choisissez donc sans façon.
> D'avoir trente croquignoles
> Ou douze coups de bâton

proves that Molière disliked policemen—however improbable it may be that, as an ex-strolling player, he should have liked them. It may well be that, in the acting profession, husbands did try to make the best of their wives' infidelities; but we do not know what Molière thought of his comic defences of cuckoldry, even when they are ennobled by the purest stoic philosophy:

> A tous événements le sage est préparé;
> Guéri par la raison de foiblesses vulgaires,
> Il se met au-dessus de ces sortes d'affaires,
> Et n'a garde de prendre aucune ombre d'ennui
> De tout ce qui n'est pas pour dépendre de lui.
>
> (*Les Femmes savantes*, vv. 1544–8)

Though Molière himself had a most immoderate devotion to his craft—that is what killed him—there are no grounds for assuming that his *raisonneurs'* advice to *sapere ad sobrietatem* was abhorrent to him. The more convinced he was that such a state was unattainable:

> Les hommes la plupart sont étrangement faits!
> Dans la juste nature on ne les voit jamais;

the more alluring an ideal it may have seemed to him. Nothing in the play forbids us to imagine this to be the case. There is only the flimsiest of evidence to suggest that it was so.[7]

A few things, however, are certain. *La Critique de l'École des femmes* and *L'Impromptu de Versailles*, written by Molière to defend himself professionally against attack, prove that witty comedy was not, for him, incompatible with polemical intent. Though only humourless bigots would find anything tendentious in the comic references to Scripture in the plays before 1664,[8] the suppression of the first *Tartuffe* left Molière in no doubt that, whatever his original intention had been, the five-act version, to his public, was something more than a funny play. Just as Dorante pleaded Molière's cause in *La Critique*, and just as Dom Juan's hypocrisy speech[9] is a blow in the battle for *Le Tartuffe*, so too, the reasoner Cléante, in his denial of *libertin* views (vv. 318–24), and in his profession of admiration for true Christians, is protesting, for Molière, that *Le Tartuffe* is not an attack on religion and piety:

> ... je ne vois nul genre de héros
> Qui soient plus à priser que les parfaits dévots,
> Aucune chose au monde et plus noble et plus belle
> Que la sainte ferveur d'un véritable zèle.   (vv. 355–8)

Is Cléante perhaps also speaking for Molière when he mocks Holy Writ? His reply 'Les sentiments humains, mon frère, que voilà' to Orgon's:

> Il m'enseigne à n'avoir affection pour rien,
> De toutes amitiés il détache mon âme;
> Et, je verrois mourir frère, enfants, mère et femme,
> Que je m'en soucierois autant que de cela   (vv. 276–9)

may, as far as he is concerned, be innocent. His reading, doubtless, has been profane, and neither Matthew, x, 34–42, nor Luke, xiv, 26–33, is the Gospel for any day on which he would be likely to go to mass. But it is inconceivable that Tartuffe, and therefore Molière, was unaware of the Scriptural background to Orgon's statement.[10] At the very least, it is safe to assert that had public veneration for holy things been close to Molière's heart, he would not have been ironical about one of the thorniest sayings of Christ. Nor, (whatever may be the significance of *Dom Juan* as a whole, and the real point, semantically, of 'Je te le donne pour l'amour de l'humanité') would he have made a joke about the fact that the prayers of the poor do not necessarily produce bread. 'If thine eye offend thee, pluck it out' is not made any easier for the poor in spirit to comprehend by Toinette's adaptation of Mark, ix, 47.[11] The most vociferous believer in the supernatural, in *Dom Juan*, is Sganarelle. The two most ardent Catholics in *Le Tartuffe* are Orgon and his foolish mother. 'Impossibile est ut non veniant scandala: vae autem illi, per quem veniunt. Utilius est illi si lapis molaris inponatur circa collum eius, et proiciatur in mare, quam ut scandalizet unum de pusillis istis'.[12] Those pious seventeenth-century souls, not all of them Tartuffes, who thought the histrion Poquelin a stumbling-block to the faithful, were not utterly deluded in so thinking.

Of course Molière is Molière because he could write plays, and not because he may have paraphrased Gassendi. Of course there is nothing strikingly novel in the ideas scattered through his pages. But, as is the case with Voltaire, the holding, and even preaching, of second-hand opinions is not incompatible with brilliant and original wit. Bernard Shaw, in error doubtless when he claimed that great art should always be didactic,[13] did prove that funny stage-plays may, in part, draw their substance from the playwright's involvement with non-theatrical issues. Critics unwilling to see anything but pure theatre in Molière identify the 'ideological' content of the plays with the audience, the public, the King, or 'the evolution of the collective consciousness'. The only man of his age *not* entitled to hold opinions, apparently, was the comedy-technician Molière!

'Chose étrange de voir comme avec passion un chacun est chaussé de son opinion'. It seems to me abundantly clear that the Molière who mocked Holy Scripture, who created the sceptic Béralde, who poured scorn on the obscurantist opponents of modern science,[14] *was* something less than *bien pensant*,[15] and that his plays *do* manifest an attitude of mind which, in the following century, informed another comic genius, Voltaire.[16] (As far as reasoners are concerned, comic by their inopportune importunity, none in Molière reaches the sublime ludicrousness of Pangloss as, speaking incontrovertible truth, he tugs at the sleeve of the licentious sailor).[17]

Eminent critics have sought to discover what causes Molière fought for, what he believed, what he felt. M. Adam sees him not, indeed, as a doctrinaire preacher, but as a man deeply involved in the problems of his age, positive, free-thinking; a believer, despite anguish and despair, in life, nature, happiness: 'La morale de Molière n'est pas dans les maximes de ses raisonneurs, elle est dans le combat qu'il a mené contre le mensonge. Elle est une morale de l'authenticité'.[18] Mr Cairncross investigates Molière's affiliations in the social structure of his time, and affirms that his fight against asceticism, tyranny and authoritarian dogma is an inspiration to us today.[19] To M. Goldmann, the socio-jansenistic undertones of 'fuir dans un désert l'approche des humains' are self-evident. For M. Guicharnaud, a grim pessimism underlies *Dom Juan* and *Le Misanthrope*:

> Parti de l'idée que le monde est rendu difficile par la mauvaise foi, le mensonge, les masques et les aveuglements, atteignant la source de ces défauts, Molière rencontre, non la bonne nature, mais un déterminisme (...) qui est l'homme privé de sa liberté, c'est-à-dire, en termes jansénistes, dans un univers séparé de Dieu depuis la Chute, l'équation définitive: Nature-Corruption.[20]

Such varying views do not cancel one another: so intense and intelligent a man as Molière could not be expected to have one single or simple reaction to life throughout his career. Nor is there anything, in or outside Molière's pages, that proves it chimerical to seek for a philosophy in 'le cercle enchanté d'un monde imaginaire' which was, indeed, created for the prime purpose of pleasing seventeenth-century French audiences. Those of us who persist in believing that a literature rooted in life may have a profundity and resonance which technique alone cannot supply, will continue to inquire where Molière stood. What his plays signified to himself will, failing new documents, never be proved. It would take legions of Doctors to establish what his plays meant to his contemporaries. And, as W. G. Moore observes, 'the study of Molière as one of the supreme manifestations of the modern spirit is perhaps in its preliminary stage'.[21]

Each interpretation of Molière is, doubtless, coloured by the social and aesthetic preconceptions of the person making it. But even that need not deter us. Célimène was not being wholly ironical when she declared:

> Et chacun a raison suivant l'âge et le goût.   (v. 975)

NOTES

[1] Act II, Sc. i.

[2] There are many examples in the later plays, e.g. *Le Misanthrope*, vv. 577–84: 'Damon, le raisonneur, qui m'a, ne vous déplaise, / Une heure, au grand soleil, tenu hors de ma chaise. / C'est un parleur étrange, et qui trouve toujours / L'art de ne rien dire avec de grands discours; / Dans les propos qu'il tient, on ne voit jamais goutte, / Et ce n'est que du bruit que tout ce qu'on écoute.' *Raisonnement* implies insolence to Arnolphe in *Les Femmes savantes*, vv. 1541–6; 'Voyez comme raisonne et répond la vilaine... La belle raisonneuse', and to Harpagon abusing La Flèche in *L'Avare*, I, iii: 'Tu fais le raisonneur. Je te baillerai ce raisonnement-ci par les oreilles.'

[3] Sc. IV.

[4] v. 1584: What possessed you to hand over the papers? vv. 1607–28: sermon on avoiding extremes. vv. 1697–9: we must act, not talk. vv. 1711–12: if only we could come to terms with Tartuffe. vv. 1731–2: can we negotiate with Tartuffe? v. 1822: we must think of something. vv. 1845–6: points out what is obvious. v. 1860: we shall think of something. vv. 1887–96: asks Tartuffe how he could possibly be such a hypocrite.

[5] 'Vous voilà vous, par exemple, vous êtes là: est-ce que vous vous êtes fait tout seul, et n'a-t-il pas fallu que votre père ait engrossé votre mère pour vous faire?' Cf. Psalm 99/100, v. 3: 'Scitote quoniam Dominus ipse est Deus: ipse fecit nos, et non ipsi nos.'

[6] Jouvet, L., *Molière et la Comédie classique*. Paris. Gallimard (1965), pp. 86–87: 'Molière lui-même avait joué Sganarelle (...) pour donner à la pièce un côté comique qui enlevait ce qu'elle pouvait avoir de dangereux dans le religieux ou l'irréligieux. Car *Dom Juan* est une pièce religieuse, parce qu'elle est la peinture de l'irréligion(...)La pièce pose, à mon avis, le problème de la religion d'un bout à l'autre.'

[7] The King, in *Psyché*, II, i, vv. 582–5, 589–91, says what Molière himself had said in his *Sonnet à M. La Mothe le Vayer sur la mort de son fils:* 'Ton deuil est raisonnable, encor qu'il soit extrême; / Et, lorsque pour toujours on perd ce que tu perds, / La Sagesse, crois-moi, peut pleurer elle-même.' This, taken with Molière's *Lettre d'envoi du sonnet*, might conceivably be held to imply that Molière thought excessive emotion unreasonable when one has *not* just lost a son, etc.

[8] *L'Étourdi*, II, v. Mascarille will not hide his God-given talent, trickery. Cf. Math. xxv, 14–30. *Dépit amoureux*, II, iv: Marinette, claiming to be a wise virgin, says 'Nescio vos'. Cf. Math., xxv, 12. *École des femmes*; Lysidas, in *La Critique de l'École des femmes*, Sc. VI, refers to accusations that the play is impious.

[9] *Dom Juan*, V, ii. The speech—the longest in the play—says more than is needed for internal dramatic purposes.

[10] Cf. also Orgon's remark: 'Enfin le Ciel chez moi me le fit retirer, / Et depuis ce temps-là tout semble y prospérer' with Math. x, 40–1: 'Qui recipit vos, me recipit: et qui me recipit, recipit eum qui me misit. Qui recipit prophetam in nomine prophetae, mercedem prophetae accipiet: et qui recipit justum in nomine justi, mercedem justi accipiet.'

[11] *Mal. Im.*, III, x.

[12] Luke xvii, 1–2.

[13] Shaw, B., *Prefaces*. London. Paul Hamlyn (1965), p. 809: 'I wish to boast that Pygmalion has been an extremely successful play all over Europe and North America. It is so intensely and deliberately didactic, and its subject esteemed so dry, that I delight in throwing it at the head of wiseacres who repeat the parrot cry that art should never be didactic. It goes to prove my contention that art should never be anything else.'

[14] *Le Malade imaginaire*, Act III, Scene iii. *Béralde:* 'et, de tout temps, il s'est glissé parmi les hommes de belles imaginations, que nous venons à croire, parce qu'elles nous flattent et qu'il seroit à souhaiter qu'elles fussent véritables.' On science, see quotation from Monsieur Diafoirus, above. The Bachelierus's speech in Intermède III of the play seems to parody part of Cicero, *Oratio cum senatui gratias egit*. (*Intermède:* 'Rendam gratias corpori tam docto. / Vobis, vobis debeo / Bien plus qu'à naturae et qu'à patri meo: / Natura et pater meus / Hominem me habent factum; / Mais vos me, ce qui est bien plus, Avetis factum medicum, / Honor, favor et gratia / Qui, in hoc corde que voilà, / Imprimant ressentimenta / Qui dureront in secula.' *Oratio:* 'Quod si parentes carissimos habere debemus, quod ab iis nobis vita, patrimonium, libertas, civitas tradita est, si deos immortales, quorum beneficio et haec tenuimus et ceteris rebus aucti sumus (…) immensum et infinitum est quod vobis debeamus, qui vestro singulari studio atque consensu (…) omnia reddidistis, ut, cum multa vobis (…) innumerabilia parentibus, omnia dis immortalibus debeamus, haec antea singula per illos habuerimus, nunc universa per vos reciperarimus. (…) Quid enim tempus erit unquam cum vestorum in nos beneficiorum memoria ac fama moriatur?') If Molière himself wrote the lines, and did base them on Cicero, then the rendering of *deos immortales* by *natura* would indicate that, on this occasion, he regarded God and Nature as interchangeable terms.

[15] Bray, R. *Molière, Homme de Théâtre*. Paris. Mercure de France (1954), pp. 25–6, gives evidence of Molière's devotional life. But, as the former would-be Jesuit Diderot says: 'notre véritable sentiment n'est pas celui dans lequel nous n'avons jamais vacillé; mais celui auquel nous sommes le plus habituellement revenus'.

[16] Cf. Gonzague de Reynold, *Le Dix-septième Siècle. Le Classique et le Baroque*. Montréal. Éditions de l'Arbre (1944), p. 207: 'L'esprit de la Renaissance—on sait lequel—revit dans La Fontaine, celui du XVIIIe siècle s'annonce dans Molière.'

[17] *Candide*, ch. 5: 'Le matelot (…) ayant cuvé son vin, achète les faveurs de la première fille de bonne volonté qu'il rencontre sur les ruines des maisons détruites, et au milieu des mourants et des morts. Pangloss le tirait cependant par la manche: 'Mon ami, lui disait-il, cela n'est pas bien, vous manquez à la raison universelle, vous prenez mal votre temps. —Tête et sang, répondit l'autre (…)'

[18] Adam, A., *Histoire de la littérature française au XVIIe siècle*, Vol. III, Paris, Éditions Domat (1952), p. 408.

[19] Cairncross, J., *Molière, Bourgeois et Libertin*. Paris, Nizet (1963).

[20] Guicharnaud, J., *Molière: une aventure théâtrale*. Paris, Gallimard (1963), p. 532.
[21] Moore, W. G., *Molière: A New Criticism*. New York, Anchor Books (1962), p. 14.

K. H. Francis

SOME POPULAR SCIENTIFIC MYTHS IN RABELAIS: A POSSIBLE SOURCE

On 15 March 1914 the eminent Cambridge scholar and translator of Rabelais, W. F. Smith, wrote in his diary: 'I am working at certain points in the Great Man, and detecting more borrowings, so that there will not be left much that is original soon.'[1] In the half-century that has elapsed since then, so many inroads have been made into the 'original' parts of Rabelais's work by commentators and students in their search for sources, that one is entitled to ask whether there are any passages left which do not show some evidence of the author's borrowings. The interest which has recently been shown in Rabelais's scientific knowledge has led to the investigation of a further and hitherto unsuspected range of source-material, so that it is now possible to say that many of the isolated curiosities and odd statements of scientific fact which are scattered throughout Rabelais's work were often accepted as true by his contemporaries not only because they were vouched for by the weight of classical authority but also in some cases because they were being perpetuated by many scholars and popular lecturers of the day.

An interesting case in point is offered by a study of the life and works of Joachim Sterck van Ringelberg, in whose *Experimenta* may be found several of the intriguing snippets of scientific lore which was being used by Rabelais at much the same period. Ringelberg himself has something of the exuberance and superhuman quality of a character from *Pantagruel*, and his life—though much shorter than that of Rabelais—was almost as full of movement and incident. There are two principal sources of biographical information concerning Ringelberg,[2] neither of which is entirely satisfactory, since they both rely almost exclusively upon anecdotes related by Ringelberg himself in the course of his work, but there emerges from these very incomplete accounts the picture of 'ung abysme de science' whom Rabelais might well have admired and indeed might well have met.

Of his early life and parentage, very little is known beyond the fact that he was born in Antwerp; even the date of his birth is uncertain, though it was probably in 1499. As a youth, he seems to have been in service at the court of the Emperor Maximilian, but at the age of sixteen or seventeen he went to Louvain to study the classics and philosophy. He remained from this time onwards very closely concerned with education, a life-long student, teacher and writer of educational treatises. His desire to communicate his ideas to others was so urgent that from about 1528 until his death (which may have occurred about 1536, but probably earlier) he travelled almost continuously in Germany, the Low Countries and France, lecturing on a variety of subjects and every day writing one or two chapters of his voluminous works. He was frequently at Antwerp and Louvain; while in Germany, probably in 1528 or 1529, he had the opportunity of putting into practice one of his favourite ideas—that only by teaching a subject can one get to know it really well, and that a scholar wherever he goes should never fail to attract an audience of patient listeners or waste the chance of speaking in public. Being unable to sleep one night on a boat journey, he passed the time lecturing to some sleepless soldiers on the structure of the universe. Ringelberg had the gift of lucid exposition, both in speech and in writing, and this doubtless accounts for the considerable popularity he appears to have enjoyed and for the high esteem in which he was held even by the most eminent scholars of the day, Erasmus among them. He is known to have lectured in Paris at the end of 1529; he then spent two months in Orléans where he had a particularly numerous following. From Orléans, he went to Bourges and lectured very successfully on scientific subjects for about a month. There is evidence of his having been at Lyons at the end of 1530 or early in 1531, whence he travelled on to Basel and eventually disappears from the historical record.

It is therefore this period in his career—from the middle of 1529 until the beginning of 1531—which is of greatest interest to the student of Rabelais. No French humanist of this time could have failed to be aware of a man whose praises were sung by André Hyperius in a public session of the Parlement de Paris and whose

name was coupled with that of Erasmus in a highly flattering
piece of verse:

> Delicium terrae gens Battava laudet Erasmum:
> Agricolam Phrysius cantet, in astra ferat:
> Barlandos referat nunc clara Zelandia doctos:
> Dorpius et magnum sit decus usque suis:
> Longolium sequitur iam Ringelbergius autor;
> Edidit hunc nobis terra Brabanta virum.
> Pierides, vestrum decus hoc redamate sorores:
> Pieridum decus hoc vos redamate, viri.[3]

Ringelberg's passionate attachment to learning and his anxiety
not to waste a moment in profitless pursuits are characteristic of
the generation of scholars to which he belonged. His range of
interests was as wide as that of Rabelais himself, and Professor
Jourda has drawn attention to the fact that Chapter III of the
Pantagrueline Prognostication is based upon a chapter in Ringelberg's *De ratione studii* devoted to a satire of astrology,[4] to mention
but one example.

According to Paquot, the collected works of Ringelberg were
first printed at Antwerp in 1527, but the oldest edition which is
at present known to exist is that published by Sebastien Gryphe
at Lyons in 1531.[5] This, however, is not a complete collection,
and so reference will be made in this article to the Basel edition
of 1541,[6] which is believed to be the earliest complete edition of
all Ringelberg's twenty-seven treatises. The most famous of
these, and the one which was most frequently printed, is the
De ratione studii. This enjoyed considerable success, not only during
the author's lifetime, but even into the seventeenth and eighteenth
centuries, and as late as 1830 it was still referred to on the title-
page of an English translation as 'the *celebrated* Treatise of J. F.
Ringelbergius'.[7] It sometimes appeared as a companion piece
to Erasmus's work which bears the same title. Ringelberg's work
is more interesting for the light it sheds upon his own methods
of study, some of which were extremely rigorous, than for any
value it may now have as a contribution to educational theory.
It seems highly probable however that this aspect of Ringelberg's
thought—that of the progressive, 'enlightened' reformer of teaching methods—would be among the first to appeal to Rabelais,
and there are other passages in the *De ratione studii* besides the
reference to astrology already mentioned which find an echo in
Pantagruel. It is incidentally worthy of note that it is this, the

earliest of Rabelais's major works and the closest in date to Ringelberg's visit to Lyons, which shows most obvious reminiscence of Ringelberg even in the passages of scientific interest which will be examined later.

In the famous Chapter VIII of *Pantagruel* ('Comment Pantagruel, estant à Paris, receut letres de son pere Gargantua, et la copie d'icelles'), there are two sentences which could have been inspired by Rabelais's reading of the *De ratione studii*. The first of these concerns the learning of languages:

> Maintenant toutes disciplines sont restituées, les langues instaurées: Grecque, sans laquelle c'est honte que une personne se die sçavant, Hebraïque, Caldaïque, Latine...[8]

In the *De ratione studii*, there is a chapter entitled 'Cuiusmodi discendae sint Artes', where Ringelberg has the following passage:

> Graeca lingua adeo necessaria, ut vix quenquam dixerim eruditum, qui eam ignoraverit.[9]

He then continues with this outline of an ambitious programme of study:

> Nec omittendæ historiæ: praestant enim et copiam orationis et rerum experientiam. Mathematicæ artes simul dignitate quadam pollent sua, tractant enim rerum sublimium descriptiones: simul ad varietatem orationis faciunt. Astronomia legem naturamque docet eorum quae ab extremo circuitu mundi usque ad elementa sunt, hoc est, pene orbem universum.

References to mathematics and astronomy are of course also to be found in Gargantua's letter, where they are given a similarly high place in the curriculum to be followed by the young Pantagruel.

The second passage in the same chapter of Rabelais to carry a (probably unconscious) reminiscence of Ringelberg's treatise is the following:

> Les femmes et filles ont aspiré à ceste louange et manne celeste de bonne doctrine.[10]

In Ringelberg's *De ratione studii*, this idea is present in a slightly different, but characteristically developed form:

> Nullae sunt fæminæ tam a Musis alienæ, quæ non unam discere queant: imo picas id efficere posse intra annos viginti, quos hæc hominum monstra uni studio impendunt, arbitror.[11]

If, as therefore seems likely, the *De ratione studii* made a deep impression upon the mind of Rabelais, it should not surprise us to find certain of the other treatises recalled from time to time.

Although very few of them have more than an antiquarian interest for the modern reader, their titles indicate the enormous versatility of the author. A large number deal with Latin composition, grammar, usage: *Elegantiæ, De usu vocum quæ non flectuntur, Compendium de conscribendis versibus, Dialectica, Rhetorica* (frequently re-edited in the sixteenth century—several copies are known dating from the 1530's and 1540's published at Antwerp, Paris and Lyons), *Liber de figuris et vitiis orationis, Sententiæ, Liber de formis dicendi, Synonyma, Opusculum de periodis.* These works can still be admired for their mastery of the Latin language and for the elegance of their composition. In view of the important place allotted to Greek in the curriculum, it is not surprising to find an *Elementa græca* among Ringelberg's treatises.

In the *Lucubrationes*, however, there are almost as many treatises on scientific subjects as on literary and linguistic ones. These can conveniently be divided into groups according to the topic treated; for example, there are four works which deal with astronomy: *Sphæra, Institutionum astronomicarum libri tres, Cosmographia* and *Liber de tempore.* Another group contains the three treatises on astrology: *Horoscopus, Astrologia cum Geomantia et Physionomia,* and *De urina non visa et interpretatione somniorum.* There are two works on mathematical subjects: *Chaos mathematicum* and *Arithmetica,* and a fourth category contains a number of works of varying kinds: *Optice* (an elementary manual on perspective), *Liber de homine* (despite its title, which leads one to expect some kind of biological handbook, this consists of little more than very elementary jottings on human physiology, psychology and ethics), *Chaos* (another collection of random notes and observations on many different subjects, not only scientific but also philosophical and literary), and perhaps the most interesting of all Ringelberg's treatises to the student of the history of scientific ideas, the *Experimenta.* Before proceeding to an examination of this work, it may be worth recalling that to his contemporaries, and indeed to writers on scientific subjects throughout the sixteenth century, Ringelberg's reputation as a mathematician and astronomer was at least as great as his fame as a writer on pedagogical subjects. Much of his astronomical work was borrowed by the next generation of theorists,[12] its popularity being partly due to the same remarkable clarity of expression which distinguished his writings as a grammarian. As a mathematician, his work in the *Arithmetica* is of little real significance, since it deals merely with the four basic processes of addition, subtraction, multiplication and division. In the *Chaos mathematicum* however he demonstrated ingenious—but of course approximate—methods of constructing a circle equal in area to a given square, and a square equal in area to a given circle. Ringelberg demonstrates his simple and elegant constructions diagrammatically, but he does not attempt to give any formal proof. Many sixteenth-century manuals of geometry nevertheless reproduced his 'solutions' to one of the most intractable problems of mathematics.[13]

The *Experimenta* make up a rather confused chapter of unrelated items, some of which belong to the realm of popular superstition and folklore; others have a definite basis of scientific fact and can be considered as simple chemical or physical experiments in the proper sense of the term; some of the entries are observations of botanical or zoological interest, while others again consist of mathematical puzzles or 'parlour games'.[14] Another group of entries are clearly meant to serve as practical household hints, such as the cure for nose bleeding with which the chapter begins, or a method of protecting clothes against moths; he describes a system whereby eggs may be cooked without the use of fire and an ingenious way of catching eels. He tells his readers how to distinguish between lead and tin in the dark; he has a cure for intoxication and information as to the best place for digging a well. He has noticed that eggs will sink in fresh water but float in brine, that the phosphorescence of rotting wood produces sufficient light to distinguish even in total darkness between objects close at hand, and the discoloration of metals by the action of acids. There are however several much less reliable 'observations', some of which Ringelberg himself admits to be based on hearsay—for example, that fighting cocks are made more ferocious by a diet of garlic, that lions are terrified by fighting cocks and fire, and that pregnant women if frightened raise their hands to their faces to prevent the unborn child from being disfigured. He quotes the well-known case in Virgil of a swarm of bees coming out of the rotting carcase of an ox. Amongst the entries which belong to the realm of pure superstition we find:

> Fama est funus occisi hominis stillare sanguine, si adfuerit interfector. Et naves mergi ni mortuorum corpora confestim ejiciantur.

He repeats the widely held—but quite false—belief that if you rub a magnet with garlic, it will lose its power of attracting iron.

It is upon this same principle that the magnetic temple doors in Rabelais, Book V, Chapter 36, were constructed, bunches of garlic being suspended to neutralize the effects of magnetism upon the doors and hold them in a state of equilibrium.[15] It is difficult to see how such a belief could logically arise, beyond the fact that to rub any magnet as weak as those generally available at this period with any substance whatever would tend to cause a loss of magnetism. Ringelberg goes on to add, with a completely uncritical acceptance of the superstition, that if you immediately dip the magnet in the blood of a ram its powers will be restored. We seem here to be very close to the world of sorcery.

The interest shown by the early sixteenth century in secret writing, codes and hidden messages is reflected in more than one place in the *Experimenta*, and it is probable that Ringelberg was acquainted with the work of the best-known contemporary authority on the subject, the *Polygraphia* of Trithemius, which had appeared in 1518. It is generally assumed that the references to invisible inks which are to be found in *Pantagruel* Chapter 24 are inspired by this work, by Pliny and perhaps other classical sources.[16] It is interesting to note however that two of the recipes quoted by Rabelais (the two least far-fetched) are also to be found in the *Experimenta*:

(*a*) Salis genus est, quod armoniacum nuncupant: hoc contusum mistumque aquæ, literas quidem albas reddit, nihil distantes a colore papyri, sed si igni admoveris, nigras.

(*b*) Ad eundem modum aluminis pulvere scripta non apparent, nisi chartam cum legere voles, merseris in aquam.[17]

Rabelais's somewhat simplified versions of these two procedures read as follows:

(*a*) (Panurge) mist (la fueille de papier) auprès du feu, pour veoir si l'escripture estoit faicte avec du sel ammoniac destrempé en eau.

(*b*) Puis la mist tout doulcement dedans un bassin d'eau fresche et soubdain la tira, pour veoir si elle estoit escripte avecques alum de plume.[18]

Panurge's investigations lead him to question the messenger who has brought a 'letter' from the *dame de Paris*, and he asks:

'la dame qui t'a icy envoyé t'a elle poinct baillé de baston pour apporter?', pensant que feust la finesse que mect Aule Gelle.'

While there is no reason to doubt, in view of Rabelais's references elsewhere to the *Noctes Atticæ* of Aulus Gellius, that he was thinking primarily of the Roman author's account of the Spartan *scytala*, a recent reading of Ringelberg's *Experimenta* would have refreshed his memory: in fact Ringelberg's chapter concludes with a lengthy description of how this method of carrying messages worked and he gives an example of how a particular message would be encoded.[19]

One of the more fascinating scientific myths twice referred to by Rabelais is that of the ivy funnel, which, it was maintained, could be used to separate wine from water. The first time Rabelais mentions this handy device is in *Gargantua* Chapter 24. The young Gargantua, accompanied by his tutor Ponocrates and his friends, takes time off from his studies in Paris to spend a day in the country.

> En banquetant, du vin aisgué separoient l'eau, comme l'enseigne Cato, *De re rust.*, et Pline, avecques un goubelet de lierre; lavoient le vin en plain bassin d'eau, puis le retiroient avec un embut, faisoient aller l'eau d'un verre en aultre.[20]

The exact nature of the process which takes place in this experiment is far from clear, and when Rabelais refers to it a second time (*Tiers Livre*, Ch. 52), he seems to strike a rather sceptical note. This is when he is describing the versatility of Pantagruelion, and protests that truth is stranger than fiction: if his readers jib at the wonders worked by this plant, then let them consider a parallel case, that of the ivy funnel used to separate water and wine which gives each back in the same proportions as they were before being mixed.

> Comment les purifieriez vous?
> J'entends bien, vous me parlez d'un entonnoir de lierre. Cela est escript, il est vray, et averé par mille experiences. Vous le sçaviez desjà. Mais ceulx qui ne l'ont sceu et ne le veirent oncques ne le croyroient possible.[21]

When in the *Experimenta* Ringelberg refers to this phenomenon, he is no more explicit than his sources, nor does he say, as he sometimes does, that he has actually seen the experiment performed. We are left with a bald statement of fact:

> Si voles scire in vinum aqua addita sit, nec ne, vasculum facito de materia hæderacea, vinum quod habere aquam putabis, in id mittito. Si habebit aquam vinum quia acrius est, modo lignum non sit nimis densum effluet, aqua manebit.[22]

What kind of a *vasculum* are we to make? Is it to be a *guobelet* as Rabelais first suggests, without any implication that the *embut*

has to be of the same material, or must the funnel itself be made
of ivy? And what of the *materia hæderacea*—do ivy leaves have any
part to play in this process of separation, or merely the wood of
the ivy plant? Unfortunately Cato is no more helpful, his wording
being almost identical with that of Ringelberg:

> Si voles scire in vinum aqua addita sit, necne, vasculum facito de
> materia hæderacea. Vinum id, quod putabis aquam habere, eodem
> mittito. Si habebat aquam, vinum effluet, aqua manebit. Nam non
> continet vinum vas ederaceum. [23]

Pliny's version at least makes it clear that the vessel should be
made of ivy wood:

> Ederæ mira proditur natura ad experienda vina: si vas fiat ex ligno
> ejus, vina transfluere, ac remanere aquam, si qua fuerit mista. [24]

If there is any foundation in fact for this remarkable claim, why,
one may well ask, do we not continue to make use of ivy funnels?
Is separation by such a process scientifically possible? The nature
of the plant cell and its walls indicates that it may be. The cell
wall is lined by a thin layer of protoplasm inside which is the
nucleus, and the remainder consists of cytoplasm, which is more
permeable to some substances than to others. It is relatively
permeable to water, less so to sugars and mineral salts, but its
actual properties vary from plant to plant. [25] If the so-called ivy
wood acts as a sieve due to this difference in permeability, one
would expect the water to pass through leaving the wine behind.
Perhaps this is what Rabelais means when he writes 'faisoient
aller l'eau d'un verre en aultre,' assuming that he intended this
remark to apply to the separation experiment.

An alternative explanation may be based upon the principle
of osmosis, though probably this method would require more
apparatus than a simple funnel to be effective. Here the separation of the liquids would be brought about by the use of a semi-
permeable membrane, which is one allowing the passage through
it of molecules up to a limiting size. All hygroscopic bodies may
be regarded as possessing a suction pressure which varies not only
with the substance itself but also with the conditions in which it
is placed. Liquids possess a diffusion pressure which will cause
diffusion of water molecules from one region to another adjacent
to it which has a lower diffusion pressure. Water will tend to
diffuse from a weak solution into a stronger one, [26] so that if the
mixture of wine and water were placed on one side of a semi-

permeable membrane with a strong sugar solution on the other side, the water would diffuse from the mixture into the sugar solution. The ivy *guobelet* might possibly serve as a semi-permeable membrane and, if we allow the wine and water to be placed inside the funnel with a strong sugar solution on the other side, it may be that the water would diffuse through, leaving the wine. Both these methods however imply the passage of the water rather than the wine. Given the information in Rabelais and his sources, it is hard to see how the experiment can be made to work. The writer has attempted to separate wine and water with two types of ivy filter and two different kinds of wine—a claret and a *rosé*. In one case a thin cross-section of ivy stem was sealed into the neck of a glass funnel, and in the other experiment a small cylindrical cup was hollowed out of the stem itself. The permeability of the wood was fairly soon demonstrated, but in neither case was there any noticeable amount of separation.

Whatever source may have inspired Rabelais's allusions to the ivy funnel, there can be little doubt that one other passage in his work appears to derive directly from Ringelberg's *Experimenta*. Once again an episode in *Pantagruel* is concerned. Chapter 27 of this work is one of the curious interludes—of which there are several in Book II—which neither advance the action nor express any particular philosophy, but serve rather as a repository for scabrous anecdotes or demonstrations of the author's versatility and inventiveness.[27] The passage in question is all the more remarkable because of its completely different tone and the extremely artificial way with which Rabelais attempts to link it to the main part of the story. After Pantagruel and his friends have set up their *trophée* to commemorate their victory over the six hundred and sixty knights, an unrelated section typical of the early Rabelais manner describes the origin of the Pygmies. Then, with another rapid change of subject, Panurge performs one of his party tricks:

> En ceste mesme heure Panurge print deux verres qui là estoient tous deux d'une grandeur, et les emplit d'eau tant qu'ilz en peurent tenir, et en mist l'un sur une escabelle et l'aultre sur une aultre, les esloingnans à part par la distance de cinq piedz; puis print le fust d'une javeline de la grandeur de cinq piedz et demy et les mist dessus les deux verres, en sorte que les deux boutz du fust touchoient justement les bors des verres.
> Cela faict, print un gros pau et dist à Pantagruel et es aultres:

Messieurs, considerez comment nous aurons victoire facilement de noz ennemys; car,—ainsi comme je rompray ce fust icy dessus les verres sans que les verres soient en rien rompus ne brisez, encores, que plus est, sans que une seule goutte d'eau en sorte dehors,—tout ainsi nous romprons la teste à noz Dipsodes, sans ce que nul de nous soit blessé et sans perte aulcune de noz besoignes. Mais, affin que ne pensez qu'il y ait enchantement, tenez, dist il à Eusthenes, frappez de ce pau tant que pourrez au millieu.'

Ce que fist Eusthenes, et le fust rompit en deux pieces tout net, sans que une goutte d'eau tumbast des verres.[28]

This is a developed, more consciously literary version of an experiment described by Ringelberg:

Mirum est, quod ipse ego sæpe numero deprehendi, magna adstantium admiratione, fustem frangi duobus impositum poculis vitreis, idque illis haudquaquam commotis. Pocula duo vitrea plena humore super sedes duas ponito, ad pedum quatuor aut quinque distantiam. Inde baculum fragilem totidem longitudine pedum super vascula cadem collocato, ita ut cyathorum margines vix attingat. Denique fuste alio robustiore impositum poculis baculum viribus totis medium percutio. Sic frangetur poculis immotis modo lignum sit, ut ante diximus, fragile.[29]

Ringelberg's mention of the effectiveness of this simple demonstration perhaps gives us a clue to Rabelais's reasons for introducing the episode. It seems likely that, having once impressed an audience with this experiment, an itinerant lecturer might well have retained it as a regular item in his répertoire. Rabelais must either have seen the experiment performed or have performed it himself to be able to describe it so clearly. In the hands of a showman with a sense of the dramatic, it can create the impression of finality one associates with a successful conjuring trick. This is the link Rabelais has seized upon to attach the episode to the main plot: the irrevocability of the broken stick matches the utter defeat of the Dipsodes in a situation which at first glance looks impossible. Undoubtedly the demonstration must have impressed Rabelais considerably: it may even have been fresh in his mind at the time of writing *Pantagruel*.

It is not without interest that a recently published junior physics manual quotes Rabelais's version of this experiment, and asks its readers to perform it for themselves and explain the result.[30] To us, of course, the scientific principle involved presents no difficulty: it is a simple problem concerning centres of gravity. The staff of a javelin would be of fairly uniform cross-section and density, and the centre of gravity would therefore be approximately at the middle point of its length. When the staff was resting upon the two glasses, each would support part of the weight, but immediately the staff was broken each half would acquire its own centre of gravity and the edge of each glass would act merely as a pivot or fulcrum about which the portions of rod would turn. The glasses, therefore, would support none of the weight and so would remain undamaged. It must have seemed however to the unsophisticated audiences of Ringelberg's lectures that there was indeed some use of *enchantement* here.

In the few passages of scientific interest here referred to, it is possible to see once again instances of Rabelais's alert and enquiring mind. If he sometimes made use of popular myths—such as the effect of garlic on magnets and the properties of an ivy funnel,—he did so because they served his purpose at those particular points in his narrative. He does not necessarily have to subscribe to the truth of these beliefs in a work of fiction, and his later scepticism about the *entonnoir de lierre* seems to indicate that he sometimes wrote of these myths with tongue in cheek. On the other hand, experiments such as the stick and glasses which involve serious principles (a comparison might be made once more with the heptagonal fountain in Book V) are seriously treated. And while it is impossible to say with certainty that Rabelais was acquainted either with the writings of Ringelberg or with the man personally, there seems to be a fair amount of evidence which points in that direction. A similarity of age, outlook, temperament, links these two men whose educational ideas have so much in common.

M. H. Bosmans's article on Ringelberg in the *Biographie Nationale de Belgique* concludes with this judgment:

> Un érudit d'un savoir encyclopédique, un esprit indépendant et original, un écrivain facile et élégant qui fit surtout preuve d'un grand talent de vulgarisation.[31]

Could not such a summary be equally applicable to Rabelais?

NOTES

[1] W. F. Smith, 'A Rabelaisian at Work'. *Adam*, XXII (1954), p. 21.
[2] Melchior Adam, *Vitæ Eruditorum, cum Germanorum tum Exterorum. Dignorum laude Virorum.* Frankfurt (1705), pp. 38 ff. and also J. N. Paquot, *Mémoires pour servir à l'histoire littéraire des dix-sept provinces des Pays-Bas.* Vol. I, Louvain (1765), pp. 442 ff.

See also the long entry 'Ringelberg' by H. Bosmans in *Biographie Nationale de Belgique*, Brussels (1906–1910), cols. 346–59. This is largely based upon the work of Adam and Paquot.

[3] Quoted by Paquot, *op. cit.*

[4] Rabelais, *Œuvres complètes*. Ed. P. Jourda. 2 vols. Paris (1962), Vol. II, p. 501. Unless otherwise stated, references will be to this edition.

[5] *Ioachimi Fortii Ringelbergii Andoverpiani opera quæ proxima pagina enumerantur*. Apud Gryphium, Lugduni, anno MDXXXI.

[6] *Ioachimi Fortii Ringelbergii Andoverpiani lucubrationes* . . . Basileæ, apud Bartholomeum Westhemerum, anno MDXLI.

[7] *The celebrated Treatise of J. F. Ringelbergius, De Ratione Studii*, translated by G. B. Earp, London (1830). A very incomplete and unreliable translation.

[8] Rabelais, *op. cit.*, I, p. 259.

[9] *Lucubrationes*, p. 20.

[10] Rabelais, *op. cit.*, I, p. 260.

[11] *Lucubrationes*, p. 76.

[12] J. C. Houzeau et A. Lancaster, *Bibliographie générale de l'astronomie*, tom. I, lère partie, Bruxelles (1887), pp. 568 and 572.

[13] Moritz Cantor, *Vorlesungen über Geschichte der Mathematik*, t. II, Leipzig (1900), p. 364, has drawn attention to Ringelberg's geometrical skill. One is reminded here of another attempt to solve a complex geometrical problem, the construction of a regular heptagon in a circle, attempted by Rabelais—following Colonna—in Book V, Chapter 42. See my article 'Rabelais and Mathematics' in *Bibl. Hum. et Ren.*, XXI (1959), pp. 85 ff.

[14] *Lucubrationes*, pp. 719 ff.

[15] See my article 'The Mechanism of the Magnetic Doors in Rabelais, Book V, Chapter 37'. *French Studies*, XIII (1959), pp. 293 ff., which attempts to explain the complex principles underlying the operation of these doors.

[16] Rabelais, *Œuvres*. Ed. A. Lefranc, Vol. IV, Paris (1922), pp. 250 ff.

[17] *Lucubrationes*, pp. 720 ff.

[18] Rabelais, *op. cit.*, I, pp. 337 f.

[19] *Lucubrationes*, p. 729.

[20] Rabelais, *op. cit.*, I, pp. 99 f. It is not clear whether there are one, two or three processes referred to here. For example, the passage after the semicolon: 'lavoient le vin...' may be an experiment completely unrelated to the ivy funnel. The Lefranc edition puts another semicolon after *avec un embut*, and adds a footnote to the effect that *faisoient aller l'eau d'un verre en aultre* means with the help of a siphon (Rabelais, *Œuvres*, ed. A. Lefranc, vol. II, Paris (1913), p. 244). Surely this implies a separate experiment? If Rabelais still intends these words to refer to the funnel, he is taking a view contrary to his Latin sources which uniformly state that it is the *wine*, not the water, which passes through the funnel. (See below.)

[21] *Ibid.*, p. 615.

[22] *Lucubrationes*, p. 721.

[23] Cato, *De re rustica*, CXI. See Rabelais, ed. Lefranc, II, *loc. cit.*

[24] Pliny, *Hist. nat.*, XVI, 35.

[25] W. O. James, *Introduction to Plant Physiology*, Oxford (1963), pp. 170 ff.

[26] *Ibid.*, pp. 196 ff.
[27] As, for example, Chapters 15, 23, 26, 32, 33.
[28] Rabelais, *op. cit.*, I, pp. 352 ff.
[29] *Lucubrationes*, p. 722. The experiment is also referred to briefly by L. Thorndike, *History of Magic and Experimental Science*, vol. V, New York (1941), p. 147.
[30] L. R. Middleton, *Junior Physics* I, London (1963), p. 104.
[31] *Loc. cit.*, col. 358.

J. C. Ireson

TOWARDS A THEORY OF THE SYMBOLIST
THEATRE

In tracing the development of a Symbolist theory of the drama,
two special problems have captured most of the attention of the
observers: the apotheosis of Wagner and the concentrated critical
work done by Mallarmé on the contemporary theatre between
1886 and 1893. In particular, critics have tended to see the notion
of a Symbolist theory of the drama as 'invented' by Mallarmé,[1]
or at any rate, initiated and formulated by him in a body of
gnomic writings, the sense of which is developed or clarified by
'disciples'.[2]

The aim of these notes is to trace, through the writings of a
number of the main authors of the nineteenth century who have
theorized about the theatre, currents of ideas which lead towards
Mallarmé and the early forms of the Symbolist drama. I am
concerned with the ideas themselves rather than with their relative
merit or with the place of authors in any group or hierarchy.

Let us first consider Mallarmé's theories of the theatre, on the
assumption that they do in fact represent a platform from which
the ideas responsible for the growth of an ambitious, experimental
lyrical drama were propagated. These ideas have been variously
summarized and have tended to be distorted according to the
perspective of the commentator. For Guy Michaud, at the time
of the writing of *Message poétique du Symbolisme*, it is the 'théorie du
drame idéal'[3] which is singled out for sole consideration, the
author selecting as his focal point the formula which is at once
a theatrical prescription and a summary of the ultimate theme of
Mallarmé's work:

> la pièce écrite au folio du ciel et mimée avec le geste de ses passions par
> l'Homme.[4]

This view characterizes Michaud's subsequent view of Mallarmé, as seen in the exemplary *Mallarmé, l'homme et l'œuvre*, where the Ideal Theatre is related to the Hindu notion of the Grand Jeu,

> réduction de l'ordre cosmique où chaque individu est mis à sa place selon son rang et sa fortune.[5]

Where more detailed and technical aspects of Mallarmé's dramatic theories are involved, the author adopts the procedure of constructing a paragraph mainly of Mallarmean snippets which, loosely connected, enable the text to proceed in elevated flashes. May Daniels sets Mallarmé's theories on drama in the general context of the Symbolist movement, which 'is mystic and universal'.[6] Jacques Robichez insists on the critical and demonstrative aspects of Mallarmé's 'campagne dramatique'[7] which, nevertheless, bring the critic to 'le cœur même du Symbolisme', the special mirror constructed by the ideal dramatist and reflecting an abstruse principle of correspondence between the inner life of the viewer (or reader) of the dramatic performance and what is hopefully left to be understood as 'beauty'.[8] In the most detailed and specialized work yet devoted to Mallarmé as a poet of dramatic tendencies and as a theorist of drama, Haskell M. Block[9] devotes a chapter to 'The Vision of a New Theater' in which he separates into a dozen themes the tessellation of ideas created by Mallarmé in the nine articles of the *Revue indépendante* (1886–7) and the three published in the *National Observer* in 1893.[10] These themes may be represented as follows: opposition of the contemporary 'living' theatre and the ideal theatre; elevation of characters to universalized and spiritual entities; the liturgical nature of the Mallarmean theatre; the social responsibility of the theatre; obscurity and effort towards cosmic reflection; 'detheatricalization';[11] the Mallarmean notion of the writer as *histrion*; preoccupation with the unique interior profundity of a central character: drama as a synthesis of arts; special importance of the dance, and of music; need for an effective poetry. The whole of this analysis, one of the most effective yet attempted, though somewhat lacking in coherent development, is set within the context of the Mallarmean notion of the ideal *Livre*, as, in fact, are most commentaries on Mallarmé's theatrical doctrines.[12]

Three great principles emerge from Mallarmé's writings on the theatre: the speculative inclusion of the drama in the idealist æsthetic; the cauterizing of the contemporary theatre in France; notes on the practicability of an experimental, rarefied and concentrated dramatic form.

Through the first of these, Mallarmé reaches towards the ineffable, the suggestion of the cosmic structures which permit the apprehension of the essentials of personal being. The second and third resemble the traditional elements of the literary programme or manifesto.

The contemporary theatre appears to offer something of a paradox to Mallarmé. This 'théâtre borné'[13] attempts a futile imitation of the sprawl and confusion of life[14] and fails because of the unsubtlety of its means. These means are the conventional speech, gestures and actions permissible to actors;[15] the idea of the stage as a replica of the real or likely settings of events;[16] its cumbersome efforts at a machine-made verisimilitude;[17] the single-minded insistence of post-Renaissance drama on the delineation of characters in complex relief;[18] the limitation of dramatic resources to the revelation of moments of crisis;[19] pandering to traditional notions of entertainment.[20] Yet, even allowing for the customary polite Mallarmean reticences over the work of named contemporaries, there are things in conventional or traditional drama which Mallarmé does not dismiss. In the comedy of manners, there is an art necessary to the satirist demonstrating a moral principle through a hypothetical situation, which appears as a 'moyen authentique de théâtre'.[21] Efforts to formulate a new theory of tragedy do not find him unsympathetic.[22] An exemplary flash set off by speculation on the dramatizing of a novel by Daudet illuminates the essential procedures of French tragedy:

produire en un milieu nul ou à peu près les grandes poses humaines et comme notre plastique morale.[23]

Classical tragedy thus approaches in two respects the ideal drama as conceived by Mallarmé; but its concern to configure types or individuals evolving within a moral situation separates it clearly from the Mallarmean theatre. The Naturalist theatre itself is not without its moments of significance for the author of *Hérodiade*. The performance of *Les Honnêtes Femmes* at the end of 1886 becomes noteworthy for Mallarmé by reason of an essential ingredient: 'sa puissante touche de poésie inévitable'. The passage continues:

K

> dans l'instrumentale conduite des timbres du dialogue, interruptions,
> répétitions, toute une technique qui rappelle l'exécution en musique
> de chambre de quelque fin concert de tonalité un peu neutre; et (je
> souris) du fait du symbole.[24]

The orchestration of dialogue, dialogue which proceeds by a
pattern of themes; the use of a vehicle which suggests a subject
beyond itself: the Naturalist theatre in its turn has run close to
the desirable formula.

The notional work of drama emerges, then, very largely from
the realizations of forerunners and contemporaries (Shakespeare,
Wagner, Banville are the principal names): insight and imagination; drama based on legend and fused with music; dramatic
poetry controlled by fantasy. Mallarmé's assessment of these
three is in accordance with principles rather than standards. If
the praise for *Le Forgeron* is immensely high, it is because of its
abstinences, its withdrawal from the material issues of the theatre
and also probably because Mallarmé is stimulated to look beyond
it, towards its virtuality, just as Wagnerian opera had caused him
to look with less comfort towards the summits of art:

> la trop lucide hantise de cette cime menaçante d'absolu, devinée
> dans le départ des nuées là-haut, fulgurante, nue, seule: au-delà et que
> personne ne semble devoir atteindre.[25]

Point by point, Mallarmé's programme establishes itself as a
meditation on desirable possibilities of transcending the traditional elements of the theatre: stage, actors, dramatic structure
and substance. In these speculations, a number of tempting
possibilities suggest themselves at the extremes of the dramatist's
art: eurhythmy; music, language tuned and elevated to represent
a metaphysical action. The evanescent hieroglyphs shaped by a
skilled dancer appeal to Mallarmé as something infinitely
subtler than the predictable poses of the actor, and as the substance of a message that can only be followed by a process of
associations. They are also analogous to language at its highest
points of connotation. Music likewise represents the point at
which spectacle and dramatic action are swept into the realm of
mentality. As for language, it can never give character to the
supreme Play, the essence of which is cosmic, the substance of
which is the disproportion between the endeavours of the artist's
mind and the inevitable human fatality.[26]

Ultimately, as Jacques Scherer indicates in the invaluable and
lucid study which prefaces the manuscript relative to the *Livre*,

the ideal Play becomes one with the ideal Book, the new Scripture; and although this quintessential Book remains 'a threatening and absolute peak', Mallarmé is surprisingly circumstantial about its function and nature. Once realized, it would need to be promulgated, and this promulgation would be effected not only by sales, but also by performances.[27]

It is here that we come to one of the most problematical aspects of Mallarmé's theory of the theatre. The ultimate and definitive Work, 'd'une pureté que l'homme n'a pas atteinte',[28] would necessarily be universal in its significance and appeal. Failing the impossible, an ambitious, elevated theatrical form is still realizable, making its own appeal to the public. The 'pièce populaire' as it exists in the nineteenth century before Mallarmé's time, sentimental, naïve, over-simplified, offers no intellectual refreshment (the term is Mallarmé's) to the working population.[29] Superior forms of the Naturalist theatre may do this sporadically;[30] but Mallarmé envisages an official, municipally organized theatre offering a 'rafraîchissement supérieur'[31] in the form of the elevated 'fiction' which would characterize the Mallarmean theatre.

This theatre, social in its intentions, moves towards archetypal forms and archetypal characters. From the point of view of characterization, *Hamlet* appears to come close to the theoretical limit with its configuration of the Prince, though it is doubtful whether, as commentators seem to think, he is for Mallarmé either the sole conceivable figure of the ideal theatre or the uniquely independent figure of the play in which he appears.[32] The recommendable pattern of characterization, noted by Mallarmé in the case of *Hamlet*,[33] is described more fully in the appreciation of Dujardin's *La Fin d'Antonia*:

> ils dessinent les uns relativement aux autres, à leur insu, en une sorte de danse, le pas où se compose la marche de l'œuvre. Très mélodiquement, en toute suavité; mus par l'orchestre intime de leur diction.[34]

An inevitable dramatic pattern, formed by the interdependent actions of characters whose motive force is reflective and poetical rather than reactive or emotionally determined; stylization, harmony: these are the qualities approved by Mallarmé. We see from the quotation how such qualities slip towards the dance and towards music and, in theory at any rate, borrow qualities from each of these forms without merging with them. At the highest attainable point of his doctrine, Mallarmé, recognizing once more the limitations of the conventional stage, together with the intangibility of music, concludes by advocating a fusion of the two ('de vague et de brutal') to produce a complex dramatized form of the Ode accompanying or evoking 'scènes héroïques',[35] ramifying into several voices or characters. This art renews, in Mallarmé's view, a tradition that was blocked by the rise of scientific humanism. It will reactivate among the people of an industrialized era the sense of wonder attached to the ancient myths. It will satisfy two further principles, those of instruction and pleasure. Inevitably, too, perhaps, the solemnized functions of poetry and the notion of a social theatre are fused to form the idea of a commemorative, ritual, theatrical art the sources of which must be looked for in the liturgical drama of past ages.

This body of doctrine, covering an immense field between theoretical limits, is, as can be seen, in many respects pertinent and practical; pertinent in abstracting defects of current drama, practical in seizing on manifestations of a new art as they appeared. But, by the very vastness and suggestive force of the concepts it embraces, it has tended to dazzle the eye of the commentator and impose itself as something unique and autochthonous. Unique it certainly is, in its relation to the *Livre*, but certainly not acaulescent. The Mallarmean theory of the theatre is prefigured in the work of Romantic and Parnassian writers and encouraged by the general state of opinion among critics towards the end of the nineteenth century.

A further complication has been added by the need felt by literary historians to establish clear divisions between movements. An example of this is afforded by Guy Michaud, the best historian of French Symbolism:

> Mais n'était-il pas alors, pour des Français qui venaient de proclamer une révolution littéraire et qui voulaient lui assurer la consécration du public, une tentation bien forte, celle du théâtre? Cette tentation, les Romantiques n'avaient pas su y résister. Les Symbolistes allaient y céder à leur tour.[36]

This is the orthodox approach of the literary historian, who carves up the chronological table of authors and works and separates them by horizontal divisions into named periods. One peculiarity of this approach is that it often tends to divide and assimilate at one and the same time. Michaud, for example, contrives to give the impression of a second 1830, an identical collective impetus, yet also of a new and separate movement.

Another historian, the lucid and concise P. Martino,[37] noting the desire of all the French schools of the nineteenth century for the 'consecration conferred by success', attributes the phenomenon to the publicity and the financial lure of the theatre, an idea which, attractive as it is, sidetracks attention away from literary problems towards an improbable sociology.

Thibaudet's description is most accurate, which envisages Mallarmé's creative work as a point of confluence of three currents: Preciosity, Romanticism, Parnasse.[38] In the case of his critical and theoretical work on the theatre, Mallarmé develops lines traced by Romantic and Parnassian writers, and is obviously encouraged by the general state of opinion among theatre critics of the late nineteenth century.

How far does this hold, for example, in the case of the arch-Romantics? If we look beyond the theatrical polemic of Hugo, the hasty vision of history, the artificial theories designed to accommodate notions of scenic and linguistic liberation with the expectations of the public of the eighteen-twenties, we find anticipations of Mallarmé. Shakespeare, an obsession of nineteenth-century literary France, yields, not surprisingly, common ground for admiration in both authors, even while allowing Hugo scope to admire precisely what Mallarmé rejects in the modern theatre:

l'émotion, l'instinct, le cri vrai, l'accent juste, toute la multitude avec sa rumeur.[39]

But *Hamlet* ('le chef d'œuvre de la tragédie rêve')[40] preoccupies Hugo almost as much as it haunts Mallarmé. Elsewhere, it is curious to see Hugo, following a road that leads through a theatre based on multiplicity, contrast, sentiment, conflict, emerge at a point where the desirable qualities of the dramatist become Mallarmean: 'profond, désintéressé, général et universel'.[41] The idea of the theatre as a mirror is common to all ages. At moments, the theatrical mirror evoked in the theoretical writings of Hugo is a Mallarmean mirror:

Attirer la foule à un drame comme l'oiseau à un miroir; passionner la multitude autour de la glorieuse fantaisie du poète.[42]

Hugo, no less than Mallarmé, is led by such an image and such an idea to the limits of art:

pénétrer sous toutes les surfaces pour extraire l'essence de tout.[43]

Hugo's scrutiny of the function and mission of the nineteenth-century theatre induces two inter-related ideas familiar to students of Mallarmé:

> Le théâtre, nous le répétons, est une chose qui enseigne et qui civilise. Dans nos temps de doute et de curiosité le théâtre est devenu, pour les multitudes, ce qu'était l'église au moyen-âge, le lieu attrayant et central. Tant que ceci durera, la fonction du poète dramatique sera plus qu'une magistrature et presque un sacerdoce.[44]

Liturgical, social, elevated, poetic (Hugo, like Mallarmé, meditates at length on the role of verse in drama), the theoretical theatre for the people becomes a theatre preoccupied with the ideal:

> il est à souhaiter que les hommes de talent n'oublient pas l'excellence du grandiose et de l'idéal dans tout art qui s'adresse aux masses. Les masses ont l'instinct de l'idéal.[45]

Equally striking, though perhaps less surprising, is the presence of a number of elements in the writings of Vigny which prefigure aspects of Mallarmé's theories. Vigny's theory of the poem is second only to Mallarmé's in elevated grace and subtlety for, if the idea, symbolized by the pearl in *La Maison du Berger*, is too stern and uncompromising in its suggestion of thought condensed from hard experience to be classified as Mallarmean, the ideas of 'l'élixir divin que boivent les esprits'[46] and of 'l'esprit pur' are analogous to Mallarmé's notions of essences and of the contact between the ideal lyrical drama and the people. We may furthermore profitably compare the ideas of the stanza 'Diamant sans rival (...)' in *La Maison du Berger* with the anticipatory passages written by Mallarmé on a future theatre.[47] *Eloa*, despite the presence of lingering neo-classical influences, may be looked upon as an experimental forerunner of the *récitation* whose development Mallarmé traces mentally through Banville's *Le Forgeron* into an idealized future. Ideas of a more negative character, noted in the *Journal d'un poète* and left undeveloped by Vigny, trace nevertheless a movement of thought similar to that of Mallarmé: a certain perversity in the attitude towards immediate and material success in the theatre;[48] distaste for comedy;[49] advocacy of the working out of a dominant idea by means of a simple and natural pattern of events and characters.[50] Elsewhere, the anomaly, briefly noted by Vigny of the two literatures,

> celle des yeux ou de la lecture, et celle des oreilles ou du chant,[51]

brings him momentarily to the problem with which Mallarmé struggles so obstinately, the relation of the printed book to the incantatory virtue of poetry or tragedy. Finally, we may note, without surprise, Gautier's judgement on *Chatterton*, the type already, in 1840, of the 'symbolical' drama:

> un drame purement symbolique, dénué de surprise et d'événements, dont la donnée est celle-ci: La poésie aux prises avec la prose, et l'idéal succombant sous le réel.[52]

Lamartine? It is true that the author of *Jocelyn* conceived, in a brief period of inspiration ('une ou deux heures d'hallucination contemplative'),[53] the design of a vast work, the 'Grand Poème'. But the longed-for sublimity and universality were of the epic type and manner. And Lamartine speculates hardly at all about the theatre. His 'tragédie moderne', *Toussaint Louverture*, is a synthesis of classical procedures (what Mallarmé calls 'les grandes poses humaines')[54] and an inherent personal attitude based on noble instincts (freedom, equality, loyalty, paternal love). Nothing in the play reveals these 'nouveaux, concis, lumineux traits'[55] demanded by Mallarmé as essential to the new theatre. Looked at from a general perspective, Lamartine's four books of lyrical and meditative poems may be seen as a multiform Ode, with its own variations of tone and metrical pattern (Mallarmé's 'orchestre intime'?),[56] its own hieratic manner. In one respect, too, the negligent and negative aspects of Lamartine's poetic expression are the act of impatience of a poet whose inspiration takes him towards a wordless monologue he calls prayer and which transcends the 'langage borné' which he notes in *Dieu*:

> Toute parole expire en efforts impuissants.[57]

This is the obverse of Mallarmé's doctrines, the despising of articulation, of the hieroglyph on the page. And yet this very force, identical to what Mallarmé has called:

> l'irascible vent des mots qu'il n'a pas dits,[58]

impels Lamartine towards the Grand Poème, but in so doing carries him out of the scope of the theatre, even of the virtuality of the Mallarmean theatre, 'inhérent à l'esprit'.[59]

Musset? He, too, foreshadows the Symbolist theory of the theatre in two respects at least: the primacy of the written composition in relation to the factors conditioning its presentation on the stage; interiority as the superior principle of the dramatist's art. The first of these ideas, as has been pointed out by May Daniels, supposes the possibility of an ideal theatre,[60] though Musset obfuscates the issues by a deliberate wilfulness and irony whenever he approaches theoretical questions. The second passes, by way of Musset's admiration for Shakespeare and Racine, through the notion of the play as a patterned exteriorization of the artist's thought (the pattern being less important than the mental play determining it)[61] towards the concept of the drama as the illumination of human sentiment and motives.[62]

> Qu'importe le combat, si l'éclair de l'épée
> Peut nous servir dans l'ombre à voir les combattants?[63]

These flashes, activated by the events of the play, in a circumambient darkness, and providing fitful visibility, represent the effort of the artist who is concerned to reveal human nature in depth ('ouvre le cœur humain').[64] This effort, which in itself belongs very largely to the moral sphere, is given an added range of effect by the work of the artist's imagination.[65] Mallarmé's idea is little different when, likewise referring to *Hamlet*, he evokes the revelations made about the character's background and motives by the apparently spontaneous gesture which kills Polonius:

> le fatidique prince qui périra au premier pas dans la virilité, repousse mélancoliquement, d'une pointe vaine d'épée, hors de la route interdite à sa marche, le tas de loquace vacuité gisant que plus tard il risquerait de devenir à son tour, s'il vieillissait.[66]

These illustrations, Musset's and Mallarmé's, serve the interests of the principle, essential according to the Symbolist formula of Mallarmé, of the 'raccourci' by which, in the theatre, concentration and evocative power are obtained:

> Un raccourci habile du héros qui le fasse dégager dans un coup de vent le secret de son habitude, c'est la manière du poète, s'il dramatise.[67]

We are concerned here with dramatists who theorize. And it is interesting to turn to the work of two writers of the earlier nineteenth century who produced copious dramatic criticism: Gautier and Nerval. In both cases, there are a number of anticipatory flashes lighting new ways of theatrical expression.

Gautier in his dramatic criticism prepares the way in a very general sense for the Symbolist theories of the theatre by his diagnosis of the state of French drama towards the mid-century: an extremely advanced stage technique;[68] relatively rare contributions from the acknowledged masters of literature;[69] the progressive disappearance of literary quality from the plays being produced.[70] In this situation, Gautier's call is for an enlargement of the theatrical horizon by the representation of modern plays from abroad[71] and above all for a poetic theatre.[72] We know that Gautier is one of the very few critics to whom Mallarmé refers specifically in *Crayonné au théâtre*,[73] and it is precisely to this general dissatisfaction with the contemporary theatre that Mallarmé draws attention, advancing down the line of Gautier's argument towards the notion of the *conventional* stage as unsatisfactory and towards the need for an arcanal, ritual element.

It might be thought that Nerval would significantly enhance this movement towards a theory of a poetic, symbolist, supranaturalist theatre, and indeed it is true, as Jean Richer reminds us, that the important function of the theatre for Nerval was the possibility of the transfiguration of reality, the access to higher states of consciousness.[74] Yet this sense emerges more clearly from Nerval's creative writings than from his journalistic articles on contemporary performances of plays. Thus, the opening of *Sylvie* presents the experience of the theatre as at once social and banal and as the occasion for an inevitable hallucination, this hallucination being the result of a confusion between a dominant remembered experience and the projection of an actress into a particular character. In one respect, (the importance attached to the power of the actress), this idea is well removed from the Symbolist notion of the depersonalized actor. But the illusion of a re-creation of the world in terms which are intensely meaningful to the individual spectator, by virtue of a magical concentration and suggestive force, becomes an inherent part of the Symbolist doctrine.[75]

In his occasional writings on the theatre, Nerval rarely strikes this same suggestive chord. His work is, however, fairly rich in perceptions of the advance of the theatre in France towards what he considered the promising complexity of the Romantic drama. He does not appear to use a personal sense of dissatisfaction with the contemporary theatre as a platform from which to gain a general view of future possibilities, as is the case with Gautier. His historical sense is centred on the movement from the eighteenth to the nineteenth century. He stresses the importance of Voltaire as well as that, more commonly recognized, of Diderot:

> La réforme théâtrale, tentée dans ces dernières années avait donc été prévue et d'avance encouragée par Voltaire. Si l'on semble réagir contre elle en remontant vers la tragédie primitive, qu'on n'oublie pas que, tout en se rattachant aux traditions du grand siècle, Voltaire poursuivait et annonçait lui-même un progrès que Victor Hugo et Alexandre Dumas ont noblement tenté d'accomplir.[76]

Diderot is seen in a perspective which leads in a straight line from the eighteenth century, through Romanticism and, by implication, towards an ideal of liberation:

> Ainsi ce n'était pas seulement le drame interne que Diderot voulait introduire, c'était aussi le drame libre, obéissant à la seule unité d'intérêt.[77]

Is there a possible Nervalian origin of Mallarmé's highly wrought comparison at the beginning of *Ballets*, where a conceit is made to join the dance of the 'star' of *Viviane* to 'la danse idéale des constellations'?[78] The visit to the Funambules recounted by Nerval in an article collected by Jean Richer is prefaced by a humorous little story about a boulevard astronomer, whose 'spectacle infiniment compliqué du firmament' is countered by the 'spectacle non moins sidéral' of the theatre.[79]

There is no need here to stress Mallarmé's affinities with Banville. Austin Gill, in a recent article, has given a welcome clarification of the evolving attitude of critics and commentators towards the role of Banville in the poetic formation of Mallarmé.[80] In the area we are considering, we have ample evidence, in the pages devoted to *Le Forgeron*, of the importance of Banville's example for the dramatic theories of Mallarmé. And the theoretical passage which follows the appreciation of Banville's dramatic poem is developed, not only by abstraction from the work itself, but also by reference to Banville's own theories. Here is an important question, which reaches considerably beyond the scope of these notes. A few main points, however, suggest themselves at once. The idea of the ode, for example, as a primitive source of dramatic writing, both tragic and comic, is in Banville and emerges from his occasional writings[81] no less than from the *avant-propos* of the *Comédies*.[82] For Banville the ode, used by the Ancients as the vehicle for celebrative and ritual utterance, exists in the modern world as lyricism, the form of language representing aspiration towards an ideal. But Banville argues chiefly in favour of the ode as the leaven of comedy; in so doing he runs parallel to some of the over-simplifications of the *Préface de «Cromwell»* and tends to emerge as the apologist of a limited form of poetic comedy. There is no doubt that Mallarmé improves and refines on these same notions when he elaborates the theory of the elevated recitative art of the dramatist of the future. For Banville the new dramatic art is to be arrived at by a revitalizing of forms no longer current or, as he puts it, 'injustement laissées dans l'oubli'.[83] This is a particularized expression of the idea forcibly uttered by Leconte de Lisle in the famous Preface of 1852,[84] and modulated forms of which pass through Mallarmé as he meditates on the virtues of a new ode bringing to life old myths. Banville harks back to Corneille:

> Dans ce Riquet à la Houppe, j'essaie de rendre à la Comédie les monologues en strophes lyriques et les scènes dialoguées symétriquement, dont Corneille nous a laissé de si admirables exemples.[85]

Corneille as a guarantor of procedures capable of enhancing modern art stands outside the field of Mallarmean theory, but is adduced by contemporary and junior theorists, by Kahn, for example, as a significant influence.[86] But Banville is fundamentally, albeit paradoxically, a modernist in a sense not permitted by the universalist theories of Mallarmé. Banville appears to accept an inevitable dichotomy in drama, between the variable and exterior elements on the one hand and the directing force emanating from the author on the other:

> Comme Henri Heine l'explique si bien, si magistralement à propos de Racine, le cadre, le costume, le milieu, les personnages ambiants sont historiques, et c'est dans cette résurrection du passé que le poète satisfait son érudition et sa fantaisie d'artiste; mais le personnage ou les personnages en qui s'incarne sa propre pensée ont forcément les idées et les passions du temps où le poète écrit.[87]

For Banville it is sufficient to be a man of one's own time; provided a dramatist has the lyrical gift, contemporary things can be given a new focus just as historical things are inevitably permeated by the spirit of the age reflected in the individual author.[88] If the anticipations of Mallarmé's theories of the theatre are clear and many in the occasional writings of Banville, the filiations of Banville's thought range outside Mallarmé. His views on the importance of Diderot and Wagner are orthodox.[89] His view of the material achievements of modern societies is that expressed by Gautier and Baudelaire and taken to extremes by Leconte de

Lisle. He has also things to say that anticipate the Symbolist view of poetry, as in his article *Poétique*, published in April, 1872:[90]

> Cependant, réduit et diminué ainsi en apparence de jour en jour, le domaine de la poésie reste toujours aussi large, aussi immense qu'il le fut à l'origine de la civilisation, car l'idéal et le surnaturel, dont elle ne peut être déshéritée, s'agrandissent pour nous en même temps et dans la même proportion que le champ des découvertes matérielles et scientifiques, si bien que la Poésie retrouve dans le monde spirituel ce qu'elle perd dans le monde terrestre, et que, plus elle se désintéresse des choses transitoires et passagères, plus l'azur s'ouvre sans limite devant le vol insaisissable de ses grandes ailes.

Almost a year before the publication of these lines, Rimbaud had set down the ideas of the *Lettre du voyant*. The basic notions (penetration of a realm of sur-reality, the immense potential of the discoveries to be made) are in the text of Banville, who does not appear from this to be as far from Rimbaud's position as the latter's *Ce qu'on dit au Poète à propos de fleurs*[91] might seem to indicate. And in Banville's notion of the clown-poet, a number of strands are brought together (Italian comedy, Illuminism, Romantic and Symbolist intimations on the nature of the poet, animism).[92]

Baudelaire? Despite the number of projects and unfinished drafts of plays,[93] Baudelaire does not appear to have been much preoccupied with elaborating a theory of the drama. His essay on Wagner has been much studied by commentators with special regard to its insights into literature and music. The number of specific references to dramatic art in its general aspects is small. One general notion which emerges from *Richard Wagner et Tann-häuser à Paris* is that of dramatic art as the coincidence of several arts;[94] it is doubtful, from the context of this observation, whether Baudelaire agrees with the premise attributed to Wagner, that drama is 'l'art par excellence, le plus synthétique et le plus parfait.' Indeed, Baudelaire rarely speculates on the theoretical limits of drama or of the theatre until he looks along the perspectives of Wagnerian art. The ideas which then engage his attention are those which arise from the Wagnerian formula rather than from a personal effort to sketch a theory.

Baudelaire's dramatic projects announce no radically new departures. The synopsis of *Idéolus* allows for a 'monologue hamlétique' which is not developed.[95] The dramatic projects generally are romantic in tone and scope, though they frequently take their references from classicism or the eighteenth century. Diderot is referred to approvingly more than once. His name is coupled with that of Balzac as one of those who strove to rejuvenate the French theatre.[96] And the imperious sweep of the Wagnerian opera does not prevent Baudelaire from catching echoes of a predictive (and contrary) observation of Diderot's:

> La vraie musique dramatique ne peut pas être autre chose que le cri ou le soupir de la passion noté et rythmé.[97]

There is no elaborated theory of the theatre in Baudelaire. There is, however, a Baudelairian sense of the theatre, as we see from the *Fleurs du Mal*:

> J'ai vu parfois, au fond d'un théâtre banal
>   Qu'enflammait l'orchestre sonore,
> Une fée allumer dans un ciel infernal
>   Une miraculeuse aurore (...)

The lines from *L'Irréparable* are familiar. They, together with other poems such as *Le Rêve d'un curieux*, represent a symbolical theatre, as one of a number of illusory possibilities of transforming reality. This is in the deepest sense the Baudelairian theatre.

> Mais mon cœur, que jamais ne visite l'extase,
>   Est un théâtre où l'on attend
> Toujours, toujours en vain, l'Etre aux ailes de gaze!

To this extent, to the extent of an impatient dismissal of the limitations of the stage and dramatic conventions and the expectation of a superior theatre, Baudelaire anticipates the poetical and experimental post-Wagnerian drama. His own instinct appears to be for a heavily formalized, hieratic art, as we see from the entry in *Mon Cœur mis à nu*.[98] And the symbolism of the *lustre*, noted in this same entry, suggests a preoccupation with a static and evocative form ('lumineux, cristallin, compliqué, circulaire et symétrique'). Jacques Scherer has analysed the complicated play which Mallarmé makes with the *lustre* in his writings on the theatre.[99] Indeed, the theme of the *lustre*, as a focal point of the theatre, a link between public and stage, lighting the proscenium,[100] a lucent centre, could profitably be traced further through the century.

All these intimations of a superior theatre are in a very general sense a development of Gautier's perception of the potential of Romantic drama:

> ces élans de l'âme au-dessus de la situation, ces ouvertures de la poésie à travers le drame.[101]

The movement towards a second theatrical revolution in the nineteenth century can, of course, be traced on other planes (technical, social), as is shown in an interesting article by Jean Duvignaud in *Cahiers internationaux de sociologie* (1961).[102] Mallarmé himself, in a footnote to a page of theatrical criticism in the *Revue indépendante*[103] advocates, momentarily, a stage technically more versatile than the *plateau à l'italienne*. Duvignaud sees the new attitude to the theatre, from about 1870 in France, as motivated by a widening of the terms of reference of the stage and by a simultaneous widening of the public in terms of class ('rapprochement de la réalité sociale et de la réalité théâtrale').[104] Viewed from this point, Symbolism is merely a part of the theatrical spectrum, the other parts being Naturalism, the restitution of the past (Wagner, Annunzio, etc.), political drama, pure æstheticism (Jouvet, Vilay, etc.). Symbolism is one of several theatrical forms that were not possible within the traditional theatre-public context, its peculiar contribution being to allegorize and individualize the deepest intuitions and aspirations of the author.

Symbolism can then, with a good deal of hindsight, be consolidated in a wide movement of enlargement of public attention to the theatre. It was also viewed, in the last two decades of the nineteenth century, as part of a movement of disaggregation, probably a commoner standpoint. Thus Doumic, in 1897, sees the characteristics of the period in negative terms:

> Aussi (...) la période que nous traversons aura-t-elle été marquée moins par l'avènement d'un art nouveau que par la lente décomposition d'un système dramatique que nous voyons se dissoudre sous nos yeux.[105]

The 'system' referred to is the composite drama according to the Romantic formula, now broken down into subsidiary forms and controlled mainly by writers who bring to the theatre the preoccupations of the non-dramatic genres. At this distance and from this perspective, the incursion of poets and critics into the theatre is seen as a defect and a manifestation of a great genre in disarray. This opinion is relatively common in the eighties and nineties[106] and forms, paradoxically, common ground for the analyses of the traditionalists and the mantic essays of the creative writers.

The opinion among scholars at the present time is that Mallarmé's theories provided the greatest single impetus towards the formation of the experimental forms of Symbolist drama[107] and that parallel efforts on the part of younger writers were the work of disciples and the offshoots of the Mallarmean doctrines. This idea requires further examination, and in greater detail than is possible here. As far as the theory of the drama is concerned, Charles Morice, of the young writers who might be considered as Mallarmé's disciples, is the only one who appears to follow the master at all implicitly. After some cursory judgements, in *La littérature de tout à l'heure*,[108] in which he echoes the current sentiments on the decline of the theatre, Morice, fired apparently by the performances at the Théâtre d'Art, after 1890, launches into a panegyric on the theatre as liturgy, developing the views set down by Mallarmé in 1887.[109] Kahn, whose theories on drama are referred to both by Jacques Robichez and Haskell. M. Block[110] in close connexion with those of Mallarmé, was less of a disciple than appears to be thought. If we accept as irrelevant the disobliging references to Mallarmé made to the reporter Jules Huret in 1891,[111] it remains that Kahn's ideas are formed more directly from Banville, Corneille, Marivaux, Italian Comedy. In his most striking article on the theatre, the only one quoted by commentators, *Un théâtre de l'avenir*,[112] he lays strong accent on comedy,[113] following Banville a good deal of the way and sketching several lively possibilities for the renewing of the forms of the theatre.[114] Above all other consideration is the need for modernity, hence the stress laid on mobility of effect and on the exploitation of the scenic possibilities of the contemporary theatre, from which Kahn does not exclude the circus ring. He also envisages a form dependent on transformations of evocative and significant scenes which foreshadows some of the work of the cinema. Parallel with this, Kahn develops a concept of the drama which, according to the author, is designed to approach the theatre of Corneille, Shakespeare and Goethe, but from which a Mallarmean notion of character none the less emerges ('des voix rythmant et allitérant leurs sensations se parlant les uns aux autres, non plus d'après les probabilités de la vie, mais d'après les intentions de leurs essences'). This definition is not significantly different from the one established by Kahn to categorize the multiple and unified 'livre de vers'.[115]

Mockel writes briefly on the theatre, and at the crucial moment (1889–1890) of the first experimentations with Symbolist plays. His reflections arise out of the reading or the representation of such works as *Les Flaireurs*, *Axël*, *La Princesse Maleine*, *Les Revenants*.[116] His starting point is the idealist concept of a superior theatre, but in its evocation, the expectation of this theatre is curiously Baudelairian:

> ce théâtre où tendent nos désirs, le théâtre où parmi les magies d'éclatants ou lointains décors un acte se dresse, que l'on sait total, et d'impareille clarté resplendit l'art comme un bolide.[117]

Solemn, remote and hieratic, this drama at one moment seems to reach back towards the antique stage, as Baudelaire also suggests. It is inconceivable without music; its driving force is poetry; its general area the universal aspects of human life; its various forms types of ballet, types of opera and superior types of pantomime. The theory is at once, in an immediate sense, Wagnerian and Mallarmean and, at a further remove, squarely in the line of the Romantic theories that constantly push forward to the notion of a drama outside the known confines of the stage.

A full evaluation of the contribution of the second Symbolist generation (those entering the literary field in about 1886) has still to be made. Moréas, Vielé-Griffin, Verhaeren, Samain, Morice, Remy de Gourmont, in addition to the dramatists of the front rank, emerge from these complex filiations, in almost every case using the drama as a natural or inevitable extension of the range of expression. This is one of the prime Romantic ideas, charted already by Hugo:

> Le drame et la poésie se pénètrent comme toutes les facultés dans l'homme, comme tous les rayonnements dans l'univers.[118]

NOTES

[1] See H. M. Block, *Mallarmé and the Symbolist Drama*, Wayne State University Press (1963), p. 130.
[2] See J. Robichez, *Le Symbolisme au théâtre*, Paris, L'Arche (1957), p. 47.
[3] *Op. cit.*, Vol. III, p. 432.
[4] *Ibid., eod. loc.* See Mallarmé, *Œuvres complètes*, Paris, NRF, Bibliothèque de la Pléiade (1945), p. 294.
[5] G. Michaud, *Mallarmé, l'homme et l'œuvre*, Paris, Hatier Boivin (1953), p. 136.
[6] *Op. cit.*, p. 23.
[7] See Mallarmé, *Œuvres complètes*, p. 1561.
[8] J. Robichez, *op. cit.*, p. 45.
[9] See above, note 1.
[10] London, 13 March, 10 June, 1 July, 1893. The articles, together with those of the *Revue indépendante*, were subsequently recast by Mallarmé. They are printed in their final form, together with a few unpublished pages, in the *Œuvres complètes*.

¹¹ This unlovely but no doubt effective term is used by H. M. Block to characterize the diminished importance attached by Mallarmé to scenic effect. See *op. cit.*, p. 88, p. 92.

¹² See also J. Scherer, *Le «Livre» de Mallarmé*, Paris, Gallimard (1957).

¹³ Mallarmé, *op. cit.*, p. 335, p. 344.

¹⁴ *Ibid.*, p. 345.

¹⁵ *Ibid.*, p. 318.

¹⁶ *Ibid.*, pp. 318–19 ('vous vous implanterez, au théâtre, avec plus de vraisemblance les paradis, qu'un salon').

¹⁷ *Ibid.*, p. 322.

¹⁸ An idea frequently touched on by Mallarmé in his pages of dramatic criticism, but not often developed in detail. See *Œuvres complètes*, pp. 338–9: 'J'observai combien supplée une humanité exacte,' etc.

¹⁹ See, for example, *ibid.*, pp. 320–1.

²⁰ *Ibid.*, pp. 314–15.

²¹ *Ibid.*, p. 341.

²² *Ibid.*, p. 321: 'Voilà une théorie tragique actuelle ou, pour mieux dire, la dernière: le drame, latent, ne se manifeste que par une déchirure affirmant l'irréductibilité de nos instincts.' This occurs in the passage on Zola.

²³ *Ibid.*, p. 319.

²⁴ *Ibid.*, p. 316.

²⁵ *Ibid.*, p. 546.

²⁶ *Ibid.*, p. 300 (on *Hamlet*): 'car il n'est point d'autre sujet, sachez bien: l'antagonisme de rêve chez l'homme avec les fatalités à son existence départies par le malheur'.

²⁷ J. Scherer, *op. cit.*, chapter VI, 'Publics et Recettes'.

²⁸ Letter to Henri Cazalis, 14 May 1867. This was, of course, said by Mallarmé about *Hérodiade* in the first instance, but remains true for the Grand Œuvre generally.

²⁹ Mallarmé's attitude towards the public is, of course, a major subject in its own right, See, for example, P. Benichou, 'Mallarmé et le public', *Cahiers du Sud*, XXX, no. 297 (1949), pp. 272–90.

³⁰ For example, the dramatized form of Zola's *Ventre de Paris* (Mallarmé, *Œuvres complètes*, p. 345.

³¹ *Œuvres complètes*, p. 345.

³² See J. Scherer, *op. cit.*, p. 40; H. M. Block, *op. cit.*, p. 91.

³³ *Œuvres complètes*, p. 301: 'dans l'idéale peinture de la scène, tout se meut *selon une réciprocité symbolique des types entre eux ou relativement à une figure seule*' (Mallarmé's italics).

³⁴ *Ibid.*, p. 326.

³⁵ *Ibid.*, p. 335.

³⁶ G. Michaud, *Message poétique du Symbolisme*, Paris, Nizet (1947), p 435.

³⁷ *Parnasse et Symbolisme*, Paris, Armand Colin (1942), p. 198.

³⁸ *La poésie de Stéphane Mallarmé*, Paris, NRF Gallimard (1926), p. 460.

³⁹ *Œuvres complètes*, Paris, Albin Michel (1934), 'Philosophie', II, p. 44.

⁴⁰ *Ibid.*, p. 129 ('William Shakespeare').

⁴¹ *Ibid.*, 'Philosophie', II, p. 17.

L

[42] *Ibid.*, 'Philosophie', I, p. 18.

[43] *Ibid.*, *eod. loc.*

[44] *Ibid.*, 'Philosophie', I, p. 15. See also p. 19: 'Au théâtre surtout, il n'y a que deux choses auxquelles l'art puisse dignement aboutir. Dieu et le peuple.'

[45] *Ibid.*, 'Philosophie', I, p. 18.

[46] *La Bouteille à la mer.*

[47] Mallarmé, *Œuvres complètes*, pp. 335–6, 345 etc.

[48] *Journal d'un poète.* Entry for the year 1834.

[49] *Ibid. eod. loc.*

[50] *Ibid.*, *eod. loc.*

[51] *Ibid.* Entry for the year 1839.

[52] *L'art dramatique en France*, Paris, Hetzel (1858), 2ème série, p. 42 (article dated March 1840).

[53] *Cours familier de littérature*, Vol. III, Paris (1857), p. 361.

[54] See above, p. 137.

[55] *Œuvres complètes*, p. 319.

[56] See above, p. 139.

[57] *Méditations poétiques.* The other language is, of course, 'le langage inné de toute intelligence' (*Dieu*).

[58] *Œuvres complètes*, p. 54.

[59] *Ibid.*, p. 328.

[60] The perspective and tone of the comment are interesting, indicative of the anti-Musset tendency of most commentators in recent years: 'Even Alfred de Musset must have had an ideal theatre in mind when writing his *Spectacle dans un fauteuil*' (*The French Drama of the Unspoken*, Edinburgh (1953), p. 1).

[61] See *La Coupe et les Lèvres*. Dédicace à M. Alfred T.: 'L'action n'est pour lui qu'un moule à sa pensée.'

[62] *Ibid.* The concentrated passage beginning. 'Par deux chemins (…)' contains these ideas, in the form of a commentary on realism and intuition in art.

[63] *Ibid.*, *eod. loc.*

[64] *Ibid.*, *eod. loc.*

[65] *Ibid.*: 'C'est pour vous qu'il y fouille, afin de vous redire
　　　　Ce qu'il aura senti, ce qu'il aura trouvé,
　　　　Surtout, en le trouvant, ce qu'il aura rêvé.'

[66] *Œuvres complètes*, p. 301.

[67] *Ibid.*, p. 339.

[68] See, for example, Gautier's account of *Les Amours de Psyché* in *Histoire de l'art dramatique en France depuis 25 ans*, Paris, Hetzel (1858), 2ème série, pp. 150–8.

[69] *Ibid.*, 2ème série, p. 247 (article of 29 May 1842).

[70] *Ibid.*, *eod. loc.*, 'Aussi le théâtre n'a-t-il plus rien de commun avec la littérature. C'est une industrie à part où la poésie, la philosophie et la critique n'ont rien à voir.'

[71] *Ibid.*, 2ème série, p. 219.

[72] *Ibid.*, 1ère série, p. 126, and 2ème série, pp. 159-60

[73] *Œuvres complètes*, p. 313.

[74] See *Œuvres complémentaires de Gérard de Nerval, II, La Vie du théâtre,* Minard (1961), Préface, p. v.

[75] There is also, in the same work (chapter XIII), a reference to the creation of a poetic drama aimed at 'conquering and fixing' an ideal in relation to which theatres are seen to be 'lieux d'épreuve'.

[76] *Œuvres complémentaires de Gérard de Nerval,* II, p. 647.

[77] *Ibid.,* p. 689.

[78] Mallarmé, *Œuvres complètes,* p. 303.

[79] *Œuvres complémentaires de Gérard de Nerval,* II, p. 708–9.

[80] '«L'Etre aux ailes de gaze» dans la doctrine esthétique de Mallarmé', in *Studi in Onore di Italo Siciliano,* Florence, Leo S. Olschki (1966).

[81] See, for example, 'L'Ode et la scène', written in March 1880, in *Critiques,* ed. V. Barrucaud, Paris, Charpentier (1917).

[82] The *Avant-propos* is dated 10 January, 1878.

[83] *Riquet à la Houppe,* 'Au lecteur', Paris, Charpentier (1885).

[84] Preface to *Poèmes antiques.*

[85] *Riquet à la Houppe,* 'Au lecteur'.

[86] One of Kahn's early projects, noted by Fénéon in 1890, is a monograph on Corneille. See J. C. Ireson, *L'Œuvre poétique de Gustave Kahn,* Nizet (1962),p. 24note 30. See also *Revue Blanche,* X (1896), p. 240: 'Nous sommes épris du *Cid* plus que de *Cinna,* de Corneille plus que de Racine, des *Burgraves* plus que du *Misanthrope,* des *Contes féeriques* de Banville, des *Vaines Amours* et de l'*Après-midi d'un Faune* plus que de l'*Assommoir*'.

[87] *Critiques,* ed. V. Barrucaud, p. 410. See also p. 411.

[88] See *ibid.,* pp. 267–8.

[89] See *ibid.,* p. 53, pp. 174–81.

[90] *Ibid.*

[91] Dated 14 July 1871. See also *Critiques,* ed. V. Barrucaud, p. 331.

[92] See, for example, *Critiques,* pp. 421–2.

[93] See *Œuvres complètes,* Paris, NRF, Bibliothèque de la Pléiade (1961), pp. 537–92: 4 plans or projects of plays, and a list of various ideas for possible dramatic development.

[94] *Ibid.,* p. 1211.

[95] *Ibid.,* p. 539.

[96] *Ibid.,* p. 622.

[97] *Ibid.,* p. 1217.

[98] *Ibid.,* pp. 1276–7.

[99] *Op. cit.,* pp. 63 ff. ('Symbolisme du Lustre').

[100] Cf. Nerval, *Les Filles du Feu,* 'Sylvie', chapter I (description of Aurélie): 'belle comme le jour aux feux de la rampe qui l'éclairait d'en bas, pâle comme la nuit, quand la rampe baissée la laissait éclairée d'en haut sous les rayons du lustre et la montrait plus naturelle, brillant dans l'ombre de sa seule beauté' (...)

[101] *Histoire du Romantisme,* Fasquelle (1911), p. 111.

[102] Vol. XXX, pp. 75–72: 'Réflexions sur la révolution théâtrale au XIXe siècle.'

[103] Vol. IV (July 1887), p. 55: 'Une salle doit surtout être machinée et mobile, à l'ingénieur, avant l'architecte, en revient la construction: que ce héros du moderne répertoire se montre un peu.'

[104] *Op. cit.*, p. 80.

[105] *Essais sur le théâtre contemporain*, Paris, Perrin (1897), Introduction, pp. I–II.

[106] See, for example, Le Corbeiller, 'Le Mélange des genres au théâtre', *Revue d'art dramatique*, XIX (1890), pp. 193–219; also, A. Filon, *De Dumas à Rostand, esquisse du mouvement dramatique contemporain*, Paris, Colin (1898).

[107] See J. Robichez, *op. cit.*, pp. 47 ff.; H. M. Block, *op. cit.*, pp. 102–3; A.-M. Schmidt, *La Littérature symboliste*, Paris, P.U.F. (Que sais-je?) (1955), pp. 100–3; G. Michaud, *Message poétique du symbolisme*, Paris, Nizet (1947), III, p. 436.

[108] Paris, Perrin (1889).

[109] 'A propos du Théâtre d'Art', in *Mercure de France* (March 1893), p. 259. Quoted by Paul Delsemme, *Un Théoricien du symbolisme, Charles Morice*, Paris, Nizet (1958), pp. 233–4.

[110] J. Robichez, *op. cit.*, pp. 46–7; H. M. Block, *op. cit.*, pp. 103–4.

[111] See Jules Huret, *Enquête sur l'évolution littéraire*, Paris, Charpentier (1891).

[112] *Revue d'art dramatique*, XV (1889), pp. 335–53. See also the letter to Jules Huret, *op. cit.*, pp. 393–401; also *Nouvelle Revue* (April 1897), pp. 576–90 ('Des tendances actuelles de la littérature'); also *Nouvelle Revue* (January 1905), pp. 245–51 ('Le théâtre des fées').

[113] The filiation here is from Banville. The clown, Pierrot, the circus fascinated Laforgue as well as Kahn. The former's sole attempt at drama (if we except dialogue forms such as *Le Concile féerique*) was *Pierrot fumiste*. Kahn explores the possibilities of grandiose spectacle in a novel, *Le Cirque solaire* (1899).

[114] They are summarized by Kahn as follows: 'Le drame; la comédie de caractère à milieu indéfini; la pantomime moderne et clownesque; l'évocation pantomimale de décors héroïques; la comédie de cirque'.

[115] Letter to Jules Huret.

[116] '*Les Flaireurs* par Ch. Van Lerberghe', *La Wallonie* (Feb.–March 1889); '*Axël*, par Villiers de l'Isle-Adam, *La Princesse Maleine* et *L'Intruse* par Maeterlinck', *La Wallonie* (June–July 1890). These articles are reprinted in *Esthétique du Symbolisme*, ed. M. Otten, Brussels, Palais des Académies (1962).

[117] *Esthétique du Symbolisme*, p. 237.

[118] Preface to *Les Rayons et les ombres*.

B. Juden

SUITE À UNE OBSERVATION DE MAFFEI SUR 'L'ESPRIT POÉTIQUE' DE RONSARD

'La réputation de Ronsard', écrivait Sainte-Beuve en 1828, 'paraît s'être soutenue plus longtemps chez les étrangers qu'en France. Le savant Scipion Maffei a loué ce poète à une époque où on avait cessé de le lire chez nous...'[1] A l'appui, le critique débutant renvoie en note à la *Ménagiana* de la Monnoye, c'est-à-dire à l'époque de Madame de Sévigné. Vérification faite, le bon Ménage a bien dit qu'il ne croyait trouver personne de son temps 'qui osât se vanter de posséder et de lire les œuvres de Ronsard'.[2] L'affirmation est loin d'être aussi simple que Sainte-Beuve voudrait le faire entendre. D'autre part, Maffei, né en 1675, était du vivant de Ménage, à peine sorti du berceau. La référence renferme donc une erreur de chronologie assez frappante. Sainte-Beuve s'en serait-il servi faute de renseignements plus précis, ou bien préférait-il brouiller la piste de ses recherches? Dans la *Bibliothèque françoise* (1784), à la fin de l'article principal sur Ronsard, l'abbé Goujet signale, pour les désapprouver, les louanges que Maffei avait décernées au chef de la Pléiade. Son commentaire s'accompagne de références précises qui permettent de retrouver les observations faites sur les mêmes propos par l'abbé Ganet et Lefèvre de Saint-Marc.[3] Il eût donc été facile pour Sainte-Beuve de consulter la plaquette que Maffei a publiée d'abord à Londres en 1736, avant de l'insérer à la fin du premier tome des *Osservazioni litterari* de 1737. Une longue défense des vers blancs y préface une traduction en italien du premier chant de l'Iliade.[4] Avant de voir dans quel contexte Maffei cite Ronsard il est nécessaire de préciser certains préjugés de l'époque envers les poètes de la Pléiade. L'auteur de *Mérope* en était sans doute au courant; il avait passé quelques mois de l'année 1733 à Paris.[5]

Prolongé par le respect pour les opinions de Malherbe et de Boileau, l'anathème qui frappait les poètes de la Pléiade visait en même temps l'inspiration et la langue poétique. Grâce aux excellentes études que Fuchs et Charlier, puis plus récemment M. Verdun-L. Saulnier, M. Claude Pichois et M. Alan Boase y ont consacré, on sait combien était lourde cette condamnation et combien la remontée fut difficile.[6] Ici il nous suffit d'examiner les arguments que la critique oppose à *l'enthousiasme* et de considérer leur effet sur le choix des bons modèles dans l'imitation des Anciens.

Vers 1670, Guéret, pouvait encore mettre dans la bouche de Desportes, une apologie très nuancée:

> S'il y a quelques mots barbares dans Ronsard, s'il a pris des libertés extraordinaires, en récompense de ces choses qui n'étoient pas des fautes dans son temps, il a de l'invention, il est plein de fictions agréables et l'on voit régner dans ses vers cette divine fureur qui fait les vrais poètes...[7]

Relevons deux faits: l'aveu que les goûts et les styles changent d'époque en époque: l'admiration non dissimulée pour la *fureur divine* qui, depuis Ficin et Pontus de Tyard, était la qualité déterminante de la haute inspiration. Par ailleurs, Guéret en reconnaît l'importance pour *l'Ode à Michel de l'Hospital* dont il cite la treizième strophe.[8] De même il tient compte d'une conséquence inévitable: le mystère de la poésie et les secrets de l'art, cachés 'sous des ténèbres savantes' au point où l'on 's'imaginait que pour être poète il fallait avoir une connaissance universelle de toutes choses...'.[9] Là, le génie poétique est clairement défini par rapport aux traditions du seizième siècle.

Pourtant, l'amour excessif de l'antiquité avait perdu ces poètes que Guéret range, en définitive, parmi les anciens.[10] La notice que Fontenelle aurait composée pour le *Recueil* de Barbin reproche également à Ronsard l'affectation 'de faire paraître de l'érudition dans ses vers'.[11] Même si, comme le soutiennent Fuchs et M. Claude Pichois, Du Bellay et Ronsard ont été exhumés pour illustrer la thèse des Modernes, on ne saurait dire que l'approbation éclate dans les textes de présentation. Un certain mérite est accordé aux grâces parcimonieusement découvertes dans le style. Tout en admettant que les *Hymnes* et les *Odes* constituent les meilleures pièces de Ronsard, l'éditeur ne juge pas à propos d'inclure un seul hymne dans le recueil, et s'abstient de toute louange pour l'inspiration du poète.

Cette omission est révélatrice d'un état d'esprit inséparable de l'estime pour 'la poésie bien disante'—et c'est précisément le genre que l'on recherche chez Du Bellay et Ronsard. Ainsi que M. Léon Gabriel Gros l'a fait remarquer, Fontenelle s'opposait à 'la fureur divine' et appliquait au poète la règle d'être maître de soi comme de l'univers, tandis que Houdar de La Motte pratiquait le refus systématique de toute inspiration.[12] L'enthousiasme doit être subordonné très étroitement à la raison, autrement survient une ivresse dangereuse:

> Ce ne sont que grands mots, précise La Motte, de fureur divine, de transports de l'âme, de mouvements, de lumières, qui mis bout à bout dans des phrases pompeuses, ne produisent pourtant aucune idée distincte.[13]

De là beaucoup d'abus, de mystification, d'obscurité et d'excès qu'il ne convient pas d'imiter. Cette critique transparaît indirectement dans l'analyse de l'Ode chez Pindare. La Motte relève des figures excessives, des 'manières de parler aussi obscures qu'emphatiques' qu'il se croit obligé d'excuser, étant donnée la réputation du poète, en se référant au goût aberrant d'une époque qui put accepter l'inintelligible dithyrambe. Envers Ronsard, il se sent beaucoup plus libre et mène sa critique bon train, d'autant plus que les ouvrages du poète n'étant plus lus, personne ne risque de vérifier ce qu'il va en dire. Il suffit de lire sa notice à la lumière de ses opinions sur l'inspiration et sur Pindare, pour s'apercevoir qu'elle est dénuée de toute bienveillance. La Motte ose ainsi avancer que Ronsard

> a imité Pindare en homme qui connaissait son modèle: jusques-là que ce qu'il emprunte d'Horace devient pindarique entre ses mains. On retrouve partout dans ses odes, ces images pompeuses, ces graves sentences, ces métaphores et les expressions audacieuses qui caractérisent le poète thébain. Il paraît même assez saisi de cet enthousiasme qui entraînait Pindare, et le mauvais succès de l'imitation vient moins d'avoir mal suivi son modèle que de n'avoir pas connu le génie de la langue française.[14]

Le dernier cliché vient renforcer l'espoir que Ronsard ne connaîtra point d'heureux retour à la gloire, ne sera jamais sauvé de l'oubli comme l'a été Pindare. C'est un parti pris chez La Motte qui en favorisant 'des Odes et même des tragédies en prose' attire, selon Amar, l'ironie de J.-B. Rousseau. Le 'grand lyrique' ne trouve pas mieux que de comparer le réformateur... à Ronsard.[15] L'aspect sérieux du procès demeure; en 1739, en

pleine séance de l'Académie des Inscriptions Louis Racine tonne
encore contre le chef de la Pléiade.[16]

D'une part les considérations sur la bonne façon d'imiter les
anciens abordent ce que Maffei va appeler 'l'esprit poétique'. De
l'autre, elles se heurtent au problème de savoir dans quelle
mesure il serait possible d'adopter les hexamètres grecs et latins
comme modèles du vers français. Allant de pair avec l'agitation
contre la rime, cette question, une des plus débattues entre les
Anciens et les Modernes, devient le noyau du *Traité de la Prosodie*
que l'abbé d'Olivet publie en 1736.[17] L'ouvrage résume toute
l'histoire des vers mesurés à l'antique depuis les précurseurs de
Baïf et de Jodelle, expose les diverses techniques, examine les
changements de prononciation, et s'efforce de prouver la nécessité
de la rime.

Il s'ensuit que tout propos sur le vers blanc ou 'libre' est d'une
vivante actualité. Dans ce climat paraît le texte de Maffei qui
reprend des arguments familiers à La Motte et à Fénelon, et vante
la supériorité des hexamètres sur les vers rimés et leurs fausses
contraintes. La rime est considérée comme étant d'origine basse,
sinon purement barbare, et Maffei soutient qu'elle transforme
la poésie en musique populaire à l'exclusion du contenu intellectuel. Il constate que la majesté et la grâce de la poésie grecque
et latine dépendent de la liaison continuelle des vers libres qui
ne sont point astreints à des repos fixes. Pour rendre plus élevée
la poésie épique et dramatique, il faut profiter de cet 'enchaîne-
ment' qui, selon Le Tasse, donne de la gravité au discours.
Voulant donner plus de poids à cette proposition, Maffei cite,
entre autres exemples, Ronsard: 'che fu pieno di spirito di Poesia,
e che tento al possibile di portare in sua lingua i pregi de gli
antichi Poëti'.[18] Pour préciser sa pensée, il s'appuie sur la *Préface
de la Franciade* où le chef de la Pléiade avait écrit:

> J'ai été d'opinion dans ma jeunesse que les vers qui enjambent l'un sur
> l'autre, n'étoient pas bons en notre Poësie; toutefois j'ai connu depuis
> le contraire par la lecture des bons Auteurs Grecs et Latins.

Maffei fait donc appel à Ronsard pour autoriser l'enjambement.
Et bien entendu la plupart de ses autres recommandations pour
éviter la langueur des vers blancs et redécouvrir le secret du
chant antique, enfreignent autant les principes du bon goût.

C'est l'abbé Ganet qui dresse procès-verbal dans ses *Réflexions
sur les Ouvrages de Littérature* pour 1738. Les idées de Maffei lui
paraissent tellement curieuses qu'une traduction du texte italien

devrait suffire à en révéler la bizarrerie mais le bon abbé prend néanmoins soin de la souligner. D'ailleurs sa défense de la rime est en quelque sorte un aveu car il croit nécessaire de la garder ... afin de pouvoir distinguer les vers de la prose. Arrivé à la mention de Ronsard, Ganet traduit en regard du texte italien:

> Ronsard qui fut rempli de l'esprit poétique et qui entreprit de transposer dans sa langue les beautés des anciens poètes...

Le commentaire est sec:

> Si M. Maffei étoit contemporain de Ronsard, je ne serois pas étonné des louanges qu'il lui donne; son siècle en fit autant. Mais depuis que tant de Critiques ont apprécié le talent de ce poète, il est étonnant que M. Maffei loue aujourd'hui sa versification.
>
> Au reste, on ne doit point être surpris du Panégyrique de Ronsard; on sçait il y a longtemps que M. Maffei l'estime beaucoup. Il est seul aujourd'hui de ce sentiment.

Donc: 'esprit poétique' signifie talent pour la versification, tous deux étant déficients chez Ronsard; et l'abbé se sent sur un terrain extrêmement solide.

Si les choses en étaient restées là, nous n'aurions pas jugé nécessaire de reproduire verbatim les propos acerbes de l'abbé Ganet. La beauté de l'affaire, c'est que le critique grincheux s'est trompé sur un point capital. En 1739, Lefèvre de Saint-Marc qui avait remplacé l'abbé Prévost à la rédaction du *Pour et Contre*, 'ouvrage périodique d'un goût nouveau', répond à l'abbé Ganet en se fondant sur la traduction de Maffei publiée par l'*Auteur des Réflexions*. Sur le sujet épineux 'que nous appelons *Enjambement*', il cite textuellement Ganet, puis va droit au but:

> Je n'examinerai pas si le *Marquis Maffei* peut se prévaloir, en faveur de la *Poésie Italienne*, de ce que *Ronsard* avoit voulu faire pour la *Poésie française*. Je ne m'attache qu'au reproche qu'on lui fait de son estime pour ce *Poète*. Je ne sais quelles sont les louanges qu'il lui donne dans d'autres Ouvrages; mais il me semble qu'il n'en dit rien ici que de vrai.
> De quoi le loue-t-il? D'avoir été *rempli de l'Esprit Poétique*...

C'est donc une appréciation de cette qualité que Saint-Marc va dégager d'une connaissance personnelle des poésies de Ronsard:

> J'ai fait autrefois la lecture de tous les *Ouvrages* de *Ronsard* avec autant de soin, que j'ai lu ce que le Siècle d'Or de notre *Poésie* a produit de meilleur; et j'ose assurer que par rapport à ce que nous appelons *Esprit Poétique*, Ronsard est un des plus grands *Poètes* que la France ait jamais eus.

Il y a déjà comparaison implicite entre l'état passé et l'état présent; notre auteur la développe, toujours favorablement pour Ronsard:

> Je vais plus loin. Elle (la France) peut le comparer hardiment, pour cette partie seule à tout ce que les *Anciens* et les *Modernes* nous offrent de plus parfait. C'est une vérité qui sera reconnue de tous ceux qui liront ce *Poète* avec la même attention que je l'ai lu.

Non qu'une petite réserve ne s'impose au sujet du style, mais l'ayant faite, Saint-Marc la retourne aussitôt contre les détracteurs, sans perdre de vue les dons réels de Ronsard:

> Cela n'empêche cependant pas que tout ce que nos *Critiques* en ont dit ne soit juste. Je ne vante en lui que les présens, qu'il avoit reçus de la Nature; et je le condamne, ou plutôt, je l'excuse de les avoir défigurés par un zèle mal entendu pour la perfection d'une *Poésie*, dont il n'avoit pas approfondi le caractère. Justement épris de ce qui fait le charme ou la richesse des *Poésies Grecque et Latine*, en possédant à fond les *Langues*; mais ne connaissant nullement le génie de la sienne, qui n'étoit encore pour ainsi dire, qu'au berceau; destitué d'ailleurs de ce goût, qui n'a commencé de se former que sous *Malherbe* et *Balzac*, et séduit par cette erreur, encore aujourd'hui trop commune, qui veut que la *Poésie* parle chez nous un *Langage* différent de la *Prose*; Ronsard crut que pour élever notre *Langue* au véritable *Ton Héroïque* il n'étoit question que d'en charger les *Vers* de toutes les *Licences* et de toutes les *Hardiesses*, qu'il trouvait dans les *Vers Grecs et Latins*.

Les formules d'usage reviennent, mais se chargent ici d'ironie au fur et à mesure que la pensée souligne habilement le contexte historique où il convient de situer les efforts de Ronsard martelant un langage à peine formé, sans pouvoir profiter des éclaircissements du goût visant à abolir la distinction entre la langue de la poésie et celle de la prose.

Alors Lefèvre de Saint-Marc noue les fils de sa plaidoirie:

> Mais doit-on faire un crime à quelqu'un, qui s'ouvre une route nouvelle dans les lieux non fréquentés, de ne pas prendre le droit chemin, pour arriver au terme qu'il se propose? S'il s'égare, ne doit-on pas le plaindre et loin d'insulter à son ignorance, louer sa résolution à s'engager dans une terre inconnue? Je voudrois que nos *critiques*, en relevant la bévue de *Ronsard*, eussent rendu justice à la force, à l'étendue, à l'élévation, à la beauté de son génie...

Les quatre attributs du génie de Ronsard, force, étendue, élévation et beauté, secondent la résolution d'un novateur zélé, épris d'un idéal très pur de la poésie. C'est exactement ce qui manque à 'l'honneur de notre Parnasse', poursuit inexorablement Saint-Marc, 'depuis la naissance du *Goût Français*'.

Avant de rechercher quels effets a pu avoir cette apologie,

admirable pour sa fermeté et—à l'époque—son originalité, il nous faut tenir compte d'une dernière observation de l'auteur. Parce que les étrangers sont aussi ignorants des subtilités du style français que les Français le sont en matière de poésie italienne, il leur arrive de penser que Ronsard et Racine parlaient la même langue. De ce fait, raisonne Lefèvre de Saint-Marc:

> Je ne serai jamais étonné de leur voir mettre Ronsard au rang de nos premiers *Poètes*. Ils ne peuvent juger que par le fond des choses.

Ce dernier trait est lancé contre la critique à la mode et la chicane perpétuelle sur les dehors de l'œuvre. Sans être totalement perdu, il n'empêchera pas le retour monotone des formules toutes faites depuis longtemps.

L'abbé Goujet en a entassé—on le sait—dans ses commentaires sur Ronsard une belle collection. Il poursuit la méthode habituelle qui consiste à annuler toute louange en y opposant un jugement écrasant fondé sur la morale ou sur les usages du bon goût.[19] S'il désapprouve les poèmes galants, Goujet admire l'art anacréontique de Ronsard comme de Du Bellay et concède que

> Le génie de Ronsard se montre dans plusieurs de ses Eglogues, comme en beaucoup d'autres endroits de ses poésies.

Aussitôt suit le repentir:

> Mais il est vrai qu'il n'a nullement connu la nature et le caractère du poème Bucolique... rien de tendre, ni de délicat...

Reste 'le défaut d'y mettre des matières élevées'.

Même tactique dans l'examen des hymnes. L'abbé commence par dire qu'ils sont 'les meilleurs de tous ses ouvrages' et qu'il y a 'du génie dans la plupart de ces pièces...'. Puis il aligne les témoins à charge pour amener l'éreintement définitif. En conclusion Goujet énumère les défauts dépistés par la critique depuis Malherbe jusqu'à Balzac afin de pouvoir reprocher à Scipion Maffei de s'être 'écarté de la vérité et des règles dans les louanges excessives données à Ronsard'. Ganet s'est, pourtant, montré trop sévère, car décrète en fin de compte l'abbé Goujet: 'on ne peut refuser l'esprit poétique à Ronsard'. Pour en avancer la preuve, il cite un fragment tiré de la notice par 'M. Lefèvre de Saint-Marc dont le goût et le discernement sont connus de tous d'ailleurs'.

Ce revirement eût été étonnant si l'abbé avait respecté le texte, mais il a choisi et faussé chez Saint-Marc le passage le plus favorable à son dessein; ce qui donne:

Les présents qu'il (Ronsard) avoit reçus de la nature *de ce côté-là étoient grands, on les aperçoit en mille endroits de ses écrits, mais il les* a défigurés, *ces présents* par un zèle mal entendu *pour une* poésie dont il n'avoit pas approfondi le caractère...[20]

Il ne faut plus excuser Ronsard, ni parler de son zèle pour la *perfection*, ni mentionner, par crainte d'une ironie perfide, cette erreur de vouloir élever la Poésie au-dessus de la Prose.

Du côté positif, Maffei et Lefèvre de Saint-Marc ont, cependant, fait admettre définitivement sous le patronage de la *Bibliothèque françoise* que Ronsard possédait de véritables dons naturels et l'esprit poétique.

De prime abord, c'est là le seul lien avec la révision du procès, qui ne semble pas s'amorcer avant 1770. Pourtant Saint-Marc continue sournoisement à défendre Ronsard et Du Bellay dans ses éditions de Boileau[21] et de Malherbe. Là où Brossette s'était montré compréhensif, Saint-Marc ne change rien, c'est le cas de la note au vers 171 de la troisième 'Satire';[22] l'apologie de l'invention est évidente dans l'éclaircissement ajouté au premier chant de l'*Art poétique*.[23] Bien plus, le critique se complaît à montrer à quel point Boileau avait suivi l'*Art poétique* de La Fresnaie-Vauquel, surtout là où celui-ci s'était fondé sur Ronsard.[24]

A cause des préventions d'époque, Saint-Marc trouve plus facile de se montrer généreux envers Du Bellay:

Il fut le premier, qui, marchant sur les traces de Ronsard, essaya de donner à nos Muses l'air et le goût de celles de la Grèce et de Rome. Il y a dans ses ouvrages moins d'invention, moins de force de génie et moins d'élévation, que dans ceux de Ronsard, mais j'y trouve plus de délicatesse; un ton de vers un peu plus naturel, un stile (*sic*) un peu moins rude. Il peut être regardé comme le restaurateur du *Sonnet* en France. Il a composé des Poésies de différents genres, et je puis dire, que parmi ses Odes, il y en a de très bien faites; mais il n'est exempt nulle part des défauts reprochés à Ronsard. Et sa Muse en françois parle grec et latin. Ce qui n'empêche pas que, dans son temps, il ne fût très digne du surnom qu'on lui donna, d'*Ovide François*. Son abondance et sa facilité le méritoient.[25]

Datant de 1747, cette édition de Boileau est réimprimée en 1772 et ce sera Viollet Le Duc qui la révisera en 1821, de la manière que nous verrons plus loin.

Entre temps Saint-Marc sort, en 1757, une édition des *Poésies de Malherbe*, rangées par ordre chronologique et la dote d'un *Discours sur les obligations que la langue et la poésie française ont à Malherbe*.[26] Là impossible d'éviter quelques réflexions sur la langue 'barbare, pédantesque, forcée' de la Pléiade.[27] L'apologie revient pourtant sous une autre forme dès que Saint-Marc aborde la question du goût, invention récente, par rapport à l'érudition qui était supérieure chez les précurseurs de Malherbe, à l'époque où les poètes

> étoient parfaitement instruits des langues savantes, et leur mémoire étoit enrichie d'un vaste fond de littérature. Quelle connaissance de l'Antiquité, quelle profusion d'érudition dans les ouvrages de Du Bartas, de Ronsard et de quelques autres! Mais ils n'avoient aucune idée de ce que c'est que le goût: et leur jugement n'étant pas dans l'habitude de réprimer la fougue de leur imagination, leurs productions n'étoient que des efforts de génie et de mémoire.[28]

Laissant planer une certaine nostalgie pour la liberté du génie poétique, Saint-Marc conserve son admiration pour 'tous ceux qui, depuis Marot jusqu'à Malherbe s'efforceront de perfectionner notre poésie...'[29]

Ce fil conducteur, mince en apparence, étant donné le contexte, est bien solide. Il y a un rapport avec la note sur Ronsard qu'en 1772 Rigoley de Juvigny ajoute à celle de La Monnoye en éditant la *Bibliothèque françoise* de La Croix du Maine.[30] Même si les observations du Cardinal du Perron sont 'fort à l'avantage de Ronsard', elles méritent quelque considération parce que Boileau n'avait jugé le poète 'que par ce qu'il avoit de ridicule, sans faire aucune attention à son génie'.

A la même époque, malgré son respect pour Boileau qu'affaiblit le désir de contredire à la fois Marmontel, La Harpe et tous les partisans de Voltaire, Sabatier de Castres donna dans le même sens:

> Malgré tous ses travers, il faut convenir que Ronsard n'a pas peu contribué à l'avancement de la Poésie parmi nous. Il est le premier de nos poètes qui ait composé des Odes; il a fait aussi passer l'Epithalame dans notre langue... Plusieurs de ses poésies se font lire avec plaisir...
> Ronsard avoit les principales qualités qui font les grands poètes. La force et le brillant de l'imagination, la fécondité de l'esprit, cette invention heureuse, qui fait l'âme de la Poésie, en auroient fait un *Génie supérieur*, si sans discernement et sans goût, on pouvoit composer de bons ouvrages...[31]

Du moins les attributs de l'esprit poétique ont-ils été remis en valeur. On remarque aussi qu'ils sont rattachés, indirectement, à l'innovation de l'Ode. Or cette tendance remonte à vingt ans en arrière et se révèle dans un texte de l'abbé Joannet. Sabatier de Castres a dû l'avoir sous les yeux.

La réhabilitation de l'ode et de Pindare se dessine avec une

conséquence pour Ronsard, que La Motte avait laissé prévoir.
En réalité, Joannet ne cherche pas à faire de fausses distinctions:

> Sans parler du sublime Pindare, de l'enjoué et tendre Anacréon,
> d'Horace qui a su réunir leurs différents genres d'écrire et de quelques
> autres Poètes anciens qui ont marché avec succès dans la route des
> Poètes lyriques; nous en avons dans notre langue qui ne le cèdent pas
> toujours à leurs modèles; Ronsard le premier Français qui ait travaillé
> avec quelque succès à leur imitation, n'a peut-être pas un génie moins
> vif, moins grand que Pindare.[32]

L'inévitable réflexion sur 'les rudesses' de la langue montre que
la difficulté de communication subsiste toujours; néanmoins,
Joannet accepte de placer Ronsard parmi les poètes lyriques
'dont la vivacité, la force, et l'imagination ont fait le caractère'.
Et Malherbe ajoute-t-il, 'avoit peut-être moins de génie'.

Autrement dit, certaines concessions se font lentement au sujet
du goût, même si on regrette que Ronsard n'en ait pas eu davan-
tage. Ce relâchement des principes transparaît aussi en 1764 dans
l'approbation donnée par l'Académie, sous la forme d'un accessit,
au poème de Chabanon *Sur le Sort de la Poésie en ce Siècle philosophe*,
renfermant l'éloge de l'enthousiasme poétique.[33] C'est d'ailleurs
Chabanon qui lit ses traductions de Pindare devant l'Académie
des Inscriptions et Belles-Lettres. Par la suite, il les réunit en
volume, avec un important *Discours préliminaire*.[34] Là s'ébauche
une justification de Ronsard, fondée sur le point capital avancé
par Saint-Marc; la perspective historique du langage et des
usages. Chabanon soutient qu'à l'époque de Ronsard les mots
empruntés au grec 'étaient vraisemblablement entendus, autrement ses ouvrages n'auraient eu aucun succès'. De même le goût
était alors moins 'perfectionné'. En tout cela la mode, observe
Chabanon, compte pour beaucoup. Le reproche le plus juste
qu'on puisse faire à Ronsard, est de tomber dans *l'impropriété
d'expression* de sorte que le style contredit la pensée. Datant
de 1772, ce texte est en avance sur les idées de Sabatier de
Castres; Chabanon va le réviser dans le cadre d'une étude sur le
progrès des langues, travail qui paraîtra en 1785, après une
nouvelle phase dans la reprise d'intérêt pour les poètes de la
Pléiade.

Ou plutôt pour la poésie du seizième siècle, comme en témoig-
nent les rédacteurs des *Annales Poétiques* lorsqu'ils tracent la ligne
de démarcation entre Marot et le nouvel idiome qu'inaugure
Du Bellay.

...le génie plus hardi de nos Poètes va apprendre aux Muses françaises, à parler comme les Muses grecques et latines. La grandeur des images, la hardiesse des métaphores, le grand secret des épithètes, sont connus. En un mot, jusqu'à présent, nous avons assisté, pour ainsi dire, aux concerts des Grâces: *nous allons entendre les accents de la Poésie.* C'est à Joachim Du Bellay, puisqu'il est né avant Ronsard, qu'appartient la gloire d'avoir commencé cette révolution.[35]

Par la *Défense et Illustration*—que l'on considère toujours favorablement—Du Bellay avait ébauché l'art de ses successeurs. Comme poète, il avait 'de la verve, de l'énergie et l'expression vraiment poétique', il était 'prompt et aigu en inventions', et chez lui, l'érudition ne paraissait pas un vice. Les éloges dépassent de loin les réserves; on corrige même la mauvaise impression laissée par l'abbé Goujet. De plus, le fait pour Du Bellay d'avoir travaillé à enrichir la langue, ne l'expose plus aux sarcasmes d'usage, on y voit plutôt une excuse d'avoir été parfois 'barbare dans son style':

C'est là l'écueil des créateurs en ce genre, et l'on peut dire à la louange de Du Bellay qu'il a su l'éviter bien plus souvent que Ronsard...[36]

Pourtant celui-ci, malgré tous ses défauts—et le rédacteur, fatigué de ses lectures en énumère une infinité—a accompli un travail nécessaire:

On doit savoir gré à Ronsard des efforts qu'il a faits pour ajouter à nos richesses poétiques: il se condamna, pour y parvenir, au travail le plus obstiné: il avoit poussé le courage et la patience jusqu'à apprendre tout Virgile par cœur: et parmi les mots qu'il a créés, il en est plusieurs de nécessaires... et l'on trouvera de sublimes expressions dans les Pièces que nous avons insérées. Tout poète, enfin, quand son goût est mûri par l'étude et la réflexion, peut lire avec fruit les poésies de Ronsard. Au reste, il avoit choisi le moment favorable pour innover.[37]

Le vœu qu'avait formulé Saint-Marc est pleinement exaucé, et pour les raisons qu'il avait exposées.

Dans deux notices importantes, l'*Année littéraire* rend compte des volumes consacrés à Du Bellay et à Ronsard.[38] La première relève en passant un plagiat de La Harpe, puis montre que Racine, Boileau, La Fontaine, Jean-Baptiste Rousseau avaient tous emprunté quelques vers aux Odes de Du Bellay.[39] La deuxième reproduit les commentaires sur le génie, la verve et l'imagination de Ronsard, insistant sur les qualités poétiques de ses vers. En somme les aspects les plus favorables sont mis en valeur et cette partie de l'article se termine sur une citation:

On doit le lire au moins comme un poète étranger; Homère et Virgile n'apprennent pas mieux que lui à faire des vers français: il faut le lire avec le même esprit qu'on apporte à la lecture d'Homère et de Virgile; il n'apprend pas si l'on veut à être poète français, il apprend seulement à être poète, si toutefois cela s'apprend.[40]

Là l'idée essentielle de *l'esprit poétique* que les *Annales poétiques* avaient exposée, mais laissée un peu en retrait, prend tout son relief. Telle est l'intention de l'*Année littéraire* car la conclusion de la notice montre comment Boileau avait empêché qu'on lise Ronsard, certifie avec étonnement que l'œuvre renferme de nombreuses beautés de tous les ordres et se prononce en sa faveur: 'il est certain que la France a eu peu de poètes qui aient eu autant de verve et d'imagination'. Une sorte de désaveu paraîtra quelques mois plus tard dans les colonnes de la revue,[41] toutefois le mal est fait, et pour des raisons que nous examinons plus loin, La Harpe ne va rien pardonner aux défenseurs de Ronsard.

En 1785, Chabanon revient à la charge avec des opinions très tranchées sur ce qui constitue les progrès du langage. Il lui semble qu'on pourrait envier à Ronsard 'son énergie et sa franchise'. A l'objection que le poète 'parla grec et latin en français', Chabanon riposte avec énergie:

> Hé nous! Faisons-nous autre chose? Notre idiome, dérivé de ces sources, ne conserve-t-il pas toutes les preuves de sa filiation? Ce que fit Ronsard pour sa langue, les Latins le firent pour la leur. Ils la teignirent, ils l'abreuvèrent de toutes les couleurs de l'hellénisme.

Et si certains néologismes ne sont pas passés dans la langue française tandis que d'autres y ont réussi, ce n'est qu'une affaire de mode, et non pas une raison de reprocher à Ronsard ses 'barbarismes'. D'autre part, observe Chabanon, si le mérite de l'œuvre est tombé 'en discrédit', c'est peut-être que la valeur n'en était pas suffisante pour faire supporter un langage vieilli. Il ne faudrait pas mettre en cause les 'vices constitutifs' de la langue même:

> En considérant que les *Œuvres* de Ronsard manquent du *mérite des choses*, et qu'elles ont fait l'admiration de Montaigne, de l'Hospital, de Du Bellay (ces hommes familiarisés avec l'idée du beau par la lecture des Anciens, qu'ils appréciaient si bien) on ne peut s'empêcher de croire que le style de Ronsard eut un mérite d'expression et d'harmonie qui fit qu'on lui pardonna tout. Dans ce cas, il eût réussi par le charme de sa langue, par l'heureux emploi qu'il en a fait, et c'est sur cette langue même, sur l'emploi bizarre de cette langue qu'on l'attaque aujourd'hui.
> Nous l'avons dit, la langue est le ministre, le serviteur de la pensée; elle en est l'outil servile...[42]

Aux yeux de ses contemporains, Ronsard avait apporté à la

langue des perfectionnements nécessaires. Dans l'esprit de Chabanon—qui se retourne contre La Motte et Fontenelle, 'faux légis-
lateurs du goût'—ce fait n'est pas dissocié de la *fureur divine* dans
le sens primitif qu'il définit à la lumière de l'*Ion* de Platon afin
de montrer comment la poésie et son expression se renouvellent
grâce à la conquête d'une nouvel ordre de connaissances. Toutefois, il se garde de relier clairement cet aspect de l'inspiration à
l'esprit d'innovation chez Ronsard. C'est sans doute pour cette
raison que son texte n'a pas effarouché l'Académie des Inscriptions qui en a autorisé la publication.

Pourtant, rien ne donne l'impression que les voix en faveur de
Ronsard aient été très écoutées. Bien entendu, Marmontel et La
Harpe criaient plus fort: leurs tirages étaient aussi beaucoup plus
considérables. Il n'est pas moins vrai que la défense de Ronsard
inaugurée par Saint-Marc, est reprise par Viollet Le Duc qui, en
1821, fait, dans son édition de Boileau, l'apologie de Ronsard le
novateur:

> A une époque où la langue n'étoit pas fixée, je ne sais jusqu'à quel
> point on peut reprocher à cet auteur d'avoir tenté de l'enrichir de
> quelques mots pris dans les langues classiques. Ensuite, il n'est pas
> exact de dire que *toutes* les poésies de Ronsard sont *chargées* de mots
> tirés du grec, au point de les rendre inintelligibles: il est de fait que ces
> exemples sont fort rares. Il eût été plus vrai et plus juste de dire que,
> parmi les expressions et tournures hasardées par Ronsard, plusieurs ont
> été admises dans notre langue poétique. Cet écrivain remarquable
> manquoit d'harmonie et d'élégance, mais il était poète. Il donna de la
> pompe et de la noblesse à notre poésie, restreinte avant lui à la bal-
> lade, au rondeau... Il sut le premier l'élever au ton lyrique et vraiment
> digne de l'Ode qu'il introduisit en France.[43]

Un an plus tard l'éditeur retouchera son texte pour l'incorporer
dans l'*Histoire de la Satire en France* insérée comme préface dans
l'édition des *Œuvres* de Mathurin Régnier.[44] Ce sont là, avant
Sainte-Beuve, les dernières preuves de ce que M. Claude Pichois
a appelé le 'courant de sympathie'.

En dépit de toute apparence, La Harpe n'a pas su y opposer
une barrière efficace, mais a peut-être réussi à en modifier un
élément essentiel. Viollet Le Duc veut bien accorder du talent à
Ronsard, sans spécifier le génie ni *l'esprit poétique*. La Harpe avait
repris la pensée de La Motte sur les méfaits de Pindare, critiqué
les vices, relevé les inventions extravagantes et 'baroques' dans
les Odes, il s'était indigné au sujet de l'ivresse et du dithyrambe.
Tout ce fiel retomba sur Ronsard, imitateur du poète thébain.[45]

M

Ensuite dans un texte plus connu, La Harpe refusa à Ronsard le génie, lui laissa le talent, encore qu'il fût 'informe et brute'.[46] Même si, comme M. C. Pichois l'a montré, Pierrot-Deseilligny reconnaît que chez Ronsard se rencontrent parfois 'de la verve et de l'enthousiasme, une imagination brillante et féconde... du sentiment, de la finesse et de la grâce',[47] Sainte-Beuve reste plus fidèle au souvenir du *Lycée*. Car, pour lui 'Ronsard se guinda jusqu'à l'ode pindarique et trébucha fréquemment'.[48]

Reste le novateur que La Harpe a durement critiqué en visant en même temps les *journalistes* grâce à qui Ronsard a failli 're-devenir le législateur de notre poésie'. En partie cette prise de position est en réaction contre l'*Année littéraire*, non seulement après l'accusation de plagiat, mais aussi en souvenir des dards de Fréron dirigés à la fois contre La Harpe et Voltaire.[49] Et l'on remarque que l'apologiste du classicisme redoute l'imitation de Ronsard; les enjambements, le vers hâché et tourmenté, la tendance à imposer à celui-ci 'un air étranger en voulant le faire paraître neuf...' Les préjugés de l'abbé Ganet reprennent vie.

Ils se transforment chez Sainte-Beuve en éloges afin de justifier les innovations patronnées par la nouvelle école: ce qui fait presque écho à Maffei.[50] D'autre part, il est évident que le critique utilise plusieurs sources: les *Annales poétiques* l'ont aidé a préparer la notice sur Du Bellay et lui ont donné un exemple précis.[51] De même il y puise une partie de ses opinions sur Ronsard. Quant à la question d'innover par l'imitation, la manière d'aborder le contexte historique semble avoir été suggéré par Saint-Marc. Chabanon et Viollet Le Duc ont pu avoir une influence sur ce jugement dont l'origine remonte à Fénelon:

> Sommes-nous en droit de nier, je le demande, que Ronsard ait été de son temps réellement sublime, et tout en cessant de le goûter et de le lire, pouvons-nous lui reprocher autre chose que le malheur d'être venu trop tôt, et le tort d'avoir marché trop vite. Un vocabulaire de choix n'existait pas en France: Ronsard en eut besoin, et se mit à l'improviser.[52]

Plus loin Sainte-Beuve réaffirme que Ronsard se rachète par le style, qu'en cela il était véritablement créateur, c'est-à-dire poète.[53] En revanche 'l'invention chez lui était à peu près nulle'. Ce qui nous ramène à l'article de l'abbé Ganet, niant l'*esprit poétique*, critiquant le fond et la forme des innovations prêtées à Ronsard pour proclamer enfin qu'on ne le lisait plus. Tout nous semble indiquer que Sainte-Beuve a dû faire la recherche dont nous venons d'esquisser les traits principaux. Pourtant, incapable de se débarrasser de la tutelle de La Harpe, il a refusé d'accréditer l'observation de Maffei sur *l'esprit poétique* et laissé aux poètes le privilège d'en découvrir le sens intérieur.[54]

NOTES

[1] *Tableau historique et critique de la Poésie et du Théâtre français au XVIe Siècle*, Paris, Sautelet (1828), 2 vols., *Œuvres choisies de Pierre de Ronsard*, préface, t. II, p. xxv.

[2] La Monnoye, *Ménagiana*, ou les bons mots et remarques critiques, historiques, morales et d'érudition de M. Ménage..., 3ème éd., Paris, Florentin Delaulne (1715), 4 vols., t. III, p. 103.

[3] *Bibliothèque françoise*, Paris, Mariette et Guérin (1743–1751), t. XII (1748), pp. 247–248: renvoie à l'abbé Ganet, *Réflexions sur les Ouvrages de Littérature*, Paris, Briasson (1738) vol. VII, pp. 313 sq.; et à Lefèvre de Saint-Marc, *Le Pour et le Contre*, t. XVIII (1739), p. 305.

[4] *Il primo canto dell' Iliade d'Omero*, tradutti in versi italiani in Londra, G. Brindley (1736)—l'opuscule est dédicacé au Prince de Galles, (suivant sans doute le précédent établi par Antoine Marie Salvini qui avait traduit en vers blancs l'*Iliade* et l'*Odyssée* et adressé une épître dédicatoire au Roi Georges Ier d'Angleterre: cf. la *Bibliothèque italique*, sept.-déc. 1728, t. III, II). Maffei a repris la totalité de sa publication, avec le même frontispice, dans les *Osservazioni litterari*, Verona, (1737), t. I, pp. 309–58.

[5] Selon Michaud, Maffei visita Paris en 1733. En 1736, il voyageait en Angleterre, fit un séjour à Londres et fut reçu Docteur *Honoris Causa* de l'Université d'Oxford (*Biographie universelle*).

[6] Fuchs: 'Comment le XVIIe et le XVIIIe Siècles ont jugé Ronsard': 3 articles, *Revue de la Renaissance*, (1908) t. VIII, pp. 228–38, t. IX, pp. 1–27; 49–72.

Gustave Charlier; 'Ronsard au XIXe Siècle avant Sainte-Beuve', *Revue des Cours et Conférences*, 41ème année, No 6, le 29 février, 1939–1940, t. I, pp. 369 sq.

Verdun-L. Saulnier, 'La Réputation de Ronsard au XVIIIe Siècle: le Rôle de Sainte-Beuve', *Revue universitaire*, mars–avril 1947, pp. 92–7.

C. Pichois: 'La Fortune française de Ronsard, Poète de "Génie", de sa Mort à sa "Réhabilitation" ': *Annales de la Faculté des Lettres d'Aix-en-Provence*, t. xxxv (1961), pp. 23–36.

Alan M. Boase, 'Tradition and Revaluation in the French Anthology 1692–1960', in *Essays presented to C. M. Girdlestone*, University of Durham, 1960, pp. 49–63.

[7] Sur Guéret, *Le Parnasse réformé* (1669) et la *Guerre des Auteurs* (1671), voir Fuchs, 2ème article cité. Signalons que les ouvrages de Guéret ont été réimprimés en 1716 en raison de leur rareté (La Haye, Neaulme). Notre citation est tirée du *Parnasse réformé* (Fuchs, *loc. cit.* et Guéret, *op. cit.*, p. 37).

[8] Guéret, *La Guerre des Auteurs*, ed. cit., pp. 65–6.
[9] *Ibid.*, p. 41, et Fuchs, 2ème article, *loc. cit.*, p. 18.
[10] Guéret, *op. cit.*, p. 67.
[11] Même si Fontenelle admet que Ronsard fut le premier en France à avoir entrepris de composer de 'grandes pièces de Poésies', c'est, d'après lui, l'érudition qui a rendu ses vers durs et peu intelligibles. Cf. A. Boase, *loc. cit.* et C. Pichois (*loc. cit.*).
[12] Léon Gabriel Gros, 'Poésie bien disante, Poètes maudits'; *Les Inconnus poétiques du 18e Siècle, Cahiers du Sud*, No 350 (1959), t. XXXXVI, pp. 3–9, (cite La Motte, Fontenelle et d'Alembert—article 'Goût', pour l'*Encyclopédie*).
[13] La Motte, *Odes... avec un Discours sur la Poésie en général et sur l'Ode en particulier*, Paris, Dupuis (1713), 2 vols., t. I. pp. 37–8; (4ème édition: le *Discours* date de 1707).
[14] *Ibid.*, pp. 64–5; cf. Fuchs, 3ème article, pp. 49 sq.
[15] 'Le vieux Ronsard ayant pris ses bésicles...', *Epigrammes*, livre II, No. xi, *Œuvres de J.-B. Rousseau*, présentées par Amar, Paris, Lefèvre (1824), t. II, pp. 276–7.
[16] Louis Racine, *De la Poésie naturelle ou de la Langue poétique*, (le 4 sept. 1739), *Mémoires de l'Académie royale des Inscriptions et Belles-Lettres* (Paris, Imprimerie Royale), t. XV, pp. 192–243, sur Ronsard, p. 194.
[17] *Traité de la Prosodie françoise*, Paris, Gandouin (1736).
[18] Maffei, *op. cit.*, p. ix, Ganet, *loc. cit.*, pp. 322–3, et Lefèvre de Saint-Marc, *loc. cit.*, pp. 304–5.
[19] *Bibliothèque françoise:* sur Du Bellay, t. XII, pp. 117–38. Cf. aussi t. I, pp. 28–9; t. VII, 107–8; 139–43; sur Ronsard, t. XII, pp. 192–248.
[20] *Loc. cit.*, p. 248—cf. le texte de Saint-Marc que nous reproduisons plus haut; nous avons souligné les modifications apportées par l'abbé Goujet.
[21] Saint-Marc a pris la succession de Brossette (Genève, Barillot, 1716, 2 vol.), comme éditeur de Boileau en 1747; la première édition en 5 volumes fut réimprimée en 1772 (Paris, Libraires associés).
[22] Edition de 1772, t. I, p. 71.
[23] *Ibid.*, t. II, pp. 239–40—cf. Brossette, t. II, p. 297.
[24] Cette tendance se remarque dans les notes aux vers 140–41 du Chant II de l'*Art poétique* et aux vers 237 et 273 du Chant III (*op. cit.*, t. II, pp. 281, 237 sq., 360 sq.).
[25] *Reflexions critiques sur Longin*, VII (1693). *Œuvres de Boileau*, t. V, p. iii, note.
[26] Cette édition comporte aussi les *Mémoires* de Racan pour la vie de Malherbe, Paris, Barbon (1757).
[27] *Op. cit., Discours*, p. 336.
[28] *Ibid.*, p. 340.
[29] *Ibid.*, p. 345.
[30] *Bibliothèque françoise de La Croix du Maine*, nouvelle édition par M. Rigoley de Juvigny, Paris, Saillant et Nyon, 2 vols. (1772), t. II, p. 317 et p. 319 (notes).
[31] Sabatier de Castres; *Les trois Siècles de notre Littérature*, Amsterdam et Paris, Gueffier et Dehansi (1772), 3 vols.; voir la prise de position énoncée dès la *Préface*, également l'article contre Palissot de Montenoy (t. III,

pp. 32–38). Sur Ronsard, t. III, pp. 199–203. Cf. M. Claude Pichois, *art. cit.*, pp. 27–9.

[32] Joannet: *Eléments de Poésie française*, Paris, Compagnie des Libraires (1752), 3 vols., t. III, p. 125.

[33] *Sur le Sort de la Poésie en ce Siècle philosophe*, Paris, Jorry (1764). Ajoutons que les *Réflexions sur le Génie de l'Ode*, d'Ecouchard-Lebrun vont dans le même sens et renferment en outre le conseil de lire l'*Ode à Michel de l'Hospital* que le futur 'Pindare' de la poésie française, considère comme un chef-d'œuvre. Le texte a paru en 1756 avec l'*Ode sur le Désastre de Lisbonne* (*Œuvres*, mises en ordre par Ginguené, Paris, Warée (1811), 4 vol., t. IV, p. 304).

[34] *Les Odes pythiques de Pindare*, Paris, Lacombe (1772); sur Ronsard, pp. 60–1.

[35] Les *Annales poétiques*, t. IV, Paris, Delalain; le volume contient des poésies de Maurice Scève, de Hugues Salel, d'Antoine de Saix et d'Etienne de Forcadel; la plus grande partie en est consacrée à Du Bellay (notice pp. 41–56 et poèmes, pp. 57–204), cf. A. M. Boase, (*art. cit.*).

[36] *Annales poétiques*, t. IV, p. 46.

[37] *Annales poétiqes*, t. V, volume que François Habert partage avec Ronsard, Paris, Delalain, (1778), p. 62, (notice, pp. 53–72 et *Choix de Poésies*, pp. 73–282).

[38] *L'Année littéraire*, 1779, Vol. V, lettre II sur le t. IV des *Annales poétiques* (pp. 39–52) et Vol. VII, pp. 171–89, lettre VIII sur le tome V.

[39] Le rédacteur de l'*Année litteraire* cite un passage d'E. de Forcadel que la Harpe avait plagié (1779, t. V, *loc. cit.*).

[40] *L'Année littéraire*, 1779, Vol. VII, lettre VIII, p. 183) cite en détail la notice des *Annales poétiques*, t. V, pp. 60–61). M. C. Pichois fait remarquer que les opinions de l'éditeur des *Annales poétiques* ont été reproduites par Désessart dans la notice qu'il a donnée en 1801 au t. V des *Siècles littéraires* (*art. cit.*, p. 30).

[41] *L'Année littéraire* Vol. VI (1780), pp. 3–34, sur les tomes VII à X des *Annales poétiques*.

[42] *Considérations sur les Langues*, ch. 3, ouvrage ajouté à l'essai: *De la Musique*, Paris, Pissot (1785), pp; 454–6.

[43] Boileau, *Œuvres*, avec les commentaires revus, corrigés et augmentés (par Viollet Le Duc), Paris, Desoer (1821), 4 vols., *Art Poétique*, ch. 1, vers 126, notes: t. II, pp. 239–40.

[44] Ce texte a été signalé par Charlier, *art. cit.*

[45] La Harpe, *De la Littérature, Le Lycée*, 1ère section, ch. 7, t. II, Paris, Agasse (1799), p. 91, note 1.

[46] *Ibid.*, *Siècle de Louis XIV* (seconde partie, livre premier, ch. 1, t. V, Paris, Firmin Didot (1821), p. 90), cf. M. C. Pichois, *art. cit.*, pp. 30–1.

[47] *Art. cit.*, p. 33.

[48] *Tableau historique, op. cit.*, t. I, p. 94. En commentant sur Du Bellay, Sainte-Beuve observe: 'du moins il ne pindarise pas; sa facilité le sauve de l'enflure pédantesque' (*ibid.*, p. 70), ce qui confirme le sens péjoratif rattaché au nom de Pindare. A vrai dire, Sainte-Beuve ressemble à Marmontel et penche pour le Ronsard anacréontique—(*ibid.*, pp. 93–4).

[49] Bachaumont signale que La Harpe a eu maille à partir avec Fréron à

plus d'une reprise, voir, par exemple, les *Mémoires* pour 1765 (notamment, t. II, p. 162).

[50] Sainte-Beuve, *op. cit.*, t. I, p. 78, sur l'alexandrin; p. 88, sur la noblesse, la gravité et l'éclat du langage.

[51] *Ibid.*, pp. 70–2. Sainte-Beuve utilise la notice sur Du Bellay et cite en outre l'exemple 'Du ceps lascif les longs embrassements', image commentée très favorablement par l'éditeur des *Annales poétiques*, (*loc. cit.*, p. 45).

[52] *Tableau*, *op. cit.*, t. I, p. 91. Cf. Chabanon, *loc. cit.*, et Fénelon, *Lettre à l'Académie:* 'Ronsard avoit trop entrepris tout à coup...'

[53] *Ibid.*, Préface du t. II, p. xxv.

[54] Signalons l'ouvrage très détaillé de M. R. A. Katz, *Ronsard's French Critics, Travaux d'Humanisme et Renaissance,* No. lxxxv, Droz, Genève (1966), paru quelques mois après la rédaction de cet article mais sans modifier l'essentiel de nos propos.

F. W. Leakey

A *FESTSCHRIFT* OF 1855: BAUDELAIRE AND THE *HOMMAGE À. C. F. DENECOURT*

In 1855, under the general title *Fontainebleau*, there appeared what must surely be one of the most notable homage volumes ever produced.[1] Its recipient was C. F. Denecourt, and among the forty-odd contributors brought together in sometimes improbable juxtaposition were numbered many of the most famous writers of the day: Lamartine, Victor Hugo, George Sand, Musset, Béranger, Gautier, Murger, Banville, Janin, together with others, such as Nerval and Baudelaire, whose fame is of more recent date. From Baudelaire, indeed, we have no less than five items: two of the finest of his 'Parisian' poems (*Le Crépuscule du soir* and *Le Crépuscule du matin*, to give them their ultimate titles); his two earliest-published experiments in the prose-poem genre; and, prefacing these, a letter to Fernand Desnoyers which is commonly regarded as his most authoritative pronouncement on the subject of Nature. Clearly then, for the student of Baudelaire the volume has great interest and merits a closer scrutiny than it has hitherto received; and where more appropriately, I would venture to ask, than in another such homage volume, dedicated to a distinguished scholar of our own century? Yet as I shall hope to show, the Denecourt *Hommage* has other and wider claims to our attention; to recall it, is for instance to recall the great work accomplished at Fontainebleau by Denecourt himself—one of the undoubted benefactors of mankind, a pioneer in the cause of conservation and 'amenity' to whom all Nature-lovers owe a debt of gratitude which the present article may serve in some small measure to repay.

I. DENECOURT AND FONTAINEBLEAU

Claude-François Denecourt was born, the eldest of a family of eleven, in 1788 in a little village of Franche-Comté; but for us his story truly begins in 1834, when after his 'banishment' to Fontainebleau two years earlier, he began to apply himself to the task which was to occupy the remainder of his long life. This task is somewhat difficult to define in a few words: thus in one biographical dictionary Denecourt is described as a 'cicerone', in another as a 'forestier et écrivain sylvestre';[2] more picturesquely, and more accurately perhaps, he was known throughout the latter part of his life simply as 'le Sylvain', and viewed almost as a form of tutelary genius presiding benignly over the whole forest and domain of Fontainebleau—a conception deriving, I suggest, like the nickname itself, from a charming essay by Théophile Gautier which figured, as we shall see, within the very volume with which we are at present concerned.

Curiously enough, it was indeed as a guide—if not precisely as a 'cicerone'—that Denecourt began his working career while still in his teens: the family having moved, on his father's death and his mother's remarriage, to a little town in the foothills of the Vosges, he there accompanied, and guided about the mountains, travellers hiring carriages from his stepfather.[3] During the period 1809 to 1814 he served, though twice wounded, within Napoleon's army;[4] thereafter, as a Bonapartist and later as a Liberal and then a Republican, he more than once fell foul of successive Monarchist governments, and finally, in 1832, shortly after being 'transferred' to Fontainebleau, was dismissed from the modest appointment he had briefly held there. What saved him, it appears, from utter despair at the wreckage of his personal life and the failure of his political ideals (and what later was to save him, yet again, after the disillusions of the 1848 Revolution), was his growing passion for the vast forest he now found 'on his doorstep'; as he himself declares, in words eloquent of his whole simple, even naïve philosophy:

> Cette magnifique forêt, si variée et aux aspects à la fois si agrestes et si pittoresques, ne tarda pas à me charmer et à me consoler de mes croyances déçues (...) Dès-lors, je me donnai tout à elle comme je m'étais donné à la politique (...) on est si heureux au milieu de ces paisibles déserts, parmi ces arbres géants et ces rochers aussi vieux que le monde! On y trouve la paix, le bonheur et la santé. Le cœur et l'âme y savourent mille jouissances délicieuses! On en revient toujours con-

tent et meilleur, car l'aspect grandiose et suave de ce jardin, comme Dieu seul sait en créer, vous charme et vous inspire la bonté.[5]

And thus it was that Denecourt applied himself—at first haphazardly, and then systematically—to exploring and charting these 'peaceful deserts' of which he speaks, until at last, in 1839, he was ready to publish a first version of the famous *Guide du Voyageur dans la forêt de Fontainebleau*, which under various titles was to run into so many editions during the ensuing thirty-six years of his life.[6] In essence, Denecourt's self-appointed task, as 'initiateur familier de la forêt de Fontainebleau',[7] was to make its beauties available and accessible to all: first, by tracing out—where necessary by *hewing* out of undergrowth or rock—the routes (ultimately totalling some 100 miles) which would lead tourists to all the various beauty spots and vantage-points he had so laboriously discovered; next, by drawing up a comprehensive map of the region in which these routes and sites would be duly plotted; next again, by offering, in his published *Guides* (each with its map attached), verbal descriptions of the itineraries to be followed; finally, and perhaps most valuably of all, by establishing a vast network of signposts with appropriate markings (names, letters, blue arrows, red stars), whereby the traveller could be led to this or that cherished spot, or at least saved from the plight of Musset and George Sand wandering lost through the forest in August 1833, i.e. in the very year following Denecourt's arrival at Fontainebleau.[8] In those early days, the forest was so wild and unfrequented that many of Denecourt's preliminary forays had to be carried out at considerable risk of life and limb; the terms 'intrepid explorer' or 'pioneer', the analogies with Columbus or Captain Cook, that recur in many accounts of his work, are to this extent by no means misplaced. From the 'portrait' sketched by Luchet, in the *Fontainebleau* volume, we gain a vivid picture of the endearing and touchingly *appropriate* physical appearance of the man: small and simply dressed, with his wide hat and round spectacles, a holly stick firmly grasped in his hand as he plunges boldly on, up hill and down dale, joyful, sure-footed, nostrils quivering, eyes always to the skies:

En voyant ainsi se découper sa silhouette aiguë dans le fond vague de l'horizon, on se rappelle les mystérieuses petites figures des gravures allemandes, qui, penchées sur les montagnes, regardent dans les villes et semblent être des messagers entre ce qu'on demande en bas et ce qu'on refuse en haut. (Luchet, *Hommage*, p. 6)

Several of the contributors to the homage volume stress—with some exaggeration, no doubt—Denecourt's curious physical 'assimilation' to the environment within which he moves: thus to Luchet, his compact, gnarled frame suggests nothing more than a juniper tree transformed into a man; to Alfred Busquet, he seems a 'human oak', as if rooted to the earth by the very structure of his legs: 'ses jambes de paysan, arquées avec force, tiennent par de vigoureuses racines au sol natal';[9] for Théophile Gautier, finally, these 'vegetable' lineaments assume, as we shall see, a purely fantastic, even wildly mythological guise of their own.

It was to be expected that Denecourt's zestful peregrinations within the forest, to say nothing of the influx of visitors that ultimately ensued therefrom, would arouse suspicions and misgivings among the conventional and parochially-minded,[10] and that these would include both the Forestry Administration and the municipality of Fontainebleau—neither of which seem to have been disposed, initially, to offer even encouragement, let alone financial support. As a result, he was obliged himself to shoulder, from his own modest resources, the major and often crippling burden of expenditure that his work entailed. The 1848 Revolution seemed for a moment, it is true, to herald a change in the official attitude towards Denecourt: Luchet having been appointed the first Republican Governor of the domain of Fontainebleau, there had arisen for Denecourt (who later, his Republican ardour rekindled, was to join with Luchet in the electoral campaign of that year) the fleeting prospect of an appointment within the Forest conservancy or inspectorate:

> En 1848, après des événements qui eurent un moment le singulier pouvoir d'arracher le sauvage voyer à ses fouilles infatigables, quelqu'un—c'était moi—proposa de créer pour lui une sorte d'inspection ou de conservation des beautés de la forêt. Cette proposition fut trouvée ridicule alors: on l'appuierait peut-être aujourd'hui, par impossible.   (*Hommage*, p. 20)

Luchet's bitterness here can in part be explained by his own discomfiture in the elections of 1848—a poor reward, this, from the citizens of Fontainebleau, for his initiative in securing the safety and maintenance of their castle and forest.[11] But we can perceive also, in this and other passages of his essay on Denecourt, the deep indignation he feels at the failure both public and private to recognize and honour his friend's achievement; and indeed the Fontainebleau volume itself was conceived, as he indicates in its

opening words, not only as a homage to Denecourt, but as a
solemn act of 'reparation' for 'ingratitude'. In the end, and to
some limited extent, reparation came perhaps to be made:
'certificates' of various kinds were awarded; an undertaking was
finally given by the Government to maintain Denecourt's work on
his retirement; the citizens of Fontainebleau, more particularly,
combined in various ways to do him (belated) homage. Thus a
medal (the work of the local sculptor Adam-Salomon[12]) was
struck by the township in his honour; the whole community, as it
seemed, turned out, in March 1875, to attend his funeral; a
square (the 'Place Denecourt') was named after him, a monu-
ment erected to him in the town cemetery.[13] In this slow and
laborious process of recognition, whereby Denecourt's name and
work were brought eventually to the notice of a wider public, the
homage volume of 1855, with its contributions from so many
illustrious pens, constitutes a first and perhaps decisive step.

II. THE HOMAGE VOLUME

The 'story' of the homage volume has been recounted by Denecourt himself, in an annexe to the 1856 edition of his *Guide*:

> En [1853], dans le courant de mai, M. Fernand Desnoyers, jeune
> poète parisien, étant venu accompagné de quelques amis se donner
> les joies de plusieurs jours d'exploration dans ma bien-aimée forêt de
> Fontainebleau, et ayant, comme M. Auguste Luchet, été saisi d'ad-
> miration en parcourant cette forêt par mes sentiers, et comme lui,
> trouvant qu'on m'avait trop peu encouragé, il voulut à son exemple
> me faire don d'un livre, mais d'un livre des *cent-et-un* ou à peu près.
>   De retour à Paris, M. Desnoyers émet par la voix des journaux sa
> généreuse idée et plus de cinquante poètes et prosateurs répondent à
> l'appel.
>   Parmi cette pléïade de littérateurs figurent les noms des écrivains les
> plus célèbres de notre époque.
>   En 1855, deux ans après ce philantropique [sic] et fraternel appel,
> le précieux volume m'était présenté au milieu d'un banquet, surcroît
> d'honneur dont me comblaient mes bienfaiteurs réunis en assez bon
> nombre et auxquels étaient venus se joindre d'autres notabilités de la
> littérature et des beaux-arts.
>   Merci donc et éternelle reconnaissance à M. Fernand Desnoyers,
> qui de cette œuvre collective a pris l'initiative et en a dirigé l'impres-
> sion.
>   Merci et reconnaissance aussi d'une manière toute particulière à
> M. Auguste Luchet qui non-seulement est le principal collaborateur de
> l'ouvrage; mais qui, en 1850, ainsi que je l'ai dit tout à l'heure, avait
> déjà par sa plume rémunéré et glorifié mes humbles créations.

> Merci et reconnaissance à tous les cœurs généreux qui ont bien voulu
> contribuer à la fondation du livre des *quarante-deux!* livre qui, je le
> répète, est la sanction et la récompense la plus belle et la plus noble que
> puissent obtenir les vingt années de travaux et de sacrifices que j'ai
> consacrées à la mise en lumière de la forêt de Fontainebleau.[14]

As far as the presentation 'banquet' is concerned, we may
amplify Denecourt's brief reference above-cited, with this more
picturesque account given by Charles de Franciosi, in a 'feuille-
ton' published on 24th August 1855 in the *Journal de Lille*:

> Il y a trois semaines environ, une joyeuse fête de famille avait
> rassemblé une vingtaine de personnes chez B..., à Paris. Le repas
> était gai, c'était le bouquet d'une bonne action. Ces chants, ces rires,
> tout cela s'adressait à un petit homme à l'œil vif, à l'air heureux,
> allègre et droit dans sa structure économe, particulièrement noueuse et
> ramassée, un genévrier changé en homme, comme dit Auguste
> Luchet.
> A ce héros de la fête, sur les cheveux duquel reposait une couronne
> de feuilles de chêne, on remit un volume magnifiquement relié:
> *Fontainebleau*. Et ceux qui avaient ordonné cette fête, c'étaient des
> littérateurs, des poètes et des chansonniers, des peintres et des chan-
> teurs. Les uns, collaborateurs du petit homme, les autres ses admira-
> teurs reconnaissants, tous ses amis.   (*Guide*, 1856, p. 295)

And the picture is completed for us by another provincial
journalist, J. Cottet, who describes how, after the presentation of
the volume 'printed on satin paper',

> ...[le] vieux Sylvain... les larmes aux yeux, a remercié tous ces
> littérateurs avec des paroles charmantes et comme le cœur seul sait
> en trouver.   (*Guide*, 1856, p. 302)

It would be pleasant to think that Baudelaire had been among the
'men of letters' present on this convivial and homely occasion—as
a respite from his long warfare with *Le Pays*, and at the very
moment when he was preparing to write, on Marie Daubrun's
behalf, to one of his fellow-contributors within the homage
volume: George Sand...[15] But to return to Denecourt's account of
the inception of the volume, it is clear that this is a somewhat
simplified and idealized version of the actual course of events.
Thus, to begin with, Desnoyers can hardly in fact have carried
through the whole enterprise single-handed: he is likely to have
had considerable 'editorial' assistance from Luchet in particular
(who having as a young man played a part in the publication, on
the bookseller Ladvocat's behalf, of the *Livre des Cent Un* above-
mentioned, had gained first-hand experience of the problems of

compiling a collective volume of this kind)—as also, to a lesser
extent, from Alfred Busquet and Philibert Audebrand.[16]
As to the actual 'gathering-in' of the contributions, the actual
response from the 'more than fifty poets and prose-writers'
mentioned by Denecourt, this can scarcely, in reality, have been
quite as immediate and 'automatic' as he implies. It would be
interesting to know how many of the items figuring within the
volume did in fact come in as the direct result of Desnoyers'
appeal through the press; certainly in at least two cases—those of
Victor Hugo and Baudelaire—personal invitations must have
been issued, as may readily be seen from internal evidence. Thus
Hugo's *A Albert Durer* is introduced in these terms:

> Un de nos amis, M. A. Busquet, avait demandé à M. Victor Hugo
> quelques vers ou quelques lignes pour ce volume. Voici la réponse du
> grand poëte...   (*Hommage*, p. 49)

(after which there follows the letter from Hugo to which I refer
again below); whilst Baudelaire, for his part, launches his famous
epistle to Desnoyers with the specific words 'Vous *me* demandez
[rather than 'Vous *nous* demandez'] des vers pour votre petit
volume(...) n'est-ce pas?' A personal approach of a still more in-
formal kind is likely to have been made to Luchet's and Desnoyers' colleagues of the so-called 'Bohème chantante' group—an
assertively bibulous but otherwise unremarkable literary faction,
who after contributing to the *Chants et Chansons de la Bohème* of
1853, were to collaborate briefly in the short-lived journal *Jean
Raisin*, as well as in an 'Almanach' of the same name and another
bearing the cognate title *Jean Guêtré*.[16a] Within the pages of the
Denecourt volume, we re-encounter almost all the members of
this group: Gustave Mathieu (by common consent its 'chef de
file'), Charles Vincent, Antonio Watripon, Édouard Plouvier,
Alfred Busquet, Philibert Audebrand, Pierre Dupont, as well as
Luchet and Desnoyers themselves.

It might at least seem, however, from the impressive picture
conjured up by Audebrand in his concluding chapter—some
forty pens, as the rallying-cry goes out, drawn spontaneously
from their 'scabbards'—that all the items published had indeed
been composed expressly for the occasion:

> ... c'est [au nom de Denecourt] que quarante plumes sont spontané-
> ment sorties du fourreau; c'est pour constater son union intime avec
> Fontainebleau et la forêt que ces écrivains, illustres pour la plupart,
> n'ont pas craint d'interrompre un jour, celui-là son drame inachevé,

cet autre son histoire ébauchée, un troisième sa strophe brillante, cet autre son roman commencé, tous la réalisation de leur rêve et l'enfantement de leur pensée.   (*Hommage*, p. 358)

The same legend recurs—in somewhat less romantic form—in several subsequent references to the volume;[17] the reality, however, was somewhat different—as may be confirmed readily enough, once again, from the internal evidence of the contributions themselves. Clearly Desnoyers and his colleagues wished to include several 'great names' within the volume, both in order to 'boost' its sales and to enhance the homage it embodied. At this point, I must mention a further naïve yet touching aspect of Denecourt's character. It was his habit to name the most cherished beauty-spots of his domain not only after national heroes, but also after artists and writers he particularly admired or wished to please. Thus on a certain venerable oak-tree is conferred the title 'le Turenne'; another and younger tree carries the inscription 'Lazare Hoche'; a cave honours Alexandre Dumas, a path Delacroix, a clump of shrubs Balzac, yet further trees Janin, Méry, Gautier, Houssaye, Diaz, Courbet; the great Hugo is not forgotten, no more than is the Parmentier who (according to Audebrand) 'invented' the potato; there is even (as Audebrand does not fail to tell us) a rock baptised 'Audebrand'...[18] It must have seemed only fitting that certain of these great figures should in return pay *their* tribute to Denecourt, and in fact, as I indicated at the beginning of this article, contributions from Lamartine, Hugo, George Sand, Musset, Béranger, Gautier and Janin, do indeed figure within the homage volume. But alas! of these only the Gautier essay answers truly to the occasion, in the sense that it alone was *newly* written with Denecourt specifically in mind. In the other cases, the authors in question merely sent—or were asked permission to reproduce—items already published elsewhere, or written clearly at some earlier date and for some other purpose. Thus the penultimate text, 'Les Adieux de Fontainebleau', is an excerpt from the opening volume of Lamartine's *Histoire de la Restauration*;[19] Janin's appeal for the conservation of the Bas-Bréau sector of the forest, was originally made in 1850 on behalf of the Barbizon artists;[20] Musset's poem *Souvenir* (with its oblique evocation of the forest as George Sand and he had known it, in that fateful week of August 1833) is reprinted from the *Poésies nouvelles* of 1850;[21] from George Sand herself comes—not indeed the more

circumstantial account of the same episode, that she was to
publish in the fifth chapter of *Elle et Lui*...—but a 'fragment'
from a letter written almost exactly four years later, during a
further stay in Fontainebleau, this time with her son Maurice.[22]
The letter from Béranger (reproduced at the very end of the
book) is at least addressed directly to Denecourt; but it was
written originally, in March or May 1854, as an acknowledge-
ment of two of the latter's *Guides* received through their mutual
friend Champfleury;[23] as for Hugo, he explains in a further letter,
addressed to Alfred Busquet, that he is unfortunately too busy to
write anything specifically for the volume, but goes on to accord
its editors permission to print (which is to say, to reprint) any
poem they may like to choose from any of his previous collections—while effectively predetermining this choice by himself
suggesting *A Albert Durer*...[24]

Desnoyers and his collaborators may well, of course, have
solicited contributions from yet other famous writers of the day; in
the event, however, although the volume was to include the
names of several writers of some independent standing and repute
(Auguste Vacquerie, Hippolyte Castille, the Breton poet Auguste
Brizeux, Méry of the Barthélémy-and-Méry 'team'), its contributors are for the most part members of what may loosely be
called the 'Bohemian-Realist circle'—taking this in its widest
extension as embracing not only Mathieu's 'Bohème chantante'
group, but also such continuing or former associates as Murger,
Champfleury, Banville, Houssaye, Baudelaire's close friend
Asselineau, and Baudelaire himself (who only the previous year,
it should be noted, had published his poem *Le Vin des chiffonniers* in
Mathieu's journal *Jean Raisin*).[25] One gathers, from certain
references made (as we shall see) within Baudelaire's letter to
Desnoyers, that initial guidance of some kind was offered to contributors in respect of subject-matter; presumably it was suggested
that articles or poems should either pay direct tribute to Denecourt, or should in some way relate to Fontainebleau and its
forest—with due licence accorded to poets to include Nature-
verses of a more general type. Certainly the majority of the items
within the volume fall more or less within such presumed pre-
scriptions. Thus we have first of all, among the more explicitly
appropriate contributions, the various 'portraits' of Denecourt
sketched by Luchet, Audebrand, Busquet and Gautier (respectively, 'Pour qui ce livre est fait', 'Le dernier chapitre', 'L'amant de

la forêt', 'Sylvain'), as also an ode in English by one Clara de Chatelain,[26] so splendidly cliché-ridden that I cannot forbear from quoting it *in extenso*:

TO THE HERMIT OF THE FOREST

Oh Fontainebleau! 'tis sweet to roam
Amidst thy dim, thy hallowed shades—
When 'neath thy forest's verdant dome
The parting daylight gently fades.

Each tree, like some historic page,
Enfolds a world of bygone lore,
The legends of a former age
Inscribed upon its branches hoar.

Yet thro' the forest vast and lone
In silent grandeur nature slept,
And o'er its rocks with moss o'ergrown,
Time's footsteps stealthily had crept.

Each floweret reared its tiny head,
Unseen to bloom and lose its hue—
The moss its fairy goblets spread,
And none but fairies quaffed their dew.

Thus solitary still it lay,
A sealed volume read by few—
For who would venture forth to stray
Within its depths, without a clue?

Thine, Denecourt, was the chosen hand
By whom each winding maze was traced,
As Moses to the promised land
Led forth the Hebrews thro' the waste.

Thine was the task to call to life,
The memories shrouded in the past—
By thee each rock, each dell is rife
With tale or legend duly class'd.

In thee all nature's worshippers
A new Columbus grateful own,
Whose heart no love of lucre stirs,
Who toils for honest fame alone.

Hail then, good Hermit, hail to thee!
By blood thy conquests are not bought—
Long may the hatchet spare each tree
With history's living archives fraught.

'Twas God who reared this leafy world
On which we feast our ravished look:—
But Denecourt has each myth unfurled,
And taught us how to read its book.   (*Hommage*, pp. 63–5)

Hail then, good poetess, hail to thee! Perhaps it is something that the editors' hatchet should have spared *thy* poem... As to the contributions relating more generally to Fontainebleau (rather than specifically to its 'hermit'), these include, firstly, descriptions of the forest or meditations arising from it (the letter by George Sand aforementioned; Murger's 'La Mare aux fées', reprinted from his *Scènes de campagne*: *Adeline Protat* of the previous year; G. de la Landelle's 'Le Val fleuri'; Desnoyers' poem *Ébauche de la forêt*); next, sketches of various Fontainebleau 'characters' (among them the two very different types of 'hunter' described respectively by Louis Lurine and Charles Vincent: 'Le chasseur d'ombres', i.e. the ghost-hunter; 'Le chasseur de vipères'); finally—the most numerous group—various 'reconstructions' of episodes from Fontainebleau's past, the most original item here being perhaps Plouvier's 'dream of history', in which the task of evocation is assigned to the Palace *carp* ('Menus-propos des carpes de l'étang de Fontainebleau'). I have mentioned already Janin's appeal of 1850 for the conservation of Bas-Bréau; another and more surreptitious republication is a curious text by Théodore Pelloquet, censuring Chateaubriand for some youthful and inaccurate verses on the forest of Fontainebleau; this text I have found to have been extracted, with suitable additions, from a guide-book, *Fontainebleau et ses environs*, published by the same writer in 1850 under his other name Frédéric Bernard...[27] What makes this piece of literary duplicity the more ironic, is that Bernard, on almost the very next page of his guide-book, had chosen obliquely to criticize Denecourt's 'rival' publications in the same field, as being needlessly detailed and confusing for the tourist... One can only hope that Bernard-Pelloquet's ultimate participation in the Denecourt homage, implied some change of heart—some recognition, if not of the other's superior merit, at least of his greater services to Fontainebleau. To these numerous items one must add, finally, three diversely unclassifiable 'pieces' sent in respectively by Paul de Saint-Victor, Champfleury and George Bell; of these I shall have more to say when discussing, in my next section, Baudelaire's own more substantial but no less unorthodox contribution.

N

Audebrand, in the opening paragraph of his *envoi*, cheerfully acknowledges the wide variousness of the book's composition:

> Ce livre fraternel est terminé (…) Chacun y a pris la parole à son tour. Il y a eu dix pages au service des formes les plus diverses de la pensée. Ainsi le lecteur y rencontre les uns après les autres l'historien, le poëte, le touriste, le conteur, le statisticien et l'humoriste; il y découvre même le critique, qui, pour cette fois, s'est fait chroniqueur. Jamais œuvre collective n'aura vu se fondre en elle tant de disparates.
>
> (*Hommage*, p. 357)

It should not however be assumed that the book in its final presentation lacks pattern of any kind; on the contrary, its editors have clearly done their best to fashion into a logical sequence the admittedly heterogeneous material they have gathered in. (Audbrand's own and confessedly 'well-worn' analogy, is of a 'Greek mosaic'.) The sub-title of the volume: 'Paysages—Légendes—Souvenirs—Fantaisies', indicates one possible classification; the grouping actually followed, however, seems rather to have been by *genre*. Thus all the *poems* are collected at the beginning, and it is presumably no accident that within this sequence Desnoyers' *Ébauche de la forêt*, with its general conspectus both descriptive and historical, is placed first, and that of the four final poems, three relate to the end of day and the coming of night (Monselet's *Soleil couchant*, Baudelaire's *Les deux crépuscules*—admittedly the twilight in the latter case is urban rather than pastoral). Of the remaining poems, a considerable number, it is amusing to note, conform more or less exactly to the type disparaged by Baudelaire in his letter to Desnoyers: 'des vers sur la *Nature*, n'est-ce pas? sur les bois, les grands chênes, la verdure, les insectes,—le soleil, sans doute?'. Thus we have, in addition to the Desnoyers and Monselet texts above-mentioned, Brizeux' *Le chant du chêne*, Nerval's *Les papillons*, Viard's *La forêt et la mer*, and Charles Vincent's *Les Fils du soleil* (interpolated within his article 'Le Chasseur de vipères'). The pattern is varied, however, by the inclusion of the two elegiac pieces by Banville (*A la forêt de Fontainebleau*) and Musset (*Souvenir*)—in both of which sentimental memories and meditations are intertwined with recollections of the natural scene—and these are followed, at a distinctly lower level of reminiscence, by two insipid sonnets of the Comte de Gramont's; thereafter, Hugo's *A Albert Durer*, Vacquerie's singularly unbucolic love poem *L'heure du berger*, Dupont's 'chanson' *La Vierge aux oiseaux*, Clara de Chatelain's ode, Houssaye's portentously symbolic *Visions dans la forêt* (subtitle: 'dédié à Platon'!), Mathieu's *Prologue d'une satire intitulée*: *le Bâton de houx*, and, finally, Baudelaire's two *Crépuscules*, complete what will be seen to be a highly uneven poetic sequence.[28]

The remaining two groupings-by-genre can be more briefly indicated: first, what might be called 'landscapes' and 'landscapes with figures' (the latter including the sketches of Fontainebleau 'characters' mentioned above, together with an account by Amédée Rolland of that first of the 'indigenous' painters of Fontainebleau, the neglected Lantara); and second, the historical 'reconstructions' aforenoted, here arranged, it would seem, in *reverse* chronological order.[29] The penultimate text, Lamartine's 'Les Adieux de Fontainebleau', would no doubt have found its earlier place within this latter, 'historical' group, had it not been for its temptingly valedictory theme; altogether more fittingly placed among the concluding items, is Gautier's 'Sylvain'—to my mind the most attractive and appropriate contribution of all. Gautier begins by recalling Heine's playful account of the unlikely and prosaic occupations to which the Gods of Olympus have been reduced in their post-Christian 'exile'. One figure, however, he explains, has been omitted from Heine's latter-day 'twilight of the gods'; this gap he can now happily fill, by revealing that the god Sylvan survives under the name (naturally!) of Denecourt, and as such presides with the utmost benignity over the forest of Fontainebleau—despite all that the local inhabitants may believe, or affect to believe, to the contrary:

> Si vous interrogez les habitants de Fontainebleau, ils vous répondront que Denecourt est un bourgeois un peu singulier qui aime à se promener dans la forêt. Et, en effet, il n'a pas l'air d'être autre chose; mais examinez-le de plus près, et vous verrez se dessiner sous la vulgaire face de l'homme la physionomie du dieu sylvestre: son paletot est couleur bois, son pantalon noisette; ses mains, hâlées par l'air, font saillir des muscles semblables à des nervures de chêne; ses cheveux mêlés ressemblent à des broussailles; son teint a des nuances verdâtres, et ses joues sont veinées de fibrilles rouges comme les feuilles aux approches de l'automne; ses pieds mordent le sol comme des racines, et il semble que ses doigts se divisent en branches; son chapeau se découpe en couronne de feuillage, et le côté végétal apparaît bien vite à l'œil attentif. *(Hommage*, pp. 347–8)

Thus under the homely 'bourgeois' disguise the lineaments of the sylvan god can on careful inspection be discerned; and it is of course through *his* godlike (yet discreet) intervention that all paths are made easy within the forest—whether to the hunted deer, or to the Barbizon artist who when confronted by a seemingly impenetrable barrier of foliage or rock, suddenly sees revealed before him the path that has been swept clear by an unseen (and godlike) hand. This same hand it is, again, that has scattered at every confusing crossroad, as if from Diana's own quiver, those little arrows that reassuringly point the direction the traveller must take; as for the occasional rustlings among the leaves, that accompany him on his journey, these he must on no account mistake for the scurryings of a rabbit or bird.... Gautier's final extravagance might almost be thought impertinent, were it not presented with such affectionate and disarming candour. Denecourt's wife (that is to say, the legal spouse that in his human form the god is obliged to take), suspicious at his long absences within the forest but having failed to surprise him in any embrace more scandalous than that lavished upon the rugged trunk of an oak, has duly reassured herself as to his fidelity; for who after all could be jealous of a mere tree? Little, however, does she understand the *true* significance of such embraces:

> Elle ne savait pas, la bonne dame, que sous la rude écorce palpite, aux approches du dieu, le tendre sein de la jeune et belle Hamadryade, qui n'a rien à refuser au maître de la forêt, et pour lui dépouille son épaisse tunique ligneuse frangée de mousse d'or. Et alors s'accomplissait le mystérieux hymen; le soleil brillait plus vif, la végétation redoublait d'activité et de fraîcheur, des bourgeons gonflés de sève éclataient sur les branches mortes, l'herbe poussait haute et drue, la source babillait sous le manteau vert du cresson, les oiseaux improvisaient de superbes chansons, et l'antique forêt reverdie et rajeunie tressaillait d'aise jusque dans ses plus intimes profondeurs.
>
> (*Hommage*, pp. 350–1)

This spirited caprice is not only by far the most effective of all the direct tributes paid to Denecourt and his work; it has also, no doubt, been among the most widely influential, for once incorporated, in 1874, within Gautier's collected *Portraits contemporains*,[30] it must have found many readers to whom otherwise even the name 'Denecourt' would have remained wholly unknown.

III. BAUDELAIRE'S CONTRIBUTION TO THE VOLUME

Baudelaire's association with Mathieu's 'Bohème chantante' group goes back, as far as its individual members are concerned, considerably farther than 1853—the year in which (for personal

reasons) he had declined the invitation to contribute to the
Chants et chansons de la Bohème.[31] Thus Dupont, for instance, was
one of Baudelaire's oldest friends; Busquet, Plouvier and Audebrand he had known from his *Corsaire-Satan* days, around 1845;
Desnoyers and Watripon (perhaps also Mathieu and Luchet),
since 1850 at least.[32] It is likely, therefore, that Baudelaire was
among the very first writers to be invited to collaborate in the
Denecourt *Hommage*; certainly one must suppose his (undated)
reply to Desnoyers to have been penned if not during the second
half of 1853, then at the latest during the early months of 1854—
rather than at the beginning of 1855, which is the date assigned to
it by Jacques Crépet in his edition of the *Correspondance générale*.[33]
Baudelaire's favourable—even generous—response, can no doubt
partly be explained in terms of personal friendships and loyalties,
but partly also by his natural eagerness to profit from this opportunity to secure further publication for his poems, at a time when
he still found such publication extremely difficult.[34] Certainly
there is nothing in the letter to suggest that Denecourt was
personally known to Baudelaire. It is true that the latter had in
the past paid several visits to Fontainebleau, where his half-
brother Claude-Alphonse (in this respect an exact contemporary
of Denecourt's!) had lived and worked since 1832;[35] moreover the
final sentence of the letter to Desnoyers, like the second sentence of
the prose poem *Le Crépuscule du soir*, might well be taken to refer to
some solitary excursion (or excursions) that Baudelaire had at
some time made to the forest:

> Dans le fond des bois, enfermé sous ces voûtes semblables à celles des
> sacristies et des cathédrales, je pense à nos étonnantes villes, et la
> prodigieuse musique qui roule sur les sommets me semble la traduc-
> tion des lamentations humaines.
>
> Dans les bois[36] comme dans les rues d'une grande ville, l'assom-
> brissement du jour et le pointillement des étoiles ou des lanternes
> éclairent mon esprit.   (*Hommage*, pp. 74, 78)

Yet surely if Baudelaire had in fact made the acquaintance of
Denecourt, he would not have failed to accord the good 'Sylvan'
some gesture of homage—even of ironic homage, as might befit
the inveterate *townsman* he plainly declares himself to be in his
letter to Desnoyers? As to the reasons why this letter should, in
addition to the four poems he had submitted, have been included
within the volume, one suspects that Desnoyers and his fellow
editors may have felt not only that the letter had great interest

and originality in itself, but also that it could serve conveniently to justify, to the recipient of the volume no less than to its readers, what otherwise might seem the extraneously *urban* nature of the first two of these four texts. It should be noted that in the volume itself as in the original manuscript, [36a] the letter to Desnoyers is linked with these two texts alone: thus under the general heading 'Les Deux Crépuscules' comes first the letter ('A Fernand Desnoyers'; signed 'C.B.'), then the poem *Le Soir* ('Voici venir le Soir, ami du criminel (...)'), then its companion *Le Matin* ('La diane chantait dans les cours des casernes (...)'); thereafter, the two prose poems *Le Crépuscule du soir* and *La Solitude* (sent at some later date, presumably) follow on quite separately, their texts being in effect continuous one with another, with the opening sentence of *La Solitude* referring back immediately to the 'friend' (one of two subject to 'crepuscular mania') mentioned in *Le Crépuscule du soir*. In the event, however, the distinctively 'urban' quality of the first two texts seems to have gone quite unnoticed by all except (fleetingly) Baudelaire's friend, Hippolyte Babou;[36b] the only other critic, A. Largent (reviewing the volume for *L'Artiste*[37]) who elects to make any comment whatsoever on Baudelaire's two poems, seems indeed scarcely to have read them at all, since he duly extends even to these bleak townscapes the insipid designations: 'légères sylphides', 'jardin de houris' [*sic*!], that he in fact applies, with perfect impartiality, to *all* the poetic 'Muses' gathered within the volume...

> Puis m'apparaissent tour à tour, comme ces riantes ou solennelles visions que M. Arsène Houssaye a si harmonieusement chantées dans ces mêmes pages, les Muses de Pierre Dupont, du comte de Grammont [*sic*] de Vacquerie, de Jules Viard, de Monselet, de C. Baudelaire... Je fuis à travers ces légères sylphides, je quitte à regret ce jardin de houris, et j'arrive aux prosateurs!

In considering Baudelaire's contribution to the *Fontainebleau* volume, I shall be concerned not so much with the texts themselves (which in their relation to the development of his Nature-philosophy, I have discussed fully in another publication),[38] as with two other questions of a more circumstantial nature: first, what were Baudelaire's reasons for sending in these particular texts, rather than others he had equally at his disposal; second, what was their significant relation to the various other contributions within the volume? In the former connexion, it must be said at once that certain of Baudelaire's assertions, in his letter to Desnoyers, are if not consciously mendacious, then at least highly disingenuous. He begins, it will be recalled, by deriding the whole genre of Nature-poetry and more especially the pantheistic cult associated with it:

> Mon cher Desnoyers, vous me demandez des vers pour votre petit volume, des vers sur la *Nature*, n'est-ce pas? sur les bois, les grands chênes, la verdure, les insectes,—le soleil, sans doute? Mais vous savez bien que je suis incapable de m'attendrir sur les végétaux, et que mon âme est rebelle à cette singulière Religion nouvelle, qui aura toujours, ce me semble, pour tout être *spirituel* je ne sais quoi de *shocking*. Je ne croirai jamais que l'*âme des Dieux habite dans les plantes*, et, quand même elle y habiterait, je m'en soucierais médiocrement, et considérerais la mienne comme d'un bien plus haut prix que celle des légumes sanctifiés. J'ai même toujours pensé qu'il y avait dans la *Nature*, florissante et rajeunie, quelque chose d'affligeant, de dur, de cruel,— un je ne sais quoi qui frise l'impudence.   (*Hommage*, p. 73)

Being thus 'prevented' from adhering to the 'strict programme' envisaged (as he chooses to assume) for the volume, he sends instead two 'urban' poems which he ingeniously justifies, as we have seen, by the suggestion that they were first conceived within the heart of the forest:

> Dans l'impossibilité de vous satisfaire complétement [sic] suivant les termes stricts du programme, je vous envoie deux morceaux poétiques, qui représentent à peu près la somme des rêveries dont je suis assailli aux heures crépusculaires.   (*Hommage*, pp. 73–4)

(Then follows the final sentence, as quoted on an earlier page.) Now the truth of the matter is that Baudelaire could very well have complied with any 'programme' requiring 'verses on Nature': he could, for instance, have sent in, from among the poems he was to publish two years later within the first edition of *Les Fleurs du Mal*, either *Le Soleil* ('des vers sur(...) le soleil, sans doute?'), or, better still, *Correspondances*—that sonnet which in its first quatrain speaks not only of the *temple* of Nature ('cette singulière Religion nouvelle'), but of its sentient pillars which in turn become the trees of a vast symbolic *forest* ('des vers sur la *Nature*(...) sur les bois, les grands chênes(...)'). Less immediately relevant to the Denecourt volume, but falling equally within the Nature-poem genre, would have been the sonnet *Tristesses de la lune*, with its tercets implying the poet's 'pious' worship of the moon, or, again, *J'aime le souvenir de ces époques nues*, with its opening section celebrating nostalgically the harmonious relationship with Nature once enjoyed by (primitive) Man.[39] Alternatively, Baudelaire could simply have contented himself with sending in the two prose poems; these, although not exactly 'verses on Nature', retain a certain relevance to the general theme of the volume, or at least are no more remote from this than are several other of the published contributions. Indeed the sentence quoted above from the opening paragraph of *Le Crépuscule du soir* ('Dans les bois *comme* dans les rues d'une grande ville, l'assombrissement du jour et le pointillement des étoiles ou des lanternes éclairent mon esprit'), might well have sufficed in itself to justify the inclusion of the two prose poems within the Denecourt *Hommage*, even without the still more appropriate concluding paragraph of *La Solitude*, with its reference to the delights of solitary contemplation of a sublime *landscape*:

> Quant à la jouissance,—les plus belles agapes fraternelles, les plus magnifiques réunions d'hommes électrisés par un plaisir commun n'en donneront jamais de comparable à celle qu'éprouve le Solitaire, qui, d'un coup d'œil, a embrassé et compris toute la sublimité d'un paysage. Ce coup d'œil lui a conquis une propriété individuelle inaliénable.
>
> *(Hommage*, p. 80)

What ulterior motives, then, may we suppose to have prompted Baudelaire's decision to contribute *additionally* the two 'urban' poems, and to accompany these with so strongly intransigent a letter of explanation? We ought first to allow, I suggest, for certain complexities or perversities of temperament: Baudelaire was always apt to react *contra-suggestibly* in situations in which a certain standard response was expected of him, and this tendency alone may have inhibited him from complying with what he calls 'the strict terms of the programme'. More important, perhaps, is the fact that this period of his life marks a decided reorientation of his aesthetic, moral and political ideas, one aspect of which was, precisely, a changed attitude towards Nature.[40] The invitation from Desnoyers may as it were have *provoked* him into clarifying and reformulating his views on this question—or rather, since the letter implies some degree of foreknowledge on Desnoyers' part ('(...) *vous savez bien* que je suis incapable de m'attendrir sur les végétaux', etc.), we may say that the invitation gave to Baudelaire a welcome opportunity of formally rationalizing his new attitude, and of assimilating to it his increasing consciousness of his role as a poet of Paris[41]—a consciousness here fostered by the contrasting 'bucolic' context of the volume as a whole. A further consideration determining Baudelaire's choice of poems for the Denecourt volume, may have been his desire to pave the way as effectively as possible for the impending publication of his long-deferred *Fleurs du Mal* volume; as with the eighteen poems printed, under that same title, in the *Revue des Deux Mondes* in the very month following the appearance of the Denecourt *Hommage*,[42] he is likely to have been seeking to 'illustrate' his poetic talent to the best possible advantage by publishing, at *this* juncture, only the very finest of his poems. Rightly, he deemed the two *Crépuscules* to fulfil these self-critical exigencies far better than would any of his more strictly appropriate 'verses on nature'. It is true that both poems had already previously appeared in print some three years earlier—but in a review (*La Semaine théâtrale*) so short-lived, and having so limited a circulation, that they could virtually be deemed unpublished; moreover he was now, in 1855, in a position to group with them two prose poems of analogous character.

In coming, finally, to the relationship between Baudelaire's texts and those of the other contributors to the volume, I must first mention that among these latter were to be found two other bold spirits, Champfleury and George Bell, who had likewise dared to diverge in some measure from what might be called the official 'line' on Fontainebleau—George Bell by brushing aside (after a perfunctory tribute to Denecourt) the beauties of the forest, and declaring his sole memory of Fontainebleau to be of a play, *Pauline*, that he once saw performed within the town theatre; Champfleury, by recounting, under a title ('Vision dans la forêt') deceptively similar to that chosen (as we have seen) by Houssaye, his prosaic tale of the bourgeois family and their cherished *pâté*, and by admitting himself to be one of those 'esprits satiriques' who are ill at ease before the spectacle of Nature, and on whose minds, as they strive to 'read' the Book of Nature, continually intrude reminders of Man and his absurdities.[42a] It will be seen from these two avowals that Baudelaire was by no means the sole disbeliever, among the Fontainebleau contributors, in what he terms the 'new' and shocking' Religion of Nature; indeed Champfleury's version of *anti*-pastoral, echoes significantly enough, at its more frivolous level, the 'humanist' sentiments of Baudelaire's letter to Desnoyers. A rather more subtle affinity with Baudelaire is displayed in the thoughtful essay by Hippolyte Castille, 'Sur la solitude', which follows, within a few pages, Baudelaire's prose poem on the same theme. Like Baudelaire (and in almost the same terms), Castille recognises the dangers or temptations (murder, rape, suicide) that may beset those who have failed to 'tame' what he calls 'le mauvais esprit de la solitude'; like Baudelaire, he affirms by contrast the salutary refreshment solitude may bring to others of stronger, more 'athletic' mind.[43] It is true that Castille has previously argued along rather different lines: for him, Man is essentially a social animal, and as such cannot long tolerate the solitude of Nature to which a primitive 'nostalgia' may at times recall him (whereas Baudelaire's conclusion is simply that the effects of solitude are entirely relative: 'elle est bonne et elle est mauvaise, criminelle et salutaire, incendiaire et calmante, selon qu'on en use, et selon qu'on a usé de la vie'.[44]) There is, however, within Castille's essay, one passage in particular that suggests what is perhaps an unexpected kinship of imagination between the two writers.[45] The forest, Castille observes, is the favoured refuge not only of poets, painters and lovers—but of suicides; and Castille's image of the hanged man, with its sudden disruption of the idyllic scene, calls immediately to mind that other 'sinistre pendu 'of Baudelaire's *Un Voyage a Cythère*:

> Mais, ô rimeurs, ô peintres, ô amants! m'expliquerez-vous, au détour du chemin, ce sinistre pendu, dont l'ombre s'allonge en travers de la route, et qui, lui aussi, est venu choisir l'aimable solitude des bois et le vert rameau d'un chêne pour cette triste cérémonie?
>
> (*Hommage*, p. 86)

Such a spectacle points for Castille the mortal 'bitterness' that solitude in Nature may at certain times assume:

> Elle se dresse comme une ironie en face de la société vivante et agissante. Elle lui envoie dans ses sauvages parfums comme un soupir de sa haine.   (*ibid.*)

This 'irony' on the part of Nature, this imagined 'hatred' towards Man, remind one not only of the famous concluding verses of Vigny's *La Maison du berger*, but also, more specifically, of Baudelaire's complaint, in the letter to Desnoyers (as also in a poem sent, a few years earlier, to Mme Sabatier: *A Celle qui est trop gaie*) against the signal 'impudence' or 'insolence' of Nature's springtime exuberance.[46]

One last text from the Denecourt volume should be cited, for its relevance to Baudelaire: this is the defence by Paul de Saint-Victor of the 'historical' school of landscape painting. It so happens that in October 1854 Baudelaire had written to Saint-Victor (whom he did not previously know), asking him to put in a good word, in his dramatic *feuilletons*, for the actor Philibert Rouvière.[47] It is probable that Saint-Victor's essay for the homage volume, was already fully written by this date; the fact remains that in taking to task the critics of the traditional 'paysage historique', he is striving to meet objections very similar to those formulated by Baudelaire in his *Salon de 1846*.[48] Baudelaire was not, of course, the sole opponent of this increasingly discredited genre; one wonders, nevertheless, in the light of their collaboration within the Denecourt volume, and of their subsequent cordial relations,[49] how far if at all Saint-Victor may have had in mind the polemical young author of the *Salon de 1846*.

The immediate motive underlying the publication of the homage volume, was to render to Denecourt much-needed financial aid for the continuation of his work, i.e. by making over to him all proceeds from the sale of a book which would thus in every sense be dedicated to him.[50] Viewed within this purely practical context, the *Hommage à C. F. Denecourt* must be deemed highly successful: within six months of publication, for instance, it had already earned its first reprint.[51] But over and above its topical utility, the volume has, as I have tried to show, a more enduring interest and value: not only does it bring together, in often suggestive juxtaposition, a number of texts of high quality and interest (Baudelaire's letter to Desnoyers, Castille's essay 'Sur la solitude', Champfleury's 'Vision dans la forêt', Gautier's 'Sylvain') which otherwise might never have come into being at all; it, further, serves to illuminate an important phase in Baudelaire's aesthetic and intellectual development, and at the same time to draw attention to an admirable yet neglected figure of nineteenth-century social history—the absurd, endearing, indefatigable and elusive 'Sylvan' of Fontainebleau.[52]

NOTES

[1] *Hommage à C. F. Denecourt. Fontainebleau. Paysages, légendes, souvenirs, fantaisies*, par Charles Asselineau, Philibert Audebrand, Théodore de Banville, Baudelaire, G. Bell, Béranger, Brizeux, Busquet, C. Caraguel, H. Castille, Champfleury, Mme de Chatelain, Fernand Desnoyers, Pierre Dupont, Th. Gautier, Benjamin Gastineau, comte de Gramont, A. Houssaye, G. Hubbard, Victor Hugo, Jules Janin, de la Landelle, Lamartine, Auguste Luchet, Louis Lurine, G. Mathieu, Méry, Charles

Monselet, Murger, A. de Musset, Gérard de Nerval, Pelloquet, Edouard Plouvier, A. Rolland, P. de Saint-Victor, Mme Adam-Salomon, George Sand, Tellier, Vacquerie, J. Viard, C. Vincent, Watripon. Paris, Hachette, 1855 (hereafter abbreviated: *Hommage*). All subsequent references to Baudelaire's prose works are, unless otherwise stated, to the edition by J. Crépet, for Conard, of the *Œuvres complètes*; individual vols. are abbreviated as follows: *FMC—Les Fleurs du Mal*, 1922; *CE—Curiosités esthétiques*, 1923; *AR—L'Art romantique*, 1925; *PPP—Petits Poèmes en Prose*, 1926; *OP—Œuvres posthumes* (with C. Pichois), 1939-52; *CG—Correspondance générale* (with C. Pichois), 1947-53. I must take this opportunity of expressing my most grateful thanks to my friend Dr J. H. B. Bennett, for his generous assistance, during the preparation of this article, in establishing or verifying numerous bibliographical references, etc.

² G. Vapereau, *Dictionnaire universel des contemporains*, 1858, p. 511; *Larousse universel du XXᵉ siècle*, T. 2², p. 766.

³ These and the ensuing particulars concerning Denecourt and his work I have collated from the following sources: 'Biographie et Profession de foi de l'Auteur', in the 16th edition of his own *Indicateurs-Denecourt* (*Le Palais et la forêt de Fontainebleau, guide historique et descriptif*), Fontainebleau, l'auteur, 1856; hereafter abbreviated: *Guide*, 1856), pp. 319-54; A. Luchet, 'Pour qui ce livre est fait', in *Hommage*, pp. 6-23; A. Joanne, *Fontainebleau*, 1867, pp. 138-45; H. Bonhomme, *Le Biographe*, I, 1873-4 [1875], 12, pp. 268-9; Roman d'Amat, *Dictionnaire de biographie française*, fasc. LVIII, 1964, cols. 1018-19 (hereafter abbreviated: *DBF*).

⁴ In the aforementioned 'Biographie' (*Guide*, 1856, p. 321), Denecourt announces the impending publication of his *Mémoires d'un Sous-Officier de la grande Armée* (cf. Vapereau, *op. cit.*, p. 512); but these two volumes seem never in fact to have appeared.

⁵ *Guide*, 1856, pp. 336, 346-7; I here combine (as did Luchet in his tribute to Denecourt, *Hommage*, p. 10) two passages relating respectively to the latter's 'discovery' of the forest, and his grateful 'return' to it after the events of 1848. This essay of Denecourt's being also a 'Profession de foi', includes a full account (and vigorous defence) of his political and religious beliefs: an obstinate faith in human progress, together with a vibrant deism.

⁶ The Bibliothèque Nationale catalogue records no less than 12 editions of the *Guide* or *Carte-Guide*, 18 editions of the *Indicateur de Fontainebleau*, to say nothing of a *Promenade dans la forêt de Fontainebleau* followed by a *Nouvelle Promenade*, etc., etc.

⁷ *Guide*, 1856, p. 352.

⁸ Cf. Musset, *La Confession d'un enfant du siècle*, Part IV, Chap. 3, and G. Sand, *Elle et Lui*, Chap. 5. Musset, in his (fictionalized) account, mentions the (pre-Denecourt) signboards which marked the roads through the forest (*Œuvres complètes en prose*, ed. M. Allem and Paul-Courant, Pléiade (1960), p. 209; cf. P. Domet, *Histoire de la forêt de Fontainebleau*, pp. 266-7). For the exact chronology of this whole much-recounted episode, see G. Sand, *Correspondance*, ed. G. Lubin, Garnier (1966), II, pp. 396-8.

⁹ *Hommage*, pp. 190-1.

[10] Luchet (*Hommage*, p. 23) cites certain complaints of an all too familiar type—such as may nowadays, for instance, be heard in Edinburgh at 'Festival time'...: 'On trouvait les habitués de ses promenades trop nombreux, funestes au bon marché des vivres, bruyants, chantants, mal élevés, trop tôt levés, trop tard couchés: un dérangement'. Cf. *Guide*, 1856, pp. 260–6, 292–3, 351; J. Levallois, *Mémoires d'une Forêt*, Paris (1875), pp. 111–14. Denecourt in his *Guide* mentions also the reproaches levelled at him from a rather different quarter. Certain Fontainebleau artists (no doubt of the Barbizon school) had declared that his newly-traced paths brought unwelcome visitors to disturb their labours, that the native wildness of the forest was thereby tamed or 'civilized'; to this, Denecourt retorted that on the contrary he had made accessible to artists vistas and aspects of the forest, of which otherwise they would have remained wholly unaware—a claim that other artists had, in fact, effectively endorsed by subscribing their aid to Denecourt, and by recording their gratitude to him in an inscription engraved in 1852 within the 'Chasseur noir' cave: 'A Denecourt, les artistes et les touristes reconnaissants'. See *Guide*, 1856, pp. 260–2, 272 n.2, 276–7, 294, 299–300, 315, and cf. Joanne, *op. cit.*, p. 143.

[11] See F. Herbet, *Auguste Luchet (1805–72)*, Fontainebleau, 1912, pp. 33–5, 52–3.

[12] Adam-Salomon's wife (whose statue, incidentally, the sculptor had already presented to the town of Fontainebleau; see *DBF*, vol. I, p. 497) had, as we shall see, been among the contributors to the 1855 homage volume.

[13] See *Le Biographe* (*art. cit.*), p. 269 and 'nota'; *DBF*, fasc. LVIII (*loc. cit.*); J. Aigoin, *Fontainebleau sous le Second Empire. Souvenirs*, Fontainebleau, 1934, p. 11. Cf., however, Champfleury's satire of 1859, *Les Amis de la Nature* (n. 52, below).

[14] *Guide*, 1856, p. 316. I have corrected to '1853' the date erroneously given as '1855' at the beginning of this passage (cf. the later phrase: 'En 1855, *deux ans après* ce philantropique et fraternel appel (...)') For an explanation of Denecourt's reference to Luchet's work on his behalf in 1850, cf. n. 16, below.

[15] Cf. *CG* I, pp. 341–6.

[16] From Busquet went out (as we shall see) the invitation to Victor Hugo, whilst to Audebrand was assigned the responsibility of eliciting a final chapter from Denecourt—or rather, as it turned out, of writing the chapter himself, Denecourt feeling such a task to be a needless diversion from his more important labours at Fontainebleau; see *Hommage*, pp. 357–9. For Luchet's role, see Herbet, *op. cit.*, p. 61, and cf. L. Badesco, 'Baudelaire et la revue *Jean Raisin*', *Revue des sciences humaines*, 1957, fasc. 85, p. 69; for the Ladvocat volume (*Paris ou le Livre des Cent un*, 1831–4, 15 vols.), and its analogy with the Denecourt *Hommage* of 1855, see Herbet, *op. cit.*, pp. 10–11, 61, and cf. *Guide*, 1856, pp. 282, 294. In 1850, Luchet had set a more immediate precedent by publishing a little booklet (*Promenade dans la forêt de Fontainebleau et itinéraire abrégé des appartements du Palais*, Fontainebleau, imprimerie de E. Jacquin) designed to assist, by its sales, Denecourt's work; see *Guide*, 1856, pp. 313–16, and Herbet, *op. cit.*, pp. 60–1.

[16a] See in this whole connection the highly interesting and informative *art. cit.* by L. Badesco, pp. 62 ff.

[17] Cf. *Guide*, 1856, pp. 281, 285, 294, 296–7, 310, 312; Vapereau, *op. cit.*, p. 512; Herbet, *op. cit.*, p. 61.

[18] Audebrand, *Hommage*, pp. 361–4; cf. Luchet, *ibid.*, p. 17.

[19] Lecou, 1851, I, 379–84 (Livre 9e, xxix–xxxii).

[20] Cf. *Hommage*, p. 96.

[21] For the poem's original publication (in 1841) and its biographical allusions, see Musset, *Poésies complètes*, ed. M. Allem, Paris, NRF–Pléiade (1962), pp. 810–12. The fact (unmentioned by Allem) that the poem was re-published in the Denecourt *Hommage* (whether at Musset's suggestion, or with his agreement), confirms conclusively—if confirmation were needed—that the forest he describes can only be that of Fontainebleau; cf. Allem, *loc cit.*

[22] Cf. *Hommage*, pp. 80–1; W. Karénine, *George Sand: sa vie et ses œuvres* (1899), II, pp. 431–2. It is intriguing to note that this 'fragment' by one of Baudelaire's *bêtes noires* among contemporary writers, follows immediately, upon the same page, his own prose poem *La Solitude...* The G. Sand text was subsequently reprinted both in *Les Sept cordes de la lyre*, Lévy, 1869, and in *Impressions et souvenirs*, Lévy (1873).

[23] *Hommage*, pp. 365–6, with dateline given as follows: 'Paris, 29 *mai* 1854'; cf. Béranger, *Correspondance*, ed. P. Boiteau, Garnier, IV, pp. 294–5 (identical text, save for curtailment of final flourish, but with date given initially as '29 *mars* 1854').

[24] *Hommage*, pp. 49–50. This letter, headed 'Marine-Terrace, 11 avril [1854]', figures neither in Vol. II (1849–66), nor in Vol. IV (s.v. Addenda), of the Imprimerie nationale ed. of Hugo's *Correspondance*; nor, again, is it mentioned by Cécile Daubray in her *Victor Hugo et ses correspondants*, Paris, Michel, 1947. Vol. II of the *Correspondance* does, however, reproduce (pp. 178–9) a letter to Busquet dated 29 October 1853, relating to a Balzac-commemoration project, and in later vols. there occur refs. to Busquet, arising from the Rhine visit on which he accompanied Hugo in 1864.

[25] See Badesco, *art. cit.*, pp. 55 ff.

[26] A prolific writer of children's tales, fairy stories, etc.; see the memoir by her husband, the Chevalier J. B. F. E. de Chatelain, *In Memoriam*, London, 1876. The ode to Denecourt had previously been published in 1854 in the *Indépendant de Seine-et-Marne*, together with a 'free translation' into French by the faithful Chevalier (see *Guide*, 1856, pp. 272–5); it re-appears in 1877 in the posthumous anthology, *Fleurs (poésies françaises) et fruits (poésies anglaises): souvenirs de feu Mme C. de Chatelain*, London, 1877. It is interesting to note that in 1863 this same Chevalier de Chatelain was to write to Baudelaire concerning the latter's Poe translations, to which he (Chatelain) had been introduced by a certain 'young friend' of his, one Stéphane Mallarmé ... —by whom he was, however, to be unkindly described, the following year, as a 'mauvais poète français habitant Londres'. See E. and J. Crépet, *Charles Baudelaire*, Vanier-Messein, 1906, pp. 342–3, and Mallarmé, *Correspondance 1862–1871*, vol. I, ed. H. Mondor and J. P. Richard, Paris, NRF–Gallimard (1959), p. 114 and n. 1.

²⁷ *Hommage*, pp. 282–9; cf. *Fontainebleau et ses environs*, pp. 94–5.
²⁸ I append further details concerning the more interesting of these verse texts. The Brizeux poem may be found in the 1910–12 ed. of his *Œuvres*, III, pp. 12–13 (under the general heading 'La Fleur d'or: histoires poétiques'); a note on p. 311 of the same vol. explains that *Le Chant du chêne* is a translation of a Breton *bardit*—already reprod. in the original, together with an alternative translation under the title *Le Chêne*, in Vol. I, pp. 150–3. Hugo's *A Albert Durer* dates from 1837 (*Les Voix intérieures*), Nerval's *Les Papillons* from 1830; this latter 'odelette' had in 1852 been collected into *Petits châteaux de Bohême*—see J. Senelier, *Gérard de Nerval. Essai de bibliographie*, 1959, pp. 78 and 155, who also notes the present reprint (p. 78, s.v. No. 84). The Dupont poem was included in 1854 in the *Chants et chansons*, III, pp. 89–91, together with the musical score (also by Dupont); a note (p. 176, n. 19) described it as having been inspired by a magnificent sunset, 'au moment de la chute des feuilles, par une des premières soirées froides de novembre'. Cf. D. Higgins, *French Studies*, III, 1949, pp. 135–6, who discerns in this poem's refrain, with its pleasing but not very original 'synæsthesia' ('On croit toujours ouïr ces phrases / Jaillir en gerbes de son chant, / Dans les roses et les topazes / Du soleil couchant'), an affinity with Baudelaire and an anticipation of the Symbolists. For Vincent's *Les Fils du soleil*, cf. Badesco, *art. cit.*, p. 83; for Musset's *Souvenir*, see also p. 182 and n. 21, above. Finally, I should perhaps add that Houssaye's poem, when published in his *Poésies complètes* (1851), had lacked the sub-title quoted above.
²⁹ With Asselineau's scholarly 'Fontainebleau avant François Iᵉʳ' (pp. 314–40) bringing up the rear.
³⁰ Charpentier, pp. 213–17, under the title 'Denecourt le Sylvain'; the art. had previously been reprinted in 1861 in *L'Almanach parisien*, and in 1865 in the 2nd edition of Gautier's *La Peau de tigre* (pp. 157–63). See Spoelberch de Lovenjoul, *Histoire des œuvres de Théophile Gautier*, II, p. 86, No. 1355.
³¹ See *CG* I, pp. 200–1 and n., 205 (letters to Vincent and Champfleury).
³² See Badesco, *art. cit.*, pp. 69, 73–4, 76–7; *Baudelaire devant ses contemporains*, textes recueillis et publiés par W. T. Bandy et Claude Pichois, Monaco, Editions du Rocher (1957), pp. 83, 86, 167 and n. 3. For Baudelaire and Dupont, see also A. Ferran, *L'Esthétique de Baudelaire*, Paris, Hachette, 1933, p. 42 (Vitu cit.) and *AR*, p. 503, and cf. Baudelaire's own reminiscences, *ibid.*, pp. 363–4.
³³ *CG* I, pp. 321–3. We have seen, from Denecourt's 'history' of the volume, that contributions were first invited in May or June 1853; but in any case, even if Baudelaire's letter and poems were not in fact among the earliest texts received, Crépet's date of early 1855 remains quite implausible. The volume, which was recorded in the *Journal de la Librairie* under the date June 2nd 1855, must presumably have gone to press considerably earlier in that same year; and however expeditious (or persuasive!) the editors may have been in gathering in the various contributions, we must assume that the receipt of Baudelaire's letter (to which, incidentally, he chose to make one revision before publication;

see *CG* I, p. 323 n. 1.) will have preceded this date by at least several months—which takes us back into 1854.
³⁴ Cf. the comment made in the course of some autobiographical notes drawn up, around 1861, for Duranty: 'Difficulté pendant très longtemps de me faire comprendre d'un directeur de journal quelconque' (*OP* II, p. 136; cf. *FMC*, pp. 303-4). Of the poems he *had* thus far succeeded in publishing, several had appeared in obscure, inappropriate or short-lived periodicals: *L'Écho des marchands de vin, Le Magasin des familles, La République du peuple, La Semaine théâtrale, Jean Raisin...*
³⁵ Baudelaire may well have visited his half-brother at the very beginning of 1855, shortly after the latter had suffered the loss of his only son; see *CG* I, 320-1. But by that time, as I have indicated, the letter to Desnoyers would already long have been written. Claude-Alphonse Baudelaire's bereavement is obliquely referred to, incidentally, in the Fontainebleau journal *L'Abeille's* review of the homage volume; enumerating the various poets who had made contributions, the critic (A. Chennevière) adds, after the mention of 'Ch. Baudelaire', the parenthesis 'un nom environné ici d'un respect douloureux' (*Guide*, 1856, p. 281). Ironically enough, therefore (in view of the somewhat strained relations obtaining between the poet and his half-brother), it is to Claude-Alphonse's 'local connections' that Baudelaire seemingly owes one of the *three sole contemporary mentions* accorded his contribution to the Denecourt volume... (He does not, however, rate as highly, on this scale, as Georgine Adam-Salomon, 'la jeune femme de l'habile sculpteur, notre concitoyen', to whose 'quelques pages d'un naturel exquis', *L'Abeille* (*ibid.*, p. 282) devotes several laudatory sentences ... For the other contemporary references to Baudelaire's contributions, see below.) Baudelaire had, of course, made a number of previous visits to his half-brother's at Fontainebleau; cf., e.g., *Lettres inédites aux siens*, ed. P. Auserve, Paris, Grasset, [1966], pp. 195-6, and *CG* I, pp. 11, 40. For Claude-Alphonse's relations with Baudelaire, and his career at Fontainebleau, see C. Pichois, 'Le demi-frère du poète des *Fleurs du Mal*. Claude-Alphonse Baudelaire, magistrat', *Le Pouvoir judiciaire*, XI, 108, Feb. 1956, pp. 4-5.
³⁶ In his next publication, in 1857, of this prose poem, Baudelaire perhaps significantly corrects this phrase ('Dans les bois') to 'Dans les *forêts*'; see *PPP*, p. 301 n. 1.
³⁶ᵃ This is reproduced in facsimile in *Baudelaire. Documents iconographiques* ed. C. Pichois and F. Ruchon, Geneva, Cailler (1960), Nos. 199 a,b,c. No corresponding MS. is known for the other two (prose) texts, but the 1855 proofs (including several corrections of Baudelaire's which were ignored by the printer but which he was able to incorporate two years later when republishing these texts in *Le Présent*) are preserved in the Bibliothèque littéraire Jacques Doucet; see Baudelaire, *Œuvres complètes*, ed. Y. G. Le Dantec and C. Pichois, Paris, NRF–Pléiade (1966), pp. 1606-8.
³⁶ᵇ *L'Athenaeum français*, IV no. 27, 7 July 1855, p. 563: 'Quant à M. Charles Baudelaire, il a donné deux pièces de vers, *le Soir et le Matin* [sic], qui ont, outre leur valeur poétique, le grand mérite de ne pas prononcer une seule fois le grand mot Nature'. For a further comment on this article of Babou's, see my forthcoming book, *Baudelaire and Nature*

(Manchester Univeristy Press), Part Two, Chap. I; cf. also J. S. Patty, 'Baudelaire et Hippolyte Babou', *Revue d'hist. litt.*, LXVII (April–June 1967), p. 265 n. 1.

[37] 5e série, XV, 11, 15 July 1855, pp. 151–2. This and other reviews of the Denecourt *Hommage* are quoted, *in extenso*, in *Guide*, 1856, pp. 278–312.

[38] In my book aforementioned, *loc. cit.*

[39] Of these various poems, *Tristesses de la lune* is known to have been composed by 1850 at the latest, and the other three are generally assumed to have been written well before that date; see *Les Fleurs du Mal*, ed. J. Crépet and G. Blin, Corti, 1950, pp. 227, 298, 300, 444, and cf. my article, 'Pour une étude chronologique des *Fleurs du Mal*', *Revue d'hist. litt.*, LXVII (April–June 1967), pp. 343–6.

[40] See my book aforementioned, *loc. cit.*

[41] Cf. his comment (in a letter to his mother, dated March 1852) on the four texts (including *Les deux crépuscules*) recently published in *La Semaine théâtrale:* '(...) ils sont très *spécialement parisiens*, et je doute qu'ils puissent être compris hors *des milieux* pour lesquels et sur lesquels ils ont été écrits' (*CG* I, 160).

[42] *Revue des Deux Mondes*, XXVe année, 2de série, X, 1 June 1855, pp. 1079–93.

[42a] For these deviations Champfleury was to earn on the one hand (with George Bell) the tentative reproaches of Largent, on the other (with Baudelaire) the firm approval of Babou; see the reviews, aforementioned, by these two critics. For Champfleury's later attitude, cf. n. 52, below.

[43] *Hommage*, p. 88; cf. Baudelaire, *La Solitude*: 'Il est vrai que l'esprit de meurtre et de lubricité s'enflamme merveilleusement dans les solitudes; le démon fréquente les lieux arides. Mais cette séduisante solitude n'est dangereuse que pour ces âmes oisives et divagantes qui ne sont pas gouvernées par une importante pensée active' (*ibid.*, p. 79).

[44] *Ibid.*, p. 80.

[45] Unexpected, in view of Baudelaire's patronizing dismissal of Castille on two previous literary occasions, in Oct. 1846 and Nov. 1851; the context in both cases was a polemic engaged between Castille and Balzac. See *OP* I, pp. 127–8 and 503; *AR*, pp. 284–5 and 531.

[46] *Hommage*, p. 73; *A Celle qui est trop gaie*, L. 17–24. In the next paragraph of his essay (*Hommage*, p. 87) Castille quotes, from his own *Histoire de la seconde République française* (1854–5), a passage which in its imagery and theme curiously recalls Baudelaire's sonnet *La Vie antérieure*: '(...) quand, sur la plage, *nos yeux se perdent parmi les profonds horizons des mers*, un soupir s'échappe de notre poitrine; on dirait que *nous nous souvenons d'une condition antérieure*, dont les sensations n'ont plus en nous qu'un écho affaibli; nous voudrions prolonger cette vague réminiscence du premier homme, perpétuée dans toute l'humanité(...)' (my italics). For Baudelaire's relations with Castille, see A. Ferran, *op. cit.*, pp. 108, 178, 528, 563, and cf. *Baudelaire devant ses contemporains* (*op. cit.*), p. 7.

[47] *CG* I, pp. 296–8 and n. 4; cf. *ibid.*, pp. 301–2, 304–7 and n. 1.

[48] Cf. Paul de Saint-Victor, 'Du paysage historique', *Hommage*, pp. 118–21; Baudelaire, 'Du paysage', *Salon de 1846*, *CE*, pp. 176–9.

[49] Cf. *CG* VI, pp. 14–15; III, pp. 116, 117, 240; *AR* p. 19; *CG* VI, p. 94. But cf. *ibid.*, III, p. 311 and n. 2–3.

[50] See Herbet, *op. cit.*, p. 61.

[51] See *Guide*, 1856, p. 311, and cf. *ibid.*, p. 302.

[52] Cf. A. Billy, *Fontainebleau délices des poètes. De la Renaissance à nos jours*, Paris, Horizons de France, p. 116: 'L'œuvre de Denecourt a vaincu l'ironie des hommes et celle du sort. Ella a duré et ainsi mérité de durer encore.' This book by M. Billy, which came to my notice only when the present article had reached proof stage, devotes a few brief pages (108–112; mostly quotation and enumeration of titles) to the homage volume, but these are followed (pp. 112–115) by a highly interesting account of the controversy surrounding the publication, in 1859, of Champfleury's satirical novel, *Les Amis de la nature*, in part directed against Denecourt; cf. also, in this connexion, my book aforementioned, *loc. cit.*

W. H. Lyons

NARRATIVE AND THE DRAMA IN MEDIEVAL FRANCE

Genre boundaries in early French literature are notoriously fluid. The student, introduced to what he is told is lyric poetry, finds himself confronted, in the *chansons de toile*, by an almost purely narrative presentation of events in the lives of personages who might well spend the rest of their fictional existence in the straggling *laisses* of a *chanson de geste*, while, in the *pastourelles*, he is faced with a frequently lengthy narrative introduction and conclusion to what is essentially a dramatic dialogue. But narrative itself is not always 'pure'. The *Chanson de Roland* is largely made up of dialogue and even the narrative, keyed predominantly in the present tense, continually threatens to erupt into dramatic form, or the narrative-dramatic recital is transfused, in the *laisses similaires*, with a solemn lyricism. Lyric features appear, also, in the religious drama (stanzaic form and the *complaintes* of the Virgin and other characters), but it is the presence of the so-called 'narrative lines', in indirect speech, that here seems most incongruous. These lines, of the same metrical form as those that make up the dialogue, but purely descriptive in content, constitute short narrative passages interrupting the dramatic intercourse in the *Resurrection* fragment,[1] the Autun *Passion*[2] and, to a lesser extent, the *Passion du Palatinus*.[3]

By its nature and origins, the religious drama and, more specifically, the drama of the Passion and Resurrection, is obviously bound to narrative, a sacred, scriptural narrative. It exists to represent a pre-existing and, at least in its outlines, a familiar *story*. It might, therefore, seem natural that it should retain some fragments of the shell from which it hatched. This is clear enough in the liturgical plays in Latin.[4] But even when its verbal form breaks free from its traditional mould, the Easter play's function is to set forth known events, not to enact experiences. In this sense, it is narrative rather than, or as well as, dramatic in character. The human explanation and motivation of these events is not its purpose. If the narrative *Chanson de Roland* takes on a dramatic quality, it is surely because it seeks to motivate and render credible human actions in human terms; since the early religious drama represents divinely ordained occurrences, the inevitability of which is not in question, it partakes of the nature of narrative.

Turning to the French drama, we find, in the *Mystère d'Adam*, a narrative element, provided by the choir chanting responsories that constitute the 'story' in its traditional form and ritual wording. In the majority of cases, this material is then given dramatic form in the ensuing vernacular dialogue. The historical order of evolution of the drama is thus respected. Occasionally, however, the order is reversed; the responsory comments on and gives retrospective justification to the dramatized version. Thus, in ll. 500–2, God, expelling Adam and Eve from Eden, pronounces sentence on them:

> Ne vus falt mais faim ne lasseté,
> Ne vus falt mais dolor ne paine
> A toz les jors de la semaine.[5]

Then follows the responsory *In sudore vultis tui*. The main point is that the sung narrative and the spoken dialogue embody the same material and echo, rather than complement, each other.

The 'narrative' passages in the *Resurrection* have quite a different relationship to the dialogue. Pilate orders his 'serganz' to see whether Jesus is yet dead:

> PILATUS
> Levez, serganz, hastivement;
> Alez tost la u celui pent,
> Saver mon s'il est devié.
>> Dunt s'en alerent dous des serganz,
>> Lances od sei en main portanz,
>> Si unt dit a Longin le ciu,
>> Que unt trouvé seant en un liu:
>
> UNUS MILITUM
> Longin, frere, vus tu guainner?[6]

Here the 'narrative' passage adds information not given in the dialogue, but which is conveyed by the action on the stage, between the two speeches. The only detail common to both dialogue and 'narrative' is the identity of the seated figure. What then is the function of these non-dramatic passages?

Monsieur W. Noomen's persuasive article, 'Passages narratifs dans les drames médiévaux français: essai d'interprétation',[7] seeks to answer this question by examining the evidence offered by all three of the early French Easter plays. It enumerates the hypotheses that have been offered in explanation of these passages.

1. They are stage-directions: 'les passages en question seraient donc uniquement destinés au "metteur en scène" et aux acteurs, et n'auraient pas été prononcés lors de la représentation publique'.[8]

2. They were recited during the performance 'dans le but d'éclairer les spectateurs sur ce qui se passait sur la scène'.[9]

3. They indicate that the 'play' was not acted but mimed by a single performer, 'qui, avec ou sans l'aide d'images, par sa gesticulation et sa diction, suggérerait la pluralité des personnages'.[10]

4. They were introduced into existing dramatic texts 'pour les adapter à la lecture'.[11]

M. Noomen's close examination of the texts themselves is intended to disprove the first, third and fourth of these hypotheses and to establish the second, with the implication that the lines in question were recited by a single reader.[12] An analysis of the so-called 'prologue' of the *Resurrection* (in reality a description of the staging of the play), characterized by the use of verbs in the present subjunctive, the future, or the infinitive preceded by *devoir*, shows that what the author is setting down is a set of preliminary stage-directions and, consequently, that he undoubtedly envisaged a dramatic performance. This 'prologue' is in all respects similar to the 'indications qu'on trouve en tête de plusieurs drames liturgiques latins; par exemple dans le célèbre manuscrit de Fleury (13e siècle), en tête de la *Conversio Beati Pauli Apostoli*'.[13]

The article then examines the 'narrative' lines in our play, which (a) do not rime with lines of the dialogue, although their language and versification 'sont sensiblement identiques à celle du dialogue';[14] (b) have their verbs 'toujours à un temps pouvant marquer une action passée (généralement le passé défini)';[15] (c) 'accompagnent le plus souvent une action qui se situe normalement entre les répliques du dialogue. Dans quelques rares cas ils indiquent simplement les personnages qui vont prendre la parole, ou ils donnent un renseignement sur la qualité ou sur les pensées d'un personnage (cf. p.e. vv. 131–2 du ms. P.)';[16] (d) in P. (C. has not been examined), are not distinguished graphically from the lines of dialogue.[17]

It is further noted (i) that the beginning of each speech and of each 'narrative' passage is marked by either a red initial or a reversed P in red at the beginning of the opening line, and (ii) that the names of the speakers, even when they are mentioned in the 'narrative' lines, are noted in the margin in black ink and also preceded by the reversed P. In these marginal indications of speakers the names, with the exception of Joseph, all appear in their Latin form. 'Tel qu'il nous est parvenu dans le manuscrit P.', concludes M. Noomen, 'le texte se présente donc comme un ensemble homogène, où chaque élément a sa fonction spécifique.'[18]

If the statement just quoted merely implies that the dramatic and non-dramatic passages in P. have not been fused in a unified narration, it is incontestable, but, before pursuing the question further, it may be desirable to make certain comments on individual points.

(a) The fact that the 'narrative' lines, riming together, do not rime ever with a line of dialogue need not have any particular significance or affect the argument for or against any of the four hypotheses. The text, in fact, exhibits throughout the 'earlier' treatment of the octosyllabic couplet, sense and rime coinciding,[19] a fact which would make such rimes less likely. But this 'compartmentalization' certainly does not strengthen the argument for considering the 'narrative' lines as part of the original. As to the linguistic similarity between these lines and the dialogue, the limited extent of the sample discourages too definite an affirmation of common authorship.[20]

(b) It is true that the verbs in the 'narrative' are always in a tense *capable* of indicating a past action, but this tense is, in some cases, the present. This occurs in ll. 123, 213 and 253[21] of P. and 138, 241, 251, 284, 287, 288, 311, 312, 345, 346, 347 and 358 of C. Some of these present forms are not associated with other verbs in a past tense (P. 253; C. 287, 288, 345, 346, 347, 348). The ambiguous *dit* occurs in ll. 122, 250, 254 and 278, and in C. in ll. 159, 288 and 312.

(c) The fact that these 'narrative' lines most often accompany ('describe' might be a more accurate term) an action taking place between the speeches is consistent with any of the four theories advanced, but perhaps gives less support to the '*lecteur* hypothesis' than to any other. A mere indication of who is to speak next would seem to favour the 'stage-direction hypothesis', while ll. 131–2 (Vers dan Joseph dunc se turna / Ne lui fu bel qu'i si parla) suggests either a stage direction or narrative adaptation.[22]

(*d*) The absence of any graphical distinction between the 'narrative' lines and those of the dialogue obviously gives no support to the argument against the third and fourth hypotheses. It might be thought to weigh against the 'stage-direction theory', were it not considered in conjunction with points (i) and (ii): in fact, each of these 'narrative' passages is marked off from the preceding and following speeches both positively, by the red reversed P, and negatively, by being accompanied by no indication of the speaker. As for the second hypothesis, if they were intended to be recited by a specific person, why is there no marginal LECTOR or CLERUS? C., not considered by M. Noomen, offers no help on this point. Here the beginning of the speech is usually marked by 'a two-line decorated capital, while the stage directions[23] are generally left with no such indication; the beginning of fifty-one speeches is, however, left unmarked in any way, and the stage directions on six occasions are begun with a decorated two-line capital letter'.[24]

It is difficult then, on the arguments advanced, to agree with M. Noomen when he says 'l'hypothèse des indications scéniques semble dès lors exclue'.[25]

> En effet [he continues], celui qui reconnaîtrait aux vers narratifs la même destination qu'aux noms de personnages, c'est-à-dire celle d'aider les acteurs à monter la pièce, devrait expliquer pourquoi une partie de ces indications sont en latin et se trouvent, dûment signalées par des moyens graphiques, dans la marge, tandis qu'une autre, partie, écrite en vers français, est incorporée au texte même de la pièce et marquée de la même façon que les répliques; en outre, il aurait à rendre plausible la circonstance que pour certaines répliques l'interlocuteur est nommé deux fois.

As to the first point, the difference in language, is it really legitimate to contrast what, for the most part, are proper names with whole passages? These names, surely, constitute a special case. They are traditional, conventional, in form, their meaning is clear in any language and they are more or less abbreviated.[26] They can be placed in the margin precisely because of their brevity. To treat whole passages of up to half a dozen lines in the same way would be difficult. The marking of these passages, like the speeches, with the reversed P can be interpreted as a mere indication that the preceding speech is not continuing. The marginal indication of the speaker, even when that information is given in the 'narrative' lines preceding his speech, need be no more than the mechanical observance of a useful convention.

M. Noomen goes on to argue against the possibility of an 'adaptation à la lecture', (a) because the passages in question probably belonged to the original (they occur in both manuscripts and do not apparently differ in language or versification from the dialogue); (b) because the 'prologue', with its instructions for staging, has not been suppressed; and (c) because the two lines (P. ll. 354–5) 'Est vus un prestre, qui out a non Levi, / Si out escrite la lei Moysi' (C., ll. 411–12, has 'Este vus un prestre ke out nun Levi, / Ke out escrit la lai Moysi') can, it seems, only be addressed to spectators.[27] The first of these points is debatable, as the evidence does not appear to preclude the possibility of an adaptation by the author himself or a contemporary. The existence of the 'prologue', on the other hand, constitutes, perhaps, the main objection to the 'adaptation' theory. The use of 'est vus' can, of course, be paralleled in purely narrative texts (e.g., *La Chanson de Roland*, ed. Ewert, l. 1187: 'Francs e paiens, as les vus ajustez'; l. 2009: 'Par tel amur as les vus desevred!').

If the arguments put forward in opposition to two of the four hypotheses advanced to account for the 'narrative' passages in the *Resurrection* seem inconclusive, those M. Noomen presents for rejecting the third suggestion, that of a mimed performance by a single actor, appear decisive.[28] The plural forms *recitom* and *appareillons* of the 'prologue'[29] would seem out of place in a dramatic monologue 'mais à la rigueur on pourrait les interpréter comme s'appliquant à une seule personne'. More significant is the enumeration of the different *lius* and *mansions* 'et notamment l'indication que Galilée soit faite "enmi la place" (ms. P., v. 22; ms. C. v. 32), ce qui implique l'existence d'une scène ayant trois dimensions'. Finally, there is the mention in the 'prologue' of characters who take no part in the dialogue (six or seven 'chivaliers' in P., the 'chevalerie' in C., the 'juerie' or 'li Jeu' accompanying Caiphas, etc.).

The remaining hypothesis, that the non-dramatic lines were recited by a *lecteur*, is favoured by M. Noomen and, as he observes, was first advanced by Marius Sepet, in different places and rather general terms. Perhaps more significant than the passage referred to by M. Noomen is the following extract from *Les origines catholiques du théâtre moderne*,[30] p. 58:

> La première transformation que l'on dut naturellement opérer dans le récit déclamé ou chanté pendant la semaine sainte, pour en faire un drame proprement dit, ce fut de dégager le dialogue de cette partie narrative qui l'enveloppait et qui était confiée à la voix du lecteur ecclésiastique (*Clerus*). Il ne faut pas croire pourtant qu'elle disparut complètement, surtout dans les premiers drames. On la conserva en la confiant soit à un lecteur unique, soit à un chœur, auxquels on conserva même parfois le nom liturgique de *Clerus*. Les paroles placées dans la bouche de ce personnage furent utilisées comme transition d'une scène à l'autre, comme résumé d'un tableau, comme explication de la pantomime des acteurs.

The author goes on to refer to the scene of the Raising of Lazarus in the Benediktbeuern play, part of which he has already given in translation.[31] This translation reads, in part, as follows:

CLERUS (c'est à dire LE LECTEUR ou LE CHŒUR)
La Seigneur, voyant les sœurs de Lazare pleurer près de son tombeau, se mit aussi à verser des larmes, puis il cria:
JESUS
Lazare, sors du sépulcre.
CLERUS
Et Lazare se dressa, les pieds et les mains liés, comme sont les morts.[32]

It will be observed that Sepet does not translate the verb CANTET that follows CLERUS in each case. The apparent relevance of this text, and of Sepet's remarks quoted above, to the argument about the 'narrative' passages in the *Resurrection* is perhaps lessened when we reflect that what we have in the Latin presentation is a choral rendering of Holy Writ, no part of which can decently be omitted. One may wonder whether Sepet's translation of *clerus* by *lecteur* has not had some influence on the fortunes of the *lecteur* hypothesis. Sepet's name is, of course, most often associated with his work on the Procession of the Prophets[33] and it is in this connexion alone, according to M. Omer Jodogne,[34] that the term *lecteur* can be properly used.

> Ce *lector* [he writes],[35] a existé en effet dans la *Procession des prophètes* de Salerne; il est appelé *cantor* à Saint-Martial de Limoges et son rôle est tenu par des *vocatores* à Rouen, des *appellatores* à Laon, et ils existent probablement dans la troisième partie de notre *Jeu d'Adam*. Mais dans aucun autre drame liturgique que la *Procession des prophètes* ces lecteurs n'apparaissent. Les textes publiés en font foi. Et, dans cette

Processio prophetarum, les *vocatores* font partie du chœur. C'est une œuvre très peu dramatique d'ailleurs, en général une suite de textes scriptuaires, dits par les prophètes qu'il faut bien appeler pour les désigner au public. Nulle part ailleurs, à ma connaissance, un lecteur n'intervient dans un drame.

The writer of the article goes on to point out that a *lecteur*, if he had existed, would have spoken in the present tense. 'Il n'aurait pas employé des parfaits, des passés composés, voire des imparfaits et des plus-que-parfaits.'[36] The passages in the Benediktbeuern play are in the past tense precisely because they are 'de simples variantes des versets de l'Evangile (Jean, XI, 33, 44)'.[37]

For M. Jodogne, then, the so-called 'narrative passages' 'ne sont que des indications scéniques s'achevant en rubriques'.[38] The proof is provided by the fact that they almost always end in a 'verbe déclaratif', usually *dire*.

Je dois imaginer [he writes], que le dramaturge, avant l'exécution de la pièce, avait rédigé un texte, recopié ensuite en rôles d'acteurs. Luimême, ou un autre, plus tard, a mis au net ce texte, versifiant peutêtre, si elle ne l'était déjà, la didascalie initiale où il aurait laissé subsister les subjonctifs, impératifs et futurs; mais il a mis en vers les didascalies intérieures et il en a converti tous les verbes au passé. Ainsi a-t-il destiné son texte à la lecture.[39]

So, for the *Resurrection*, we seem to arrive at a rejection of two of the traditional hypotheses and a reconciliation of the two remaining ones.

It was in discussing the 'narrative' elements in another drama that F. Schumacher arrived, apparently, at the same conclusion: an originally dramatic composition had been transformed into a narrative by the remodelling of stage-directions.[40] The Autun *Passion* presents both resemblances to and striking contrasts with the *Resurrection*. Of the two versions, only B (the *Passion de Biard*) contains 'narrative' lines and its text shows other variations from that of the much shorter R (the *Passion de Roman*). Like the *Resurrection* fragment, the Autun *Passion* begins with a prologue. But here we can omit the inverted commas, for it is a true prologue, not a set of stage-directions, and its forty lines (in B) combine, in a sermonizing style, a *résumé* of the reasons for the incarnation, of the life, death and resurrection of Jesus and exhortations to the public to remain silent and profit by the performance. It concludes with a promise of 'vii ans de vray pardon' to whoever will maintain a becoming silence. The first eight lines read:

Ouyés, les bons, entendés moy,
Je vous commandes de par le roy,
De par Pilate le prevost,
Que vous ne disiés ung seul most,
Et ne veullés feres moleste,
Quar nous veullons monstret l'ystoyre
De la passion Jhesucrist,
Si comme nous trouvons en escripst.

In R we find a prologue substantially the same in content, though in place of *monstret l'ystoyre* in l. 6 it reads *fere la feste*, obviously the original reading.[41] The change from the first person singular to the plural in this and the following lines makes it almost certain that a dramatic performance by a number of actors was originally envisaged.

In the main body of the text itself the speeches are preceded by appropriate indications in prose. The 'play' begins with the despatch of Peter and John to seek accommodation:

Parle JHESUS a saint Perre et a saint Jeham.

Pierre et Jehan, or en venés,
Ligierement vous en alés,
A ung hoste que troverés
Et de per moy le salués
Et ly dictes qu'en sa mayson,
Moy et tous mes compaignon,
Qu'i nous veulles esbergier.
Je sçay qu'i l'octroyra volentier.
Alés il toust ligierement.
            Parle SAINT PERRE a Jhesucrist.

Syre vostre commandement
Et vostre volunter ferons
A chiere ly.
            Parle SAINT PERRE a l'oste.

Le roy des cieulx saul et begnie
L'oste et sa compaignie!   ll. 41–54

The rubrics, or stage-directions in prose, of course, furnish no information other than the identity of the speaker and of the person addressed. The verb (*parler* or *respondre*) is always in the present tense (it is omitted before l. 971). Before l. 126 the rubric is simply 'La complainte MAGDELENE' and before ll. 1189, 1314 and 1948 'La complainte NOSTRE DAME'. What happens (the movement from one *lieu* to another) between l. 52 and Peter's salutation of the host is unrecorded.

The first 'narrative' lines occur in the middle of the host's speech of welcome to Jesus:

Et tous ceulx qui tiendront ta voye
Arons de paradis la joye.
Et puis se tourna vers saint Pierre
Et ly dy: Amys debonnayre,
Faictes seoir toutes ses gent,
Quar je sera vostre servant.
Et puis va a a Jhesu dire:
Sire maistre, que tout conduicte   ll. 96–103

Unlike the 'narrative' lines in the *Resurrection*, these are completely incorporated with the rest of the text, without any distinguishing marks, often rime (imperfectly at times) with lines of the dialogue, and even overflow into these lines. Elsewhere one of them may have no rime and, in one place, they interrupt the rime between two lines of dialogue (ll. 361–4). In the passage corresponding to that quoted above, R simply omits lines 98–99 and l. 102 and the remaining part of the speech.

As the *cœna* at which, according to Saint John, the anointing of the feet took place, is here identified with the Last Supper, the next speaker is Mary Magdalene. Her monologue, introduced by the rubric 'La complainte MAGDELENE' begins at l. 126 in B and, after twenty-two lines, is interrupted by a further 'narrative' passage of five lines:

Incontinant par l'uyt entra,
De soubz la table se bouta.
Apres se mys a genoillon,
Et faisant son oroyson
En telle manieres, disam:
Doulx syre, qui formaste Adam   ll. 148–153

Once more, the corresponding speech in R, containing only 16 lines compared with B's 72, shows no trace of the five 'narrative' lines, nor does it include the 'lyrical' passage, the *complainte* itself (ll. 153–191).

It is clear that these 'narrative' lines would perform no useful function for an audience watching a staged production. Whatever information they contain would in any case be conveyed by the actors' movements. They may instruct the actors as to these movements but, in the first passage quoted (ll. 98–9), this information could be given more simply by a conventional rubric, interrupting the host's speech, as in R ('Or parle L'OSTE a seint Pierre' before l. 84, corresponding to l. 100 of B). It is difficult, in fact, to see what many of these lines, however their function is understood, add to the text, although the omission of others would now destroy the sense. These contain, in indirect speech, statements made by characters in the play, either in answer to a question asked in direct speech—

> Seigneurs, que vous en est advis?
> *Et tous d'une voye dire ensemble*
> *Qu'i le failloit en la croix pandre—*   ll. 429–431

or making a statement which is answered by the following speech:

> *Apres ung Jüïfz est venus*
> *Qui luy dit que l'avoit veü*
> *Avec le filz Marie*
> *Et qu'i estoit de sa compaignie*
> *Et Pierre piteusement luy dit:*
> Amy, je ne say que tu as dit.
> Saches, je ne le cognoys.
> *Apres la chambeliere de l'ostés*
> *A saint Pierre a raconter:*
> Je te cognoys a ta parole,
> Je te cognoist, tu es d'escole.
> *Et puis avec adjurement*
> *Regnia son maistre plainnement.*
> *Et puis de la se departir.*
> *Incontinan le cog chantir,*
> *Et des paroles se racordy*
> *Que son maistre luy avoit dy,*
> *Et s'en ala en une cavernes*
> *En grand doleur et grand larmes,*
> *Et soit griefment deconfortant,*
> *Et telles paroles disant:*
> Las, chetis, j'ay mal esploitier
> Quant mon seigneur j'ay regnïer.   ll. 494–516

In this part of the text, beginning at l. 441 and ending at l. 524, in which Peter and John follow the Jews and their prisoner, but finally abandon their master, 'narrative' lines occur in profusion, accounting for half the total (ll. 468, 471, 476–8, 484–7, 491–2, 493–8, 501–2, 505–14), whereas in the text as a whole they make up only one-ninth. Yet this is an episode lending itself naturally to dramatic rather than narrative treatment and requiring little commentary. The long 'narrative' passages from l. 1009 to 1023 and from 1033 to 1052, describing, respectively, the journey to Calvary and the raising of the cross are more understandable.

Their content is unsuited to dramatic treatment or visual representation yet irresistible for the didactic author.

At times, the 'narrative' seems to betray, if not an incomprehension of, at least an indifference to, the meaning of the dramatic content:

> *Adonc Judas sen point de comfort*
> *Avec ung las se mys a mort*
> *Et puis leurs dit a tous ensemble:*
> Bonnes gens, laissés vostre noyse,
> Quar il n'y a que baret et rayson.
> Je suis Judas et sen rayson
> Traÿson j'ay faictes trop grand
> Pour la somme d'ung petit argend.
> Bien le vous este aperceüz!
> Las, je me suis bien deceüz!
> Ce que j'ay fait me demeura:
> Ill y a trucherie et barat.
> Helas, desus tous les marchant
> J'en suis ung le plus meschant,
> Quar j'ay vanduz trante denier
> Mon seigneur qui estoit droicturier.
> Helas, que j'ay faicte grant offande!
> Pour quoy je me veul aler pandre,
> Quar panduz seray sen mantir,
> Et tart sera le repantir.   ll. 610–629

The nature and distribution of these individual lines and extended passages of description seem, then, to point to a clumsy rewriting and inflation of a dramatic text in order to make of it a didactic narration that appears to defy theatrical presentation. M. Noomen maintains, however, that the 'narrative' passages in the Autun *Passion* have 'sensiblement la même fonction que dans la *Résurrection*, sauf qu'elles sont ici, dans la plupart des cas, plus visiblement indispensables à la marche de l'action, et que les détails psychologiques et autres sont plus nombreux'.[42] He admits that, as the 'narrative' lines and prose identifications of speakers do not occur together, the former might be considered as stage-directions, but observes that this explanation is universally rejected, 'en effet, l'enchevêtrement des vers en question dans le dialogue exclut de penser à des indications scéniques'.[43] Yet, as we have seen, this is precisely what a number of these lines are (ll. 98–9, 696, 749, 760–1, 796–7, 806, etc.). The form of the prologue rules out the possibility of considering the text as a 'poème de jongleurs destiné à la récitation... c'est bien une seule personne qui débite le prologue, ce sont, en revanche, plusieurs acteurs qui "montrent l'ystoyre".[44] The suggestion that the work, in its present form, is an 'adaptation à la lecture d'une pièce primitivement dramatique' is considered untenable, again because of the prologue: 'pourquoi le remanieur, tout en introduisant 230 vers nouveaux, aurait-il laissé intact le prologue, avec son début:

Ouyés, les bons, entendés moy.' [45]

Moreover, one of the 'narrative' passages begins:

Or *escoutés* comme se complain
Le filz de Dieu en la croix estant
Et parle a tout le monde et dit   ll. 2057-9

Once more, it is argued, we are 'par élimination, réduits à l'hypothèse du lecteur'. 'Seule l'hypothèse du lecteur permet de lire sans préjugé le prologue et de rendre compte de tous les détails: elle seule aussi explique le mot *escoutés* dans le vers narratif 2057.'[46]

There is one obvious objection to this elegantly logical demonstration. In the case of the Autun *Passion* we know, as we do not know in the case of the *Resurrection*, that extensive rewriting, including the insertion of the lines under discussion, has taken place. This is accepted by the editor of the text[47] and her conclusions are not questioned by M. Noomen. The passages, in general, would not help an audience to follow a performance and, in those places where their presence is now essential to the exposition, it seems that they have replaced part of the original dialogue. What they do, in places, introduce is a hortatory, sermonizing note. Is it not thus, perhaps, that we should interpret l. 2057? Not every sermon, written or spoken, containing the phrase 'listen to the words of Christ on the cross' is accompanied by a dramatic performance. The *escoutés* of the *Passion* seems no more conclusive than the *est vus* of the *Resurrection*.

There remains the third drama of the passion and resurrection that contains a narrative component. The *Passion du Palatinus* is preserved in a single manuscript which contains neither title nor prologue and indicates the speakers in only thirteen instances, although the copyist seems to have set out with the intention of marking the beginning of each speech with a large initial in red.[48] Of the 1996 lines in the printed text, six are 'narrative' in form: lines 395, 396, 402, 513, 1004 and 1005. They appear as follows:

1.

MARQUES

Pour le grant Dieu, fai dont errant!
Et si alons par tout querant
Que il n'ait coutiau ne gaïne.
(Et si le fiert tout maintenant   395
La paume sus l'oreille li tant.)   396
Qui t'a feru? Or le devine!
Encuse le apertement,
Ou il ira ja autrement.
Puis que tu ne veus deviner,
Il te covient au roy parler.
(Parole n'a parolé.)   402

2.

UNS JUIS

Et tu qui es, se Diex t'aït,
Es tu des deciples Jhesucrit?
(Et lors saint Pierre respondi:)   513

SAINT PIERRE

Gentil sire, par foy, nenil!
Onques ne le vi ne il moy,
Foy que je doy, sire, vo loy.

3.

SAINT JEHAN

Douz pere, je ferai ton plesir,
Grant duel ai quant te voi morir.
(Et li douz gracieus dit   1004
Qu'il avoit suef a son ami:)   1005

JHESU

SITIO

For the sake of completeness, one might perhaps add:

4.

JHESU

Hely, Hely, lama zabatani?   1018
(Hoc est: Deus meus, quare me dereliquisti?)[49]

ANNAS

Caÿfas, n'as tu donc oÿ
Comment il a huchié Hely?

This text seems to shed little light on our problem and to offer little scope for speculation. The editor is concise in her comment on the source of the 'narrative' lines and the nature of the work:

Elle présente, il est vrai, des vers narratifs et, comme elle s'est évidemment inspirée de la *Passion des Jongleurs*, qui est un poème narratif, on peut être tenté de lui attribuer le même caractère, mais: 1° précisément aucun des vers narratifs de la *Passion du Palatinus* ne provient de la *Passion des Jongleurs*, et 2⁰ de ces vers narratifs (395–6, 402, 513, 1004–5), le vers 513 seul rime avec un vers dramatique, le vers 402 est sans rime et trop court, les vers 395–6 se trouvent entre deux vers rimés du dialogue et les vers 1004–5 forment un couplet estropié; la conclusion s'impose alors que ces vers narratifs sont adventices et que nous avons affaire à une œuvre vraiment dramatique.[50]

Elsewhere she is even briefer, but more explicit as to the function of these lines: 'A few narrative lines have made their way into the play, but these seem to be versified stage-directions contributed by the copyist.'[51] This description seems adequately to characterize l. 402 and also ll. 395–6, which make explicit what is only implicit in the following lines of dialogue. Lines 1004–5 offer a gloss on the following scriptural quotation, while the Latin phrase following l. 1018, if it is considered at all in this context, simply reproduces the scriptural gloss on the Hebrew.

M. Noomen, while he would endorse Mrs Frank's description of the text as a play to be acted, contests the stage-direction diagnosis. Why introduce only six such indications into a play of almost 2,000 lines? Moreover, the lines seem to be linked to specific scenes: the interrogation of Jesus (ll. 395–6 and 402), Peter's denial (ll. 513) and the passion on the cross (1004–5). The rare indications of speakers also seem to occur in groups, almost half appearing in the two *planctus*.[52]

> Tout porte à croire que ces vers, et probablement aussi les noms des personnages, ne sont pas des éléments adventices, mais bien plutôt des vestiges d'une pièce antérieure, modèle ou source de la *Passion du Palatinus*... Dans cette pièce antérieure les vers narratifs, probablement en plus grand nombre, ont pu avoir une fonction analogue à ceux de la *Résurrection* ou de la *Passion d'Autun*.[53]

Whether the groupings discerned by M. Noomen are significant or not, it is clear that they cannot affect the main point at issue between him and Mrs Frank: were the six 'narrative' lines intended, in this play or in some possible source, as stage directions, or as commentary to be recited during a performance? That this text seems to add no new element to the discussion is not surprising. Of the three plays considered, the *Passion du Palatinus*, with its meagre half-dozen 'narrative' lines, its lack of a prologue and its infrequent indications of speakers, appears the most parsimonious in the clues it offers. Yet, thrown into relief by the very scantiness of the evidence, there is one feature that obtrudes itself insistently. This is the temporal situation of the

P

actions described in the 'narrative' lines. The tenses form a progression, starting with the present in ll. 395–6, as the action
interrupts the speaker's flow of words, proceeding to a present
perfect to describe Jesus's continued silence in l. 402, then to a
simple past for the decisive *respondi* introducing Peter's notorious
denial in l. 513 and the final *dit* with its associated *avoit* in ll. 1004–
1005. This variation in tense confronts us with what perhaps constitutes the main difference between the dramatic and the
narrative techniques. The present is the dramatic tense, the past
the narrative tense. Of course, the category of person is involved
also, but to a lesser degree. If we include stage-directions, on the
printed or the written page, or commentary accompanying a
broadcast play, in our conception of the drama, we imagine them
in the present indicative. But this is a modern attitude. In the
liturgical drama we find the jussive subjunctive. Here the author
is standing back from his 'story', giving instructions for actions
that are *to be* performed. This tradition is continued by the sub-
junctives and futures of the *Mystère d'Adam* and the 'prologue' of
the *Resurrection*. But there is another possibility. If the play represents what *did* happen, the temporal situation of the *real* events
may replace, in whole or in part, that of the reconstruction, and
stage-directions will then slip into the past tense. This at least is
what seems to occur in another 'early' Easter play, probably
intermediate in date between the Palatinus and the Autun
Passions, which seems relevant to our problem—the Provençal
Passion.[54]

In the *Passion provençale*, the stage-directions are in prose,
written in red ink in the same hands as the rest of the text.[55]
Often they simply identify the next speaker: *Jhesus ditz a sant
Pey e a sant Johan; Jhesus dis al sec; Respon Yzacar enaissi* (preceding
ll. 15, 24 and 161 respectively). The verb of saying is frequently
in the past tense: *Simon respondec a Jhesu; Los diables disoron a Jhesu*
(before ll. 414 and 1724). But information other than the identity
of the speaker may be included: *Roboam cridec en auta votz; Lo sec
fe sa lauzor a Dieu; Ara parlet Caifas mes los Juzeus et ditz Roboam enay-
shi* (before ll. 99, 41, 61). In addition to prescribing the manner
of speech or the position of the speaker, the rubrics describe
actions: *Lo Lazer resusitet he dit a Jhesu; Ara los Juzeus guarda la us
l'autre he la us s'en ira apres l'autre. E Jhesus dit a la femna enaysi*[56]
(before ll. 170, 289). Some develop into extended descriptions:

Ara es mogut Jhesus del loc de la Magdalena e intrec s'en al Temple e gitet de foras tot quant y trobec e.l rector del Temple ab II homes vestit de suzaris blancs e Jhesus dit lor enaysi (before l. 230). *Ara es Jhesus devant Jherusalem ab mot enfans he los us despulheron lors vestiduras, estenderon las denant e los autres eshiron li ab rama d'arbres davant he disoron li aquestas coblas* (before l. 328). *Ara responderon totz amen e sezian encara a la taula e mentre que manjavan la Magdalena venc ab une brustia d'enguent e gitic ne sobre Jesu e dit aquestas coplas* (before l. 374).

These prose passages, with their verbs in the simple past tense (*intrec, gitet, trobec, despulheron, estenderon, eshiron, disoron, responderon, venc, gitec*) or the imperfect (*sezian, manjavan*) are descriptions of past actions and, hence, essentially narrative. Yet they are stage-directions, as is evident from the invariable inclusion of a verb such as *dit* or *disoron*. The author is aware of the actors' presence on the stage (*ara es mogut Jhesus del loc de la Magdalena...; ara es Jhesus devant Jherusalem...*), nevertheless he is dominated by the 'pastness' of the events they imitate. These rubrics have not undergone a refurbishing in verse, as seems to have happened in the case of the *Resurrection*, or a further transformation into mere description clumsily forced into the structure of the dialogue, like the passages in the Autun *Passion*, but their ambiguity is no less obvious.

Past and present, one suspects, are equally in the minds of the authors, revisers or copyists of all these plays, precisely because of the nature of their material. Stage-directions become narrative passages, first in tense and then in form. We are in the presence, not so much of the destruction of one function by another, but of the co-existence of both functions in a single text. Our embarrassment by the presence of a prologue (or 'prologue') and indications of speakers together with 'narrative' passages, in the plays we have been considering in such tedious detail, would probably have seemed very odd indeed to those who wrote them. As Schumacher observed, 'les limites entre le drame et la narration ont été souvent un peu vagues'.[57] And why not? The concept of the genre is a convenience, not an eternal truth, and the laws of the filing-cabinet do not necessarily apply to literary production, especially in medieval France.

NOTES

[1] *La Seinte Resurreccion*, Oxford, Anglo-Norman Text Society (1943).
[2] *La Passion d'Autun*, ed. Grace Frank, Paris, SATF (1934).

[3] *La Passion du Palatinus*, ed. Grace Frank, Paris, CFMA (1922).

[4] See the passage from *Les origines catholiques* quoted below, p. 209.

[5] *Le Mystère d'Adam*, ed. Paul Aebischer, Paris, TLF (1963).

[6] *La Seinte Resurreccion*, ll. 85–93 of the Paris version (P.). The Canterbury text (C.), ll. 97–105, is almost identical.

[7] *Revue belge de philologie et d'histoire*, XXXVI (1958), pp. 761–85.

[8] *Loc. cit.*, p. 762.

[9] *Ibid.*

[10] *Ibid.*

[11] *Ibid.*

[12] *Ibid.*, pp. 772, 785.

[13] *Ibid.*, pp. 766–7. M. Noomen refers to the text in K. Young, *The Drama of the Medieval Church*, Oxford, Clarendon Press (1933), Vol. II, p. 219. This text in fact begins 'Ad representandum Conversionem Beati Pauli Apostoli...', whereas the *Resurrection* uses the verb *reciter* (P.: En ceste manere recitom / La seinte resurreccion. C.: Si vus avez devociun / De la sainte resurrectiun / En l'onur Deu representer / E devant le puple reciter).

[14] *Loc. cit.*, p. 764.

[15] *Ibid.*

[16] *Ibid.*

[17] *Ibid.*

[18] *Ibid.*, p. 765.

[19] *La Seinte Resurreccion*, p. lxxiii, 'The author of the Fragment is markedly conservative in his handling of the couplet, avoiding overflow except when the correspondence of couplet and sense can be restored either by the immediate use of a single line complete in itself . . . or by a set of three lines.'

[20] This, of course, is not to question the great weight that must be accorded to the opinion of the late Professor M. K. Pope. A careful reading of her observations on this point, on p. cxxiv of the introduction to the A.N.T.S. edition, particularly when taken with what she says on pp. lv–lvi, leaves one with the impression that all that can be affirmed of the linguistic evidence is that it is not inconsistent with common authorship of both dialogue and 'narrative' lines.

[21] 'Tant cum l'oinnement li baut.' The glossary of the edition, p. 66, gives this as 'ind. pr. 3' of *bailler*. The note on p. 56 reads 'the form *baut* (*balt*), ordinarily the third singular of the present subjunctive of *baillier*, is more probably to be explained as an analogical form of the present indicative, made on the model of the forms of *baillir* and *faillir*, with which verbs it has many forms in common. The A.N. predilection for analogical forms is notorious.'

[22] Nothing corresponding to these lines occurs in C.

[23] This section of the introduction, written by the late Professor J. M. Manly, uses the term 'stage directions' to describe the 'narrative' lines.

[24] *La Seinte Resurreccion*, p. xxii.

[25] *Loc. cit.*, p. 765.

[26] *La Seinte Resurreccion*, p. xxii.

[27] *Loc. cit.*, p. 765.
[28] *Ibid.*, p. 766.
[29] P., ll. 1,3.
[30] Paris, P. Lethielleux (1901).
[31] On p. 33.
[32] The Latin text will be found in K. Young, *The Drama of the Medieval Church*, I, p. 524.
[33] Marius Sepet, *Les prophètes du Christ, étude sur les origines du théâtre au moyen âge*, Paris (1878).
[34] Omer Jodogne, 'Recherches sur les débuts du théâtre religieux en France', *Cahiers de civilisation médiévale*, VIII (1965), pp. 1–189.
[35] *Ibid.*, p. 188.
[36] *Ibid.*
[37] *Ibid.*, p. 189.
[38] *Ibid.*, p. 187.
[39] *Ibid.*
[40] Fr. Schumacher, 'Les éléments narratifs de la *Passion* d'Autun et les indications scéniques du drame médiéval', *Rom.*, XXXVII (1908), pp. 570–93. Cf. *La Passion d'Autun*, p. 14, n.1, 'Schumacher n'a pas fait prévoir ses conclusions assez nettement dès le commencement de son article, où, en réalité (p. 571), il promet de soutenir l'hypothèse que "les éléments narratifs ne seraient que des indications scéniques mises en vers".'
[41] *La Passion d'Autun*, p. 13 n.
[42] *Loc. cit.*, p. 768.
[43] *Ibid.*
[44] *Ibid.*, p. 769.
[45] *Ibid.*, p. 770.
[46] *Ibid.*, p. 771.
[47] *La Passion d'Autun*, pp. 12–14, especially p. 13, 'La conclusion s'impose donc que les vers narratifs de B représentent des additions à un texte primitivement dramatique.'
[48] *La Passion du Palatinus*, p. iv.
[49] The MS. has 'Homo est Deus'. Fr. Schumacher, *loc. cit.*, p. 592 n., quotes the same phrase from the Benediktbeuren *Passion:*
'Jeus videns finem dicit clamando:
"E-ly, E-ly-lama sabactany, hoc est Deus
Deus meus, ut quid dereliquisti me?"
(Ici, il est vrai, le scribe a remarqué la faute, car d'après une note de l'éditeur, les deux mots "hoc est" paraissent avoir été biffés dans le manuscrit.)'
[50] *La Passion du Palatinus*, pp. iv–v.
[51] Grace Frank, *The Medieval French Drama*, Oxford, Clarendon Press (1954), p. 128.
[52] M. Noomen (p. 771) corrects the total number in the text, given by the editor as 12, to 13.
[53] Noomen, *loc. cit.*, p. 772.
[54] *La Passion provençale du manuscrit Didot*, ed. William P. Shepard, Paris, SATF (1928).

[55] See introduction to the edition, p. xi.
[56] 'La dernière phrase de cette rubrique est par exception écrite en noir', according to the editor (p. 14 n.).
[57] *Loc. cit.*, p. 582.

I. D. McFarlane

GEORGE BUCHANAN AND FRANCE

Harold Lawton is one of the few *seiziémistes* in his generation to have stressed, both by exhortation and in his own research, the importance of Neo-latin studies in the French Renaissance. Since, moreover, his interests have lain especially in the field of Renaissance drama, I should like here to reconsider the *années françaises* of one of the greater Latin dramatists of the century—George Buchanan.

A proper understanding of Buchanan can be achieved only by a fuller knowledge of his many years in France. His outlook and his humanist ideals were shaped more particularly by his sojourns in Paris and Bordeaux; and it is remarkable how he maintained throughout his life the connections he had formed with scholars and humanists on the continent—at least where religious attitudes made this possible. Hume Brown's standard biography, balanced and well-informed as it is, tends to ignore many of Buchanan's humanist contacts, and it is significant that, except for Paris University Archives, none of the various manuscripts relating to the Scotsman and preserved in French libraries is mentioned by him.[1] There are still many gaps in our knowledge; here I shall try to bring together both material fairly easily accessible, but not normally within the purview of scholars interested in Scottish humanism, and also a number of relevant *inédits*. I shall confine myself to a consideration of the *milieux* in which Buchanan moved, and shall leave aside scrutiny of such important matters as the development of his religious ideas or of his poetic compositions. Our knowledge of Buchanan's *années françaises* is based on the following sources: (i) his own published works, especially the poems, and desultory autobiographical references elsewhere; (ii) the manuscripts of his poems, which contain a goodly

amount of *inédits* and important variants (including the addressees);
(iii) liminary verse contributed by Buchanan to writings by
friends; (iv) contemporary references, both in published and unpublished sources: under this rubric one must include references
in humanist books published in France, about which we shall be
better informed when all the volumes of the *Bibliographie parisienne*
have appeared.[2]

I *The first period.* This may be said to cover the first two stays in
Paris, where Buchanan studied and took his degree, and also
began his tutorship to Gilbert Kennedy. Of the first sojourn
(1520-2 approx.) we have little knowledge, except his own statement that he worked much at Latin verse composition.[3] The
second stay is longer and more important—Buchanan says it
lasted ten years, but his statements about dates are often rather
loose.[4] He returned to Paris in the wake of his teacher John
Major, who was himself picking up the threads of his earlier
academic career: clearly Buchanan's hostility to his teacher must
have developed later. The Scotsman's autobiography skates
rapidly over this stage of his existence; certain details are well
known, the taking of his degree, activity in the University (as, for
instance, procurator of the German nation), and teaching duties
at Ste-Barbe, which was well famed for its stress on Latin verse
composition, and boasted teachers such as Guy de Fontenay, and
in Buchanan's time, Martin Dolet.[5] A few points may however
be stressed: (*a*) though it is difficult to say to what extent he was
affected by Lutheran propaganda at that time, Buchanan admits
that he was so attracted.[6] No doubt he went as far as many other
humanists who hoped that religious liberalism would mean more
intellectual freedom and a more inward religion—the Erasmian
outlook, in fact. (*b*) Among the humanists connected with Ste-
Barbe were the men due to form the shock-troops summoned by
Tartas to run the Collège de Guyenne; Buchanan will maintain
touch with many of these humanists. (*c*) In a letter to Daniel
Rogers, Buchanan asserts that he translated the *Medea* into Latin
so as to perfect his knowledge of Greek, and it has therefore been
assumed by some that he acquired his Greek later in life.[7] But
there is evidence that Buchanan was highly proficient in the
language by the end of the 1520s. Not only does he tell us in his
first examination by the Inquisition that he learned both Latin
and Greek at Paris,[8] but the archives of Paris University describe

him before 1530 as 'cet homme capable, le doctissime en grec
et en latin'.[9] This suggests that he knew a number of leading
Hellenists: Jacques Toussaint, whose influence on the younger
generation was great and who encouraged his pupils to translate
from the *Greek Anthology* into Latin;[10] Pierre Rosset, author of
a number of poems in heroic metre inspired by Mantuan, but
respected by young humanists and known as a teacher of Greek.[11]
Rosset also wrote liminary verse for Badius' edition of Hector
Boece's History of Scotland, published in 1527 (n.s.). The
efflorescence of Latin poetry in the middle 1530s owes much to
the teaching of the preceding decade in Paris, and it is difficult
not to imagine Buchanan on some terms of acquaintanceship
with these scholars. (*d*) We know little of Buchanan's teaching
at this time, but he must have made some mark rapidly,
since Gouvéa was very glad to snap him up for the Collège de
Guyenne when he returned to France. Moreover, he showed his
sympathies with new pedagogic ideas by his translation of Lin-
acre's *Rudimenta*, dedicated to Gilbert Kennedy and printed in
1533.[12]

II *The second period (1539–47)*. Buchanan returned to Scotland
c. 1535, still as tutor to Kennedy and 'escaped' via England to
France in 1539.[13] Whether he was offered a teaching post at
Bordeaux while he was still in Paris or already in the Midi is
a moot point.[14] His third sojourn in France may conveniently
be divided into the Bordeaux period, and the rather obscure
years 1543–7 before he left for Portugal.

The main outlines of the Bordeaux stay have been described
by Gaullieur and Hume Brown;[15] we know about his colleagues
at the Collège de Guyenne, Nicolas Grouchy, Guillaume Guérente, later Elie Vinet,[16] and also Antoine de Gouvéa;[17] we have
some information about friends and patrons in Bordeaux society,
F. Belcier, Innocent de Fontaine, Briand de Vallée, Ptolomée
de la Taste.[18] The relations between Buchanan and Scaliger have
been described in some detail,[19] and we know that he made
friends with Biron and the Longa mentioned in a poem.[20] We
know less about the students he taught, except Montaigne; but
we can add the name of Bernard Poey du Luc.[21] We can also
point to Buchanan's friendship with Jean Binet, the uncle of
Ronsard's biographer.[22] This humanist also taught at the Collège
de Guyenne and enthusiastically composed Latin verse; he was

a friend of Gélida, Toussaint, Guillaume Budé, and knew Sebastian Gryphius at Lyons.[23] At this time he had rather close connexions with Orléans and its *sodalitium*, and one may wonder whether Buchanan's links with that town, close enough later on, did not develop to some extent at this stage. A number of other question marks arise about this stay in the Midi: did Buchanan already know Toulouse (where Adrien Turnèbe was teaching)? and was he in any way connected with Marguerite de Navarre's entourage at Nérac?[24] One may also recall that the de Mesmes family came from the South-West.[25]

The years 1543–7 have been described as the silent ones.[26] Buchanan himself is chary of reference to this part of his life. Broadly speaking, apart from a stay in Toulouse, to which he alludes in the *Historia*,[27] he appears to have spent most of the time in Paris, among other things teaching at the Cardinal Lemoine, where Gélida was Principal, though there is nothing to warrant the legend that Turnèbe and Muret were also on the staff at the same time.[28] From Buchanan's own writings we know of his friendship now with Adrien Turnèbe and Charles Estienne;[29] he was seeing his *Medea* through the press of Vascosan, and was also teaching Greek to David Pa(i)nter.[30] Many of his friends were connected with Vascosan's *officina*, and these links continued after his return from Coimbra; for a time, moreover, he stayed in Vascosan's house and no doubt served as a corrector.[31] And something more can be said about the *milieux* which he frequented during these years.

(*a*) It is now that Buchanan came to know Beza well. It is unlikely that the two men could have been on close terms earlier, since Beza left Orléans about the time Buchanan settled in Bordeaux. The evidence for this friendship occurs in Beza's liminary letter to a volume of verse by himself and Buchanan:

. . . Reuersus enim Aurelia Lutetiam, ibique velut in gymnasio totius orbis florentissimo, nactus quibuscum in omni studiorum genere me exercerem, prout sese variae offerebant animi a grauioribus studiis relaxandi occasiones, quædam præterea eiusmodi scriptituram: ita quidem (absit verbo inuidia) doctissimis illius academiæ hominibus, quos amicissimos habebam, comprobata (cuiusmodi tum erant, Ioannes Stracelius, Adrianus Turnebus, Georgius Buchananus, Ioannes Teuius, Antonius Goueanus, Mellinus Sangelasius, Salmonius Macrinus) ut eos meminerim, quum Francisci Genethliacon scripsissem, uno consensu primas in epigrammate scribendo ultro mihi tribuisse.[32]

Obviously no one's spectrum of friendships overlaps completely with that of another, but it is striking that in this list only Strazel and Salmon Macrin are not explicitly mentioned in Buchanan's works. Given Macrin's connexions with the Du Bellay family, Jean de Lorraine, the Morel *salon*, not to speak of his literary standing from 1528 (when Buchanan was at Paris), or for that matter of the Calvinist leanings of his children,[33] I find it hard to believe that Buchanan and he had no contacts.[34] The friendship with Beza continues of course, but it also prompts one to ask whether Beza did not help the Scotsman to establish further contacts with Orléans humanists. We know that Germain Audebert obtained an early copy of Buchanan's *Læna*, probably about 1544;[35] and later Buchanan is in touch with many Orléanais: Florent Chrétien, the Groslots, Pierre de Montdoré, the Hatté family, and of course Pierre Daniel.[36]

(*b*) Buchanan, though teaching at Cardinal Lemoine, was also in search of patronage, and indeed was himself much sought after. In his Defence before the Inquisition, he mentions several persons who showed interest in him.[37] He refers to the bishops of Tarbes and Condom; and, what is perhaps more interesting, he mentions Jean de Gagn(a)y, at whose house he claims to have spent some months. Gagny was an orthodox theologian who died in 1549, but he claims the interest of literary historians on two counts: he published an anthology of Italian humanist poetry *c.* 1546,[38] and, more relevant here, he brought out in 1547 a Latin verse translation of 75 Psalms, a publication all the more attractive for the theory he developed in his preface on the value and function of psalm paraphrase.[39] He spent some time in defending his priority over Marcantonio Flaminio, whose paraphrases appeared earlier in print, but was apparently not aware that François Bonade had led the field as early as 1531 with a complete verse paraphrase.[40] This leads one to ask whether Buchanan had shown any interest in Psalm paraphrase before the Coimbra experience; moreover, many humanists, including Macrin, Bourbon and Sussannée, had tried their hand at the genre, and Flaminio was not unknown in France. Among other patrons were Lazare de Baïf, under whose roof Buchanan spent some months, and who also engaged Charles Estienne and Jacques Peletier du Mans for tutorial purposes; Charles de Marillac, bishop of Vienne,[41] to whom the humanist addressed a poem, and who was a friend of the Brissac family and of Michel de l'Hôpital; cardinal Jean de Lorraine, a notable patron of letters until his death in 1550; and François Olivier whom Buchanan had earlier addressed on behalf of the Collège de Guyenne.[42]

(c) From what has just been said, two points emerge. On the one hand, Buchanan seems to have caught the attention of a number of persons highly placed at court before he left for Portugal. And on the other, Buchanan was already well known to various persons connected with what was to become the Pléiade. This is shown in part by his friendship with Lazare de Baïf (and presumably Jean-Antoine, though his name never occurs in Buchanan's writings), by a connexion with Jean du Bellay which must have started before the cardinal left for Rome in 1547 after falling out of royal favour, and perhaps too with Jacques Peletier du Mans.[43] It is remarkable how quickly Buchanan enters the swim on his return from Portugal; he may well have known Muret before Coimbra, and we know that Joachim du Bellay translated into French verse the *Adieu aux Muses* in 1551, that is when Buchanan was away.[44]

Once again, there are question marks. Did Buchanan ever meet François Rabelais? It seems that he wrote an epitaph on the author of *Gargantua*, though this does not prove acquaintance; it is not dissimilar in spirit from Ronsard's epitaph.[45] Did he know Tiraqueau, the friend of Rabelais, but also of many humanists with whom Buchanan was connected, as can be seen from the liminary verse to successive editions of his *De legibus connubialibus?*[46] What we do know is that Tiraqueau possessed a copy of Buchanan's *Jephthes*.[47] I leave aside the question of Buchanan's contacts with Scotsmen in France at that time.[48]

Though I have raised more queries than I have solved, I think that these details help to fill in our picture of the 'silent years'. It emerges that these were no *Wanderjahre*, as Ruddiman suggested, though Buchanan may well have made excursions into the provinces; on the contrary, his teaching commitments and the network of connections he built up at this time in the capital suggest that the sojourn was fairly continuous. Some contacts were to come in useful later, and there is evidence that Charles de Lorraine was already benevolently inclined to Buchanan and to the younger French poets.

III *The third period (from 1552).* Buchanan returned to Paris probably towards the end of 1552: according to his own statement, his arrival coincided with the raising of the siege of Metz.[49] Except for the periods he spent in Piedmont and Italy as tutor to Timoléon de Cossé, Paris was to remain his residence until 1560, and indeed in 1557 he obtained 'lettres de naturalité'.[50] The contacts he enjoyed during these years were exceedingly important, not only for his poetic activity, but for the development of his thought, both religious and political. Here again, we are handicapped by a lack of sufficiently precise dates—though new dates have recently come to light; but a fairly clear picture of Buchanan's mode of life does emerge, and I shall set out under separate headings details of the various circles in which he moved; this seems more satisfactory than attempting a chronological presentation.

(a) Passing reference may be made to a matter that is important but ill-documented: his relations with both Scotsmen and Marian exiles. His brother Patrick was towards this time appointed tutor to the Regent's children in Paris. We assume that Thomas Randolph, later one of Buchanan's best English friends, first met him tutorially in Paris, but of older Marian exiles with whom he may have been connected, I have gleaned nothing.

(b) When Buchanan was in Paris in 1543-7, we noted his association with Vascosan. I think that he renewed these ties on his return from Portugal. It is true that his first book to appear, the *Jephthes* was printed by G. Morel,[51] but the second edition of the play bears Vascosan's imprint; and of course the *Alcestis*, the *privilège* of which is dated 1553, was also published by him. Other ties with the printer suggest themselves. For instance, it is Vascosan who publishes Nicolas Grouchy's *De comitiis romanorum* in 1555, and some of the work of another old colleague, Guérente, appears through him. Moreover, Vascosan's tastes in publishing must have commended themselves to Buchanan: on the one hand, he prints a considerable number of mathematical and astronomical treatises, at a time when Buchanan was starting on the *De Sphæra*, and on the other, his interests veer sharply after 1554 towards historiography, also at a time when Buchanan was already collecting material for his *Historia*.[52] Another piece of evidence is worth mentioning; when Vascosan publishes an *Epître* concerning the Maréchal de Brissac, the prefatory letter contains information about Buchanan's tutorship in Italy.[53]

Before we leave the Vascosan milieu, something should be said

about Nicolas de Grouchy, usually neglected by biographers, but
undoubtedly a very important friendship in Buchanan's life.
They had probably met first at Sainte-Barbe, they were later
colleagues at Bordeaux, they formed part of the group that went
out to Coimbra. After that time, we have less direct evidence of
maintained contacts, but when Buchanan pays a visit to Paris
in 1567, he stays with Grouchy at Dieppe on the way home.[54]
In other words, this friendship lasted over 35 years. I suspect that
when Buchanan was in Paris during the 1550s, he did see something of Grouchy, even though the latter had settled in Nor-
mandy. They had similar connections in high places—some of
Grouchy's work is dedicated to Michel de l'Hôpital and Henri de
Mesmes; Florent Chrétien also knew him, for he wrote a distich
on the Grouchy-Sigonius quarrel.[55] Grouchy furthermore knew
Patrick Adamson, with whom Buchanan was then on friendly
terms.[56] The interests of both humanists overlapped substantially,
though Grouchy, as editor of Aristotle, was of a more philosophical turn of mind. His pedagogic ideas, which are set out in
the *Præceptiones dialecticæ* (published in 1552 by Vascosan, and
dedicated to Guérente and Patrick Buchanan) harmonize in
many ways with the Scotsman's;[57] he was also interested in
astronomy, and in 1554, again through Vascosan, published his
edition of Aristotle's *Meteorologicorum libri IIII*. But his life's work
centred on the book he published in 1555, the *De comitiis romanorum libri III*. This volume develops the thesis that the rulers of
Rome were the instruments of the people and not its masters:
the following extract from the Preface shows this briefly:

> Respublica Romanorum quandiu fuit libera, ex tribus illa quidem
> Reip. generibus (quemadmodum docet Polybius) constabat βασιλεία
> ἀριστοκρατία δημοκρατία; Sed merito tamen maximam partem ob-
> tinuisse mihi uidetur δημοκρατία. Quanquam enim regiæ potestatis
> species quædam in Consilium imperio, in Senatus uero potestate opti-
> matum principatus quodam modo agnosceretur: populi tamen tanta
> erat auctoritas supra omnes magistratus, & Senatum, ut non immerito
> dici possit omne imperium, omnem maiestatem illius Reip. penes
> populum fuisse . . . Iam uero de capite ciuis, ominoque de libertate ac
> iure ciuitatis, nullius erat nisi populi iudicium . . .[58]

This work, whose appearance was noted by Ferreri in a despatch
that also refers to Buchanan's being already engaged on his
Historia,[59] had a considerable impact in Protestant circles. It
went through several editions, and an epitome was later published
in a volume containing writings by Hotman, at Basel.[60] It offered

a historical justification of the Calvinists' democratic view of the ruler as representative of the people. Buchanan, presumably, saw the work in this light too, for in 1575 a copy of the work was bought for the library of the young James VI.[61] Grouchy eventually declared himself for Protestantism and on the verge of death was offered a post at La Rochelle. I suspect that Buchanan's close and lasting connection with Grouchy may have played some part in the formation of his political and religious thinking.

(c) Another important milieu for Buchanan was the Pléiade. I have suggested that the foundations of his ties with these poets were probably laid before he left for Portugal, and before indeed the Pléiade came properly into being; it is striking how quickly he took up the threads on his return. We know that he enjoyed immediately the patronage of Marguerite de France, a warm protectress of the Pléiade;[62] he also tells us that he was pressed by his friends, as soon as he arrived, to write a poem on Metz in rivalry with Mellin de St-Gellais, the court poet, an invitation that caused him slight embarrassment, as he was on good terms with the man.[63] These 'friends' must be members of the Pléiade who at this time were quarrelling with St-Gellais. What is important is that Buchanan is seen as a useful ally, of sufficient standing too to serve as a ceremonial poet. Moreover his poems were already circulating, for Pierre des Mireurs refers to his *Pro Læna*.[64] For part of this period he was teaching at the Collège de Boncourt, and he made his impact both as a scholar and as one interested in drama. It is no doubt this dramatic interest which links Buchanan with La Péruse,[65] Jacques Grévin,[66] possibly Estienne Jodelle,[67] and, with a wider spectrum of interests, Marc-Antoine Muret.[68] Our knowledge of his friendship with Muret is scanty; we know that Buchanan wrote liminary verse for the latter's *Juvenilia* almost immediately after his return to Paris,[69] but it is possible that the two had met earlier. When the *Juvenilia* appeared, Muret was fairly closely connected with the Brinon circle, and it is probable that Buchanan was too; indeed, a number of the humanist poets in that group were also involved in the *Tombeau* of Marguerite de Navarre, and, given Buchanan's poems alluding to the queen, one wonders whether he might not have been a contributor himself, had he been in France at the time.[70] Muret left Paris under a cloud in 1554, and shortly afterwards settled in Italy, but Buchanan continued to have a high regard for his scholarship—for instance, a copy of Muret's

edition of the Latin elegists was to be found in James VI's
library.[71] I have not found any explicit reference to links between
Buchanan and Jean-Antoine de Baïf or Jacques Peletier du Mans,
though the latter may well have known the Scotsman: he was a
close friend of Vascosan, staying at his house for some months,
he was well known to Beza *c.* 1547, a friend of Gélida, and later
connected with the Brissac family; he was very interested in
mathematical and scientific matters, and became, for a short
while, principal of the Collège de Guyenne. Of Buchanan's
relations with Ronsard, we have De Thou's testimony that the
poet was well acquainted with Antoine de Gouvéa, Turnèbe,
Muret and Buchanan, whose urbanity he praised;[72] of Jean Dorat
I shall say something presently.

Of all the members of the Pléiade, Joachim du Bellay was
surely the one closest to Buchanan's heart. They very probably
met before Buchanan left for Portugal; and though they cannot
have had much time to see each other between the Scotsman's
return to Paris and Du Bellay's departure for Rome in 1553, they
were in constant touch during the last few years of Du Bellay's
life, being frequent visitors to the Morel family. In the French
poet's writings, there are several references to, and apparent
borrowings from, Buchanan. First of all, there is the *Adieu aux
Muses*, a translation of an elegy which Du Bellay had completed
before Buchanan returned to Paris in 1552, since it was published
in that year.[73] Then, he translates an Ode relating to the siege
of Metz.[74] In the *Regrets* there is a sonnet addressed to the Scotsman, in which specific reference is made to his drama.[75] And in
the *Antiquitez de Rome*, there are two poems which owe something
to the *Fratres fraterrimi*.[76] If one looks at the Latin poems which
Du Bellay was writing in Rome and after his return to Paris,
we see that he was handling themes very similar to those to be
found in Buchanan: some verse on Calais and the Guise family,
the marriage of François the Dauphin; epitaphs (usually hostile
pasquilli) on Popes, and notably Julius III, two poems connected
with the Brissac family, and two epitaphs on the young Monluc.[77]
There is thus a very close parallelism of inspiration between the
two poets at this stage: one may even see a thematic similarity
between Buchanan's *Desiderium Lutetiæ* and Du Bellay's *Patriæ
desiderium*, though I have not detected textual resemblances.[78]

When Du Bellay returns to Paris, his friendship with Buchanan
develops strongly, at literary level, in two contexts. In the first

place, from 1558 onwards there is a very sharp increase in encomiastic verse relating to the court and to military events, both in the vernacular and in Latin.[79] It is clear that the members of the Pléiade (with Dorat in the van) are much involved, that this propaganda is stimulated in particular by the Guise family, with its political ambitions, but also by Michel de l'Hôpital, who contributes a number of Latin compositions himself, and that one publisher is more active in this field than any other— Fédéric Morel. A good conspectus of these compositions on the Latin side may be found in the volume which Charles Utenhove published in Basel c. 1568 and which contained verse by Michel de l'Hôpital, Adrien Turnèbe, Jean Dorat, Buchanan and the editor himself.[80] Some of the themes developed are: the capture of Calais, the marriage of François to Mary Queen of Scots, and military exploits with which the Guises are associated. That Buchanan should be on such excellent terms with the Guises has occasioned surprise; but the cardinal de Lorraine had been good to him before his journey to Coimbra, Buchanan was still in favour of the 'auld alliance', his poetic activity in ceremonial verse ranks parallel with that of his friends in scholarship and in the Pléiade, and he had still not reached a clear-cut religious attitude.[81] Like his friends, he went along with the Establishment: the Colloque de Poissy had not yet taken place. Du Bellay's part in all this encomiastic activity is also very considerable, but though a few poems belonging to this context may be found in his Latin volume, it is essentially in the vernacular that he deploys his energies.[82]

In the second place, Buchanan's friendship with Du Bellay is strengthened by their welcome at the house of Jean de Morel, where Charles Utenhove was a tutor to the three precocious children of the household.[83] Du Bellay was on intimate terms with the Morels during the last years of his life, and he dedicated to Jean de Morel his fine *Elegia*, memorable not only for its literary qualities, but for its autobiographical value.[84] A literary consequence of these humanists' friendship with the Morels appears in the *Allusiones* of Utenhove, also published in the Basel volume, and containing some verse by Du Bellay and Buchanan.[85] Buchanan does not make overt reference to Jean de Morel in his writings, though he must have known him not later than his return from Portugal; but he maintained some interest in Camille: there is a poem addressed to her in the *Miscellanea*,[86] and in the

Q

Utenhove edition (Basel, 1568?) a further poem was originally intended for her.[87] The Scotsman also promised to let her have a copy of his Psalm paraphrases when they were published.[88]

Among the people Buchanan seems to have met in the Morel household we may number Florent Chrétien, who was tried out unsuccessfully as a tutor to the Morel children after Utenhove's departure.[89] There was also Guillaume de Calvimont, to whom Buchanan was tutor at some stage, and whose connections with the Morel household are apparent in the volume of verse he published in 1571.[90] The Calvimonts had family connections in the South-West, and Buchanan may have known older members when he was teaching in Bordeaux.[91] It is not impossible that G. de Calvimont is responsible for the poem signed 'G. C.' in the first edition of Buchanan's poems published by (?)Estienne.[92]

(d) The Morels, in their heyday, were closely associated with the Pléiade, but religious differences—the Morels seem to have had Calvinist leanings, and Camille herself went over to Geneva later in life—probably kept away some poets, such as Ronsard, after a time. Moreover, the Morels were interested in scholarship rather than in poetry, and this may be one reason why Buchanan found their salon congenial. He had close links with the leading humanists of the day, both French and foreign. On some of these links we have clear evidence, though detail is lacking. One would like to know how well Buchanan knew Ramus, who in 1567 besought the Scotsman to do what he could to further the cause of mathematics at St Andrews.[93] In the Aristotelian context, it is likely that Buchanan would side with his friend Antoine de Gouvéa rather than with Ramus, but it must not be forgotten that Ramus persuaded several members of the Pléiade to do some homework for one of his books.[94] Then, Buchanan wrote a poem to Louis Le Roy, in which he thanked him warmly for help given.[95] Since Le Roy was in a permanent state of financial distress and with a rather precarious foothold at court, I am surprised by Buchanan's fulsomeness; but Le Roy does appear to have been patronised by men known to Buchanan—Jean du Bellay, Charles de Marillac, Michel de l'Hôpital, Jean de Monluc and others. I should like to find out more about possible links between Buchanan and Pierre Paschal the historiographer royal; what is certain is that Paschal had in his possession a copy of one of Buchanan's *Silvæ* which he communicated to his friend Geoffroy de Malvin.[96] Jean Dorat makes no reference, that I know, to

Buchanan in his published work, but I think he has the Scotsman in mind when he is writing to his friend Jean de Maledent (Maludanus), a lawyer with South-West connections and a good friend of the De Mesmes family: 'Mouet me socij nostri Georgii exemplum de quo scies ex illis quicum isthic norunt omnia mandata mea a te exhausta sunt diligenter.'[97] Undated, this letter also mentions Toussaint, Daniel Rogers and the De Mesmes. Gifanius, in a letter to Buchanan, alludes to the recent appointment of Dorat as *poeta regius*.[98] We can assume that Dorat and Buchanan knew each other well: not only their scholarly interests (notably on the Greek side), and their pedagogic enthusiasms, but also their activity as court poets must have brought them together, though in the long run religious differences, especially after the St-Barthélemy which Dorat defended raucously, may have cooled their relations. Of Turnèbe's links we have gleaned a little evidence already; to this should be added the text in the *Adversariorum tomi III*, where he praises Buchanan's scholarship.[99] Pierre de Montdoré was surely known to Buchanan from the early 1550s—he was another scholar whose works were published by Vascosan, and after Buchanan had returned home for good, we have evidence of their continuing friendship, strengthened also no doubt by Buchanan's religious evolution. Other scholars with whom Buchanan was connected include of course Elie Vinet of Bordeaux, and Pierre Daniel of Orléans,[100] but also, in all probability, Elie André of Bordeaux, associated with Henri Estienne, Denis Lambyn, and Léger Duchesne.

The most interesting of these scholarly contacts is, however, Henri Estienne II. We have little evidence about the origins of their friendship, though Buchanan may have known him, as he knew Charles Estienne, before the journey to Portugal; but the chronology of Estienne's travels at this time reduces the opportunity of their meeting. At all events, Estienne knew the Scotsman by 1556. It was in that year that Estienne was preparing his Anthology of Psalm paraphrases, in which various countries were to be represented: Italy produced two contributors, Flaminio and Rapizzo, Germany was represented by Eobanus Hessus, France *faute de mieux*, as the editor tactfully explained, by Salmon Macrin, and Scotland by Buchanan,[101] to whom Estienne later gave the title *nostri sæculi poeta facile princeps*. He thus acquired the *primeurs* of the psalm paraphrases, of which he published eighteen. These texts, incidentally, were reprinted by Léger Du Chesne in the anthology he published in 1560.[102] Next, Henri Estienne won Buchanan's collaboration for Latin versions of certain Greek poets he was editing, versions which subsequently reappeared in the collected poems.[103] It is reasonable to suppose that Buchanan wrote these translations specially for the purpose, though one may wonder whether he had not tried his hand at this type of composition, as did pupils of Toussaint, in the 1520s. Estienne, like other Frenchmen at this time, had advance knowledge of Buchanan's poems, for in the *Apologie pour Hérodote*, which came out shortly before the first edition of the *Franciscanus*, he discusses or mentions the following poems by the Scotsman: (i) the epitaph on Jacques Dubois, the celebrated physician whose avarice was a by-word, and on whom Buchanan wrote some time before his death;[104] (ii) the poem beginning *Esse Lutheranum* which is used as an example of the dissolute state of the Roman Catholic Church, and in which the man's name is different from the one used by Buchanan in the printed version;[105] (iii) a line is quoted from another of the *Fratres* poems, with a variant not found in the first edition.[106] The presence of these variants suggests that his manuscript sources were different from those used by Pierre Daniel for the first edition. Even after that date, Henri Estienne's links with Buchanan remained very close. He publishes, of course, various editions of Buchanan's poems, including the 1569 edition which contains variants not found elsewhere;[107] he refers on various occasions to Buchanan or his works in prefaces scattered throughout his publications; and on Buchanan's part there is an undated letter to Henry Scrymgeour, then a professor at Geneva, asking the latter to convey greetings to Estienne and Beza.[108]

Another scholar-poet, on occasion closely connected with Henri Estienne, is Florent Chrétien; he crosses Buchanan's path frequently, but we are still ill-informed about him.[109] Only Irving, of Buchanan's biographers, allows him decent space, and I cannot do more than bring together what little evidence is available. Chrétien was a friend of the Morels, Estienne, Turnèbe, Ronsard, Jodelle and Daniel. He would attract Buchanan by his scholarly interests (especially in Greek), by his satirical talents—many of Buchanan's friends have this streak, Turnèbe, Gouvéa, Scaliger, —and by his religious sympathies. He interests us particularly because he is the first translator of Buchanan: he published a version of the *Jephthes* in 1567, and in the same year a rendering of portions of the *Franciscanus et Fratres*. A letter from Chrétien to

Pierre Daniel dealing chiefly with scholarly matters, shows that
he is still in touch with the Scotsman after his return home:

> Audi amice ni properas hoc quoque. Accepi paucis diebus de Scotia
> usque literas a Buchanano nostro, tuo & meo, ad quas non ita pridem
> responsum dedi. Ille tibi (si nescis) plurimam salutem . . .[110]

Chrétien also contributed some Greek versions to the first edition
of the Psalm paraphrases. It is likely that Buchanan wrote
liminary verse for an edition of the pseudo-Denys by Chrétien
which does not appear to have survived.

Of Buchanan's other contacts in France, leaving aside
Duplessis-Mornay and Languet, as well as foreign scholars and
friends of the Pléiade like Melissus (Schede), we do not know
much. There remains one interesting contact—Montaigne, whom
Buchanan taught at Bordeaux. In his *Essais*, the Frenchman
writes:

> Bucanan, que ie vis depuis à la suite de feu Monsieur le Mareschal de
> Brissac, me dit qu'il estoit après à escrire de l'institution des enfans, et
> qu'il prenoit l'exemplaire de la mienne: car il avoit lors en charge ce
> comte de Brissac que nous avons veu depuis si valeureux et si brave.[111]

Of this Paedagogion, if Buchanan got down properly to work at
all, nothing has survived; but the extract shows that Montaigne
came across him in the 1550s. There is moreover an unpublished
poem by Buchanan addressed to the three Montaignes.[112] Montaigne had a high regard for Buchanan's poetry;[113] he read some
of his later works, such as the *De Iure Regni*,[114] and he owned a
copy of the *Historia*, recently acquired by the National Library of
Scotland.[115]

Buchanan returned to his homeland in 1560; he maintained
touch with former friends by correspondence and by third
parties, and especially when the De Mesmes, circle were gathering
material for an edition of the poems.[116] However, he was to
undertake a final trip to France in 1566–67. The evidence for
this journey is indisputable: (i) the statement already mentioned
in connection with Grouchy;[117] (ii) Daniel Rogers' statement that
he met Buchanan in France in 1566;[118] (iii) the fact that he
could only have met certain people, such as Fruter, on that
occasion;[119] (iv) the reference to his return to Scotland in state
records.[120] It has been reasonably suggested that Buchanan went
abroad in order to deal with the forthcoming edition of his
poems, but there is evidence that Buchanan was sent on government business.[121]

I have confined myself to biographical matters; it seems to me important that more evidence of this nature should be assembled before one goes on to consider the development of his thought or the composition of his poetry. On many points, further enlightenment is very necessary, but I hope that I have brought out sufficiently the great importance of these *années françaises* for Buchanan.[122]

NOTES

[1] P. Hume Brown, *George Buchanan, humanist and reformer*, Edinburgh (1890). I hope to publish, in the near future, information about these manuscripts, preserved for the most part in the Bibliothèque Nationale, Paris.

[2] *Imprimeurs et libraires parisiens au XVIe siècle*, Vol. I, Paris (1964).

[3] *Opera Omnia*, ed. Ruddiman, Leiden (1725), Vol. I, fol. g 2 r°. This statement is made in the *Vita*.

[4] *Vita, ibid.*, fol. g 2 v°–g 3 r°.

[5] J. Quicherat, *Histoire de Sainte-Barbe*, Paris (1860), Vol. I, *passim*.

[6] *Vita, Opera Omnia*, Vol. I, fol. g 2 v°.

[7] *Epistola* xxvii, *ibid.*, Vol. II, p. 755.

[8] J. M. Aitken, *The Trial of George Buchanan before the Inquisition*. Edinburgh and London (1939), pp. 96–7.

[9] Quoted by Quicherat, *op. cit.*, Vol. I, p. 160.

[10] See, for example, N. Bourbon, *Nugarum libri octo*, Lyons, S. Gryphius (1538), where frequent reference is made to Toussaint, and many versions of *Greek Anthology* poems may be found.

[11] P. Rosset, a disciple of Baptista Spagnuoli, died *c.* 1532 (see H. Sussanée's *Deploratio* in his honour published in 1532; the only copies I know of this *plaquette* are preserved in the Bodleian, Oxford). He composed a number of hagiographic poems, and was edited posthumously by the same Sussannée.

[12] I have traced 19 editions between 1533 and 1559. One wonders whether this textbook was not used at the Collège de Guyenne for a period.

[13] On this, see P. Hume Brown, *op. cit.*, pp. 100 ff.

[14] See J. M. Aitken, *op. cit.*, pp. 64 ff.

[15] P. Hume Brown, *op, cit.*, pp. 105 ff.; E. Gaullieur, *Histoire du Collège de Guyenne*, Paris (1874), *passim*. For the stay at Bordeaux we have a *terminus a quo*, in that Buchanan addressed Charles V on behalf of the College on 1 December, when the Emperor was on his way through France. As for the date of departure, Buchanan's own statements are conflicting, but he probably left some time in 1543. On all this see Aitken, *op. cit.*, p. 92.

[16] Buchanan's friendship with Vinet lasts until his death; cf. the relevant letters in the *Opera omnia*, Vol. II, also J.-A. de Thou (Thuanus), *Historiæ sui temporis*, Vol. IV, London (1733), p. 99. On Grouchy see below. Guérente is a more shadowy figure, very devoted to Grouchy.

[17] Antoine de Gouvéa does not mention, to my knowledge, any con-

nexion with Buchanan in his writings; but they were colleagues at Bordeaux, and I think that they were still in contact after the return from Portugal. Gouvéa was linked with the Mesmes circle, and in 1567 some Latin poems by Buchanan and himself appeared in the *Lena* printed by Desplanches of Dijon (only known copy in the B.N. Réserve).

[18] Ptolomée de la Taste is the least well-known of these men, but he is presumably a member of the family mentioned *passim* in Fleury Vindry, *Les parlementaires français au XVIe siècle* (fascicule containing Bordeaux entries). Two poems to him will be found in B.N. mss. fçs., 22561, pp. 58 and 69 (add. Ptolomée de Luxe, Seigneur de la Taste).

[19] Vernon Hall, Jnr., *Life of Julius Caesar Scaliger (1484–1550)*, in *Transactions of the Amer. Philosophical Soc.*, n.s. 40, pt. 2, (1950), pp. 130–1.

[20] *Opera omnia*, Vol. II, p. 347. Biron and Longa are mentioned together in the Defence before the Inquisition quoted by Aitken, *op. cit.*, pp. 136–7. Aitken, rightly, identifies Biron with Arnaud de Gontaut, baron de Biron, who was later a strong supporter of Henri de Navarre. Guillaume de Lur Longa is also correctly identified by Aitken as a senator of Bordeaux (p. 112); to this one may add the information given by Fleury Vindry, *op. cit.*, that he was the son of Bertrand de Lur-Longa and Catherine de Gontaut Biron, and so closely related to 'Monsieur de Birom'. Longa was not only a member of the Parlement de Bordeaux, but later in life a 'conseiller au Parlement de Paris'. He died in 1556. A Jehan de Gontaut Biron edited Livy in 1556 (in Paris). When Buchanan has broken with the Guise family, he will substitute Biron's name for Guise's in his ode *Ad Herricum II . . .* (Incipit, *Cælo vetustas intulit Herculem*, *Opera Omnia*, Vol. II, p. 413).

[21] P. Bénétrix, *Les origines du Collège d'Auch (1540–1590)*, Paris (1908), p. 120, refers to a decastich by this writer on Buchanan. Poey du Luc (also called Puymonclar) is found later in Paris, and, among other things, contributes liminary verse to the *Orlando Furioso* printed by Vascosan in 1555.

[22] B. N. nouv. acq. lat. ms. 2070, fol. 110 v°, contains a liminary poem by Buchanan for Binet's *Vindemia*, dated 1539.

[23] *Ibid.*, fol. 120 v° and *passim* for Gélida, fol. 121 r° for Budé, fol. 125 r° for Gryphius, fol. 127 r° for Toussaint, Binet was friendly with various humanists connected with Orléans including the Neo-latin poet Jean Dampierre.

[24] Buchanan addressed a poem to Marguerite de Navarre, *Opera Omnia*, Vol. II, pp. 361–2 (in the Killigrew ms., B.N. nouv. acq. lat. ms. 106, fol. 91 r° this poem was originally addressed to Jeanne d'Albret). The well-known Epithalamium for François and Mary Queen of Scots, printed in 1558, seems to have begun life as an incomplete poem to Henri de Navarre (see B. N. mss. lat. 8141, fol. 24 r°).

[25] Henri de Mesmes was one of the persons instrumental in collecting Buchanan's poems for publication in the 1560s; see relevant letters published by John Durkan, *Bibliotheck*, IV, 1963, pp. 69 ff. in his art. 'George Buchanan: some French connections'.

[26] J. M. Aitken, *op. cit.*, p. 135.

[27] Mentioned by Aitken, *ibid.*, p. 98 n.

[28] R. Trinquet, 'Recherches chronologiques sur la jeunesse de Marc-Antoine Muret', *Bibl. d'Humanisme et Renaissance*, xxvii (1965), pp. 272 ff.

[29] *Opera omnia*, Vol. II, p. 316.

[30] Aitken, *op. cit.*, pp. 26 and 96. Vascosan was a son-in-law of Josse Bade, and was therefore also related by marriage to Robert Estienne. During Buchanan's 'silent' years, 1543-7, Vascosan was publishing the works of many of the humanist's friends: A. Turnèbe (edition of Pliny's *Natural History*), J. Sturm; also books by Latomus, Sylvius, Ramus, Cabedo's translation of Aristophanes' *Plutus, plaquettes* by Nicolas Bourbon. An edition of Lucian (1546) contains some liminary material by Joan. Ribittus, a friend of Binet, who was working in the field of history. Io. Ferreri, whose testimony is sought by the Inquisition concerning Buchanan, also publishes through Vascosan.

[31] *Ibid.*, p. 98 n.

[32] *Theodori Bezæ Vezelii Poematum Editio secunda, ab eodem recognita. Item, ex Georgio Buchanano aliisque variis insignibus poetis excerpta carmina, presertim epigrammata.* H. Estienne, 1569, p. 5.

[33] *The Registers of the Protestant Church of Loudun, 1566–1582*, ed. C. E. Lart, n.p. (1905), pp. 2, 15, 47.

[34] On Salmon Macrin see my article 'Jean Salmon Macrin (1490–1557), *Bibl. d'Humanisme et Renaissance*, xxi (1959), pp. 55–84 and 311–49, and xxii (1960), pp. 73–89. He was considered the finest Neo-latin poet in Renaissance France, and was a protégé of Philippe de Cossé, the Du Bellays and the cardinal de Lorraine.

[35] Bibliothèque municipale d'Orléans, ms. 1674, pp. 225–31. This valuable ms., at one time in the Phillips collection, contains an early *état* of Beza's Latin poems, and also many other compositions of contemporary humanists. I have no proof that Audebert and Buchanan knew each other personally, though this is likely. Later in his life Audebert was in touch with the De Mesmes circle.

[36] On Florent Chrétien and Pierre de Montdoré, see below; Buchanan refers to his friendship with the Groslot family in a late letter, *Epistola* lix *Opera omnia*, II, 768; and there is a ms. poem *Ad Hattæos fratres*, dated 1565, and mentioned by J. Durkan, *art. cit.*, in the Bibl. Nationale ms. lat. 8140, fol. 101 r°. The Hattés were a strongly Calvinist family; one member wrote liminary verse for one of Audebert's Latin poems, and was also secretary to Henri IV. Many of Buchanan's Orléans contacts had Protestant leanings.

[37] Aitken, *op. cit.*, p. 28.

[38] *Doctissimorum nostra ætate Italorum epigrammata* . . . Paris, N. Le Riche (?1546).

[39] *Psalmi Davidici septuaginta quinque in lyricos versus* . . . *redacti*. Paris, N. Le Riche, 1547. In my article on Salmon Macrin, *BHR*, xxi, pp. 334–5, I have summarized the theories developed by Gagny in his letter-preface.

[40] *Eximii prophetarum antistitis regia Dauidis oracula*, Paris, C. Wechel (1531).

[41] Buchanan addressed a poem to him, *Opera omnia*, II, p. 359.

[42] *Ibid.*, II, p. 317.

[43] On Peletier du Mans see below.

[44] On Joachim du Bellay see below.

[45] This poem is to be found in the Dijon edition of the *Læna*, mentioned above, fol. 6 r⁰, but attribution is not certain:

Vina, ioci, crapulæ, Rabelæso adcurrite, namque hic
Perstitit in vestra stansque cadensque fide.

[46] The 1546 edition, for instance, had liminary verse from the hand of Michel de l'Hôpital, Jacques Peletier du Mans, Claude Cottereau. Tiraqueau had been a friend of Briand de Vallée.

[47] Mentioned by J. Bréjou, *André Tiraqueau (1488–1558)*, Paris (1937), p. 55.

[48] Aitken, *op. cit.*, p. 141, has something on this; there is room for further research.

[49] *Vita*, in *Opera omnia*, I, fol. h 3 r⁰.

[50] Mentioned by J. Durkan, *art. cit.*, p. 68 (for 'fils du Ch. de Brissac' read 'fils du S(ieu)r de Brissac).

[51] We do not hear of Guillaume Morel printing other works of Buchanan; but Fédéric Morel had become Vascosan's son-in-law not later than 23 November 1552 (see Charles du Bus, *La Vie et les œuvres de Michel Vascosan*, p. 45. This work has not been printed; a typescript has kindly been shown to me in the Réserve of the Bibliothèque Nationale).

[52] Letter from Giovanni Ferreri to Robert Reed, 2 May 1555, in *Papal Negotiations with Mary Queen of Scots during her reign in Scotland 1561–1567*, ed. J. H. Pollen, Edinburgh, 1901, p. 416. Antoine Mizault, some of whose work found its way into James VI's library, was writing on astronomy in the 1550s and publishing through Vascosan.

[53] *Epistre en vers français enuoyée de Rome sur la venue de Monseigneur le Mareschal de Brissac*, Paris, Vascosan, 1556. Though the title-page gives no indication of authorship, the letter is clearly by Guillaume du Maine who writes to Timoléon de Cossé: 'Monsieur, je suis bien aise d'auoir entendu par Monsieur Buccanan vostre precepteur, & plusieurs autres dignes de foi la bonne affection que vous auez à l'estude...', fol. 3 r⁰. Du Maine was Reader to Marguerite de France; but, though his name is often found in collections of humanist verse, rather little is known about him. This *Epistre* is one of three publications issued for him by Vascosan in 1556.

[54] Vte E.-H. de Grouchy et Emile Travers, *Etude sur Nicolas de Grouchy et son fils Timothée de Grouchy, sieur de la Rivière*, Paris, 1878, p. 141.

[55] Sc. de Sainte-Marthe, *Elogia*, in *Opera*, 1616, Vol. II, p. 92.

[56] Adamson wrote verse for the first edition of the *Franciscanus*, fol. D iv v⁰.

[57] This work, a copy of which is held by the Mazarine, is essentially a résumé of Grouchy's teaching in Coimbra.

[58] *De Comitiis Romanorum libri III*, Paris, M. Vascosan, 1555, (*privilège* 'vii idus Februarij MDLIII'), p. 3.

[59] See note 52.

[60] *Epitome de comitiis Romanorum* in F. Hotman, *Commentarius verborum juris*, Basel, 1558, and under a slightly different title, Basel, 1563, and Venice, 1564.

[61] *The Library of James VI, 1573–83*, p. xlvi, in *Miscellany of the Scottish Historical Society*, Vol. I, Edinburgh (1893).

[62] See Buchanan's dedication to the first edition of the *Alcestis*.

[63] *Vita*, in *Opera omnia*, I, fol. h 3 r°. Buchanan addressed a poem to him, *ibid.*, II, p. 375. In B.N. ms. lat. 8141, 67 v° there is a further poem to St-Gellais which was later published in two separate parts and addressed to Mary Queen of Scots, *Opera*, *II*, pp. 394–5.

[64] Munich, Staatsbibliothek, Cod. Monac., 10383, Vol. 33, fol. 198 r° ff.

[65] In his *Ode a Ge. Bucchanan, La Médée, Tragedie, et autres diuerses poesies* . . . Poitiers, les de Marnefz & Bouchetz freres, n.d. (perhaps 1555), La Péruse makes three points: he refers to Buchanan's 'graue vene' which is specially suited to ceremonial and encomiastic verse, advises him not to delay the publication of his fine poetry, and says flattering things about Buchanan's 'Corinna'. This name does not occur in the humanist's verse, but it may be the forerunner of Neæra, who has metrically the same value.

[66] Jacques Grévin owes some debt to Buchanan in this respect, and Buchanan wrote liminary verse for his *Théâtre*, 1562, fol. IV. Grévin was also a friend of Florent Chrétien who sends him some liminary verse, *ibid.*, pp. 220–2, and also of the Protestant surgeon Rasse des Nœux, whose collection of contemporary poetry (propagandist, erotic and satiric) is preserved in the B.N. under mss. fçs, 22560–5. Since this collection contains many Buchanan poems (including at least one *inédit*), one wonders whether Rasse des Nœux did not know the Scotsman personally.

[67] See Enea Balmas, *Un poeta del Rinascimento francese, Etienne Jodelle*, Florence (1962), pp. 260–5 and 393–4.

[68] There are two early editions of the *Juvenilia*, 1552 and 1553.

[69] Buchanan's poem is reproduced in the *Opera omnia*, II, p. 169.

[70] Among the contributors to the first *Tombeau* were Nicolas and Gérard Denisot, Pierre des Mireurs, Mathieu Pac, Jean Dorat, Charles and Louis de Sainte-Marthe, J.-A. de Baïf, Jacques Goupil (a friend of Patrick Buchanan). The second *Tombeau* (1551) also included Nicolas Bourbon, Salmon Macrin, J. P. de Mesmes, Ronsard, etc.

[71] *The Library of James VI*, (. . .) *op. cit.*, p. xxxvii.

[72] See note 16.

[73] *Œuvres poétiques de Joachim du Bellay*, ed. H. Chamard, Vol. IV, pp. 190–200.

[74] *Ibid.*, Vol. V, pp. 277–82. Chamard thinks that Du Bellay must have written this version in March–April 1553, before leaving for Italy.

[75] Sonnet No. 187.

[76] See H. Chamard, *Joachim du Bellay 1522–1560*, Lille (1900), p. 295. The two sonnets concerned in the *Antiquitez* are No. 8 and No. 18. But is it clear who influenced whom?

[77] The most convenient edition of Du Bellay's Latin poems will be found in *Poésies françaises et latines de Joachim du Bellay*, ed. E. Courbet, Paris (1919), vol. 1, pp. 419–535.

[78] The *Patriæ desiderium* will be found in the Courbet edition, vol. I, pp. 445 ff.

[79] For 1558 alone, I have noted 28 *plaquettes* of Latin verse.

[80] The Buchanan section has the title *Franciscanus & fratres quibus accessere varia eiusdem & aliorum Poemata quorum & titulos & nomina xvi, indicabit pagina* . . . T. Guarinus, Basel, s.d.

[81] J. Durkan, *art. cit.*, p. 69, refers to Buchanan's enjoyment of the prebend of Muneville-sur-Mer in 1558. No doubt this charge came his way through the influence of the Brissac family. Philippe de Cossé (+ 1550), a well-known patron, had been bishop of Coutances, and intrigue had arranged for Etienne Martel to hold the bishopric until Artus de Cossé reached a suitable age.

[82] See, more especially, Vol. V and VI of the *Œuvres poétiques*, *passim*.

[83] On Utenhove, see W. Janssen, *Charles Utenhove, Sa vie et son œuvre (1536-1600)*, Maastricht (1939); on the Morel family, see S. F. Will, 'Camille de Morel: a Prodigy of the Renaissance', *PMLA*, li (1936), pp. 83-119. Relevant manuscript material will be found in the Bibliothèque Nationale and the Staatsbibliothek, Munich (Camerarius Collection).

[84] *Ad Janum Morellium Ebrodunensem Pyladen suum, Xenia . . . seu Allusiones*, 1569, fol. 16 r°.

[85] The Buchanan poems will be found on fol. 2 and 22.

[86] *Opera Omnia*, Vol. II, p. 425.

[87] This poem was subsequently addressed to Henry Killigrew, *ibid.*, Vol. II, p. 373.

[88] B.N. mss. lat. 8589, fol. 39 r°-40r°, letter from David Rizzio to Jean de Morel. Also mentioned in S. F. Will, *art. cit.*, p. 117, n. 131.

[89] W. Janssen, *op. cit.*, p. 23.

[90] *Gulielmi Caluimontani . . . Syluarum liber primus*, Paris, D. Du Pré, 1571. On fol. 22 v° there is a hexastich addressed *Ad Georgium Bukananum Scotum Præceptorem suum*. On fol. 2 r° there are two poems to Calvimont from Camille Morel, not mentioned by S. F. Will.

[91] Some members of the Calvimont family are listed *passim* in Fleury Vindry, *op. cit.*; and one Calvimont was very outspoken against Lutheran tendencies developing in the Collège de Guyenne.

[92] *Franciscanus . . .* fol. D iv v°. On fol. 4 v° of Calvimont's volume, there is a poem addressed *Ad Gulielmum Caluimontanum Iureconsultum*.

[93] In his *Proemium mathematicum*, Paris, Wechel, 1567, p. 60. I am grateful to my colleague Mr Peter Sharratt, of Edinburgh, for this reference. W. S. Howell, *Logic and Rhetoric in England 1500-1700*, New York (1961), p. 188, refers to the early penetration of Ramism at St. Andrews, but doubts whether Buchanan played much part: (*a*) his own suggestions for the academic programme still call for much Cicero and Aristotle; (*b*) Buchanan was a close friend of Antoine de Gouvéa, a notorious opponent of Ramus. In France, Périon was one of the staunchest supporters of Cicero and early attacked Ramus' attitude; but Nicolas Grouchy, in his edition of Aristotle, is critical of Périon.

[94] The *Dialectique*, 1555.

[95] *Opera Omnia*, Vol. II, p. 362. There is no mention of Buchanan in A. H. Becker, *Loys Le Roy de Coutances*, Paris (1896), or W. Gundersheimer, *The Life and Works of Louis Le Roy*, Geneva (1966). Le Roy was closely connected with Joachim du Bellay when he was working on his translation of the *Symposium* (1560), for the poet provided a great number of the French renderings of classical poets quoted in the commentary. Le Roy's first translation was printed by Vascosan in 1551.

[96] P. Courteault, *Geoffroy de Malvyn, 1545-1617, Magistrat et humaniste*

bordelais, Paris (1907), p. 193. Courteault does not include the transcription of Buchanan's *Desiderium Lutetiæ*, which stops at l. 83, but since the author of this letter, which bears no indication of year, died on 16 February 1565, he must have had a ms. copy before Buchanan's poems were printed. The letter is to be found in the Archives Municipales, Bordeaux, under Delpit 210, fol. 257 r°.

[97] B.N. nouv. acq. lat. 10327, fol. 23 r°.

[98] *Opera Omnia*, Vol. II, p. 726.

[99] Book I, ch. 2, col. 3 in the 1604 edition. Ruddiman has reproduced the relevant passage in *Opera Omnia*, Vol. I, fol. k 4 v°.

[100] A monograph on Vinet would be welcome; on Pierre Daniel we already have books by L. Jarry and Hermann Hagen. Elie André contributes to the same volume of Greek poets edited by H. Estienne in 1560 as does Buchanan (see n. 103).

[101] *Dauidis Psalmi aliquot, latino carmine a quatuor (sc. quinque) poetis quos quatuor regiones Gallia, Italia, Germania, Scotia, genuerunt (Salmonio Macrino, M.A. Flaminio, Eobano (sc. Eobano Hesso); & G. Buchanano, ita et Iouita Rapicio)* . . . Paris, H. Estienne, 1556, p. 4.

[102] *Flores Epigrammatum ex optimis quibusque authoribus*, Paris, J. de Marnef, 1560. The second of the two volumes carries the title *Farrago*, and it is here that the paraphrases will be found, together with the ode on the fall of Calais. I am grateful to my colleague Mr Brian Jeffery for bringing this information to my notice.

[103] *Pindari, Olympia, Pythia, Nemea, Isthma, Cæterorum octo lyricorum carmina* . . . 2 vols. (Geneva?), 1560. This work is reprinted frequently, and there is also a Plantin edition of 1567.

[104] *Apologie pour Hérodote*, ed. P. Ristelhuber, Lisieux (1879), Vol. I, p. 308.

[105] *Ibid.*, Vol. I, p. 42.

[106] *Ibid.*, Vol. I, p. 141.

[107] See above, note 32.

[108] *Opera Omnia*, II, p. 728. Henry Scrymgeour, the uncle of both James Melville and Peter Young, was appointed to the chair of civil law in Geneva in 1563 and died in 1572.

[109] *La France Protestante*, ed. Haag, 2nd. ed., Vol. IV, cols. 362–75.

[110] Bongars collection, Berne, ms., Vol. 141, fol. 140 (undated).

[111] Montaigne, *Essais*, I, xxvi (in P. Villey's edition, Paris (1922), Vol. I, pp. 223–4).

[112] B. N. mss lat., 8141, fol. 59 r°, *Ad michælem thomam petrum eiquenios Montanos Burdigalenses*. Mentioned by J. Durkan, *art. cit.*, p. 67.

[113] *Essais*, II, xvii (Villey, ed. Vol. II, p. 448). He quotes from the *Baptistes* in III, v (Villey, Vol. III, p. 81) and from the *Franciscanus*, III, x (Villey, Vol. III, p. 313).

[114] *Essais*, III, vii (Villey, Vol. III, p. 178).

[115] His edition was the 1582 Edinburgh one (Arbuthnet).

[116] See *art. cit.* by J. Durkan.

[117] When Buchanan visited Grouchy in 1566 (n.s. 1567), he brought news from Montdoré with whom he had been staying. The Grouchy letter on all this is quoted in Grouchy and Travers, *op. cit.*, p. 141.

[118] Rogers refers to the fact that Buchanan showed (him, the sense implies)

the *Baptistes* in Paris 1566; see B. N. fonds Dupuy, ms., Vol. 951, fol. 52 r°:

... Ex Georgij Buchanani poematibus hæc edita sunt: ... Epigramma in Tragœdiam quendam D. Greuini, ... Carmen egregium scripsit in Dionysium Christiani Florenti ...; edenda ... Ioannis Tragoedia quam ostendit in Parisiis 1566.

[119] Ruddiman reproduces the Fruter references in *Opera Omnia*, Vol. I, fol. 1 2 v° and II, pp. 721–2.

[120] T. Randolph to the Earl of Leicester, *Cal. State Papers, Scotland 1509–1603*, II, p. 835 (dated 29 January 1566).

[121] In the B.N. copy of the first edition of the *Franciscanus* (press-mark: Yc 9635), there is a transcript of an unpublished letter from Buchanan to Cornelius Musius (fol. D iv v° ff.): the latter was a Netherlands poet who was a friend of Salmon Macrin in the 1530s and was martyred in 1572. This letter, which from internal evidence, must belong to 1567, is, apart from minor variants, the same as the one mentioned by J. Durkan, *art. cit.*, p. 68 as being extant in the libraries of Leiden and Troyes. Since Buchanan says he returned 'legatione', this confirms the implication from the *Cal. State Papers* that he went on government business. I give the B.N. version of the letter as it is fuller than the ms of Leiden; the words in italic are missing in the Leiden copy, which however has 'doctissimos' after 'viros'. *Cornelio Musio Monasticæ vitæ laudatori. Georg. Buchananus S.*

Cum nuper legatione apud Gallorum Regem defunctus in Scotiam patrium Regnum (*Leiden* patriam Regiam(?)) contenderem in urbe Parisiorum aliquot dies subsistens, forte tua, Musi, musis inuitis & contra morem Latinorum effusa Poemata incidi, legi, risi. & quia parum opportune franciscanum meum Typographo excudendum emanciparem submoleste tuli, iam mihi non esse integrum, eadem opera contra tuam vitam solitariam aliquid attexere. Mitto tamen nunc ad te, & Reuerendissimum *Episcopum* Ruremondensem Lindanum, Itemque ad M. Doncanum Franciscani mei tria, ut excusa sunt, exemplaria, totius Panopliæ (qua in patriam reuersus, Beatam *illam* vestram solitudinem, & totam denique Monachorum cohortem, semel oppugnare atque expugnare meditor) rudem quamdam ac crasse informatam adumbratamque imaginem. Lunium & Susionem viros (doctissmos *Leiden only*) qua ratione adduci potuerunt ut nomen vestris nugis suis ascribi paterentur. Credo equidem importunitate vestra illorum expugnatam esse humanitatem. Hæc an Musi tibi tuisque denuntiata *esse* volui, ne ærum futurarum essetis imprudentes. Vale et cum pinguibus tuis aqualiculis causam monacham sartam atque tectam (tectamque *Leiden*) ita uti facis, tuere.

[122] I am grateful to the following libraries for providing me with microfilm material: Bibliothèque Nationale, Paris, Bibliothèque Municipale, Orléans, Archives Municipales de Bordeaux, Universiteitsbibliothek, Leiden, Stadtbibliothek, Berne, Staatsbibliothek, Munich. I record my gratitude to Dr J. K. Cameron for advice and scrutiny of the typescript, Mme J. Veyrin-Forrer for putting me on the track of manuscript material, and Professor H. Trevor-Roper for interpretation of an important point.

C. A. Mayer

CLÉMENT MAROT AND LITERARY HISTORY

Can literary history be separated from absolute value judgements? In the case of Clément Marot it would appear not. All the traditional criticism of him as a light and superficial poet is solidly based on historical consideration. Even worse, it can be shown that factual mistakes in literary history have had a very large and mainly detrimental influence on the traditional judgements of his poetry. Few, if any, poets or writers seem to have been so ill-treated by posterity.

There is, however, an analogy in the case of Hector Berlioz, whose work, owing to historical errors, was subjected to systematic, albeit illogical and contradictory, denigration. Although eminent musicologists like Romain Rolland, Ernest Newman and Cecil Gray defended him, it was not until fairly recently that his reputation as a great composer was safely established. Attacks on him, tending to dismiss him as a charlatan, were commonplace; again and again it was asserted that his compositions lacked melodic line, were weak in counterpoint, etc. This led Berlioz's most recent biographer, Jacques Barzun, to devote a whole chapter to an eloquent refutation of these baseless criticisms,[1] and to protest against the 'numerous assertions that run counter to evidence'.[2] 'Similar contradictions', he exclaims, 'flat, fatal to logic and almost to sanity, rose up in one's path as one went to explore Berlioz's life, character and ideas'.[3] Quite rightly Barzun sees in 'this debunking treatment... part of a deep-seated anti-Romantic movement with primarily political and religious motives'.[4]

Marot's position is very similar indeed. Here too, partly because of religious and political motives, the artist's true merit has gone unrecognized. Apart from rank prejudice this state of affairs is due partly to confusion between literary appreciation, literary history and ordinary history. In the case of Marot it can indeed be shown that value judgements are based entirely on literary history, but on mistaken literary history, where every statement can be proved to be wrong.

Thus implicit or explicit in almost all existing works on Marot is an impressive looking list of defects of his poetry. There is of course no question of denying that Marot has defects; since this is not the place to make a proper revaluation of his poetry I shall only mention the many and grave accusations which run counter to evidence and which can thus be rebutted.

The first and most frequent criticism is that Marot is not serious: he writes poetry for fun. Whether expressed through the faint praise of the 'élégant badinage', or through taking him to task for not having treated serious subjects, or again through claiming that, unable to write epic poetry, Marot was good only in his shorter poems, and more generally in the lighter vein, the accusation of lack of depth is always there. Even when Du Bellay and Ronsard are said to have returned to Marot's type of poetry the implication is frequently that his poetry was simple, familiar, lacking nobility and true poetic inspiration.

Many of these charges are self-contradictory. Thus, even for a great poet, to be endowed with a sense of humour is no fault. In being unable to write a great epic Marot was not different from other Renaissance poets with the sole exception of d'Aubigné. Similarly, as regards short poems, Du Bellay is certainly outstanding in his sonnets, Ronsard's most popular poems are not the Pindaric Odes, but sonnets and light odes; so that the reproach made against Marot could indeed with equal justification be made against the Pléiade. Altogether this is largely a matter of individual taste. Here again we can turn to the example of Berlioz and his treatment by his critics. Thus a reviewer wrote that he preferred one single recitative from Bach's Saint Matthew Passion to the heroics of the 'March to the Scaffold'. Barzun replies that it would be as valid to say that one prefers one simple recitative from L'Enfance du Christ to the dramatics of the chorus shouting 'Barabbas'.[5] In fact this kind of judgement merely shows that the critic prefers short and light poems to long and serious ones, and is meaningless as a value judgement. Nor can there be any suggestion that Marot's poetry is generally light in either subject-matter or manner. Marot's eloquent protest against judicial torture, the first such protest in France, can hardly be dismissed as banter or considered as light-hearted:

> O chers Amys, j'en ay veu martirer
> Tant que pitié m'en mettoit en esmoy!
> Parquoy vous pry de plaindre avecques moy
> Les Innocents qui en telz lieux damnables
> Tiennent souvent la place des coulpables.[6]

Equally grave and moving are his condemnations of religious persecution, whether they are expressed by means of scathing sarcasm, as in the third coq-à-l'âne:

> Ilz ont esté si bien rotys
> Qu'ilz sont tous convertiz en cendre.[7]

or by compassion for the victims:

> Puys tost apres, Royal chef couronné,
> Sachant plusieurs de vie trop meilleure
> Que je ne suys estre bruslés à l'heure
> Si durement que maincte nation
> En est tombée en admiration,
> J'abandonnay, sans avoir commys crime,
> L'ingrate France.[8]

All the more courageous if one considers that it was written by the exiled poet in his epistle to the King responsible for these very same persecutions.

Nor can his attacks on the Catholic Church, on the Sorbonne, on the monastic orders and on the corruption of justice be dismissed as light banter. The subject matter of the majority of Marot's works is very serious indeed and does not justify the label: poetry for fun.

The same is true of his manner. The grave tone and lofty style of the speech of Death in the *Déploration de Florimond Robertet* written in 1527 are not only the best example of religious poetry from Marot's pen, but can, from the point of view of rhythm and style, be compared to Ronsard's *Hymne de la Mort*. In fact Marot's poem may well be preferred to that of Ronsard:

> Prie à Dieu seul que par grace te donne
> La vive foy dont sainct Pol tant escript.
> Ta vye apres du tout luy abandonne,
> Qui en peché journellement aigrit;
> Mourir pour estre avecques Jesuchrist
> Lors aymeras plus que vye mortelle.
> Ce beau souhait fera le tien esprit.
> La chair ne peult desirer chose telle.

R

L'ame est le feu, le corps est le tyson;
L'ame est d'en hault, et le corps inutille
N'est autre cas q'une basse prison
En qui languist l'ame noble et gentille;
De tel prison j'ay la clef tressubtille;
C'est le mien dard à l'ame gracieux,
Car il la tire hors de sa prison vile
Pour avec foy la renvoyer es cieulx.[9]

The elegiac poems composed during the poet's first exile, especially those written at Venice in the summer of 1536, are also marvellous examples of serious lyricism, of sustained grave tone. The three great epistles, *Au roy, du temps de son exil à Ferrare*,[10] *Au roy, de Venise*[11] and *A la royne de Navarre*[12] can all be quoted *in extenso* in support of this claim.

Finally Marot's translation of the Psalms owes its undoubted success to his ability to render adequately in French the exalted lyricism of Hebrew poetry. It should be pointed out that Marot's Psalm translation enjoyed a success unequalled by any other literary work during the sixteenth century, since well above 500 separate editions of it are known between 1539 and 1600. Almost as soon as the first edition appeared Marot's psalms were adopted by the French Protestants. Not only did they continue to be sung in Protestant temples until the revocation of the Edict of Nantes, but even to-day they are sung in many churches. Nor need one believe that the success of the Psalms was due entirely to the fortuitous reason of the emerging of the Huguenots and of the religious wars. In fact these poems in their musical setting were popular among the Catholics as well. If in the early part of this century there was a tendency to dismiss Marot's translations as of little poetic value, and if the rather facile argument that Marot could not equal the richness and burning passion of the Hebrew original was used again and again,[13] a comparison with other Psalm translations shows Marot's consummate artistry and true lyricism.

Just as important in this respect is Laumonier's discovery that for his Pindaric odes Ronsard, in spite of his claims of independence from any native source, took the metrical arrangement of every one of his poems from Marot's Psalms, so that the real invention of the main lyrical metres of French poetry is due to the latter. It is no doubt largely the consistent under-rating of Marot which led to this fact, disturbing as it was to conventional literary history, being successfully played down. Thus P. Villey stated:

'Après avoir créé, dans ses Psaumes, l'instrument du lyrisme, il ne semble même pas s'apercevoir de ce qu'il vient de faire',[14] so that the more or less untenable theory of unconscious creation, especially untenable in the case of innovation in poetic structure and form, is used to shore up an otherwise crumbling literary misconception.

Another frequent reproach, implicit to a certain extent in the previous one, is Marot's alleged so-called 'low' conception of poetry, and of the role of the poet. Indeed the belittling of Marot is an integral part of the praise given to the Pléiade for having introduced the new ideal of poetic inspiration. One should remember, however, that this ideal was clearly expressed by Thomas Sebillet in 1548 in his *Art poétique*[15] based entirely on Marot's poetry. Du Bellay's *Deffence et Illustration de la Langue françoise* was due largely to the anger to which the young poets of the Pléiade were aroused when they found their most cherished ideas expressed in Sebillet's pamphlet before they could prove their own worth to the public. Their subsequent exaggerations are due to a large degree to this publication. It should thus be obvious that there was in fact little new in the ideas of the Pléiade, except for their misunderstanding of Plato's irony concerning poetic inspiration.

Marot may at the beginning of his career have given the impression that he shared the inferior conception of poetry with which the Rhétoriqueurs are usually credited. However, the passage on which this assumption is based and in which poetry is praised merely for being innocuous, and the poet encouraged to be no more than the faithful servant of a powerful prince, comes from the epistle *Au roy, pour succeder en l'estat de son pere*,[16] where these ideas are placed in the mouth of the poet's dying father, the Rhétoriqueur Jean Marot. It may thus well be that Marot is here being consciously archaic, expressing the ideas of his father and not his own. In any case, from 1536 onwards there are numerous examples of Marot claiming to bestow immortality on those he celebrates in his verse.

One need not insist too much on this point, since the Rhétoriqueurs have certainly been maligned in this respect. The idea of immortality through poetry was not unknown in the fifteenth century.

One might add, however, that, whether original or not, Marot forestalls Du Bellay in his conception of poetry not only as a means of bestowing immortality on those he celebrates but as a therapy, as a way of alleviating his own suffering.

Thus, in one of his last epistles, written during his second exile, shortly before his death, there occur these lines:

> Ne voy tu pas, encore qu'on me voye
> Privé des biens & estatz que j'avoye,
> Des vieulx amys, du païs, de leur chere,
> De ceste Royne & maistresse tant chere
> Qui m'a nourry, & si, sans rien me rendre
> On m'ayt tollu tout ce qui se peut prendre,
> Ce neantmoins, par mont & par campaigne,
> Le mien esprit me suyt & m'acompaigne?
> Malgré fascheux, j'en jouyz & en use;
> Abandonné jamais ne m'a la Muse.[17]

One of the most frequent criticisms is Marot's lack of knowledge. Taking up Boyssonné's 'Marotus latine nescivit', most critics have pointed out that Marot did not know Greek and that his knowledge of the authors of antiquity is no different from that possessed by medieval scholars. It is indeed true that there is no trace in his poetry of any imitation from Horace or Juvenal; yet there is no doubt whatever about his imitating Catullus and Martial, who were both practically unknown in the Middle Ages.

Above all Marot's manner of imitating the Ancients is different from that of the Middle Ages. By taking from Catullus the genre of the epithalamium and from Martial the epigram, by following Virgil in the use of imagery and Ovid in the expression of nostalgia, Marot is the real initiator of the intelligent imitation of the Ancients which was to become Classicism.

Nor is his ignorance of Greek perfectly obvious. Whether or not he read Greek authors in the original, there is no doubt whatever that he was familiar at least with Theocritus, Moschos and the Pseudo-Moschos, whom he imitated directly in his first eclogue.[18]

I have already described as faint praise 'élégant badinage'. This is not to deny that Marot possesses this quality, nor that Boileau was right in singling it out for commendation. It is, however, most interesting to study the origin of this cliché and more particularly to ascertain the reason for Marot's comparative popularity in the seventeenth century.

First of all, it is a fact that Marot's popularity remained constant throughout the sixteenth century in spite of the Pléiade. Between the end of 1544, that is to say after the poet's death, and 1600, about 100 editions of his works, not counting the separate editions of the Psalter, were published. This shows, by the way, how wrong it is to dismiss Marot as the last poet of the Middle Ages, since two generations of a reading public that liked and admired the works of Ronsard and Du Bellay still found an obvious pleasure in the poetry of Marot. That Marot was held in high esteem by the intellectuals at the end of the century is also borne out by critics such as Pasquier, La Croix du Maine, Du Verdier and Fauchet.

In the seventeenth century his popularity no doubt diminished, but less so than that of other Renaissance poets. Whether or not lyrical poetry existed in the classical period, whether or not the seventeenth century was capable of appreciating true lyrical poetry, these are questions which cannot be discussed here. Suffice it to say that not a single one of the Renaissance lyrical works found favour in the classical period. It is therefore not in the least surprising that Marot's serious lyricism should not have been admired. Nor could his satire full of attacks on the Catholic Church be read with pleasure by any except Protestants at a time which saw the revocation of the Edict of Nantes.

If Marot escaped the fate of Ronsard and Du Bellay, if his works continued to be read and if critics like Boileau, La Bruyère and later Bayle held him in high esteem, it is no doubt largely because they found in his poetry something which they could appreciate, something akin to their own spirit: wit.

To begin with, the *précieux* literature, for reasons which some-how escape us, brought back the discarded *genres* of *Rondeaux* and *Ballades*, so that Marot's earliest works became fashionable. Moreover, with the development of salon life and literature Marot's *badinage* came to be the only facet of his work which could be appreciated by the seventeenth-century public. Thus at the time when Boileau came to write his *Art poétique* the labels of 'familiar', 'naïve', 'witty', would appear to have already been firmly affixed to Marot.

One can go further. From the *Art poétique* it is clear that Boileau had no direct knowledge of any French poet before Marot. Though the meaning of his lines on Villon:

Villon sut le premier, dans ces siècles grossiers,
Débrouiller l'art confus de nos vieux romanciers[19]

has never been explained quite satisfactorily, there can be little doubt that this passage precludes the possibility of Boileau having actually read Villon. In fact, it would appear that for Boileau Marot was very much the first French poet. His judgement is therefore most certainly preconceived in more ways than one. For not only was Marot appreciated as a light and witty poet exclusively already before Boileau, but for him Marot, being in the remote past, was endowed with all the characteristic features of a primitive artist. Hence no doubt the insistence on wit and *badinage* as well as on 'naturel' and 'naïveté' which are found in all appreciations of Marot during the seventeenth and eighteenth centuries.[20]

Thus, the label of 'élégant badinage' really tells us more about the seventeenth century than about Marot. The lighter side of Marot being the only one which the seventeenth century was able to appreciate, one may well say that the praise of Marot as a witty and light-hearted poet is based to a large extent on a seventeenth-century misconception. In any case, if it be a value judgement, it can of necessity only be a historically conditioned, and thus a relative and not absolute, value judgement.

With the rehabilitation of Renaissance poetry by Sainte-Beuve something of a paradoxical situation arose. Marot, though, as we have seen, in a very partial way, never ceased to be appreciated; whereas the poets of the Pléiade were to all intents and purposes forgotten. By re-discovering them, Sainte-Beuve caused the bogus revolutionary declarations of Du Bellay in the *Deffence* and of Ronsard in the preface to the *Odes* to be taken seriously. Thus arose the mistaken idea that French poetry started with the Pléiade, that there was no poetry worth speaking of before 1549 and that Marot, witty though he might be, was continuing the outmoded style of the Rhétoriqueurs, writing old-fashioned poetry in old-fashioned *genres*, etc., etc. It was thus that clichés like 'poetry for fun' began to receive currency. It should be added that Sainte-Beuve himself was guilty of none of these mistakes and realized the true greatness of Marot. Yet insufficient knowledge of literary history caused his discovery, or rehabilitation, of the Pléiade to have the unfortunate effect of belittling Marot.

To show how mistaken the claim of the Pléiade is, it suffices to enumerate briefly Marot's innovations, more particularly in respect of *genres*. Because of Du Bellay's condemnation of the fixed form *genres* like *Rondeaux*, *Ballades*, and *Virelays*, it was and still is frequently believed that Marot's main output was indeed in these *genres*. Even to-day one finds Marot sometimes referred to as 'le poète des Rondeaux'. It must therefore be pointed out that Marot did not write a single *virelay*, and that after 1527 he more or less gave up the *rondeau* as well as the *ballade*,[21] so that Du Bellay in this respect as in others, more or less condemns what had already been dead for two decades.

In discussing this question of *genres* one must beware of falling into the somewhat naïve attitude of Du Bellay in believing that there is intrinsic merit in a given *genre*. There is nothing to support his view that *rondeaux, ballades*, etc. are bad in themselves and that the sonnet is necessarily good.

On the positive side, it is clear that practically all the *genres* which Du Bellay recommends and which according to him were as yet 'inconnus de la Muse françoise' had in fact been introduced by Marot, since he undoubtedly wrote the first French elegies, the first eclogues, the first epithalamium, and probably the first French epigram and the first French sonnet. Thus all the *genres* of the Pléiade were already practised by Marot, with the exception of the Ode. Yet, as Sebillet pointed out, it is difficult to find a valid definition which distinguishes the Ode from the *Chanson*, or the *Cantique*, the two lyrical *genres* cultivated by Marot.

A particular example of a historical error affecting very strongly the general appreciation of Marot's poetry is in respect of his Petrarchism. It has until very recently been firmly held that Marot was not influenced by Italian poetry until his stay in Ferrara.[22] Before 1535, according to accepted literary history, there was no real imitation of Petrarch in French poetry.[23]

In fact the first known French poem imitated closely from an Italian Petrarchist poet, in this case from Serafino Aquilano, is a *Rondeau* by Clément Marot's father Jean Marot:

S'il est ainsi que ce corps t'abandonne.[24]

It would have been somewhat surprising if Clément had not taken up his father's only innovation. It is precisely in his early poems, composed in the main before 1527, that Petrarchist inspiration is most evident.[25] The *genres* which the poet uses exclusively for his Italianate love poetry are the *rondeau* and the *dizain* or *huitain* which in 1538 he was to call *épigrammes*. Strangely enough the *chansons*, which like many of the *rondeaux* are love poems, appear to reproduce far more closely typically medieval love themes than the latter *genre* where Marot welds most successfully Italian and French tradition. It is in the *rondeaux* that are to be found all the most characteristic devices of Petrarchist poetry, the antitheses, the fire and water, heat and ice images, the conceits of the exchange of hearts, the heart and the body, nature sympathizing with the lover's suffering, the wounds inflicted by the cruel lady, and the unhappy lover cherishing his suffering.

Marot, though having abandoned more or less completely the *rondeau* as a *genre* after 1527, went on to compose *dizains* and *huitains* in the Petrarchist manner before his exile at the end of 1534 as well as during his stay at Ferrara in 1535 and 1536. However, this particular inspiration disappears from his poetry practically after his return from Italy. Thus—rather paradoxically— Marot was influenced by Italian sources before he went to Italy and he abandoned Italianism after having spent almost two years at Ferrara and Venice. This apparent paradox is not particularly difficult to explain. Italianism was the fashion in France at the beginning of the century and there is nothing surprising at all in Marot following this fashion. The Italian poets whom he imitated were men like Serafino, Tebaldeo and Olimpo di Sassoferrato, that is to say the late fifteenth-century 'precious' poets against whom, under the influence of Bembo, there was a strong reaction in Italy during the first half of the sixteenth century. Marot, coming into contact with Italian literary circles, as he probably did at Ferrara, must have realized that the type of Petrarchism he had followed was completely out of fashion. It is not surprising that he abandoned it.

The reason for the error in this respect was mainly the confusion of literary history and history proper. Marot having gone to Italy in 1535, critics were tempted to look for Italian influence in his poetry after this date only and to ignore the possibility of such an influence in anything composed before that date. The same mistake can be seen in the frequently used argument that Petrarchism reached England before it did France since the first English Petrarchist Thomas Wyatt went to Italy a few years before Marot! It is no doubt for this reason that frantic efforts were made to show that Wyatt in his rondeau 'If it be so that I forsake thee' imitated Serafino directly, and not indirectly through Jean Marot's 'S'il est ainsi que ce corps t'abandonne', as he so clearly did.[26]

Naturally Du Bellay's condemnation of the *rondeau* as 'espicerie' contributed to the error, since no one would have thought that this despised *genre* could, in its last flowering, have been the vehicle of a new fashion in French poetry, and one which Du Bellay himself was to exploit.

This then is a perfect example of mistaken literary history resulting in complete failure to appreciate a whole set of poems. For it is not only that Marot's Petrarchism in his *rondeaux* was never properly noticed, but that the fact that they were considered medieval and that Du Bellay condemned the very *genre* of the *rondeau* caused these poems to be dismissed as of little interest. Those, who, for whatever reason, wished to give Marot the 'debunking treatment' used the *rondeaux* especially as evidence of Marot being behind the times, whereas those who liked Marot—and here is another paradox—have played down this particular *genre* as well as most of Marot's early compositions. Hence, one way or the other, Marot's *rondeaux* were considered to be bad poetry. Yet many of these poems have quite an astonishing freshness and beauty. Marot has succeeded in renewing in a remarkable fashion the somewhat trite clichés of the 'precious' Italian Petrarchists. Like Ronsard's later in the century, Marot's imitation of poets like Serafino, Olimpo and Chariteo is successful and frequently his poems are superior to their sources.

To show the particular charm of Marot's Petrarchist poetry the rondeau *D'ung soy deffiant de sa Dame*[27] is a good example:

Plus qu'en aultre lieu de la ronde
Mon cueur volle comme l'Aronde
Vers toy en prieres et dictz;
Mais si asprement l'escondis
Que noyer le fais en claire unde.   5

Dont ne puis croire (ou l'on me tonde)
Que ton cueur à m'aymer se fonde
Quand tous biens me y sont interdictz
    Plus qu'en aultre lieu
Car il n'y a Princesse au Monde   10
Qui m'aymast d'amour si profonde
Comme celle que tu me dys,
Qui ne m'ouvrist le Paradis
De jouyssance où grace abonde
Plus qu'en tout oultre lieu.   15

Marot's imitation is never slavish. Indeed at times he even changes a Petrarchist theme quite considerably, as for instance in the rondeau *De celluy qui ne pense qu'en s'Amye*[28] where he gives a most significant twist to the conceit of the exchange of hearts:

Toutes les nuyctz je ne pense qu'en celle
Qui a le Corps plus gent qu'une pucelle
De quatorze ans sur le poinct d'enrager,
Et au dedans ung cueur (pour abreger)
Autant joyeux qu'eut oncque Damoyselle.   5

Elle a beau tainct, ung parler de bon zelle
Et le Tetin rond comme une Grozelle.
N'ay je donc pas bien cause de songer
    Toutes les nuictz?
Touchant son cueur, je l'ay en ma cordelle,   10
Et son Mary n'a sinon le Corps d'elle.
Mais toutesfois, quand il vouldra changer,
Prenne le Cueur, et, pour le soulager,
J'auray pour moy le gent Corps de la belle
    Toutes les nuictz.   15

I hope to have shown that the traditional appreciation of Marot is largely, if not entirely, conditioned by history of literature. This first conclusion should go a long way towards putting us on our guard against the facile belief that history and literary appreciation could ever be separated. Those who still hold Marot in low esteem may sincerely believe that they are making a pure absolute value judgement whereas their taste, their entire approach have in fact been conditioned by generations of critics who based their view of Marot almost entirely on history.

The particular interest of Marot's case is that the literary history is palpably untrue, and is based, as in the example of Petrarchism, on the most rudimentary confusion between history and literary history or on lack of knowledge and misunderstanding.

Finally appreciation and value judgement are based, in Marot's case, to a large extent on previous judgements which are due to the special conditions prevailing in the seventeenth century.

The study of Marot thus tends to show that it might be well to realize the practical impossibility of pure value judgement, which in turn shows the importance of searching for truth in literary history.

NOTES

[1] J. Barzun, *Berlioz and the Romantic Century*, 2 vols., London, Gollancz (1951).
[2] *Ibid.*, p. 4.
[3] *Ibid.*

[4] *Ibid.*, p. 7.
[5] *Ibid.*, p. 17, n. 32.
[6] *Œuvres satiriques* ed. C. A. Mayer, London, The Athlone Press (1962), I, *L'Enfer*, vv. 284–8.
[7] *Œuvres satiriques*, IX, v. 168–9
[8] *Epîtres*, ed. C. A. Mayer, London, The Athlone Press (1959), XXXVI, vv. 186–92.
[9] *Œuvres lyriques*, ed. C. A. Mayer, London, The Athlone Press (1964), VI, vv. 325–40.
[10] *Epîtres*, XXXVI.
[11] *Epîtres* XLIV.
[12] *Epîtres*, XLVI.
[13] Cf. J. Plattard, *Marot, sa carrière poétique, son œuvre*, Paris (1938), p. 205.
[14] *Marot et Rabelais*, Paris, Champion (1923), p. 146.
[15] *Art poétique françoys*, STFM, Paris (1910).
[16] *Epîtres*, XII.
[17] *Epîtres*, LVI, vv. 71–80.
[18] *Œuvres lyriques*, LXXXVII.
[19] *Art poétique*, I, v. 117–18.
[20] Cf.: 'J'ai profité dans Voiture,
Et Marot par sa lecture
M'a fort aidé, j'en conviens.'   (La Fontaine)
Marot, par son tour et par son style, semble avoir écrit depuis Ronsard: il n'y a guère, entre ce premier et nous, que la différence de quelques mots.
Il est étonnant que les ouvrages de Marot, si naturels et si faciles, n'aient su faire de Ronsard, d'ailleurs plein de verve et d'enthousiasme, un plus grand poète que Ronsard et que Marot.   (La Bruyère)
On peut dire sans le flatter, non seulement que la poésie française n'avait jamais paru avec les charmes et avec les beautés naturelles dont il l'orna, mais aussi que dans toute la suite du XVIe siècle, il ne parut rien qui approchât de l'heureux génie, et des agréments naïfs, et du sel de ses ouvrages.   (Bayle)
Le nom de Marot est la première époque vraiment remarquable dans l'histoire de notre poésie, bien plus par le talent qui brille dans ses ouvrages, et qui lui est particulier, que par les progrès qu'il fit faire à notre versification.
On remarque chez lui un tour d'esprit qui lui est propre. La nature lui avait donné ce qu'on n'acquiert point: elle l'avait doué de grâce. Son style a vraiment du charme, et ce charme tient à une naïveté de tournure et d'expression qui se joint à la délicatesse des idées et des sentiments. Personne n'a mieux connu que lui, même de nos jours, le ton qui convient à l'épigramme, soit celle que nous appelons ainsi proprement, soit celle qui a pris depuis le nom de madrigal, en s'appliquant à l'amour et à la galanterie.   (La Harpe)
[21] See *Œuvres diverses*, ed. C. A. Mayer, London, The Athlone Press (1966). pp. 6–10.
[22] See J. Vianey, *Le Pétrarquisme en France au XVIe siècle*, Montpellier (1909).

[23] Cf. V.-L. Saulnier speaking about Marot's elegies: 'Nous sommes en un temps qui n'est pas encore celui du pétrarquisme français'; *Les Elégies de Clément Marot*, Paris (1952), p. 96.

[24] See C. A. Mayer et D. Bentley-Cranch, 'Le Premier Pétrarquiste français, Jean Marot,' *Bibliothèque d'Humanisme et Renaissance*, t. XXVII (1965), pp. 183–5.

[25] On this question see C. A. Mayer et D. Bentley-Cranch, 'Clément Marot poète pétrarquiste', *Bibliothèque d'Humanisme et Renaissance*, t., XXVIII (1966), pp. 32–51.

[26] Cf. A. Foxwell, edition of the *Poems of Sir Thomas Wyatt*, London (1913), and S. Baldi, *La Poesia di Sir Thomas Wyatt, il primo petrarchista inglese*, Florence (1953), p. 221. Cf. also C. A. Mayer et D. Bentley-Cranch 'Le Premier Pétrarquiste français, Jean Marot', *art. cit.*

[27] *Œuvres diverses*, Rondeau XLII.

[28] *Œuvres diverses*, Rondeau XLIII.

Ruth Murphy

RABELAIS, THAUMASTE AND THE KING'S GREAT MATTER

Rabelais' use of reality, his embodiment of historical, geo-
graphical and local fact into the texture of *Pantagruel* is sufficiently
known to need no elaboration, and though the activity of seeking
out the reality underlying his fiction is non-literary, its results
have contributed much to a fuller appreciation of the text. Indeed,
too rigid a separation of disciplines may lead to later generations,
through ignorance of events or failure to relate them to a work
of literature, remaining baffled by some allusion whose point
would have been immediately obvious to the writer's contemporaries.

This appears to be the case with Chapter XIII [XVIII–XX] of
Pantagruel, relating the visit of the learned Englishman Thaumaste
to Pantagruel, and his disputation with Panurge. What is this
enigmatic episode really about? Is it simply an illustration of
Pantagruel's intellectual gigantism? Why then does it occur in the
sequence of chapters devoted to Panurge (X–XIV [XIV–XXII]),
and why should it be Panurge who undertakes the dispute rather
than Pantagruel himself, as in the lawsuit? Granted, *Non est
discipulus supra magistrum*, as Thaumaste points out; but in this case
the master prepared himself for the coming debate very differently from his disciple. Indeed, his feverish bout of study, which
caused Panurge to fear for his health, departs so much from the
confident ease with which he accomplished his other feats that it is
hard to read the episode as just another in their series.

Alternatively, is it a satire of the doctors of the Sorbonne? But
why then should Rabelais have Thaumaste specifically reject their
mode of disputation?[1] Why too should he have the scholars discuss
problems of magic, alchemy, geomancy, astrology, and the

kabala, all matters one would scarcely associate with the Sorbonne? Or is it a satire on adepts of the occult sciences listed, intended to decry their learning as so much nonsense? This certainly seems a possibility, given Rabelais' attitude to astrology and the like. But here two difficulties immediately arise. One would expect that any Englishman suited by his learning and renown to the role of Thaumaste would not even now be far to seek; whereas this English Agrippa must lie buried, if he lie at all, very deep in the annals of history.[2] Further, if one temporarily limits attention to the kabala, then it is of the German Reuchlin one thinks, of the Cologne disputes surrounding his work, and of the judgement passed on it by the Sorbonne in 1514.[3] But would these disputes be fresh enough in Rabelais' and the public mind to give real point to the chapter, and in any case would the point not have been lost on the popular reader or hearer, unfamiliar with these academic debates and unable to see in the chapter any more than buffoonery? Further, would Rabelais, stressing as he did in Gargantua's letter the value of Hebrew for the study of scripture, so have burlesqued one of the great advocates of Hebrew? And if he did, why present the German Reuchlin as an Englishman?

It has been suggested the original of Thaumaste may be Thomas More, but this idea has rightly been rejected.[4] Although the textual change from *ung grandissime clerc* to *un sçavant homme* would accord both with the change in More's situation between 1532 and 1534 and with the deeper knowledge of English affairs Rabelais must have had after accompanying Jean du Bellay to Rome, and though in general terms More was well fitted to be the eminent English scholar who visited Paris, nevertheless there is nothing in Rabelais' text which specifically indicates More, and much that taken literally would exclude him. Further, More's repute as a humanist and his friendship with Erasmus make it improbable that Rabelais would cast him in the occasionally undignified role of Thaumaste.

However, the strongest argument against Thaumaste being based on More lies in the fact that More was not among the learned Englishmen who in 1529 and 1530, on the orders of Henry VIII and with the support of Francis I, visited Paris with the express purpose of persuading the Faculty of Theology to give an opinion on one particular abstruse matter: the divorce of Henry VIII and Catherine of Aragon.

Over a period of nine months or more, there occurred in Paris individual consultations and stormy faculty meetings; bribery, threats and political pressure were freely used to obtain a decision favourable to Henry in what rapidly became known as 'the King's Great Matter'. It is our contention that, rather than in any specific English scholar, the key to the Thaumaste episode is to be found in these events, in this chapter of Anglo-French relations which is now forgotten but which was notorious in its day. This explanation of the episode has in its favour a high degree of historical probability, and is satisfying in that it shows the Thaumaste episode to have a point which Rabelais' contemporaries could not fail to grasp.

How Henry came by the idea of a divorce from Catherine of Aragon is hard to say.[5] Catherine attributed it to Wolsey; Henry credited the French ambassador with the notion; since Wolsey was hand-in-glove with the French, the allegations are not incompatible. Moreover, early in 1527 relations with the Emperor, Catherine's nephew, were at a very low ebb, while a close Anglo-French alliance against him was in preparation. Political considerations may well have played their part in this complex affair from the very start.

What Henry's true motives were in seeking the 'divorce' will of course never be known. Were his scruples of conscience about the validity of his marriage genuine, or was his main preoccupation the dynastic one of begetting a (legitimate) son to succeed him? Even regardless of origin and motives however, the affair is a labyrinthine tissue of theological, legal, political, diplomatic and military threads. The discussions in the French universities occurred during its second phase, after July 1529 when the legatine court went into recess and the case was advoked to Rome, and before January 1531 when the writ of Praemunire was served on Convocation.

The first phase had lasted just over two years. In April 1527, Henry consulted some of his trusted advisers about the legality of his marriage to Catherine; in May, at a secret court in Westminster, he had himself accused by Wolsey, the Cardinal Legate, and Warham, Archbishop of Canterbury, of having lived for eighteen years in incestuous intercourse with his late brother's widow. Perhaps because of Warham's scruples, perhaps because news arrived while the court was sitting that Rome had been sacked and the Pope was in the hands of the Emperor, it was found only that the marriage seemed open to doubt and merited the strictest examination. Other bishops consulted, perhaps not realizing what was expected of them, gave answers unfavourable to Henry. The first strategem had failed, and the Pope must obviously be informed. In consequence, when Wolsey went to France shortly afterwards (July 1527), part of his diplomatic business was to enlist the support of the French for a commission of cardinals to replace the Pope during his 'captivity'; this tactic also failed, but another part of his plan did not.

Though France could not openly give support to Henry while the French princes were still held in Madrid, nevertheless she could send an army into Italy, and did so. On the success of that army was to depend the success of the next development in the King's matter. In February 1528, Stephen Gardiner and Edward Foxe were sent to the Pope to request that he grant to Wolsey and a special legate powers to pronounce final judgement in the case. In April, French military successes aiding, the Pope granted the request, appointing Cardinal Campeggio as the special legate, but giving him specific instructions not to take final action without reference to Rome, and to procrastinate all he could.

And delay he did, both in travelling to England—so much so that by the time he arrived in October 1528 the military situation in Italy had been reversed once more in favour of the Emperor—and in starting proceedings. The hope in Rome seems to have been that Henry would soon tire of Ann Boleyn and that the whole matter would go by default. Finally however the legatine court sat at Blackfriars on 18 June 1529. Catherine, appearing in person, appealed against the court. At the next session three days later she made her well-known appeal to the king's conscience. On June 25 another dramatic moment occurred when Bishop Fisher protested against the forging of his signature and seal on a list of bishops who had allegedly endorsed the king's position.

Before the court could conclude its business, politics and the vacation intervened. In June, a French army led by the Count of Saint-Pol had been defeated at Landriano, and the Pope had come to terms with the Emperor in the treaty of Barcelona. On July 23 Campeggio convened the court to announce that it would go into recess until October. A week later, news arrived that the case had been advoked to Rome. A week later again came the crowning blow to Henry: the signing at Cambrai on 5 August of the Ladies' Peace, by which Francis I settled all his differences with the Emperor.

So ended the first phase in the development of the King's Great Matter. If all was not yet lost, neither had anything been gained, and from Henry's point of view the situation was black. The theological nub of the matter was whether Henry's marriage to Catherine was valid in the sight of God, since she was the widow of his brother Arthur. Two apparently conflicting biblical books were invoked: *Leviticus* xviii, 6 and 16, and xx, 21:

> Omnis homo ad proximam sanguinis sui non accedet, ut revelet turpitudinem ejus. Ego Dominus.
> Turpitudinem uxoris fratris tui non revelabis; quia turpitudo fratris tui est.
> Qui duxerit uxorem fratris sui, rem facit illicitam, turpitudinem fratris sui revelavit; absque liberis erunt.

and *Deuteronomy* xxv, 5–6:

> Quando habitaverint fratres simul, et unus ex eis absque liberis mortuus fuerit, uxor defuncti non nubet alteri; sed accipiet eam frater ejus, et suscitabit semen fratris sui; et primogenitum ex ea filium nomine illius appellabit, ut non deleatur nomen ejus ex Israel.

For the king, Gardiner was to argue that *Deuteronomy* was a temporary disposition limited to particular circumstances, but that *Leviticus* was of permanent value.[6] On the other hand the Bishop of Bath, John Clerk, 'had the courage to declare that the passage of Leviticus does not refer to the widow of a late, but to the wife of a living brother, that it does not relate to a marriage but only emphasizes the prohibition against adultery in a case where it seems particularly shocking, that the prohibition of canon law is consequently not based upon the passage and can derive no authority from the Bible'.[7] John Fisher agreed with Clerk. From Catherine's point of view, *Leviticus* and *Deuteronomy* were irrelevant: to the end, her main line of defence was that her first marriage had never been consummated; she was therefore Henry's wife by a valid marriage.

Henry did not answer Catherine's objection, but preferred legal arguments concerning the validity of the papal bull of 1503 granting a dispensation to marry. His lawyers had found in it what appear to be defects of substance capable of rendering it invalid. When news arrived from Spain that a papal brief had been discovered, also permitting the marriage, of the same date as the bull but without its defects, there was consternation in Henry's camp, and everything was done, but without success, to obtain the original of this brief.

s

It was apparently only in the second phase of the affair, when the case had been advoked to Rome and was being touted round the universities that the validity of the dispensation was questioned in a more fundamental manner, to wit: could the Pope dispense the positive law of God? If the Bible forbad a man to marry his brother's widow, what right had the Pope to give a dispensation to the contrary? So far was Henry from raising this question during the first months of the affair, that he requested from the Pope a dispensation to marry again before the matter was judged, and another dispensation allowing this new marriage to be valid within the first degree of affinity: the latter being necessary because, since Anne Boleyn's sister Mary had been his mistress, under canon law he was related to Anne in the same degree as he was to Catherine if she had been Arthur's wife. When the matter was taken to the universities however, it was put in the form of two questions, the first concerning the lawfulness of the type of marriage concerned, and the second questioning the Pope's power to dispense:

> ... dubium nobis propositum, quod est tale, utrum jure divino pariter et naturali illicitum sit homini Christiano relictam fratris sui etiam absque liberis sed matrimonio jam consummato, defuncti ducere uxorem; et an Pontifici liceat super hujusmodi Nuptiis dispensare.[8]

During the sixteen or so months which followed the disgrace of Wolsey and preceded the emergence of Thomas Cromwell, Henry's chief object seems to have been to obtain from learned men and institutions at home and abroad, by fair means or foul, opinions in favour of his divorce, in the hope of swaying the Pope.

The canvassing of the French scholars and universities took place between September 1529 and July 1530, that is during the time Guillaume and then Jean du Bellay were in France overseeing the progress of the matter in that country. First, Ghinucci, the bishop of Worcester, arrived in Paris on 11 October on his way through to Italy, declared his commission to Francis the following day, and on 15 October took leave of the king, who desired him to speak of Henry's matter to the Pope.[9] He was followed, we may conclude quite rapidly, by George Boleyn (Ann's brother) and Dr John Stokesley who were sent on a mission to Francis, replacing Sir Francis Bryan: they were to prevent a Franco-Scottish alliance; to prevent a General Council; to obtain opinions favourable to Henry's 'divorce'; and to get copies of the original text of the treaty of Cambrai.[10]

Although, according to Chapuys, it was rumoured from the beginning of September that George Boleyn was to form part of a new embassy to France,[11] it is difficult to ascertain exactly when he and Stokesley actually went to Paris. All the evidence however points to their having left England early in October 1529,[12] and if they travelled with Ghinucci, as Chapuys reported that they would,[13] they must have been in Paris on 11 October, in time to engage in individual discussions with some doctors before the Sorbonne debated the matter on 21 and 22 October.

Stokesley in particular was charged in the instructions with consulting the learned men whom Langey had reported as being favourable to the King's cause:

> Upon the King's great matter they shall say, the King has sent Stokesly, who shall declare his opinion and that of other learned men, and shall say that, as De Langy at his late being here had said that divers in those parts were of similar opinion, he had special charge to consult them, and he shall do his best to obtain opinions favorable to the King.[14]

His discussions did not always have the desired result: this information Chappuys had by the admission of Langey himself, in a conversation which took place in England early in February 1530:

> In the course of conversation we touched on the subject of Dr. Stokesley, and his attempt to gain the decision of the Paris doctors in behalf of the King. At first they denied it, and then excused it, and then said that several who had been consulted by Stokesley had given their opinions against him. De Langey spoke so precisely, that I believe he had orders from his master to interest himself in this matter; and I am confirmed in it by a letter from an English resident in Paris.[15]

Whether Langey's admission referred to attempts made by Stokesley before the first Sorbonne discussions or to subsequent activity on his part cannot be determined. He was however introduced by Langey to the First President Jean de Selve, to the bishops of Lisieux and Senlis and to some doctors of the Sorbonne, and individual approaches were made to people thought to be favourable to Henry.

Then on 21 October there was held a meeting of theologians appointed to give their opinion on the case; a relation of this meeting is extant in a letter from Ambrosio de la Serna to Catherine's physician.[16] De la Serna's account of the address given by the First President and of a speech by the Spaniard Dr Garay could be taken as implying that there had already been a meeting of some sort. Be that as it may, the meeting was a stormy one. The First President Jean de Selve addressed the assembly, reporting a letter received from the King of England complaining of the injuries (agravios) he had received from the Emperor, and protesting his own (de Selve's) impartiality. Then the Bishop of Lisieux rose, 'uttered certain complaints and threats', accused the Imperial ambassadors of being misinformed by slanderous letters about him and other members of the University, and threatened those responsible, particularly Garay and Moscoso, with legal action.

After much 'wrangling and disputing', a scrutiny of the votes was finally taken, not without disagreement over the scrutineers. When, next day, the President informed Garay and Moscoso that scrutiny of the votes revealed a majority in Henry's favour, they challenged *inter alia* the interpretation put on the conclusion many had come to: 'Summus pontifex non poterat dispensare nisi in rebus arduis....' These votes, according to Dr Moscoso, ought to be counted in the Queen's favour, not the King's. As Bourrilly writes:

Des protestations énergiques accueillirent le résultat du scrutin: deux Espagnols, Garay et Moscoso, le syndic de la faculté de théologie, Noël Béda, se firent remarquer par leur véhémence: ils contestèrent la sincérité du vote, l'exactitude du chiffre des voix favorables et la validité de l'opération, puisque la première partie de la conclusion qu'on avait interprétée en faveur du roi d'Angleterre pouvait aussi justement être considérée comme favorable à la reine Catherine d'Aragon.[17]

Disapproval of the proceedings was not confined to the academic opposition: despite Francis' backing of Henry's case, a dominican friar recently arrived in Paris

had seen and heard at the court of the most Christian King of France Madame d'Alençon and other ladies and gentlemen greatly shocked and scandalized at what had taken place. That Princess had even said to him these very words, 'If the Paris University had given no other proofs of partiality and violence than those shown in this present case, that would be sufficient for me to look upon its future conclusions as completely erroneous and false.[18]

The faculty was not to discuss the matter again until 1st February 1530. The intervening months had not however seen a cessation of activity; both sides had continued their intriguing.

Stokesley must have been busy, for on 29 December Jean du Bellay wrote to Montmorency that he had never seen Henry or his party in so favourable mood, largely because of the ambassadors' reports of what the French theologians had done. He warns Montmorency however about Noël Béda: 'il y a ung Béda de ce nombre qui est ung très dangereux marchant, et ne seroyt grant besoing d'en avoir beaucoup de telz en une bonne compagnye'.[19] Montmorency sent for Béda at Chantilly and informed him of the king's wishes; this did not however stop Béda and Garay from collecting signatures in favour of Catherine. A German doctor, Gervais Wain, had already been brought in to help in 'persuading' the theologians to decide for Henry; now Béda's manoeuvres necessitated counteraction. In this Stokesley seems to have had some success, as he reports to Wiltshire on 16 January 1530 that the doctors won over by Béda have recanted, and that they, the English party, have the inquisitor Valentinus Lemini in their favour.[20]

Nevertheless it seems clear from this letter that stronger influence was needed if they were to be quite certain of their ends, since he states that the presence of Langey was necessary. It seems also that an appeal had been made to Francis I to state his position openly, and even perhaps to address a faculty meeting. 'If the French King or Lysott[21] will show themselves to the faculty, the matter might pass in a month, though Lysott strongly favours the Pope'.

What the score was at that time we can learn by the ubiquitous ear of Chappuys:

> I have been told by the landlord of the house where the French ambassador lives that he has heard him say that the King, his master, had caused several learned Parisian doctors to be written to in support of this divorce and that 35 of them had already declared in favour of it; that the subject had been much argued, and that among the said doctors were some, who fearing lest they might lose the preferments they held under your Majesty, did not venture to give an opinion in the matter; and that a promise had been made to them in the name of the two kings (i.e. Henry and Francis) that in such case more valuable benefices should be bestowed upon them. The number of doctors they have found ready for this purpose is certainly not large, but on the other hand, the amount of crowns they have been obliged to disburse has been really enormous.[22]

Henry however was dissatisfied with the doctors of Paris, in comparison with those of Italy. Langey was only able to persuade him out of thinking that Francis had not done enough to recommend the matter to them by showing him a letter from Gervais Wain reporting some progress.[23]

At this stage in the proceedings, towards the end of January, Stokesley leaves the French arena to continue his work in Italy. In Stokesley's own letter of 16 January we see a hint perhaps that the matter was to pass into other hands; du Bellay, we learn, 'sent such letters as he had to Mr Poole,[24] but none to us'.

On February 1st, the faculty met again. Dr Jacques Barthélemy who at the October meeting had been aligned with Béda and Garay, complained of the way doctors were still being individually consulted and their opinions collected. Unanimously the faculty forbad this practice, under pain of exclusion, and renewed the prohibition three days later. For the next four months the struggle continued, but behind the scenes. Langey, who had given Henry an undertaking that he would obtain a favourable decision from the Sorbonne, spent a few days in Paris at the beginning of March, and returned at the end of the month primarily for the purpose of forwarding the King of England's 'matter'. His tactics in the cause were described by the Spaniard Garay:[25] Langey would assemble ten or twelve doctors for dinner, and then persuade them to sign a prepared document stating that the Pope had not the right to dispense in the case of such a marriage, which was contrary to divine law. No less than thirty doctors had been brought to sign by these methods.

The final act, the collective conclusion, was delayed, largely because the French princes were still held by the Emperor; in these circumstances Langey hesitated to make use of his ultimate weapon, the letters he had from Francis I, for fear of provoking the Emperor. But arrangements for the return of the Princes were finally made on 26 May, and a general assembly of the Sorbonne was called for 7 June 1530.

Garay seems to have respected the oath not to reveal what happened in the discussions of the assembly, but his general comments to the Emperor are worth noting:

> Many doctors have been summoned to this Council, and the utmost violence and wickedness prevail. Several who were in favour of the Queen are either dead or absent and dare not speak, so that there is not the liberty of action required in a case of such importance.[26]

Thanks to Langey however we have an eye-witness account of the first part of the proceedings.[27] After explaining why he had

finally been obliged to present Francis' letters of 7 May to the
faculty, he lists those present at the congregation:

> ...y assisterent Messieurs les Evesques de Senlis, Abbés de Premontré,
> de Chailly, de Missy, de saint Martin, de Laon, de Vendosme, de
> Foucambault, et autres Abbés; plusieurs Doyens, Archidiacres et
> Chantres d'Eglises Collegiales, Prieurs generaux, Provinciaux, Minis-
> tres et Gardiens de l'Ordre des quatre Mendians, tous Docteurs de
> cette Université et Faculté, gens de sçavoir, capacité et auctorité, et
> tous assemblez et venus par vostre commandement...[28]

Then follows an account of his own masterly address to the assembly: Henry's scruples of conscience about his marriage, which he
held to be 'chose damnable et indispensable' for reasons which the
English ambassadors would expound, led him despite his own
certainty to seek the opinion of the Sorbonne which he held in
such esteem:

> luy pour icelle reverence et reputation de leur jugement, voulloit bien
> entendre leur opinion et determination en cette matiere, non point en
> forme de jugement, ce qu'ils pourroient craindre d'entreprendre, mais
> seulement par forme de Conseil et doctrinalement...[29]

He had therefore asked Francis to request their opinion. The
ambassadors of the emperor, 'd'autre part aussi vostre bon frere,
et allié à present', had also frequently requested Francis to see
that the Queen was not wronged by any unjust judgement given
by the learned men of the realm. Francis, therefore, knowing that
he could not before God refuse the counsel of his scholars to his
two allies, and thinking that both the emperor and Henry would
accept what was right in conscience and before God, had caused
the Faculty to meet,

> ...en tel et si suffisant nombre, que pieça ne fut en pareil, les priant &
> neantmoins enjoignant qu'en se recommandant à Dieu, apres la
> celebration d'une Messe du saint Esprit, ils eussent à bien veoir les
> articles qui sur cette matiere leur seroient proposés, iceux debatre &
> discuter, toutes les faveurs ou apprehensions cessantes: Et aprés meure
> deliberation, comme en tel cas est requis, en conclure et determiner ce
> que Dieu leur inspireroit en leurs consciences & leurditte conclusion et
> determination, ils baillassent és mains à qui par cy après vous leur
> ordonneriez de la bailler.[30]

As Langey comments to Francis, not even the emperor, had he
been present, could have found fault with (calomnier) his address.
To maintain a semblance of impartiality, after Béda had spoken of
how Francis wished to meet the wishes of Henry, Langey spoke
again stressing that the Emperor too was an ally, and that the

matter should be determined 'sans faveur mais selon Dieu et vérité'. Whereupon he departed 'pour les laisser plus librement conclure de ce qu'ils avoient à faire'. The rest of the narration he presumably obtained from some doctor less scrupulous than Garay about his oath of silence.

When the discussion began, three opinions were expressed as to whether the Faculty should accede to Francis' request. The first to speak were obviously in Henry's favour:

> Les premiers deliberans furent d'avis que vostre Requeste estoit si juste et raisonnable, que non seulement à vous, mais à la plus vile ou estrangere personne du monde, ne se pouvoit selon Dieu reffuser, et à cette cause que promptement vous debvoient obeïr...[31]

Doubtless it was the imperialists who introduced the following delaying tactics:

> ...autres furent d'advis qu'estant la Faculté subjette au Pape, duquel ils ont tant de beaux Privileges, et veu qu'en cette matiere il est question de la puissance du Pape, ils ne debvroient parler sans envoyer par devers luy sçavoir son intention, à tout le moins envoyer devers vous, sçavoir si vous seriez de cest advis.[32]

A third section suggested a compromise, that of writing to Francis, but beginning the discussion meanwhile.

Some of the doctors, obviously the pro-Spanish, would only approve the second course of action, reminding the assembly that the Pope had forbidden discussion of the matter and had already twice admonished Henry and those concerned with the matter about having it discussed. This brought forth a strong reply from 'aucuns personnages d'authorité', reminding the faculty that its privileges depended on the king as well as the Pope, pointing out that to suggest that the Pope had forbidden "consolation et remede" to be given to a suffering Christian conscience was an attack against the Pope's honour, and finally, referring to some unrecorded words about Henry, that

> c'estoit tres-mal parlé telles outrageuses paroles en telle Compagnie, et sans montrer en quoy, d'un tel Prince allié du Roy leur Prince et Seigneur...[33]

who had moreover shown himself a good Christian Prince and zealous defender of the unity and peace of the church.

At this point tempers broke; an incident occurred, and the meeting came to a tumultuous close:

> ...durant lesquels propos, et cependant que leur Bedeau recolligeoit les noms et opinions des deliberans, pour veoir quel seroit l'opinion de

la plus grande partie, se leva un desdits sieurs nos Maistres, qui luy arracha le Roole des poings et le deschira, et sur ce point se leverent en trouppe, et avec grand et desordonné tumulte, commencerent aulcuns à cryer que c'estoit assez fait et parlé et que la plus grande et plus saine partie estoit d'avis de n'en deliberer sans escrire à vous, Sire, et au Pape. Ainsi se departit la Compagnie...[34]

The English ambassadors, who were walking in a gallery, saw them leave 'en tel desordre et crierie', and heard all that was being said. They interpreted what had happened in bad part, blaming Langey for not taking seriously enough their warnings about Béda and his accomplices, and began writing to Henry and Wiltshire. Fearing the political consequences Langey spoke to the First President who sent for Béda, Barthélemy, Tabary 'et aulcuns autres principaux autheurs de cette discorde et brigue' and finally got them to agree to meet again the next day and to adopt at least the third opinion, that of beginning deliberations while waiting for Francis' reply.

On 9 June the faculty therefore met again, and agreed to start discussions the following Monday, 11 June, and to send their conclusion under seal to Francis 'pour la bailler à qui bon vous semblera'. (This last point was important; as Garay had discovered to his disadvantage, possession of the original documents was capital.) The English ambassadors however were still not fully satisfied that the faculty really intended to come to a conclusion, and Langey admits that their fears were not groundless:

lesdits Ambassadeurs... m'ont dit rondement qu'ils connoissent bien que tout ce qui est conclu, est seulement pour paistre de paroles le Roy leur Maistre et eux et leur tenir le bec en l'eauë, sous couleur qu'on parlera de la matiere, mais qu'ils sçavent bien qu'on n'en fera aucune conclusion, et n'est Sire, du tout sans fondement qu'ils le disent; car il en y a aucuns qui presque publiquement se vantent que d'un an la chose [ne] sera vuidée.[35]

Béda had been publicly talking in that vein, so once again the First President sent for him and wrung from him a promise not only not to prevent the king's letters being obeyed, but also to do all he could to see that the affair took its course, 'sans bruit ne scandale'.

Langey advises Francis, if he values English friendship, to write to the dean of the faculty Maistre Dominique le Mercier, 'homme desirant vous obeïr', commanding him to expedite the matter. He reports too that the bishop of Senlis (Guillaume Petit) is eager to see Francis both to tell him about the way the faculty is governed and to beg him to subject it to a much needed reform; further, some are of the opinion that once the Princes have been restored,

> fissiez telle demonstration de ceux qui vous ont mis en cest accessoire, que par cy aprés les autres en fussent plus sages,[36]

a suggestion which Langey does not comment on but doubtless approves.[37]

As had been decided, the faculty met on Monday, 11 June, to begin its deliberations. Langey, replacing the indisposed First President, presented further letters from Francis, dated 27 May. While he was there the English ambassadors arrived, one of whom revealed English suspicions of French intentions by a forthright warning not to try to dupe the king of England, backed up by a scarcely-veiled threat of political disaffection: the faculty should proceed

> de sorte que le Roy mon maistre congneust par effect que toutes amitiez abandonnées, il s'estoit declaré amy de Prince non ingrat, et qui ne luy voulust refuser ce qu'à personne du monde selon Dieu ne peut estre reffusé.[38]

Langey, ever fearful of the possible political consequences, that is, of England breaking with France and transferring her friendship to Spain—'que par l'advenement d'ung tiers se fissent amis Herode et Pilate'[39]—thought Francis should be informed of this happening so that he could take steps to ensure that Wiltshire did not write about it 'trop crument' to Henry, and so that the French ambassador to Henry, Joaquim de Vaux, could be suitably instructed.

When Francis learned what had happened in Paris, he was predictably angry; he ordered Lizet to threaten Béda with the royal wrath. As to whether the Pope should be consulted, he needless to say rejected the suggestion, which would have been contrary to the rights and privileges of the realm.[40] After this, the doctors clearly had no option but to proceed to a definitive conclusion. This they did at meetings held at the end of June and the beginning of July. On 2 July they finally reached their decision; by fifty-three votes to forty-seven, they agreed a determination according to which both divine and natural law forbad a man to marry the widow of a brother deceased without children, and the Pope could not dispense for such a marriage. Julius II's dispensation of 1503 was illegal, and the marriage of Henry and

Catherine was null. A certified copy of the document was despatched to Henry on 6 July.[41]

Though the adverse party continued its struggle in various ways for another month, all it achieved was a few days' delay in the sealing of the determination. The forces against which they were fighting were too strong, for they were opposing not theologians who held different views on certain kinds of marriage or on papal authority, but men of power like Guillaume du Bellay, for whom the king of England's divorce was not a matter of theology, but just one element in a complex struggle for the balance of power in Europe.

To what extent were the intrigues which surrounded the Sorbonne's discussion of the matter repeated elsewhere? On 5 April 1530, Orléans decided in Henry's favour; on 23 April Poitiers decided against him, as did Angers on 7 May, despite Dr Gervais Wain.[42] On 24 May, the faculty of canon law in Paris, 'à la requête de Reginald Pole et sur la sollicitation pressante du roi d'Angleterre lui-même',[43] pronounced in Henry's favour, as did Bourges on 10 June, and Toulouse on 1 October.[44] Was there any repetition of what had occurred when, in June and August respectively of the following year, the law faculties of Orléans and Paris declared that Henry was not bound to appear at Rome?[45] These questions cannot be answered here; it is enough to have seen the theologians of Paris individually and collectively approached, bribed, threatened and subjected to political pressures over a period of nine months, and finally, after stormy meetings, coming to the conclusion desired, the whole to a background of political diplomacy dominated by Langey.

It is perhaps Langey's dominance in the matter, particularly during the last few months, that causes the English envoys to be cloaked in near-obscurity. Not that they were dominated by him; rather, there seems to have been considerable tension and mistrust, as the English pressed for the Sorbonne to meet and conclude, and Langey procrastinated, hesitating to make open use of Francis' letters before the French princes were restored, and yet fearing to delay too long lest Henry should recall his ambassadors and come to terms with the emperor to the disadvantage of France.

The obscurity which surrounds the activities of these Englishmen does not mean that they remain anonymous; who they were has in part emerged.

In the first few months, we saw George Boleyn and John Stokesley engaged on the matter, the latter leaving for Italy about the end of January, the former leaving Paris for the court midway through January[46] and returning to England in February.[47]

Next there appeared Reginald Pole, kinsman of Henry and future cardinal, 'one of the most learned men known',[48] who had gone to Paris in October 1529 to continue his studies, with an exhibition of £100 from Henry;[49] who had, perhaps in January 1530,[50] been commanded by Henry 'ut cum Parisiensibus causam [suam] agerem';[51] whose biographers have differed as to the extent and willingness of his involvement in the matter[52] but whose participation in itself is undeniable.

There was also Sir Francis Bryan, who had been given leave to return to England in October 1529 when Boleyn and Stokesley went to Paris;[53] he was among those commissioned in February to restore the *fleur de lys* and the indemnity, and was then once again accredited as ambassador to France.[54] Bryan was in France from early March to late August of 1530,[55] and of him, in connection with the Sorbonne discussions, Langey expresses the fear that Henry would withdraw him before the decision was reached if the matter was delayed too long;[56] he is not however named as the ambassador who threatened the doctors with the political consequences of not concluding.

Lastly we can name Dr Edward Fox, the future bishop of Hereford, who in February and April 1530 had been concerned in obtaining favourable decisions from Cambridge and Oxford,[57] and was employed on several missions concerned with the divorce; he was sent to Paris in May 1530, in response, it is said, to Pole's request that Henry send someone better qualified than himself to treat of his matter.[58] He crossed the channel on 25 May,[59] and was in Paris at the end of June.[60] On 7 July, Pole, writing to Henry, speaks of the great diligence and prudence Fox had used in withstanding the opposition.[61] Fox himself was the bearer of the letter and was back in England by 20 July.[62]

Away from Paris, after George Boleyn's departure, there was John Wellisbourne (Welshebourne), gentleman of the privy chamber, who was sent in March in embassy to the French king;[63] doubtless it was he who was at Poitiers on 26 April.[64] On May 16 he reported to Henry from Angoulême that he could not discover what was happening or intended; there were daily discussions, but much secrecy.[65] He remained in France until 19 December,[66]

when he was replaced by Sir Francis Bryan.[67] Also with the
French king from early May until August[68] was Thomas Boleyn,
earl of Wiltshire and Ormond. He may have been in Paris in
June;[69] whether he was or no, Henry was competently represented in that city.

Further research may reveal in more detail what part was
played, in Paris and elsewhere, by these and perhaps other
English ambassadors, in furthering the King's Great Matter,
during the consultation of the French universities. For our
present purpose, it is sufficient to establish that there were such
men in France engaged on that matter while the events we have
been describing took their course.

We return now to Rabelais and Thaumaste, and to our
suggestion that the Thaumaste episode is based on the events we
have recounted. That Rabelais was in Paris in 1530 there is little
doubt,[70] nor that when in the capital he frequented 'la gent
scolaire de l'Université'.[71] It seems therefore more than likely that
Rabelais knew of this affair which was being spoken of, by Garay's
report, in every tavern in Paris.[72] Two years later, Rabelais
writes of the visit of a learned Englishman to Paris to dispute of
difficult matters; can there be any doubt but that in this episode,
he was alluding to the matter of which there had been such protracted and stormy discussions, and which was still unresolved?

Looking afresh at Rabelais' narration, we find several details
which conform with our hypothesis. First, Maistre Alcofribas
refrains from explaining what Thaumaste's propositions were and
what the signs meant, because

> l'on m'a dict que Thaumaste en feist un grand livre, imprimé à
> Londres, auquel il declaire tout sans rien laisser. Par ce, je m'en
> deporte pour le present.[73]

Now, in 1530 there had come from the press of Thomas Berthelet
in London a quarto volume bearing the title:

> *Gravissimæ, atque exactissimæ illustrissimarum totius Italiæ, et Galliæ Aca-*
> *demiarum Censuræ, efficacissimis etiam quorundam doctissimorum virorum*
> *argumentationibus explicatæ, de veritate illius propositionis, Videlicet quod ducere*
> *relictam fratris mortui sine liberis ita sit de jure divino et naturali prohibitum:*
> *ut nullus Pontifex super hujusmodi Matrimoniis contractis sive contrahendis*
> *dispensare possit.*[74]

In it the opinions of the Universities of Paris (faculties of theology
and canon law), Toulouse, Orléans, Bourges, Bologna, Padua and
Pavia were presented, followed by a treatise probably written by

Dr Edward Fox with the assistance of Dr John Stokesley (now elect of London) and Nicholas de Burgo. An English translation, thought to be by Dr Cranmer, was to follow:

> The determinations of the moste famous and moste excellent univer-sities of Italy and Fraunce, that it is so unlefull for a man to marie his brothers wyfe, that the pope hath no power to dispence therwith.[75]

This was not the only book about the matter to be printed, but it was the 'official' version, the public printed record of the results of months of negotiation. We may well assume that this was the book of which Maître Alcofribas had been told.

The next point concerns Panurge's apparel:

> Or notez que Panurge avoit mis au bout de sa longue braguette un beau floc de soye rouge, blanche, verte et bleue, et dedans avoit mis une belle pomme d'orange.[76]

This short passage, to which Rabelais deliberately draws our attention, presents details which, considered individually, could be regarded as coincidental, but which taken together form what is surely a conscious heraldic reference to the English royal house.

The combination of colours, in the order given by Rabelais, seems meaningless, but when paired white with green, and blue with red, the colours become significant. White and green were the colours of the house of Tudor;[77] as such they were the livery colours of Henry VII and Henry VIII;[78] as such they appear as the background colours of non-armorial royal badge-bearing pennon-banners and standards[79] of the time.

Blue and red on the other hand had been the 'ground' colours of the English royal arms since Edward III took *Quarterly France Ancient and England*;[80] Henry IV's change to *Quarterly France Modern and England*,[81] which remained the royal arms in Henry VIII's reign,[82] did not affect the blue and red. A Tudor manu-script gives pennon-banners of Edward III[83] which use blue and red as the background to badges, and similar standards not only for Edward III and IV but also for Henry VII.[84] (This last standard moreover, like that of Edward III, is fringed red and blue, indicating the livery colours.)

What Rabelais appears to have done is to take the ground colours of the royal arms and the livery colours predominantly used as background in Tudor badge-bearing ensigns, and mix them together in an impressionistic allusion to the royal house of England. The mixing may not even be random however, since the order he gives, if read as quarters, would endow the said royal house with a new banner which one could describe perhaps as *Quarterly England and Tudor*.[85] This notion may be fanciful, but there seems little doubt that the choice of colours was not made at random.

Any doubt there is must be undermined when we examine the way Panurge bears the colours, as a tuft or small fringe. It was common heraldic practice for some types of ensign to have a fringe in the livery colours.[86] Standards in particular seem to have been so fringed; those we have referred to all show a fringe, usually (since the badge is associated with the livery colours)[87] of the same colours as the background. It is difficult not to associate Panurge's tuft of colours with these fringes; one is tempted even to the conclusion that, in his own way, he is bearing the livery of England.

The *pomme d'orange* carried by Panurge continues the heraldic allusion. Its relevance to Henry's matter is absolutely clear; like the other *pommes* it was traditionally a symbol of love. As Belleau wrote in his commentary on Ronsard, 'Toute sorte de pommes et principalement les oranges sont dédiées à la Volupté, aux Graces, et à l'amour'.[88] More than that however, it is possible that Panurge's *pomme d'orange* not only has its usual symbolic value, but is intended to recall the *pomme de Grenade*, which likewise symbolized love:—'L'amour à la Grenade en symbole estoit joint'[89]—and which Catherine of Aragon, before going to England, had adopted as her badge.[90] As such it was incorporated into royal coats of arms,[91] and figures, entwined with the double rose of Lancaster and York, on a non-armorial ensign.[92]

Individually, any one of these three details, the colours, their mode of display, and the symbolic orange could be ignored as meaningless or coincidental, but the three together form a coherent heraldic pattern of allusion to England, Henry and Catherine that cannot lightly be dismissed as fortuitous. Nor is this all; Rabelais takes up the story two chapters later.

Panurge's victory over Thaumaste gained him public repute in Paris and made him welcome among the ladies, with the result that he attempted to gain the favour of one of the great ladies of the city.[93] The fact that his success in the disputation should win him popularity with the ladies and be the cause of his undertaking the exploit recounted in chapter XIV [XXI–XXII] shows a continuity of theme which supports our argument. Beyond this general continuity, there is one point of particular relevance:

> et la [sa braguette] feist au dessus esmoucheter de broderie à la Romanique.[94]

A la Romanique however is the 1534 version; originally, Rabelais had written *à la Tudesque*. This change in a small detail must be significant; in the context of Henry's divorce, *à la Romanique* is indeed meaningful, (to the extent that it could indicate Rabelais' opinion in the case), and in retrospect at least, the opposition Romanique/Tudesque suggests that Tudesque may have been a pun on Tudor.

It could be considered that Panurge's choice of the *braguette* rather than another part of his clothing to make his heraldic display is too typical of him to be of particular significance, but a passage like the following, where Panurge's gestures clearly allude to sexual activity, confirm that the choice had some bearing on Henry's affair:

> A quoy Panurge tira sa longue braguette avecques son floc, et l'estendit d'une couldée et demie, et la tenoit en l'air de la main gauche, et de la dextre print sa pomme d'orange, et, la gettant en l'air par sept foys, à la huytiesme la cacha au poing de la dextre, la tenant en hault tout coy; puis commença secouer sa belle braguette, la monstrant à Thaumaste.[95]

On a different level, a further aspect of the episode which concords with our interpretation is the non-verbal form taken by the disputation, and Pantagruel's insistence on silence: between himself and Thaumaste, he stresses, there should be neither 'debat ny tumulte',[96] and from the crowd he demands calm and quiet.[97] In this insistence it is easy to see an allusion to the tumultuous faculty meetings which had occurred in reality. Further, the secrecy which had not surrounded those meetings was guaranteed by Thaumaste's method of discussion; in Rabelais' account, even the academic audience understood very little, though they still managed to disagree.[98]

Thaumaste chose this form of debate because the matters he wished to discuss were so difficult that words were inadequate; through Thaumaste's choice, Rabelais too may have implied that the matters under discussion were very arduous. On the other hand however he may have wished to imply that they were ridiculously simple, that there was in fact no real problem: his stress on the occult, and the solution by Panurge, incline one to the latter interpretation. Both views could be—and in fact were—applied to Henry's matter.

Finally, besides this ambiguity of comment, the sign argument offered another more fundamental advantage over a verbal disputation. The Sorbonne as we saw had forbidden individual consultations; there had likewise been papal prohibitions,[99] and in 1532 the matter was still *sub iudice* in Rome. It had not yet indeed been settled in England, since Henry's marriage to Anne and Convocation's decision in his favour take place the following year. In these conditions, a dispute by signs gave Rabelais a means of alluding to the matter while yet respecting the necessary silence, and this in turn allowed him to make comic reference to the need for silence itself. This is surely the sense of the books on the unspeakable which Pantagruel studied: Plotinus' *De Inenarrabilibus*; the imaginary *Peri Aphaton* (sur les choses indicibles) by the equally imaginary D'Ynarius, in whom one recognises *denarius*; and the fictitious *Peri Anecphoneton* (sur les choses qu'il faut taire), the attribution of which to a satirical poet is a clear indication of Rabelais' intention.[100]

In conclusion, we can affirm not with absolute certainty, but with a degree of probability which carries strong conviction, that Rabelais' Thaumaste episode is based on the 'divorce' of Henry VIII and Catherine of Aragon. The simple chronological sequence: 1529–30, protracted and tumultuous discussions of the matter in Paris, during Rabelais' probable stay there; 1532, redaction and publication by Rabelais of a burlesque episode in which a great English clerc visits a scholar in the Sorbonne to discuss abstruse matters;—this sequence of events separated by so short an interval of time, is in itself sufficient to suggest that the events are related in no accidental way. When in Rabelais' narration of the episode we find details that, with all the appearance of deliberate artistry, form a coherent pattern of reference consonant with such a relationship, we can but conclude that the Thaumaste chapters of *Pantagruel* are not a pointless though entertaining sketch, but a deliberate and sustained allusion to the Great Matter of the King of England.

NOTES

[1] A. Lefranc, *Œuvres de François Rabelais*, IV, p. 210, ll.53–55.
[2] In L. Thorndike, *A History of Magic and Experimental Science*, Vols. V–VI,

The Sixteenth Century, New York (1941), and R. T. Gunther, *Early Science in Oxford*, Oxford (1923), there is no trace of an Englishman whose interests would fit him to figure as Thaumaste. As for the kabala, there appears to have been in England a general lack of interest: cf. F. Secret, *Les Kabbalistes chrétiens de la Renaissance*, Paris (1964), p. 228.

[3] A. Renaudet, *Préréforme et humanisme à Paris*, 2nd ed., Paris (1953), pp. 641 ff.

[4] Lefranc, *op. cit.*, IV, p. 207, n. 3; G. Ascoli, *La Grande-Bretagne devant l'opinion française*, Paris (1927), pp. 61–2.

[5] Besides the standard histories of the realm, we have relied mainly for our account of the first phase of the affair on P. Friedmann, *Anne Boleyn, a chapter of English History, 1527–1536*, London (1884); G. Constant, *La Réforme en Angleterre*, Paris (1930), (references to the English ed., Vol. I, London 1934); G. Mattingly, *Catherine of Aragon*, London (1942). For sources and bibliography see Constant, *op. cit.*; Mattingly, *op. cit.*; Fliche et Martin, *Histoire de l'Eglise*, Vol. 16, Paris (1950); E. G. Léonard, *Histoire générale du protestantisme*, Vol. 1, Paris (1961). For the Sorbonne discussions of the question see V.-L. Bourrilly, *Guillaume du Bellay, Seigneur de Langey 1491–1543*, Paris (1904), chapter III, *L'Affaire du divorce de Henry VIII en Sorbonne*, a reliably documented account. The printed *Letters and Papers, Foreign and Domestic, of the reign of Henry VIII* are referred to in our notes as *L.P.* with volume number; the *Calendar of State Papers, Spanish* as *Cal. Span.* with volume number. Except when page number is given, reference is to item number.

[6] Fliche et Martin, *op. cit.*, p. 323.

[7] Friedmann, *op. cit.*, I, p. 86. See also P. Janelle, *L'Angleterre catholique à la veille du schisme*, Paris (1935), pp. 111–31, for Fisher's arguments for the queen and Gardiner's for the king.

[8] From the reply of the theology faculty of Angers. Le Grand, *Histoire du divorce de Henri VIII, roi d'Angleterre, et de Catherine d'Aragon*, Vol. III, *Preuves*, Paris (1688), p. 508.

[9] *L.P.*, IV, iii, 6007–9.

[10] *Loc. cit.*, 6073.

[11] *Cal. Span.*, IV, i, 132, 152.

[12] *L.P.*, IV, iii, 5983, 5996, 6026; V, p. 315; *Cal. Span.*, IV, i, 160. From this evidence it is reasonable to infer that their instructions, which appear in *L.P.*, IV, iii, after papers for November, were drawn up early in October.

[13] *Cal. Span.*, IV, i, 160.

[14] *L.P.*, IV, iii, 6073.

[15] *L.P.*, IV, iii, 6199.

[16] *Cal. Span.*, III, ii, 578.

[17] Bourrilly, *op. cit.*, p. 95.

[18] *Cal. Span.*, III, ii, 578. Marguerite was later to refuse to meet Anne Boleyn, when Henry and Francis met at Boulogne in October 1532 (Friedmann, *op. cit.*, I, p. 169).

[19] Legrand, *op. cit.*, pp. 421–5. *L.P.*, IV, iii, 6109.

[20] *L.P.*, *loc. cit.*, 6147.

[21] Pierre Lizet, who had replaced the deceased de Selve as First President

on 20 December. Lizet seems to have received instructions from Montmorency early in February (Bourrilly, *op. cit.*, p. 96).

22 *Cal. Span.* IV, i, 255.

23 *L.P.*, IV, iii, 6169.

24 I.e. Reginald Pole.

25 *Cal. Span.*, IV, i, 315.

26 *Cal. Span.*, IV, i, 353.

27 Legrand, *op. cit.*, pp. 458–71. 9–12 June 1530.

28 *Loc. cit.*, p. 459.

29 *Loc. cit.*, p. 460.

30 *Loc. cit.*, p. 462.

31 *Loc. cit.*, p. 463.

32 *Loc. cit.*, pp. 463–4.

33 *Loc. cit.*, p. 465.

34 *Loc. cit.*, p. 465.

35 *Loc. cit.*, p. 467.

36 *Loc. cit.*, p. 469.

37 In August 1530, an enquiry into the conduct of Béda and his fellows was in fact started; Lizet however opposed it and it seems not to have had any result. (Cf. Bourrilly, *op. cit.*, p. 106.)

38 Legrand, *op. cit.*, p. 470.

39 *Loc. cit.*, p. 459.

40 *L.P.*, IV, iii, 6459.

41 Friedmann, *op. cit.*, I, p. 119; Bourrilly, *op. cit.*, pp. 103–4.

42 'L'ambassadeur (anglais) qui est nouveau venu est encore à Poitiers pour avoir l'Université pour luy. Demain va maistre Gervais secrètement à Angers pour faire le pareil.' Jean du Bellay to Berthereau, 26 April 1530 (Musée Condé, série L, Vol. V, f. 288–9; quoted in Bourrilly, *op. cit.*, p. 100, n. 2).

43 Bourrilly, *op. cit.*, p. 100.

44 Friedmann, *op. cit.*, I, p. lv.

45 *Loc. cit.*, pp. lix–lx.

46 *L.P.*, IV, iii, 6147.

47 Friedmann, *op. cit.*, I, pp. liii, 118.

48 *L.P.*, IV, iii, 6033.

49 *L.P.*, V, p. 315.

50 See above, p. 270 (note 24).

51 *Pro ecclesiasticæ unitatis defensione, libri quatuor*, Rome (1538), f. LXXIX.

52 See Constant, *op. cit.*, p. 260; R. Biron and J. Birennes, *Un prince anglais cardinal légat au XVIe siècle. Reginald Pole*, Paris (1922), pp. 42–5; W. Schenk, *Reginald Pole, Cardinal of England*, London (1950), pp. 23–5.

53 *L.P.*, IV, iii, 9996–7, 6073.

54 *Loc. cit.*, 6227, 6234.

55 *Loc. cit.*, 6255, 6603.

56 Legrand, *op. cit.*, p. 459.

57 *Dictionary of National Biography*.

58 Constant, *op. cit.*, p. 261.

59 *L.P.*, IV, iii, 6022, ii.

60 *L.P.*, IV, iii, 6481.

[61] *L.P.*, IV, iii, 6505.

[62] *Loc. cit.*, 6523.

[63] *L.P.*, V, pp. 318–19.

[64] See note 42.

[65] *L.P.*, IV, iii, 6389.

[66] *L.P.*, V, p. 322.

[67] *L.P.*, IV, iii, 6665.

[68] Bourrilly, *op. cit.*, p. 99, n. 4. *L.P.*, IV, iii, 6571, 6579.

[69] *Loc. cit.*, 6455 is a very mutilated letter dated 15 June from Paris, and said to be from Wiltshire to [Norfolk]. We have not examined the original, but its content as given in the printed text, compared with Langey's letter to Francis of 9–12 June, suggests that it may be addressed to Wiltshire rather than be written by him.

[70] Plattard, *op. cit.*, chapter VI.

[71] *Loc. cit.*, p. 70.

[72] *Cal. Span.*, IV, i, 315.

[73] *Œuvres*, IV, p. 228, l.45–9.

[74] B.M., C.37. f. 2.

[75] Thomas Berthelet, London (1531), 8o; B.M., C.21.b.43. J. G. T. Graesse, *Trésor de livres rares et précieux*, article *Divortium*, records two other English editions, both from Berthelet: one of 1530, in-16, the other of 1531, 40.

[76] *Œuvres*, IV, p. 217, l.165–7.

[77] *Boutell's Heraldry*, revised by C. W. Scott-Giles, London (1950), p. 211, where white is given as argent, the technical term.

[78] Mattingly, *op. cit.*, pp. 32, 118.

[79] For the difference between pennons, banners, standards etc., see Lt.-Col. R. Gayre of Gayre and Nigg, *Heraldic Standards and other Ensigns*, Edinburgh and London (1959). For examples of 1) pennon-banners 2) standards with white and green, see 1), Lord Howard de Walden, *Banners Standards and Badges from a Tudor manuscript in the College of Arms*, The de Walden Library (1904), p. 10 (cf. Gayre, *op. cit.*, plate IVd), p. 14; 2) de Walden, *op. cit.*, pp. 77–80, 99. Richard II had used the same colours; cf. *loc. cit.*, pp. 5, 71 (Gayre, *op. cit.*, plate VIII (a)).

[80] I.e. in non-technical terms: *facing*, upper left (1) and lower right (4), blue strewn with gold fleurs de lis; upper right (2) and lower left (3), red, with three gold lions passant guardant.

[81] As in note 80 except that three fleurs de lis only figure on the blue.

[82] *Boutell's heraldry*, ed. cit., p. 210. De Walden, *op. cit.*, pp. 12, 13.

[83] De Walden, *op. cit.*, pp. 3, 4, (Gayre, *op. cit.*, plate IV, e, f.)

[84] *Loc. cit.*, pp. 72; 61–3; 100.

[85] I.e., *facing*, upper left and lower right, red and blue respectively; upper right and lower left, white and green respectively.

[86] Cf. Gayre, *op. cit.*, pp. 26, 36, 48.

[87] *Loc. cit.*, p. 99.

[88] Cf. Ronsard, *Les Amours*, ed. H. and C. Weber, Paris (s.d.), p. 687. See also G. de Tervarent, *Attributs et symboles dans l'art profane*, Geneva (1958), article *Pomme*.

[89] Ronsard, *Amours diverses*, XLI, ed. cit., p. 475. See also G. Ferguson,

Signs and symbols in Christian Art, O.U.P. (1961), chapter II, article *Pomegranate*.

[90] Mattingly, *op. cit.*, p. 316.

[91] De Walden, *op. cit.*, pp. 11, 16, 20.

[92] *Loc. cit.*, p. 15.

[93] *Œuvres*, IV, p. 229, ll.1–11.

[94] *Loc. cit.*, ll.6–7.

[95] *Loc. cit.*, p. 223, ll.93–98.

[96] *Loc. cit.*, p. 212, l.28.

[97] *Loc. cit.*, p. 216, ll.134–140.

[98] *Loc. cit.*, p. 222, ll.74–6; p. 220, ll.43–7.

[99] L. Pastor, *History of the Popes*, 4th ed., vol. 10, London (1938), p. 274. Friedmann, *op. cit.*, I, pp. liii–lv.

[100] *Œuvres*, IV, pp. 213–14, n.41, n.45, n.47.

G. Rees

NATURE IN APOLLINAIRE'S *ALCOOLS*

To write on the Apollinaire of *Alcools* as a nature poet may seem voluntarily paradoxical. He confessed 'moi, j'aime les décors de notre temps'[1] and his feeling for the contemporary revealed to him a whole new range of expression which is predominantly urban. The stanza from *La Chanson du mal-aimé* is only one example of his recognition of the relevance of his own age:

Soirs de Paris ivres du gin
Flambant de l'électricité
Les tramways feux verts sur l'échine
Musiquent au long des portées
De rails leur folie de machines

but yet there are in *Alcools* a number of important poems which take their structure or their central images from nature. The frequency varies.[2] Common enough in the earliest poems of Monte Carlo, Stavelot and Paris up to 1901, nature images play a large part in the Rhineland poems of 1901–2. The Paris–London poems of 1902–4 often have recourse to nature as a source of poetic material for the expression of frustrated emotion but the Montmartre poems of 1905–8 largely ignore it. The last poems of the volume in date (1909–12) reveal a return to the awareness of nature.

Apollinaire is far from a Romantic poet in his treatment of nature and if echoes of his predecessors recur it is because, as he wryly put it himself, 'les poètes personnels rappellent parfois d'autres poètes'.[3] This is not to say that Apollinaire had recourse to nature only in his lyrical or Verlainian moods; indeed the technique of shock images is used considerably earlier in images taken from traditional sources than in those using modern impedimenta. The splendid line from *Vendémiaire*:

Je suis ivre d'avoir bu tout l'univers

is no more than a factual statement of Apollinaire's enormous appetite for the whole world around him. André Breton wrote: 'Accordons... au poète un don prodigieux d'émerveillement'[4] and this is confirmed by André Rouveyre who, knowing him intimately, suggested that his personal *devise* should be 'J'émerveille'.[5] Apollinaire is reticent about his own leanings and statements like: 'Les grands poètes et les grands artistes ont pour fonction sociale de renouveler sans cesse l'apparence que revêt la nature aux yeux des hommes'[6] may not represent more than an exercise in that æsthetic rhetoric of which Apollinaire was at times over-fond. To what extent may *Le Poète assassiné* be regarded as a work of concealed autobiography? André Rouveyre suggested that in this work Apollinaire 'a prêté à son héros Croniamantal bien des traits—mais portés à une intense fulgurance—de sa personne morale, exposée dans un bouleversant et frémissant truchement'.[7] There is, in a chapter entitled *Pédagogie*, a passage which has a certain significance in explaining Apollinaire's attitude towards nature. Croniamantal, then an orphan, has been cared for by the Dutchman Janssen, a much-travelled, erudite and philosophical man. A good deal of the tuition has taken place out-of-doors in the country house near Aix:

> Dès que Croniamantal eut six ans, M. Janssen l'emmena souvent dans la campagne le matin. Croniamantal aimait ces leçons dans les sentiers des collines boisées. M. Janssen s'arrêtait parfois et montrant à Croniamantal des oiseaux voletant l'un près de l'autre ou des papillons se poursuivant et s'ébattant ensemble sur un églantier, il disait que l'amour guide toute la nature. Ils sortaient aussi le soir par le clair de lune et le maître expliquait à l'élève le destin secret des astres, leur cours régulier et leurs effets sur les hommes.
>
> Croniamantal n'oublia jamais qu'un soir lunaire de mai, son maître l'avait mené dans un champ à la lisière d'une forêt; l'herbe ruisselait de lumière laiteuse. Autour d'eux, les lucioles palpitaient; leurs lueurs phosphorescentes et vagabondes donnaient au site un aspect étrange. Le maître attira l'attention du disciple sur la douceur de cette nuit de mai:
>
> —Apprenez, disait-il... apprenez tout de la nature et aimez-la. Qu'elle soit votre nourrice véritable dont les mamelles insignes sont la lune et la colline.[8]

It would be unwise to interpret this as a literal description of Apollinaire's own upbringing—there are no traces of a M. Janssen in his youth—but the inclusion of such an extract in a chapter entitled *Pédagogie* can be taken as an indication that Apollinaire was not a purely urban man, in the mould of Baudelaire.

The earliest poems of *Alcools* such as *Clair de lune* (the first poem published), *Merlin et la vieille femme, Le Larron* and *L'Ermite* reveal a marked influence of those Symbolist techniques of which Apollinaire was a skilful imitator when he so wished. A minor but lasting influence is to be found in the names of flowers which roll sonorously through certain of the texts. Apollinaire stated baldly 'Je déteste les fleurs' (*Signe*) but Mme Jeanine Moulin has drawn attention to the names of flowers attached to the women in his life: 'Annie Playden, "marguerite exfoliée" des premiers espoirs, Marie Laurencin au regard couleur de colchique, Louise Coligny "rose atroce" de l'attrait charnel, Madeleine Pagès, candeur et fierté des "lys", Jacqueline Kolb, "rose thé" que dorent les flammes du foyer, telles sont les fleurs dont se compose la gerbe des amours apollinariennes.'[9] The flowers which decorate his earlier poems have ancient, resonant names and less personal associations: *la marjolaine, les pas d'âne, l'aubépine* of *Merlin et la vieille femme; l'anémone* and *l'ancolie* of Clotilde; the *saules gris* and *romarins* of *Rhénane d'automne*; the *épine, myrte, lilas, thym* and *lavande* of *La Maison des morts* and the *colchiques* of the poem of that name. That there is here an influence of the poetry of Remy de Gourmont (one of Apollinaire's early supporters) is hardly to be doubted. Gourmont's *Litanies de la rose* (1892) and *Fleurs de jadis* (1893) reveal great ingenuity in the handling of the names of flowers for their sonorous effect. This was a game of which Gourmont soon tired, as he admitted in a preface to *Divertissements*, a collection of his verse which appeared in 1914 and from which he omitted these earlier exercises: 'il y a très peu dans ce recueil de poésies purement verbales, que domine le plaisir de régir le troupeau obligeant des mots, dont on sent bien que l'obéissance m'a découragé à mesure que je m'assurais de leur docilité excessive'.[10] For Apollinaire too these fine flower names are not symbols nor are they *mots-clef*. They diminish in frequency as he found his own assured voice and are replaced by the 'vagues poissons arqués fleurs surmarines' of *Le Voyageur*.

This use of a vocabulary of nature description in common employment amongst his immediate predecessors is offset by an unexpected originality of vision and style which is inherent in Apollinaire's temperament rather than an accretion of his Montmartre days and friendship with the Cubist painters. His boyhood companion Toussaint Luca quotes two of Apollinaire's earliest poetic attempts, both signed with his then pseudonym of

Guillaume Macabre. A sonnet on the death of Pan is written in measured alexandrines well-stuffed with classical allusions; it is followed by a poem in free verse on Mardi Gras.[11] The coexistence of two different poetic styles and modes of vision is shown then to be present from Apollinaire's earliest days as a writer and this happy dexterity extends beyond the handling of verse forms. In later days when Apollinaire had been acclaimed leader of the *avant-garde*, he rationalized this instinctive duality. A letter of 18 October 1915 states boldly: 'La meilleure façon d'être classique et pondéré est d'être de son temps en ne sacrifiant rien de ce que les Anciens ont pu nous apprendre';[12] and the well-known closing lines of *La Jolie rousse*:

> Je juge cette longue querelle de la tradition et de l'invention
> De l'Ordre et de l'Aventure

reiterate the same theme. All this comes later when Apollinaire, an experienced poet at the height of his powers, begins to relate his work to wider fields of art and æsthetics; in the earlier poems he is working on a less wide scale of reference and yet his images, starting as they do from hackneyed materials of nature imagery, sometimes incorporate a surprise twist, startling, witty or simply incongruous. Thus the red sun in the opening stanza of *Merlin et la vieille femme*:

> Le soleil ce jour-là s'étalait comme un ventre
> Maternel qui saignait lentement sur le ciel

and later in the same poem a kind of jocularity elbows a traditional 'poetic' image:

> Le soleil en dansant remuait son nombril
> Et soudain le printemps d'amour et d'héroïsme
> Amena par le main un jeune jour d'avril.

The snow-covered trees of *Les Femmes* (dated 1901) assume an unexpected aspect:

> Ce cyprès là-bas a l'air du pape en voyage
> Sous la neige

as does the Madonna of the last stanza of *Rhénane d'automne* (1901)

> A nos pieds roulaient des châtaignes
> Dont les bogues étaient
> Comme le cœur blessé de la madone
> Dont on doute si elle eut la peau
> Couleur des châtaignes d'automne.

Such poetic points are not difficult to score, for the impact of the image is superficial and purely decorative. In *Les Sapins*, one of the *Rhénanes* series and signed 1901, the whole structure of the poem depends on a sequence of comparisons, mainly visual in their origin. The chapter entitled *Voyage* in *Le Poète assassiné* describing Croniamantal's travels along the Rhine[13] contains a kind of scenario for this poem although it is impossible to determine chronological priorities. The elements are all present—the 'vieux rabbin prophétique', the 'violent coup de vent', the 'rafales de neige', the carols and Christmas trees—but as disorganized *choses vues*, lacking the tension, the association and, above all, the *relevance* which the poem confers on them. Mme M.-J. Durry sees in this poem 'surtout un exercice de langage'[14] but this is to overlook the extraordinarily imaginative chain of associative images which range over a wide field of reference and encompass not only the most unexpected visual effects but also include a kind of cosmic view of the pine tree in its relationships with man. The first lines:

Les sapins en bonnets pointus
De longues robes revêtus
Comme des astrologues

are triggered off by the visual implications of a form and then, following up the fantastic train of thought set off by the *astrologues*, the pine trees have magical powers and supernatural powers attributed to them. They are poets; they are magically transformed into Christmas trees; they are musicians and cherubim; their use in medicine transforms them into doctors. There is a kind of superior logic in this which is visual rather than verbal in its origin although the tightly-knit five-line stanzas confer an unbreakable unity on the poem. It is a poem without *arrière-pensée* and its joyous, witty celebration of the trees reveals an uncomplicated response to nature. Apollinaire never noted this as one of his favourite poems and it is a poetic structure which is rare in his work. He came to dislike the *littérature d'images* which he thought too easy: 'On s'est habitué aux images,' he wrote in 1915.[15] 'Il n'en est plus d'inacceptables et tout peut être symbolisé par tout. Une littérature faite d'images enchaînées comme grains de chapelet est bonne tout au plus pr (*sic*) les snobs férus de mysticité. C'est à la portée de tout le monde'. In *Zone*, first published in 1912, a similar technique is employed to deeper effect. Once again the associative link between the two elements of the image is imaginative and highly original but here nature is integrated into the life of a modern city. The images:

> Bergère ô tour Eiffel le troupeau des ponts bêle ce matin

and:

> Maintenant tu marches dans Paris tout seul parmi la foule
> Des troupeaux d'autobus mugissants près de toi roulent

link a contemporary urban immediacy with an ancient pastoral allusion in an unexpected association. The surprise is evident as is the illustrative force and both are profoundly relevant to the central theme of the poem. The actuality of the *décor* is fused with the past and the unchanging nature of man and his suffering are placed into a new perspective. These images are more than decoration; they are also comments on the human situation and are part of the 'lyrisme neuf et humaniste' for which he strove.

Apollinaire's stay in Stavelot in the Belgian Ardennes and in the Rhineland as tutor to a German family brought him for the first time into contact with Northern landscapes. Here he met the English girl Annie Playden with whom he fell in love only to be rejected; the impact of a new landscape coincided with a period of sentimental unhappiness. Is there an obscure atavism in Apollinaire's recognition of the beauty of the forests and of the Rhine as a poetic force? Although his mother was of Polish origin his upbringing had been entirely Mediterranean. Further, his love of legend had, in one sense, predisposed him towards an appreciation of a river which is particularly rich in myth.[16] M. Décaudin notes acutely that, 'dès son arrivée, Apollinaire a été sensible à un pittoresque rhénan qui n'est nullement livresque mais se compose de *choses vues* par l'observateur sans cesse en quête d'inattendu qu'il est'.[17] It is certainly true that, even in a poem like *La Loreley*, the Rhine is more than a simple *décor folklorique* in the minor Symbolist style. The *Nuit rhénane* alludes briefly to the song of the boatman witnessing

> ... sept femmes
> Tordre leurs cheveux verts et longs jusqu'à leurs pieds

and the legend sets up sinister echoes through the brief passage, but the Rhine is not the subject of any great set-pieces, either descriptive or narrative. Apollinaire had always possessed the gift of poetic concision and his later statement: 'il s'agit de vitesse, de raccourci, le style télégraphique nous offre des ressources auxquelles l'ellipse donnera une force et une saveur merveilleusement lyriques'[18] is a formulation of his own poetic practice and his gift of evoking a landscape in a few words, which whilst not being syntactically elliptic in all cases, can convey a sense of the country which is remarkable. In *La Synagogue* Ottomar Scholem and Abraham Loeweren

> vont à la synagogue en longeant le Rhin
> Et les coteaux où les vignes rougissent là-bas

and the same aspect of the Rhineland appears in *Nuit rhénane*:

> Le Rhin le Rhin est ivre où les vignes se mirent
> Tout l'or des nuits tombe en tremblant s'y refléter.

The wind in the trees is evoked in *Rhénane d'automne*:

> Le vent du Rhin ulule avec tous les hiboux

and in *Les Femmes*:

> ... La forêt là-bas
> Grâce au vent chantait à voix grave de grand orgue

Le Vent nocturne which ranges over a wider field of cultural reference succeeds in expressing the same sound with an equal brevity:

> Oh! les cimes des pins grincent en se heurtant.

These descriptive grace-notes occur in poems in which nature has a large part to play and yet it is clear that there are no traces of Romantic pantheism nor excessive intrusion of personal memories. If, occasionally, the landscape is an 'état d'âme', it is never described for itself alone and is never deserted. Landscape for Apollinaire is always a landscape with figures and his descriptions are incidental rather than an end in themselves. Nature is the accomplice of man and has no existence outside the framework of human life. The seasons pass but emotion always remains in the forefront:

> Ah! tombe neige
> Tombe et que n'ai-je
> Ma bien-aimée dans mes bras   (*La Blanche neige*).

Two lines from *Les Collines* (a late poem of *Calligrammes*) reveal how he related this sensitivity to nature particularly to his early days:

> Jeunesse adieu jasmin du temps

and:

> Adieu jeunesse blanc Noël

but even in his youth Apollinaire displays a remarkable discretion. In a letter to Lou, dated 3 October 1914, he makes this remarkable confession: 'J'avais voulu déjà écrire un poème pour vous. Il m'eût été trop personnel et n'eût dépeint que les sentiments que vous avez éveillés en moi et aussi de votre grâce'.[19] This apparently out-giving poet has his own reticences and his feelings have a decent veil. It is a part of Apollinaire's own reaction against a poetry that is too personal that he seeks to place a certain æsthetic distance between the original emotion and its ultimate poetic expression. It is for this reason that his landscapes, however personal they may be to him in relation to a given episode in his sentimental life, are always made more general and less personal by the eruption of figures other than himself and his love. His effort is not to generalize by claiming universal validity for individual human experience but rather to set this individual human experience in the context of a world from which man is never absent. Unlike the Romantics who remain alone in the centre of their moral and emotional universe, Apollinaire feels himself to be a man amongst others, undergoing in his turn the experiences which are part of the human condition. Even in a poem like *Les Colchiques* of which Mme M.-J. Durry writes: 'Lenteur, langueur, tant aimées par la poésie symboliste... *les Colchiques* en sont impregnées,'[20] the reflective melancholy of the first stanza comparing the colour of 'les colchiques' to the colour of his woman's eyes and ending as it does with the line:

> Et ma vie pour tes yeux lentement s'empoisonne

is sharply broken by the boisterous interruption of:

> Les enfants de l'école viennent avec fracas
> Vêtus de hoquetons et jouant de l'harmonica.

This effectively lowers the emotional temperature and masks the too-poignant revelations of a real sadness. Sometimes the interruption is more discreet as in *Automne malade* where the desperation of an autumn dying into winter is cast in an emotionalized pure landscape until the last Verlainian lines:

> Les feuilles
> Qu'on foule
> Un train
> Qui roule
> La vie
> S'écoule

in which the 'train qui roule' ejects the poet and his readers from the closed world of private emotion into a world outside. There is a more muted intrusion in *Le Vent nocturne*:

Les villages éteints méditent maintenant.

In *Mai* the *tziganes* make a brief appearance and in *Les Sapins* the references to human figures (*grands rabbins, vieilles demoiselles, médecins divagants*) add a wittiness and a curious precision to his descriptions. The poem *Automne* has a particularly fine use of figures. The misty, vague Verlainian landscape (similar in its irreality to *Colloque sentimental*) reveals the peasant singing a song of love and infidelity. The ancient task of the cultivation of the soil and the ancient human experience of love and infidelity are not emphasized or linked, but the poem of eight lines condenses in a most suggestive form the dialogue between permanence and transience which lies at the heart of some of Apollinaire's most brilliant poems.

In one of the *Lettres à sa marraine* written in 1916, Apollinaire says: '... j'ai toujours désiré que le présent tel qu'il fût perdurât. Rien ne détermine plus de mélancolie chez moi que cette fuite du temps. Elle est en désaccord si formel avec mon sentiment, mon identité, qu'elle est la source même de ma poésie'.[21] But all men are conscious of the passing of time and poets have constantly turned to this theme. The fine lines of Joachim du Bellay (quoted from H. W. Lawton's edition) may stand as an example of an approach which may be found in poets before and since:

N'attendez donq' que la grand' faulx du temps
Moissonne ainsi la fleur de voz printemps,
Qui rend les Dieux & les hommes contens:
    Les ans, qui peu séjournent,
Ne laissent rien, que regretz & souspirs,
Et empennez de noz meilleurs desirs,
Avecques eulx empruntent noz plaisirs,
    Qui jamais ne retournent.   [*A une dame*][22]

R. Champigny, in an interesting article,[23] has drawn attention to the subtle attitudes of Apollinaire towards time. There are no overt regrets as are found in the Du Bellay verse just quoted, but a marked and normal consciousness of the irremediable passing of time, of man's impermanence, of his consciousness of eternity. Yet there are ways in which man can partake of a feeling of permanence and one is in his experience of those emotions which are an unchanging part of the human condition. Nature betrays the same contradictory characteristics for, if it is in itself eternal, its own annual rhythms ordain its death and rebirth. Apollinaire is not a philosophical poet and it is in confidences less frank than the quotation to his *marraine* that his ideas are hidden. The poem *Mai* is at first sight a conventional pastoral. Its opening stanza describes a boat trip down the Rhine in high spring:

Le mai le joli mai en barque sur le Rhin
Des dames regardaient du haut de la montagne
Vous êtes si jolies mais la barque s'éloigne
Qui donc a fait pleurer les saules riverains

Vous êtes si jolies mais la barque s'éloigne and the poet, in the grip of the moving river, can never return to recapture what he has irrevocably lost. The river, like time itself, is unconquerable. The next line too looks over its shoulder:

Or des vergers fleuris se figeaient en arrière

and the spring itself fades in 'les pétales tombés des cérisiers de mai' and the 'pétales flétris' to increase the effect of the past tense in 'celle que j'ai tant aimée'. The tenses are not the brutal past historic but the less precise imperfect and past indefinite. The movement of the river adds its own note of irresistible but gentle force. The *Pont Mirabeau* uses a similar symbolism. The brief poem *L'Adieu* reflects the same subtle change of tense to mingle past, present and future in its five short lines:

J'ai cueilli ce brin de bruyère
L'automne est morte souviens-t'en
Nous ne nous verrons plus sur terre
Odeur du temps brin de bruyère
Et souviens-toi que je t'attends.

The triumph of memory, death yet hope, past and future are mingled and the fine synæsthesia 'odeur du temps brin de bruyère' link them together. The impact of nature in these poems is to bear witness to Apollinaire's own feelings on the passing of time and to enable him, although not explicitly, to detect and mirror for us the permanence and transience that he detects in nature. *Adieu* denies pessimism and yet faithfully recalls the sadness of much human experience.

In *Signe* Apollinaire wrote:

Je suis soumis au Chef du Signe de l'Automne

and later:

Mon Automne éternelle ô ma saison mentale.

The apocalyptic capital letters should not tempt us to think of Apollinaire as a 'poète maudit' but it is undeniable that the season of autumn is the most frequent setting of his nature poems. It provides him with an obsessive image:

L'automne est plein de mains coupées
Non non ce sont des feuilles mortes   (*Rhénane d'automne*)

Les mains des amantes d'antan jonchent le sol   (*Signe*)

Tes mains feuilles de l'automne   (*Marie*)

Mme M.-J. Durry writes: 'L'automne règne, qui fut la saison des romantiques, mais que les symbolistes se sont annexée, saison baudelairienne, saison verlainienne, saison de leurs descendants'[24] but it is clear that Apollinaire is not a poet of despair. If, as the evidence seems to prove, Apollinaire is above all a man of the forests, it is in the autumn that the trees fascinate him and they become an easy symbol of dying hope and frustrated love. If autumn is cruel:

Oh! l'automne l'automne a fait mourir l'été   (*Automne*)

it becomes itself a victim in its turn:

Automne malade et adoré   (*Automne malade*)

and:

Pauvre automne
Meurs en blancheur et en richesse
De neige et de fruits mûrs   (*ibid*)

It is in lines like these that Apollinaire approaches most closely to the landscape as an 'état d'âme' and it is perhaps the least original part of his response to nature.

Apollinaire possesses considerable skill as a parodist as the *Aubade chantée à Laetare un an passé* shows. Set in *La Chanson du mal-aimé* it celebrates happiness in love in a sixteenth-century style; its stylistic difference from the remainder of this poem ironically underlines the realities of the 'mal-aimé' as the idyllic natural setting contrasts with a harsher contemporary mood.

The truth is that Apollinaire does not find in nature as did Hugo, Wordsworth and the other Romantic poets, that release and challenge which leads to lyrical meditation. In *Le Brasier* he specifically rejects the 'grand'plaintes végétales' as subjects for poetry. The majestic themes of nature have no attraction for him and indeed in *L'Esprit nouveau* he talks of more insignificant yet equally revelatory sources—the 'mouchoir qui tombe peut

U

être le levier avec lequel il [le poète] soulèvera l'univers'. As a poet conscious and appreciative of the weight of his past, he draws on nature for the sentimental poem and the record of his love affairs is frequently marked in this way. His obsession with the passing of time finds a convenient symbolism to hand in the recurring cycles of nature. But even in his poems of love, employing a traditional *décor*, Apollinaire is attentive to cover his tracks and the distance of detachment for which he strives, between the finished poem and the personal experience which is at once its theme and its origin, is aided by a stylistic deviousness which often takes the form of surprise. To find this tension in a poet who is truly sensitive to nature and yet who is reticent in his self-revelations is rare.

The traditional dichotomy of Apollinaire is well documented by his own writings and statements of intent as an endless dialogue between the past and the present, tradition and innovation. There is another dichotomy in Apollinaire which has its own importance: the oscillation between lyricism and prophesy. In *Les Collines* (*Calligrammes*) which Scott Bates has argued persuasively[25] is Apollinaire's final *art poétique*, the prophetic strain is clear:

Habituez-vous comme moi
A ces prodiges que j'annonce
A la bonté qui va régner
A la souffrance que j'endure
Et vous connaîtrez l'avenir.

The *prodiges*, *bonté* and *souffrances* are only incidentally to be found in nature and it is not exclusively in this field that Apollinaire can find the explanation of the world which he had come to seek. But Apollinaire's old universal appetites remain with him and in *Sur les prophéties* (*Calligrammes*) he reserves his own rights:

Il y a avant tout une façon d'observer la nature
Et d'interpréter la nature
Qui est très légitime.

NOTES

[All quotations from *Alcools* and *Calligrammes* are taken from: Apollinaire, *Œuvres poétiques*, Paris, Gallimard, Bibliothèque de la Pléiade.]

[1] *Tendre comme le souvenir*, Paris, Gallimard (1952), p. 113.
[2] The difficulties of dating some of the poems of *Alcools* are well known. In so far as I use chronological references I have relied on the pioneer

work of LeRoy C. Breunig ('The Chronology of Apollinaire's *Alcools*' in *PMLA*, LXVII, 7 (1952), pp. 907–23) together with more recent suggestions made by Mme M.-J. Durry in *Alcools*, Paris, Société d'Edition d'enseignement supérieur, 3 vols. (1956–64) and M. Décaudin, *Le Dossier d'*Alcools, Geneva, Droz; and Paris, Librairie Minard (1965).

³ *Lettres à sa marraine 1915–1918*, Paris, Gallimard (1951), p. 41.

⁴ In *Les Pas perdus*, Paris, Editions de la Nouvelle Revue Française (1924), p. 28.

⁵ In *Apollinaire*, Paris, Gallimard (1945), p. 105.

⁶ *Les Peintres cubistes, méditations esthétiques*, Geneva, Cailler (1950), p. 21.

⁷ *Op. cit.*, p. 84.

⁸ *Œuvres complètes de Guillaume Apollinaire*, ed. M. Décaudin, Paris, Balland et Lecat, (1965) Vol. I, p. 249.

⁹ In Guillaume Apollinaire, *Textes inédits*, Geneva, Droz; Lille, Librairie Giard (1952), p. 3.

¹⁰ Paris, Mercure de France, p. 13.

¹¹ A. Toussaint Luca, *Guillaume Apollinaire, souvenirs d'un ami*, Monaco, Editions du Rocher (1954), pp. 29–31.

¹² *Lettres à sa marraine*, p. 35.

¹³ *Le Poète assassiné* in *Œuvres complètes de Guillaume Apollinaire*, Paris, Balland et Lecat (1965), Vol. I, p. 279.

¹⁴ *Op. cit.*, III, p. 89.

¹⁵ *Tendre comme le souvenir*, p. 55.

¹⁶ A full discussion of Apollinaire and the Rhine, together with a further bibliography, will be found in P. Orecchioni, *Le Thème du Rhin dans l'inspiration de Guillaume Apollinaire*, Paris, Lettres Modernes (1956).

¹⁷ M. Décaudin, *op. cit.*, p. 21.

¹⁸ *Tendre comme le souvenir*, p. 48.

¹⁹ André Rouveyre, *op. cit.*, p. 131.

²⁰ *Op. cit.*, II, p. 151.

²¹ P. 72.

²² Joachim du Bellay, *Poems*, edited by H. W. Lawton, Oxford, Blackwell, (1961), p. 53.

²³ 'Le Temps chez Apollinaire' in *PMLA*, LXVII, 2 (1952), pp. 3–14.

²⁴ *Op. cit.*, II, p. 145.

²⁵ In *Guillaume Apollinaire, Revue des Lettres modernes* (1962).

Marjorie Shaw

SHAKESPEAREAN PERFORMANCES IN PARIS IN 1827-8

So much has been written about the importance and the influence of the performances by English actors in Paris in the years 1827-8. Critics such as F. Baldensperger, steeped in a most detailed knowledge of the period, wax lyrical about the atmosphere of the time, the excitement and the enthusiasm, the eager discussions and the comparisons of one performance with another of the same role, the following which Harriet Smithson soon acquired in Paris and of course the passion she inspired in Hector Berlioz, and every critic writing of the period quite correctly devotes several pages to the performances.[1]

J. L. Borgerhoff's study, *Le Théâtre anglais à Paris sous la Restauration*[2] is a most scholarly piece of work and all these subsequent critics have drawn on it almost exclusively. One must insist on the fact that Borgerhoff himself was scrupulously fair and put all his cards on the table. For instance, in his Chapter IV, entitled *Le Répertoire*, he gives precise details of the text of each play actually performed and he has compared this with a standard English edition. The conclusion in each case was that for some reason each play was 'modified', some 'much modified'. Either the company of actors was insufficient in actual numbers and therefore some twenty-two characters were perforce omitted from the cast of *Richard III* or else that some scenery had been too cumbersome to transport so that one lot had to do service for two plays with the result that *Richard III* was played in the same set as *Othello*.[3] In every case the text was considerably cut and even altered. Thus the King and Queen of Denmark became a duke and duchess, and several minor characters were omitted altogether.[4]

No doubt these mutilated texts must be compared to those previously offered on the French stage in translation. One of Talma's greatest successes (apart from Cornelian and Racinian roles) had been in *Othello* as rendered into French by Jean-François Ducis (1733–1816), a role which he played for the first time on 26 November 1792 and which, says his English biographer, 'he would retain all his life'.[5] But in Ducis' *Othello*, the hero, no longer a Moor, had acquired a 'yellow, coppery complexion' less liable to frighten the ladies, and the character of Iago was radically changed, his villainy only being discovered at the end of the play. An alternative ending to the play was provided in which both Desdemona (rechristened Hédelmone) and Othello are still alive at curtain fall.[6] Only perhaps *Hamlet* without the Prince of Denmark would be more difficult to imagine.

Only if we remember such facts as these is it possible to understand the enthusiasm of those audiences in 1827 and 1828 who felt that they were in the presence of 'the real Shakespeare' at last.

We should perhaps be on our guard nevertheless when trying to assess the influence of these performances on individual writers. I would like to suggest that the influence of these performances on Hugo, Vigny and the rest was in proportion to their individual readiness to accept what was offered, and that Hugo in particular exploited the influence rather than submitted to it. We know that Berlioz was overwhelmed by his passion for Harriet Smithson (who appears to have reached the height of her powers during these performances in Paris). He subsequently married her and was able therefore to sublimate at one and the same time his love for her and his taste for the poetic atmosphere of *Romeo and Juliet* in his compositions. Details of texts used and of interpretation of individual parts would be of minimum interest to him.

Vigny, on the other hand, was a mature writer who had after all reached his thirtieth birthday six months before the performances began. Moreover we know him to have been capable of reading and translating from the original text before the English actors arrived in Paris. His translation and adaptation of *Romeo and Juliet*, in collaboration with Emile Deschamps, was begun before the end of the year 1826. His translation of *Othello* may well owe something to the performances, however, since he appears to have adopted all those cuts in the text which the

English actors were themselves accustomed to make, even though he had worked from a copy of the 1630 folio. Annie Sessely, in her study of *L'Influence de Shakespeare sur Alfred de Vigny*, Berne, 1927, thinks that the translation may have been begun *after* the first performances. Baldensperger, in his series of articles on Vigny,[7] demonstrates how deeply Vigny was involved in the visit of the English actors to Paris, and how anxious he was therefore for the success of the visit. He also shows that Vigny

> se servit de ses adaptations shakespeariennes pour indiquer ce qu'il demandait à la muse (p. 105)

that is, as a demonstration of what he considered to be suitable poetic language for modern tragedy. Nowhere does he suggest that Vigny needed to come under the influence of Shakespeare in order to become a dramatist himself, and Annie Sessely comes to precisely the same conclusion:

> ... la lutte pour la réforme du théâtre une fois terminée, Vigny est revenu à sa réserve habituelle. Le nom de Shakespeare ne figure plus officiellement à son programme littéraire. C'est pour lui seul, désormais, qu'il continue à l'étudier,... Quant aux effets de l'influence shakespearienne sur lui et son œuvre, ils peuvent se résumer en un effort vers une plus grande liberté, et de forme, et de pensée. Le poète anglais a donné au poète français, à un moment décisif, l'impulsion nécessaire: Vigny lui doit en grande partie la conscience de son originalité et la capacité de l'exprimer. Peut-on demander autre chose à un maître?'[8]

There was of course no reason why Vigny should not continue to read and enjoy Shakespeare for himself once *Le More de Venise* had played its not inconsiderable part in the Romantic battle, and we know indeed that he did so. He met Macready again when he was in London during the winter of 1838–9 and probably saw him perform in *The Tempest* and *King Lear* which Macready was playing at the time, as well as in the title role of Bulwer's play *Richelieu*, in which Macready based his interpretation on Vigny's novel *Cinq Mars*.[9] P. Flottes[10] maintains that one of the last books Vigny read before his death was a volume of Shakespeare's historical plays.

However that may be, Annie Sessely's conclusion, after examining Vigny's dramatic development in considerable detail, is undoubtedly the right one; that Vigny worked away from Shakespeare, and approached more and more closely to the classical ideal with *Chatterton*, and then ceased to write for the theatre altogether.

One more point made by Annie Sessely in this study may well be underlined anew. She stresses the advantages to be gained strategically—in the Romantic battle to achieve acceptance in the theatre—by presenting a play the subject matter of which is already familiar to the audience, who could therefore give more attention to the language and the form of the play. The weak point of this argument (but which does not invalidate it completely nevertheless) lies in the un-Shakespearean nature of the plot of *Othello* as Ducis had allowed it to be known to Parisian audiences. Some of the public would presumably have read the prose renderings of Shakespeare, Le Tourneur's for example, re-issued by Guizot in 1821, but we must assume that few would indeed have read the original English.

The main point which we need to keep in mind is surely the fact that Vigny, involved as he may have been in the experiment and no doubt inspired to further efforts by specific performances, did not have to wait for these to take place before making a close acquaintance with at least some of the Shakespearean plays and before knowing enough English to be able to read and understand them in the original.

It would at first sight appear possible that Hugo, on the other hand, was inspired, as a direct result of some of the earliest performances, to write a fuller preface to his play *Cromwell* than perhaps he had originally intended. The only evidence to prove this is a letter written to his friend Victor Pavie, dated September 24, 1827 (by which date performances of *Hamlet, Romeo and Juliet* and *Othello* had already been given) in which we note the following:

> Dans quinze jours, vous recevrez *Cromwell*. Il ne me reste plus qu'à écrire la *préface* et quelques *notes*. Je ferai tout cela aussi court que possible; moins de lignes, moins d'ennui.[11]

In fact he began his Preface a week later on 30 September, completed it by the end of October, and the whole volume (play and preface) appeared on 5 December 1827.[12] It would seem therefore that little reliance can be placed on this letter as evidence. Either Hugo did not want his friend to know what he intended to write, or, less likely, he only realized the full possibilities of what he might write after the letter was written. Now from the point of view of the performances, there was only one of a Shakespearean play during the time that Hugo was actually writing the preface. *Othello* had been given a second performance on 25 September 1827 and *Romeo and Juliet* would receive its third performance on 8 October.

What knowledge of Shakespeare had Hugo at the time he composed his Preface? A. R. Oliver in his *Charles Nodier*,[13] makes the point that when Hugo went with Nodier and Dumas to the Coronation of Charles X, the young writers wiled away an evening reading to each other, that Hugo was amazed at Nodier's impromptu translation of *King John*, and that up to that date (May 1825) Hugo had little knowledge or appreciation of Shakespeare. There was indeed no particular reason why he should have had such a knowledge. Most of his attention so far had been turned towards the other Mediterranean countries, and more especially towards Spain. We must believe, however, that in the ensuing months there were several reasons why the ambitious young writer should take more note of the literature of the people on the far side of the English Channel. Stendhal's second pamphlet *Racine et Shakespeare* appeared in March 1825, exactly two years after the first one. All the decade of the twenties in France was remarkable for the amazing success enjoyed by Walter Scott and for the fact that all the Waverley novels were translated into French almost as soon as they appeared in English. Both Hugo and Vigny, having made their reputations first of all as poets, were to publish novels in the year 1826, before turning their attention to the theatre. It is surely safe to assume some degree of concerted action between friends on this score. And since at this date Vigny was indeed Hugo's friend and the relations between the two poets were never to be more cordial, there was also the fact of Vigny's knowledge of English, and his English connexions, to rouse Hugo's interest in English literature.

How much can we judge from the *Préface de Cromwell* itself of Hugo's knowledge of Shakespeare and his plays at the time of the writing of the Preface? It is possible to argue that Hugo's knowledge of Shakespeare at the time may have been quite superficial, and that in fact all Hugo was anxious to do was to use the name of Shakespeare effectively and appropriately. Does one feel, when reading the Preface, that Hugo is anxious to spur his readers on to read Shakespeare, either in the original or in translation? Certainly not. Hugo is above all concerned that his readers should be favourably disposed towards the 'new drama' which he proposed to write. But he does need a good name to fit his argument.

In his sweeping history of poetry in three major periods, Hugo sees each of these periods epitomized by the Bible, Homer and Shakespeare respectively, and following as this does on his analysis of 'le grotesque' and the contrast with 'le sublime', one must admit that Shakespeare's is an eminently suitable name to use:

> Shakespeare, c'est le drame; et le drame, qui fond sous un même souffle le grotesque et le sublime, le terrible et le bouffon, la tragédie et la comédie, le drame est le caractère propre de la troisième époque de poésie, de la littérature actuelle.[14]

It is obvious that Hugo had no need to see many (or indeed any) of the plays performed in order to realize the advantages to his argument of using Shakespeare's name in this way. Given the fact that Shakespeare had written both tragedies and comedies, and that he was notorious in France (since the time of *Les Lettres sur les Anglais*, 1734) for having indulged in the unpleasant, uncouth, and in fact frankly barbarous habit of including comic scenes—and all sorts of other irregularities—in his tragedies, and of having flagrantly violated all the rules of 'le bon goût', this use of Shakespeare's name tells us nothing of Hugo's own personal acquaintance with the works themselves.

If we look a little more closely at the *Préface* and note the plays and characters which Hugo specifically mentions, we are confronted by a very short list. In discussing 'le grotesque' he has already stated categorically:

> Certes, les euménides grecques sont bien moins horribles, et par conséquent bien moins vraies, que les sorcières de *Macbeth*.[15]

Please note the 'par conséquent'. This would seem to be a conclusion which might at least be questioned. A few pages farther on, Hugo makes another categorical statement, the full effect of which is undoubtedly in its progression towards a climax:

> Chose frappante, tous ces contrastes se rencontrent dans les poètes eux-mêmes, pris comme hommes. A force de méditer sur l'existence, d'en faire éclater la poignante ironie, de jeter à flots le sarcasme et la raillerie sur nos infirmités, ces hommes qui nous font tant rire deviennent profondément tristes. Ces Démocrites sont aussi des Héraclites. Beaumarchais était morose, Molière était sombre, Shakespeare mélancolique.[16]

Souriau expresses mild surprise at this statement about Beaumarchais, while Pierre Grosclaude, editing the text for Les Classiques Larousse, suggests that it is just not true as far as Beaumarchais and Molière are concerned, but makes no comment on its application to Shakespeare. Do we in fact know enough about Shakespeare's personality (as distinct from his genius) to be able to assert that he was 'mélancolique' or that he was not? Such evidence as there is would seem to point to a period of considerable depression, during which the great tragedies were written, but that he emerged from this to write the last plays, culminating in *The Tempest*.

The very next paragraph is interesting also, since here Hugo is enumerating those characters which embody 'le grotesque'. Amongst this list of examples, drawn from French and German literature as well, are several Shakespearean ones, Juliet's nurse, Richard III, Osrick (*sic*) and Mercutio. 'Le grotesque' in action will also account for Macbeth's meetings with the witches, Romeo's meeting with the apothecary and Hamlet's with the gravediggers, and will also be responsible for King Lear and his fool braving the storm together in a scene where 'le grotesque [mêle] sa voix criarde aux plus sublimes, aux plus lugubres, aux plus rêveuses musiques de l'âme'.[17]

Now these are certainly apt examples to fit Hugo's argument of the use and indeed of the 'suprêmes beautés' of 'le grotesque' in the theatre. They still do not demonstrate a particularly profound knowledge of Shakespeare. Why was there no mention of some at least of the following: Caliban, Bottom, Autolycus, the Bastard (from *King John*), Falstaff, as well as of the Ghost of Hamlet's father, and indeed the various apparitions in *Macbeth* and *Richard III*? It is perhaps relevant to note that the first three Shakespearean plays to be presented by the English company in September 1827 were *Hamlet, Romeo and Juliet* and *Othello*. *King Lear* would follow in January 1828, *Richard III* in February and *Macbeth* in April. Most of Hugo's examples were therefore taken from the plays actually performed during the first month.

There are several more references to Shakespeare in the remainder of the *Préface de Cromwell*, but it is possible to argue, on the evidence of the *Préface* itself, that Hugo had only a general conception of some of Shakespeare's plays, particularly the four great tragedies. It is obvious that he had a good, general, wide-ranging knowledge of literature, but even some of his references to Classical literature (in which he might well be expected to be better-grounded than in Modern European literatures) are very general and not always very orthodox.[18]

Whatever may or may not have been the limitations of Hugo's

actual acquaintance with Shakespeare's plays, it is evident that he made use of Shakespeare's name, and used it effectively, as a rallying point and as a name 'to be conjured with'. He could still have believed firmly in the antithesis of 'le sublime et le grotesque' and in the necessity of including both in 'le drame moderne' without in fact coming under the influence of Shakespeare himself at all, as represented by the actual performances in Paris in September 1827. A. R. Oliver, in his biography of Charles Nodier, has an interesting and informative chapter on the relationship between Hugo and Nodier, and more especially the episode of the journey to Rheims for the Coronation of Charles X (already referred to) with particular reference to the reaction of Hugo to Nodier's translation of *King John*, and the steps which Hugo subsequently took to efface the record of his astonishment and pleasure at this reading, for fear it would seem that he had been unduly influenced and that in fact he owed more to Nodier (and indirectly to Shakespeare) than he was prepared later on to admit.[19]

Géraud Venzac, in his study on *Les premiers Maîtres de Victor Hugo*, devotes some interesting pages to Hugo's school-days and more particularly to his formation during the twenties both of the century and of his age, drawing particular attention to the fact that after 1830 Hugo is, understandably enough, really only interested in his own writings:

> Victor Hugo rejette en effet dès lors tout modèle: il n'est que de remarquer par exemple le profond oubli dans lequel sombre et s'éteint Chateaubriand, après 1830, aux yeux de Victor Hugo; son absence éclatante de *William Shakespeare*, et le splendide isolement de la statue que Hugo s'érige à lui-même au cœur de son siècle. Témoigne dans le même sens, le peu d'intérêt que Victor Hugo porte à l'œuvre des autres.[20]

F. Baldensperger[21] insisted that the writer of *Victor Hugo raconté par un témoin de sa vie* passes over the incident of the Shakespearean performances so lightly in order not to give away just how much Hugo did owe to this influence.[22] I should like to suggest that though this may well be fundamentally true, the reverse may also be partially true, that Hugo was not in fact basically interested in Shakespeare or in individual Shakespearean plays, but chiefly in what he, Hugo, could extract from the situation for his own purposes, and that he did exploit the situation, the enthusiasm aroused by the performances, and that he did use the name of Shakespeare in *La Préface de Cromwell*, as effectively as we have seen, without in fact having acquired a detailed knowledge of even the most obvious of the plays.[23] Has anyone undertaken to study 'La Vie intellectuelle' of Hugo as Del Litto has done that of Stendhal? The volume of G. Venzac does not go far enough. He is chiefly interested in what Hugo learned at school and in what he retained of that education.

J.-B. Barrère has just reprinted in book form several of his articles on Hugo published originally during the years 1946–54, and one of these examines Hugo's debt to English writers, including of course Shakespeare. Barrère insists on the importance of Shakespeare's influence in the Romantic theatre as a whole, on the possibilities of 'le grotesque' suggested to Hugo himself, and on the fact that Hugo 'semble déjà deviner qu'il y a dans cette œuvre tout un univers qui en fait "la sommité des temps modernes" '.[24] The remainder of his chapter is devoted to the much more detailed knowledge of Shakespeare which Hugo acquired during his exile in Jersey and Guernsey while his son was occupied with his translation of the plays. 'Le Shakespeare de ses années romantiques n'est évidemment pas le même que celui de Guernsey'.[25]

Let us now turn from Hugo and the text of his *Préface de Cromwell* to the list of the actual performances given, as quoted by J. L. Borgerhoff and reproduced in an appendix. Several interesting facts strike one as worthy of note: firstly, the small number of Shakespearean plays actually performed; secondly, the small number of performances of these few Shakespearean plays given during the ten months the English actors were in Paris; and thirdly, the comparative swamping of Shakespeare amidst a host of other plays, some of which even shared the bill with Shakespeare on occasion. Indeed, on several occasions, the English actors collaborated in special performances given both by the Théâtre Français and by the Opéra Italien. In all some thirty other English plays were performed. Of these we note particularly:

Massinger, *A New Way to pay Old Debts.*
Otway, *Venice preserved.*
Rowe, *Jane Shore.*
Fielding, *The Wedding Day.*
Goldsmith, *She Stoops to Conquer.*
Sheridan, *The Rivals* and *The School for Scandal.*
Howard Payne, *Junius Brutus.*
Knowles, *Virginius.*

The remainder are plays now completely forgotten. Several of these were performed only once, and the vast majority only two, three or four times, while *The Weathercock*, and *The Wedding Day* and Knowles's *Virginius* reached the grand total of five performances each. The greatest success was scored by Harriet Smithson in Rowe's *Jane Shore* which reached a total of thirteen performances, nearly twice as many as any of the plays performed during the ten months between September 1827 and July 1828.

Had the performances taken place in 1727 instead of a century later, I suppose one would have been surprised at the high number of plays by Shakespeare. But 1827 was not only post-Garrick but a period favoured by such notable actors as those who did indeed come to Paris, Charles Kemble, Abbott, Terry, Kean (at that time near the end of his career) and finally Macready. Mrs Siddons had already retired from the stage in 1812. All of these, as well as Garrick, had made their reputations in many Shakespearean parts, and though Shakespeare was less generally regarded as quite such an outstanding genius of the theatre as he is today, nevertheless he was better known—at least by name—in France than most other English dramatists.

A grand total of seven plays (out of the Shakespearean canon of thirty-seven plays) and of thirty-three performances (including one gala performance of Acts IV and V only of *Romeo and Juliet*) is certainly slight. The range of the plays chosen is also very limited. Apart from the four 'great' tragedies and *Romeo and Juliet*, *Richard III* is the only history and *The Merchant of Venice* the only comedy to be performed. Of these seven plays *Richard III*, *Macbeth* and *King Lear* received only three performances each, *Romeo and Juliet* four, all at the beginning of the season and including the gala performance already alluded to, *The Merchant of Venice* and *Othello* six performances each and *Hamlet* seven, and (like *Othello*), both at the beginning and at the end of the season.

No doubt the choice of play was largely determined by the actors available. So we notice that Kemble during the one month of September 1827 played Hamlet three times, Romeo twice, and Othello twice, while Abbott, a star of much less magnitude, also played Hamlet and Romeo twice each. Kean did not arrive until May 1828 and played Othello three times, Lear twice, Shylock four times and Richard III once only. Terry, in January, played Lear and Shylock once and twice respectively, while Macready, having appeared for seven performances, three in *Macbeth*, in

April, returned at the end of June to appear in five plays, includ-
ing two performances of *Hamlet*, one of *Othello* on 21 July (the last
Shakespearean performance) and the last performance of all,
Jane Shore on 25 July 1828.

There can be no question of the interest aroused by these performances. The newspapers reported and commented on practically every one, royalty were present on more than one occasion,
and the writers, musicians and artists certainly patronized them.
The actors of the Comédie Française also showed considerable
interest in their colleagues' performances. There was after all a
great deal to interest them in the different style of acting as well
as in the different style of the plays chosen. So great were the
technical differences as practised in London and in Paris, that
Garrick had been much in demand, when he visited Paris in
1751, to demonstrate this by giving the dagger speech from
Macbeth, for example, in the salons where he was received.[26]

In the same way, Talma, who had spent some years as a child,
and later, as a youth and young man, in London, claimed, when
he visited London at the height of his career in 1817, to have
learned a great deal from his English colleagues and was anxious
to impress on his fellow actors of the Comédie Française the
necessity to achieve a more naturalistic style of acting.[27]

There can therefore be no doubt as to the importance of these
performances of Shakespeare by English actors in Paris during the
winter 1827–8 in the history of the French theatre and in the
history of Romanticism in particular. I submit however that it is
too easy to read into the event after-effects which might have
taken place anyway, and far too easy to lose sight of the limitations of the performances as they took place. I would not wish to
detract in any way from the approval expressed of the courage
of those concerned, the initiative shown, the obvious goodwill and
the enthusiasm displayed by the actors in an attempt to suit
their wares to the taste of their audiences, and so on. But I would
like to suggest that we remember more than is usually done the
'negative' side, that is, the few plays chosen, the mutilated texts
used, the relatively few performances of Shakespeare in a grand
total of eighty-two, spread over a period of ten months, and many
of them in a notoriously small theatre.[28]

Thus, though Nodier could write at the time: 'L'établissement
du théâtre anglais à Paris est un des événements de l'époque,'[29]
it was an event which had little immediate impact on the major

dramatic writers, and was exploited by them, particularly by Hugo, rather than an influence suffered by them. This is of course excellent, for did not Hugo say in his *Préface*:

> Le poète . . . ne doit donc prendre conseil que de la nature, de la vérité et de l'inspiration qui est aussi une vérité et une nature . . . Que le poète se garde surtout de copier qui que ce soit, pas plus Shakespeare que Molière, pas plus Schiller que Corneille.[30]

NOTES

[1] A. Dubeux, *Les Traductions françaises de Shakespeare*, Les Belles Lettres (1928); F. Baldensperger, 'Les Années 1827–1828' in *Revue des Cours et Conférences* (15 March 1929); René Bray, *La Chronologie du Romantisme*, Nizet (1932); F. C. Green, *Minuet*, London, Dent (1935); G. Ascoli, *Le Théâtre romantique*, Centre de documentation universitaire, Tournier et Constans (1937); Philippe Van Tieghem, *Les Influences étrangères sur la littérature française (1550–1850)*, P.U.F. (1961); Jean Jacquot, *Shakespeare en France: mises-en-scène d'hier et d'aujourd'hui*, Le Temps (1964) to mention only some of the most obvious ones.

[2] J. L. Borgerhoff, *Le Théâtre anglais à Paris sous la Restauration*, Paris, Hachette (1912).

[3] See Borgerhoff, *op. cit.*, p. 58.

[4] See also H. P. Bailey, *Hamlet in France*, Geneva, Droz (1964), pp. 36–8.

[5] H. F. Collins, *Talma, a biography of an actor*, Faber and Faber (1964), p. 86.

[6] For full details see E. P. Dargan, 'Shakespeare and Ducis', *Modern Philology* (1912), Vol. X, 137–78, and also H. F. Collins, *op. cit.*, p. 85–6.

[7] 'Alfred de Vigny et les littératures étrangères', *Revue des Cours et Conférences*, December 1924–December 1925, but particularly Lecture VII, *RCC*, December 1925, pp. 97–109.

[8] Annie Sessely, *L'Influence de Shakespeare sur Alfred de Vigny*, Berne, (1927), pp. 117–18.

[9] See *The Diaries of William Charles Macready, 1833–1851*, edited by William Toynbee, Chapman and Hall (1912), 2 vols. See Vol. I, pp. 477–503.

[10] P. Flottes, *Alfred de Vigny*, Perrin (1925), p. 300.

[11] Hugo, *Correspondance, 1815–1835*, Paris, Calmann-Lévy (1896), p. 67.

[12] For details concerning the writing of the play and its preface, see Hugo, *Théâtre I*, éd. Imprimerie Nationale, p. 478 sqq.; M. Souriau, *La Préface de Cromwell*, Boivin (1897); and also Hugo, *Théâtre complet*, I, Bibliothèque de la Pléiade, pp. 1734–9.

[13] Syracuse University Press (1964), pp. 151–2.

[14] Hugo, *Théâtre complet*, I, Bibl. de la Pléiade, p. 422; *La Préface de Cromwell*, éd. Souriau, pp. 213–14.

[15] *Ibid.*, I, p. 419; éd. Souriau, p. 202.

[16] *Ibid.*, I, p. 427; éd. Souriau, p. 229.

[17] *Ibid.*, I, p. 427; éd. Souriau, p. 230-1.

[18] *Ibid.*, éd. Souriau, pp. 181–2 and 189–90.

[19] A. R. Oliver, *Charles Nodier: Pilot of Romanticism*, Syracuse University Press (1964), pp. 151–2.

[20] G. Venzac, *Les premiers maîtres de Victor Hugo*, Bloud et Gay (1955), pp. 348.

[21] 'Les années 1827–1828 en France et au dehors', IX, in *Revue des Cours et Conférences* (15 March 1929), p. 643.

[22] *Victor Hugo raconté par un témoin de sa vie*, Hetzel et Quantin (1885), Vol. III, p. 78. 'Ces admirables drames admirablement joués remuèrent profondément M. Victor Hugo qui écrivait dans ce moment la préface de *Cromwell*; il l'emplit de son enthousiasme pour "ce dieu du théâtre en qui semblent réunis, comme dans une trinité, les trois grands génies caractéristiques de notre scène, Corneille, Molière, Beaumarchais." '

[23] See Borgerhoff, *op. cit.*, p. 181. Hugo, writing the Preface a year earlier, might conceivably not have included Shakespeare at all.

[24] Jean-Bertrand Barrère, *Victor Hugo à l'œuvre. Le poète en exil et en voyage*, C. Klincksieck (1965), p. 76.

[25] *Ibid.*, p. 71.

[26] Carola Oman, *David Garrick*, Hodder and Stoughton (1958), pp. 142–50.

[27] A. Dubeux, *Les Traductions françaises de Shakespeare*, Les Belles Lettres (1928), p. 35 and also H. F. Collins, *Talma* (1964), pp. 20–6, and 292–7.

[28] Borgerhoff, *op. cit.*, pp. 57 and 99, speaks of 'l'exiguïté de la salle Favart'. There was also the period from 8 October 1827 (*Romeo and Juliet*) until 27 December (*Hamlet*)—a period of more than eleven weeks—during which no performance of a play by Shakespeare was given, as well as the period during which no performances at all were given, in March 1828.

[29] Nodier, 'Sur le théâtre anglais à Paris', *Mercure de France du XIXe siècle*, Vol. xix, p. 33, quoted by Borgerhoff, *op. cit.*, p. 179.

[30] Hugo, *Théâtre complet, I*, Bibl. de la Pléiade, p. 434; *La Préface de Cromwell*, éd. Souriau, pp. 253–5.

x

J. P. Short

THE CONCEPT OF FATE IN THE TRAGEDIES OF RACINE

The concept of fate in the tragedies of Racine is a large subject and it would be presumptuous to claim that a full treatment of it is to be given here. All that will be attempted is an examination of some assumptions that are frequently made about this aspect of Racinian tragedy. The reason for the attempt being made is a feeling of unease concerning the validity of certain of these assumptions and a desire to see how far it is justifiable to assert that the tragic view of life which Racine presents in his tragedies depends on the concept of a blind and remorseless fate pursuing men and women.

It would obviously be desirable at the outset to make clear what is meant by fate in this discussion but any effort to arrive at a satisfactory definition quickly makes apparent the difficulties and ambiguities which surround the whole subject. Words denoting the idea of fate such as *destin*, *fortune* and *sort* are common in Racine, but do not always mean the same thing. Compare, for example, Hippolyte's reference to Thésée:

J'ignore le destin d'une tête si chère;[1]

with Thésée's own remark later in the same play:

Avec quelle rigueur, destin, tu me poursuis![2]

The word *fatal* itself varies in intensity of meaning and sometimes means simply 'catastrophic' or 'deadly', without necessarily any idea of inevitability being implied.[3] Some characters talk of themselves as victims of fate[4] and others confronted by cruel circumstances which they are powerless to control apostrophize the gods or *le ciel* in the hope of finding comfort when none is to be had from fellow human beings.[5] All that can be deduced from such examples is that the concept of fate can be adapted to a number of different uses according to the demands of a particular subject or particular situation. This is not, however, the core of the problem. This lies in the view that the tragedies of Racine present a world in which men are at the mercy of a cruel fate which is indifferent to their sufferings and which they are unable to alter by their own efforts. Such a view does not necesssarily depend on the particular dramatic use of the words signifying fate but on the interpretation of Racine's approach to his subjects and his treatment of them. What it is wished to investigate here is whether this is a completely acceptable view or whether it may not be, in some cases, misleading. The matter is important because it is concerned closely with the very nature of the tragic in Racine.

The subjects which Racine chose for his tragedies vary, but they all seem to have at least one aspect in common. This is the desire to show an innocent individual (using the word to mean 'good' as well as 'guiltless' and taking these words in their conventional moral sense) as a victim or potential victim of events over which he or she has no control.[6] It is precisely in the creation of such circumstances that the idea of fate is so convenient and is so often used to explain Racine's tragic view of life. If it is thought that the destinies of mankind are at the mercy of forces beyond its control, then it is obvious that there is plenty of material for the creation of such situations. The sources upon which Racine drew for some of his subjects offer material of this nature. Greek tragedy, including that of Euripides, can be thought to depict man as a victim of forces, called gods, who are masters of his destinies and use him as they will.[7] Yet it is hardly necessary to point out that the manner in which this material is used by Racine precludes the automatic assumption that he takes over the Greek view of fate. The denouement of *Iphigénie* or the changes made in the treatment of his sources in *Phèdre* are sufficient to show that. It would be wrong to assert at this point that there is no idea of fate in Racine's treatment of Greek material, but it would be equally wrong to assume that, because he uses this material, there is. A similar statement must be made concerning Jansenism and its place or influence in the tragedies of Racine. There is not space to go into this matter in detail, but it is essential to refer to it. The contention that, because Racine was educated at Port-Royal, his plays are imbued with the doctrines of Jansenism needs rather more evidence to support it than has been hitherto forthcoming.[8] It can quite easily be shown, if this were thought either necessary or desirable, that Racine's presentation of man and his place in the universe is perfectly explicable in terms of conventional Christian doctrine without having recourse to specifically Jansenist interpretations. Men and women in these tragedies are judged, for instance, according to the ordinary yardsticks of Christian morality, and the good and the bad are easily identifiable. It is far too sweeping to attribute Jansenist views on the corruptibility of human nature and the inevitable damnation of the great majority of human beings to Racine and claim that his tragedies portray such a view in their presentation of men and women predestined to suffering and death. This view requires that a great deal of what Racine actually created must be discounted, and the justification for such a view is not always plain to see. It is better to consider what is actually in the plays themselves, to see how Racine used the material he took from his various sources rather than to start from prepared positions which assume that these tragedies reflect either the fatalism of Greek tragedy or the ideas on predestination of Jansenism.

There are in the tragedies several characters who regard themselves as victims of fate, and who seem to have some points of similarity. Taxile, Oreste, Antiochus are all unhappy lovers who tend to blame fate for their unfortunate situations. Of these Oreste is most frequently cited as an illustration of Racine's presentation of a man overwhelmed by a malignant fate that relentlessly pursues its victim, refusing to relinquish its hold until it has achieved its aim. However, it must be remembered that Oreste is based on the Orestes of antiquity who, in the passage from Virgil which Racine quotes in the preface to *Andromaque*, is *Furiis agitatus*. The reason that Orestes was pursued by the Furies was because he had murdered his mother Clytemnestra.[9] This is not mentioned by Racine: in *Andromaque* it is love for Hermione that constitutes the unhappy fate of the character whom Racine called Oreste. In Euripides Orestes kills Pyrrhus more to avenge the insult offered to his family by the latter's treatment of Hermione than because Hermione had formerly been promised to him.[10] Racine simply transfers the well-known aspect of the Orestes of antiquity to his portrayal of an unhappy lover. Before Oreste, Taxile, in *Alexandre*, had cried:

> Quoi? la fortune, obstinée à me nuire,
> Ressuscite un rival armé pour me détruire?[11]

The theme of the unhappy lover who blames his misfortunes on fate is by no means unknown in the tragedy of the seventeenth century. That Racine should have chosen to present Oreste in this manner is not at all surprising, and it would be foolish to try and deduce from this that he had certain views about fate. This is borne out if the presentation of Antiochus in *Bérénice* is considered. Here again the unhappy lover is portrayed, but this time with no well-known prototype in antiquity. Antiochus too sees himself as a victim of fate:

> Qu'ai-je donc fait, grands Dieux? Quel cours infortuné
> A ma funeste vie aviez-vous destiné?[12]

but it is difficult to accept that Antiochus is chosen by fate as an example of the wrath of the gods with mankind. In fact it is, perhaps, significant that the main victims in this tragedy are very much conscious of their power to direct their own destinies. Titus describes suicide as a way of succumbing to fate. Talking of Romans who are the victims of numerous misfortunes, he says:

> Lorsque trop de malheurs ont lassé leur constance,
> Ils ont tous expliqué cette persévérance
> Dont le sort s'attachait à les persécuter,
> Comme un ordre secret de n'y plus résister.[13]

but he does not accept this in that he decides to face his tragedy and not to obey the dictates of fate. With Antiochus it is clear that a formula is being used, but where the real heart of the play is concerned, other values come into play. Similarly, in *Mithridate* Xipharès believes that his love for Monime is doomed never to reap its reward. In a moment of despair Xipharès, like Oreste and Antiochus before him, sees himself as a victim of fate:

> Je suis un malheureux que le destin poursuit;[14]

but once more it is obvious that these are words only meant to express an attitude and have no real depth of meaning. It is not therefore unduly implausible to suggest that in the context of these characters the concept of fate is little more than a convenient method of portraying the sufferings of unrequited love when such sufferings are borne by characters who are presented as otherwise virtuous. All the characters who have been mentioned, with the possible exception of Taxile, have the qualities of heroes as they appeared in seventeenth-century French tragedy.[15] They deserve to be loved in that they are brave, selfless and meritorious. That they are not loved must, therefore, be explained in some other way, and the convenient way to do it is to attribute the fault to fate. No conclusions which are valid can be drawn from this type of character about the concept of fate in Racine.

What conclusions can be reached by considering the plays which are based on subjects taken from Greek tragedy? *La Thébaïde*, Racine's first published tragedy, seems a clear example of fate at work. The two sons of Œdipus destined from birth to be enemies must work out their fate. The tragedy is filled with cries of woe at the cruelty of fate—the cruelty of the gods which make men their playthings—pawns to be used and thrown away at the whim of those in control. However, it is possible to show that, far from emphasizing the aspect of fate in the play, Racine does a great deal to attenuate it. Jocaste tries to influence events but cannot do so and finds relief in her apostrophizing of fate— but this is because she is a character who is slightly outside the main course of the action. It must be remembered that in a drama characters must act, must do, and if they have nothing to do then they must talk. This is precisely what happens with Jocaste who does little beyond bringing her sons together. She inveighs against the cruelty of fate because it is the only way her feelings can gain relief. In some of his plays Racine provides an object on which frustrated characters can turn their hatred and thus find relief. Where no such character exists then relief can be found by execrating the unknown—the eternal cry of mankind against cruel happenings that are seemingly inexplicable. But this is not to assert that fate is to be considered the moving factor in the play. There is a very clear indication that Racine considered the play to be a play about human motives and that its outcome is the result of human motives. It is not sufficient to say that a play shows fate at work when all it shows is the working out of a situation created by the nature of the human beings who participate in it. For *La Thébaïde* is a play about ambition rather than a play about fate. Etéocle is a king who is determined to remain a king. Polynice is equally determined to be king. The combat between the two brothers is shown to be inevitable from the start, not so much because of their hatred but because of their ambition. Jocaste herself has more faith in the powers of human beings to change events than she has in the power of destiny. For instance, when she learns that Créon has decided to support her efforts for peace she says:

> Non, puisqu'à nos malheurs vous devenez sensible,
> Au sang de Ménécée il n'est rien d'impossible.
> Que Thèbes se rassure après ce grand effort:
> Puisqu'il change votre âme, il changera son sort.[16]

Also, far from trying to emphasize the fatal nature of the hatred which separates the two brothers Racine deliberately shows that it is not motiveless but has a very strong cause—the power which goes with kingship. It is worth-while noting here that a passage which is sometimes quoted as evidence that, from the very outset of his career, Racine was concerned with the effects of fate on man was not, in fact, added until the edition of 1697 (the last to be prepared by Racine himself before his death in 1699).[17] The lines in question are these:

> Triste et fatal effet d'un sang incestueux!
> Pendant qu'un même sein nous renfermait tous deux,
> Dans les flancs de ma mère une guerre intestine
> De nos divisions lui marqua l'origine.[18]

The fact that Racine, in 1697, considered that the fatalistic nature of the hatred between Etéocle and Polynice needed to be emphasized seems to argue that, in 1664, such an interpretation of this hatred was not foremost in his mind. In fact, what seems to be clear is that he had tried to reduce the amount of the action which could be thought to be attributable to fate. Etéocle says further on in this same speech:

> On dirait que le ciel, par un arrêt funeste,
> Voulut de nos parents venger ainsi l'inceste.[19]

One notices the 'on dirait' which softens down the otherwise bald assertion that the hatred of the brothers was due to supernatural causes. The whole of this play shows Racine taking a subject which in his sources was treated from the point of view of the effect of fate on man[20] and turning it into a play about the working of human emotions and motives based on the nature of the human beings who participate in the action.

A more testing case is that of *Iphigénie*. Here is portrayed direct interference by supernatural powers in human affairs. Men are shown being urged, in spite of themselves, to commit a dreadful crime. It is interesting, however, to consider for a moment the nature of the subject which Racine is treating in this play. The situation in which Iphigénie finds herself, condemned to death for no reason at all by her own father, is not easily imaginable in any ordinary terms. It is a supreme example of the type of situation which Racine liked to treat, but it is a situation which would be impossible to invent because of its incredibility. It is only possible if use is made of the supernatural and Racine is prepared to use this because it is in his source, but only on his own terms. As he tells us in the preface, he wants the situation without having the destruction of Iphigénie as its outcome. His solution to this difficulty is that it is not Iphigénie who is killed: another victim is found. It is Eriphile who is really condemned, it appears, and she is made to deserve her death. In other words Racine refuses to accept the interpretation of a universe where fate strikes down wholly innocent people. Eriphile is an invented character and Racine could make her 'telle qu'il m'a plu'. Fate, then, by this interpretation, is shown to be much less blind than one might suppose in its choice of victims. In this play too Agamemnon refuses to accept the decrees of the gods. He reviles his fate and tries to overcome it and refuses to believe that the gods would condemn his daughter and, of course, he is right as it turns out. The sacrifice which the gods seemed to have demanded is not the one that they really want. Iphigénie is saved (for the reasons that Racine gives in his preface) and Eriphile is condemned, but the fate of Eriphile is as arbitrary as that of Iphigénie, and therefore Racine tries to make her deserve her death. Eriphile is an invented character, but she is not made completely innocent and good like Iphigénie. Thus she is made worthy of the fate that befalls her and therefore fate, by that very interpretation of its actions, is shown to be acting here as a judge, dealing out punishments or rewards and using standards which are those of a conventional morality. If, in this play, Racine meant to show a world dominated by fate, then he has not succeeded. What is shown is a world in which goodness is rewarded and evil punished. It is of no importance to say that Eriphile is guiltless in that she is a victim of passion which she could not control. Racine obviously intends Eriphile to be considered as living on a moral plane considerably lower than that of Iphigénie. Compare the behaviour of Iphigénie when she thinks

Y

that Achille is not going to marry her and is, instead, in love with Eriphile with that of Eriphile herself in the same situation.[21] In the code of the play Eriphile is guilty for falling in love with Achille and behaving as she does. The conclusion is that, in this play, Racine seems to be showing that the characters who act evilly in his tragedies do so because they are evilly inclined and this side of their nature emerges when they are thwarted or frustrated. Thus it is through their passions that their capacity for evil-doing is given the opportunity to be realized; they are not driven to do evil because they are overcome by their passions. It also follows that the very fact that Racine used this solution shows that he is not primarily interested in the tragic implications of death. The tragedy is what happens in the play, not the consequences of what happens. The notion that there is a fate which overhangs mankind, driving it on inexorably to its predestined end, demands as a corollary the notion that such a conception can only be of importance to a tragic dramatist who wants to prolong interest in the characters he creates by leaving question-marks over them after the completion of the action of his play. Racine is not interested in this as we know from the preface to *Britannicus*.[22] The end of a Racinian tragedy is death for some, life for others, but death or life is not what is of primary interest. What is of interest is what happens in the play—how the characters suffer, how they react, how they show their feelings in one way or another. They are only concerned with their ultimate fate in so far as it affects what happens to them now. Surely this is the explanation of the dénouement of *Iphigénie*.

Phèdre, the next tragedy taken from a Greek source, presents, from this point of view, problems of a similar nature. This is the play which is the most difficult to assess, perhaps, because it raises in a very acute form the whole question of the role of fate in the tragedies of Racine. Did he intend to present Phèdre as the victim of fate and, if he did, what is meant by fate in this context? Phèdre is presented differently from Antiochus or Xipharès; but how? She, like them, is shown as seeing herself as a victim of fate but her case is not comparable with theirs. Is Racine, in this character, postulating that there is a force over which men have no control and which can be called fate, and that there is nothing that can be done about it? As far as *Phèdre* is concerned it would seem that the answer to this question must be indefinite and far from clear. It is certainly not clear enough for a definite affirmative answer to be given, as is generally done.[23] The crux of the matter is the accusation made of the innocent Hippolyte. That Phèdre is not responsible for the fact that she fell in love with Hippolyte is indisputable. This is the result of forces over which her body has no control although her will is strong enough not to yield to the demands that her body makes upon her. There can be no doubt that this is how Racine presents his character at the outset of the tragedy. He shows there that, although human beings may be at the mercy of their passions in that they cannot prevent themselves from falling in love with somebody who does not love them, at least they need not be at the mercy of the results of these passions. Phèdre successfully combats her desire for a long time. The circumstances in which she is at last brought to confess it and act on it need not concern us here except to suggest that Racine is not completely convincing in his attempt to portray her yielding as involuntary. In none of this has Phèdre shown herself to be anything other than deserving of pity. But the accusation of Hippolyte is a different matter altogether. This is an act based on human motives and human fears and it is completely independent of any supernatural cause. Phèdre is afraid of Thésée's knowing what she has done, and she is also ashamed of what she has done. Are these feelings enough to justify the enormity of what is done? It has long been recognized that this is a difficulty in the development of the action.[24] How much clearer is Euripides. Phèdre commits suicide and leaves a letter in which she accuses Hippolyte. She does this with the specific intention of doing him harm.[25] She makes a blameworthy decision to revenge herself on Hippolyte. It is not the result of fate but the result of a decision voluntarily taken. Now in Racine no such clear-cut decision is taken. Is it certain that Racine intended Phèdre to be considered guiltless here? Only if this is certain can it be positively asserted that Phèdre is presented as an innocent victim of fate and that Racine intended her to be so considered. The decision must be taken if the tragedy is to have meaning, for Hippolyte must be killed—the victim of a false accusation. Once the accusation is made, however, Phèdre is in a completely different moral situation. As she is responsible for the accusation, she is open to be judged. If her actions are then considered to be wrong her actions no longer come under the general protection of fate, but must be seen at a much more human level. From this point on, then, Phèdre is not a victim of fate, she is a victim of her own actions. There is a difference in these concepts in spite of appearances. That Racine seemed to be aware of this difficulty may perhaps be shown by referring to the jealousy scene. Here Phèdre has come to take a positive step of her own. She will, perhaps, try to undo the evil that has been done, but before she is able to say anything that might save Hippolyte she learns something that prevents her from speaking. She remains silent once more, therefore, and fails to save either Hippolyte or herself. In this way, the dénouement of the tragedy can take its course; Hippolyte is killed, Phèdre commits suicide. The tragedy is accomplished but the question that has still to be answered is whether Racine is presenting, in *Phèdre*, the view that humanity is overshadowed by vast powers outside its control driving it on to catastrophe and misery, or whether he is not rather trying to show the disasters of one particular person forced by a combination of circumstances, passion and voluntary action into a catastrophic situation. The two concepts may not seem completely self-excluding but, in fact, they represent interpretations which are very different. On the one hand there is the vast general question of the place of humanity in the scheme of things and, on the other, the place of one individual in the scheme of humanity. In other words, does Phèdre represent humanity or does she represent herself? It is tempting to consider that Phèdre is a universal figure, but is it a valid picture? Phèdre is a unique figure whose sufferings we are called upon to pity but not necessarily to share. Racine presents his tragedies to us as spectacles infinitely sad, infinitely haunting, infinitely pitiful but not necessarily as commentaries on human destiny in general. It would, of course, be absurd to pretend that Racine's tragedies are not written with the behaviour of humanity in general in mind and how else indeed could he ever have created reactions which chime in so well with what we know is true? Of course Racine's tragedies betray a world of cruelty and uncertainty but does this cruelty and uncertainty lie in the undeserved blows of fate? In *Phèdre* is not Racine saying, weep for this woman, consider her case, see her misery and pity it? Is he also saying, weep for humanity, here is a typical case of what it is like to be a human being at the mercy of forces which cannot be controlled? How then does this throw light on Racine's concept of Fate? In this way: the view that there is a fate which pursues some people to their doom depends on the view that man is a victim of forces

beyond his control. Now this is patently not the case in some
other plays of Racine. Why save Iphigénie? Why save Andromaque? If the tragedian is concerned to present us with a view
of the universe which implies a blind unreasoning fate, then
there is no reason to distinguish between characters judged from
a human moral standpoint. Whatever may be thought, Racine
presents his characters as right or wrong from a human standpoint—a set of moral rules promulgated by human beings. Thus
Phèdre's behaviour, when she accuses Hippolyte, is wrong only
from a human standpoint and her reasons for doing this do not
seem to have a great deal to do with fate. If Phèdre is a completely innocent victim of fate then she should be shown being
driven to her catastrophic end by forces over which she has no
control at all, although it would be ill-advised to assert categorically that this is not what is meant to happen. However, one could
point here to *Iphigénie*, a play where it might have happened but
which is deliberately changed so that it does not happen. It
is perhaps not unfair, then, to say that the working of fate in
Phèdre tends to be a reflection of what a human being thinks
ought to be the right way that human affairs should go.

Is any further light thrown on the question by *Esther* and
Athalie? These two plays present a special aspect of the problem
because of the role played in them by the God of the Bible.
Racine is here concerned with a supernatural force that has the
power to direct events. How far does Racine make the action
of these plays depend on the assumption that the fate of the
characters is not in their own hands but in the hands of a supernatural power over which they have no control? *Esther* cannot be
said to provide very much useful evidence on this point. The
contrast between black and white, between right and wrong is
too rigidly determined here for there to be much doubt on the
matter. Whatever may be thought of the methods used by Mardo-
chée to obtain influence over Assuérus and the role played by
Esther in these intrigues, it is impossible to think that these figures
represent a valid commentary on the way human affairs are
managed. Obviously events are directed towards a certain end
but no valid conclusions can be drawn from this except perhaps
this: that when Racine writes a tragedy based on the belief that
human events are susceptible to supernatural control, the result
is the least convincing of his presentations of such events.
Athalie, on the other hand, does offer matter for speculation on the

lines that have been followed hitherto. We are asked to understand that a situation has arisen from human action which must be now resolved by divine intervention. This is the situation which Racine presents at the outset of *Athalie*, and this implies that Athalie is fighting God on more or less equal terms. She is not a victim, she is the loser in a battle where the issue might have been in doubt. This is what makes *Athalie* so interesting. If the play is considered simply as a battle between the ruling power and a rival element a satisfactory interpretation of the action is completely possible. The only overtly supernatural event in the play is the dream of Athalie so that again the situation is found where the supernatural aspect is played down as far as possible —and this in a play where the fate of Athalie is in the hands of the God in whom Racine believed. It is because of the dream that Athalie comes to the temple in the first place. The dream is the device by which the action is started, and it must be stated that the device is primarily a dramatic one.[26] It is quite clear moreover that Athalie conducts her battle on the human plane, and if she is defeated in the end it is because her adversary has at his disposal weapons which she has not got. It is a measure of Athalie's power and greatness that she considers God as the only fit rival to herself. She scorns Joad at the conclusion when she cries:

Impitoyable Dieu, toi seul as tout conduit.[27]

The corollary of this, however, is that God is put on the same level as Athalie. It is true that Athalie is defeated but her defeat is not, as it were, a resounding defeat for humanity. There is no sense of the inevitability of doom in Athalie's downfall. It is an event in human affairs which does not carry with it any sense of despair or terror. Even in this play Racine does not paint a background of the helplessness of humanity in face of the might and power of the forces seemingly ranged against it.

The tragic world of Racine is not one in which a blind fate strikes down completely guiltless men and women. It is perhaps true that such a concept of a cruel world, hostile to mankind and in which human beings find themselves cast without their permission and driven along by forces outside their control is an appealing one. The reaction to such an interpretation is one of immediate assent and recognition. Yet paradoxically such a view is in some ways a comforting view, much more comforting and comfortable than the view which sees man, certainly as an alien being in the world, but also capable by enormous effort and without any help, of shaping the world to his own ends and not necessarily the impotent victim of the meaninglessness and dumb enmity which surrounds him. There can be tragedy or tragic struggle when a man realizes that he is able to control his destiny and that he does not have to succumb to a blind fate; that, indeed, such fates do not exist but that man is a completely free agent and able to make decisions and choices which do have consequences and the consequences which they are meant to have. Is it going too far to suggest that it is in this area of interpretation that the tragic in Racine should be sought? It can be argued that what Racine's tragedies are about is the fight for existence and that he is concerned with people engaged in this fight and who are helped or hindered by their passions. This further raises the question whether the passions are not the manifestation in man of the uncontrollable forces which can be given the name of fate? The answer to this question is not and cannot be straightforward for the reason that, sometimes, Racine depicts people who are perfectly well able to control their passions and direct their activity into paths where it is not harmful and at others people who are incapable of this. Is this because these latter cannot or because they will not? It is convenient to suggest that if they cannot it is because they are victims of fate. Is it possible to suggest that this is too easy and over-simplified an interpretation and that the reason really is that they will not? The equating of fate with passion is not justified when the whole of Racinian tragedy is taken into account. Rather does there emerge from it a world in which men and women, with the capacity for doing good or ill, are given the opportunity of using this capacity through their passions. Any tragic consequences which follow from their attempts to fulfil themselves spring from the decisions taken by them and need not be ascribed to fate. This view in no way detracts from the profoundness or beauty of Racine's tragic imagination but helps, perhaps, to delimit, and therefore sharpen, the area in which that imagination worked.

NOTES

[1] *Phèdre*, l. 6. The edition of the tragedies of Racine to which reference is made is *Racine: Œuvres complètes*, edited by R. Picard, R. Groos and E. Pilon, Editions de la Pléiade, Paris (1951). Line references, which are lacking in this edition, have been added.

[2] *Ibid.*, l. 1003.

[3] See, for instance, *Mithridate*, l. 1341, where Monime speaks of her *fatal amour* or *Bajazet*, l. 1125, where Atalide says, *moment fatal* or *Phèdre*, l. 25, where Hippolyte talks of the *inconstance fatale* of Thésée.

[4] These tend to be men who love but who are not loved in return such as Taxile, Oreste, Antiochus or a lover like Xipharès who believes marriage to the woman he loves impossible.

[5] These tend to be women. Some obvious examples are Jocaste, Atalide and, of course, Phèdre.

[6] This is looking at one aspect of the plots of the plays only, but it is the dominant aspect in plays such as *Andromaque* and *Iphigénie* and very important in *Mithridate* and *Bajazet*.

[7] Cf. H. D. F. Kitto, *Greek Tragedy*, London, Methuen (1939), pp. 250–1.

[8] Many references to Racine's Jansenism are of too general a nature to be valuable, but even such detailed works as F. J. Tanquerey, *Le Jansénisme et les tragédies de Racine*, Paris, Boivin (1937) or the passages on Racine (pp. 446 ff.) in J. Paquier: *Le Jansénisme*, Paris, Bloud (1909), are far from convincing.

[9] Cf. the *Oresteia* of Aeschylus and the *Electra*, *Orestes* and *Iphigenia in Tauris* of Euripides.

[10] Cf. Euripides, *Andromache*, ed. Louis Méridier, Paris, Les Belles Lettres (1960), ll. 881–1009.

[11] *Alexandre*, ll. 1261–2.

[12] *Bérénice*, ll. 1297–8.

[13] *Ibid.*, ll. 1411–14.

[14] *Mithridate*, ll. 1218.

[15] Cf. J. Scherer, *La Dramaturgie classique en France*, Paris, Nizet (1950), pp. 20–22.

[16] *La Thébaïde*, ll. 771–4.

[17] See, for example, G. Truc, *Jean Racine*, Paris, Garnier (1926), pp. 29–30 and G. Le Bidois; *La vie dans la tragédie de Racine*, 6e édition, Paris, Gigord (1929), pp. 142–3.

[18] *La Thébaïde*, ll. 921–4.

[19] *Ibid.*, ll. 927–8 (1664 version).

[20] Cf. the *Phœnissæ* of Euripides and the Œdipus trilogy of Sophocles.

[21] Iphigénie reviles Eriphile but is mainly concerned with saving her dignity and her *gloire* (Act II, scene 5) while Eriphile is determined to do harm if she can.

[22] Cf. the passage in the *Première Préface* where Racine is replying to the critics of Act V, scene 6 (which he did subsequently remove): 'J'ai toujours compris que la tragédie étant l'imitation d'une action complète . . . cette action n'est point finie que l'on ne sache en quelle situation elle laisse ces mêmes personnes'.

[23] Cf. Thierry Maulnier, *Racine*, Paris, Gallimard, (1947), p. 197 or J. C. Lapp: *Aspects of Racinian tragedy*, University of Toronto Press, (1955), p. 26.

[24] Cf. the discussion devoted to this in J. Pommier: *Aspects de Racine*, Paris, Nizet, (1954), pp. 205–20.

[25] Euripides, *Hippolytos*, ed. Louis Méridier, Paris, Les Belles Lettres (1960), ll. 724–31.

[26] Dreams are frequently used as dramatic devices in 17th century tragedy as, for example, in *Polyeucte* and the *Mariane* of Tristan l'Hermite amongst others.

[27] *Athalie*, l. 1774.

LIST OF SUBSCRIBERS

Ian W. Alexander, Department of French, University College of North Wales, Bangor.

D. J. Allsop, 49 Paxton Road, Chesterfield.

L. J. Austin, Jesus College, Cambridge.

Enea Balmas, Facoltà di Lettere, Università di Padova, Italy.

Mrs Annie Barns, St Anne's College, Oxford.

H. T. Barnwell, Department of French, Queen's University, Belfast.

C. Stuart Barr, Department of French, The University, Leeds.

Blanchard W. Bates, 240 East Pyne Hall, Princeton University, New Jersey, U.S.A.

S. H. Baxter, Department of Modern Languages, Carleton College, Northfield, Minnesota 55057, U.S.A.

Mrs Marie Blewitt (née Ross), 10 Patterdale Road, Harwood, Bolton.

J. M. Brogan, Department of French, The University, Manchester.

Mr and Mrs H. V. W. Buckler, 4 Canterbury Drive, Sheffield 10.

G. S. Burgess, Department of French, Queen's University, Kingston, Ontario, Canada.

C. A. Burns, Department of French, The University, Southampton.

E. D. W. Chaplin, Lincoln House, London Road, Harrow.

John Christie, Department of French, The University, Nottingham.

Mrs R. Clark, 19 Agawam Road, West Acton, Massachusetts 01720, U.S.A.

P. W. Clinning, 8 Beacon Close, Aspatria, Cumberland.

Miss Yvonne M. Copley, 24 Fairhaven Road, St Annes-on-Sea.

Rodney J. Cox, 36 The Fairway, Alsager, Stoke-on-Trent.

Colin Duckworth, Bedford College, Regent's Park, London.

Mrs Simone Eastman, Avignon, 40 University Road, Highfield, Southampton.

Miss Dorothy P. Ellis, 27 Pearson Road, Odsal, Bradford.

R. Fargher, St Edmund Hall, Oxford.

Miss Alison Fairlie, Girton College, Cambridge.

A. G. Fokerd, 102 Dore Avenue, North Hykeham, Lincoln.

Albert M. Forcadas, Department of Romance Languages, The University of Alberta, Edmonton, Alberta, Canada.

E. T. B. Francis, The University, Sheffield.

K. H. Francis, Department of French, Royal Holloway College, Englefield Green, Surrey.

G. Gadoffre, Department of French, The University, Manchester.

K. S. Geary, 30 Lordswood Square, Lordswood Road, Harborne, Birmingham.

Victor E. Graham, The University, Toronto 5, Canada.

Miss E. C. Haber, Flat 2, 1 Montpelier Terrace, Brighton.

C. A. Hackett, The University, Southampton.

H. G. Hall, 18 Abbey End, Kenilworth.

Miss Kathleen M. Hall, Department of French, The University, Southampton.

Mr & Mrs R. E. Hallmark, 30 Sheringham Road, Kings Norton, Birmingham.

P. F. Hardy, 17 Ivydene, West Molesey, Surrey.

Miss M. I. Henderson, 3 Glebe Court, Highfield, Southampton.

Richard W. Hill, 46 Gainsbro' Drive, Adel, Leeds.

W. J. Hitchens, 32 Wilson Road, Sheffield.

Miss Yvonne Hoggan, Department of French, University College of Wales, Aberystwyth.

P. C. Hoy, Merton College, Oxford.

Mrs Margaret Ihringer, Hockley House, Ashover, near Chesterfield.

A. R. Jones, 39 Frederick Road, Sutton Coldfield.

K. Lloyd Jones, University College of North Wales, Bangor.

Miss Pamela N. Jones, 29 Bath Street, Port Sunlight, Cheshire.

Rhys S. Jones, St David's College, Lampeter, Cardiganshire.

P. J. M. Jourda, Rue Montcalm 5, Montpellier, France.

Gerard de Jubecourt, Department of Modern Languages, The University, Calgary, Alberta, Canada.

B. Juden, Department of French, The University, Sheffield.

Miss Pauline M. Kelly, Hillcrest, Southlands Grove, Bingley, Yorkshire.

R. C. Knight, The Library, University College, Swansea.

W. H. Lakin, 9 bis, Building Jourdan, Paris XIVe, France.

M. Lucien Lang, 78 Avenue Georges Clémençeau, Reims 51, France.

John C. Lapp, Stanford University, California, U.S.A.

T. E. Lawrenson, The University, Bailrigg, Lancaster.

David C. Lawton, 18 Carrfield Avenue, Long Eaton, Nottingham.

G. C. and S. M. Lawton, 160 St John Street, London E.C.1.

William P. Lawton, 19 Kings Avenue, Prestatyn, Flintshire.

A. L. Leigh, 277 Haunch Lane, Kings Heath, Birmingham.

John Lough, 1 St Hild's Lane, Gilesgate, Durham.

W. I. Lucas, Department of German, The University, Southampton.

Miss Patricia I. Maguire, The University, Hull.

I. D. McFarlane, Department of French, The University, St Andrews, Fife.

D. B. McNeill, Connaught Hall, Swaythling, Southampton.

Francis J. Melville, 62 Swain House Road, Five Lane Ends, Bradford.

Mrs V. T. Mocquard, St Helena School for Girls, Sheffield Road, Chesterfield.

E. Moles, Department of French, The University, Glasgow.

Mrs Elizabeth M. Moss, 58 Albert Road, Heeley, Sheffield.

A. Naaman, Faculté des Arts, Université de Sherlbrooke, Sherlbrooke, Quebec, Canada.

Miss Jill Nelmes, 73 Walter Street, Tredegar, Monmouthshire.

Miss Joyce Newman, 2a Salters Lane South, Darlington, County Durham.

D. E. Newton, 16 Lawson Avenue, Gatley, Cheadle, Cheshire.

Rowland Parker, Cottage on the Green, Foxton, Royston, Hertfordshire.

C. E. Pickford, Department of French, The University, Hull.

Mrs Patricia Place (née Bailey), 18 Lilly Hall Road, Maltby, near Rotherham.

Miss Susan M. Pollard, 30 Lapwing Lane, West Didsbury, Manchester.

Frank Port, 10 Stanley Park Avenue, Rhyl, Flintshire.

D. M. Powell, 1 Victoria Avenue, Evesham, Worcester.

Arthur G. Quarrell, 58 Endcliffe Vale Road, Sheffield.

A. W. Raitt, Magdalen College, Oxford.

Miss Delyth Rees, 59 Newland Park, Hull.

Professor & Mrs Garnet Rees, 59 Newland Park, Hull.

R. A. Sayce, Worcester College, Oxford.

Wilfred L. Saunders, 12 Whiteley Wood Road, Sheffield.

Jean Seznec, All Souls College, Oxford.
David J. Shaw, Rutherford College, University of Canterbury at Kent.
Miss Marjorie Shaw, Department of French, The University, Sheffield.
Miss Margaret Simpson, 10 Sandhall Cottages, Ulverston, Lancashire.
Mr & Mrs Jeremy Skipper, Linden Wood Cottage, Wrotham Road, Fairseat, Kent.
M. C. Spencer, Sidney Sussex College, Cambridge.
F. E. Sutcliffe, Department of French, The University, Manchester.
L. C. Sykes, The University, Leicester.

L. W. Tancock, Department of French, University College, London.
Merlin Thomas, New College, Oxford.
J. Ridley Thompson, 55 Harewood Avenue, Bridlington, Yorkshire.
Gilbert Todd, Wayside Cottage, Sibford Ferris, near Banbury.

Kenneth Varty, Department of French, The University, Glasgow.
Eugène Vinaver, Department of French, The University, Madison, Wisconsin, U.S.A.

Mrs Lilian Waites, 20 Repton Road, Earley, Reading.
S. Weintroub, Department of Physics, The University, Southampton.
D. B. Wilson, 86 Gilesgate, Durham.
W. L. Wilson, Department of German, The University, Southampton.
B. Woledge, University College, London.
Miss Barbara Wotton, Faculty of Arts, The University, Southampton.

Miss Margaret L. M. Young, The University, Manchester.

LIBRARIES

Aberdeen, King's College.

Basel, Romanisches Seminar der Universität.
Bonn, Universitätsbibliothek.
Brighton, The University of Sussex.
Bromley, Stockwell College of Education.

Cambridge, Churchill College.
  Jesus College.
  Magdalene College.
Canterbury, The University of Kent.
Coventry, The University of Warwick.

Doncaster, The College of Education.
Dundee, The University.
Durham, The University.

Englefield Green, Royal Holloway College.

Glasgow, The University.

Hull, Brynmor Jones Library, The University.

Köln, Romanisches Seminar der Universität.

Leeds, James Graham College of Education.
Leicester, The University.
London, Birkbeck College.
    Queen Mary College.
    University College.
    Westfield College.

Montreal University, Faculty of Letters Library.

Ottawa, Carlton University.
Oxford, Christ Church.
    St Anne's College.
    St Hugh's College.

Paris, The Sorbonne.
Peterborough, Ontario, Trent University.

Saarbrücken, Universitäts-Bibliothek.
St Andrews, The University.
Salisbury, University College of Rhodesia.
Sheffield, The University.
Southampton, La Sainte Union College.
Stanford, California, The University.

Toronto, St Michael's College.

Uppsala, Romanska Seminariet.

Winchester, King Alfred's College of Education.

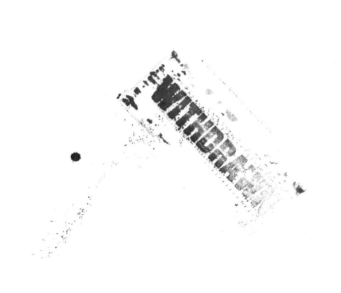

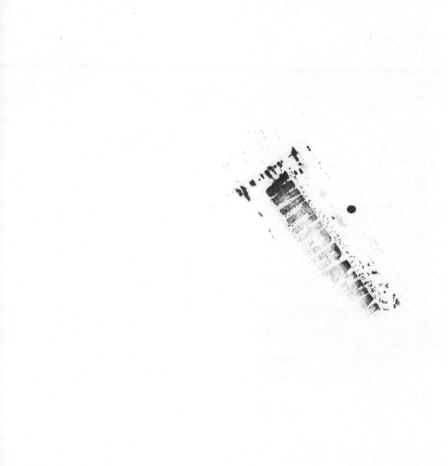